'This book comes at a critical time when the values that underpin our democracy and its institutions, including schools, are under growing threats from the forces of globalisation. It recognises the urgent need for us to reconceptualise education, including the role of citizenship education, in ways that provide young people with the knowledge, skills and values not only to promote democracy but to protect and defend it. It also draws attention to the crucial role that that the education system plays in such a reconceptualization. Only a truly national education service can guarantee that all young people are educated to be the knowledgeable, responsible and reflective, active citizens that are and will be required to tackle with confidence the challenges of learning, working and living in 21st century societies. We ignore such a reconceptualization at our peril.'

—**David Kerr,** *Consultant Director of Education, Young Citizens and Head of ITT, University of Reading*

'The cumulative experience of the writers of this book is enormous. They have seen the system from so many different perspectives and their insights are fascinating. All of the writers are committed enough to offer their effort through a deep concern for the lasting health of the education system. It is a book well worth reading and it merits serious thought and action. In education we are trying to influence individual opportunity and build life-long habits and prospects so that today's children can make a positive difference to their world. As for the best way to do that, let's make decisions wisely.'

—**Mick Waters,** *previously Director of Curriculum at the UK government's Qualification and Curriculum Authority*

EDUCATION SYSTEM DESIGN

This book highlights decisions governments have to make about their public education systems, the options they have before them and the consequences of their decisions. As well as covering issues such as values, curriculum, teacher training, structures and so on, the book addresses education planning for epidemics, pandemics and disasters.

Education systems provide the foundations for the future wellbeing of every society, yet existing systems are a point of global concern. *Education System Design* is a response to debates in developing and developed countries about the characteristics of a high-quality national education service. It questions what makes a successful system of education. With chapters that draw on experience in education systems around the world, each one considers an element of a national education service and its role in providing a coherent and connected set of structures to ensure good education for all members of society.

Key topics include:

- Existing education systems and what a future system might look like
- Inclusion and social justice
- Leadership and teacher education
- Policy options, and the consequences of policy changes

This book suggests an education system be viewed as an ecosystem with interdependencies between many different components needing to be considered when change is contemplated. It is a vital book for any stakeholders in educational systems including students, teachers and senior leaders. It would be particularly useful to policy makers and those implementing policy changes.

Brian Hudson is Emeritus Professor and former Head of the School of Education and Social Work (2012–2016) at the University of Sussex, Honorary Professor and former Associate Dean for Research at the University of Dundee (2009–2012) and currently Senior Professor at Karlstad University, Sweden. His particular research interests are in mathematics education, ICT and learning, curriculum studies and subject didactics. He is a board member and former chair of the Teacher Education Policy in Europe (TEPE) network (https://twitter.com/TEPEnetwork); was the main organiser of the WERA (www.weraonline.org) International Research Network on *Didactics –Learning and Teaching* and is currently an Associate Editor of the *Journal of Curriculum Studies*. He was awarded a National Teaching Fellowship in 2004 and Honorary Network Membership of the European Education Research Association (https://eera-ecer.de) Network 27 on *Didactics – Learning and Teaching* in 2016.

Marilyn Leask has held roles in central and local government, universities, schools and research institutes. She is visiting Professor at De Montfort and Winchester Universities, UK, and is committed to supporting international collaboration between teachers and educational researchers for the benefit of learners everywhere. In 1992, she initiated the Learning to Teach in the secondary school series of textbooks which she co-edits. She is co-chair of the Education Futures Collaboration Charity which oversees the MESHGuides initiative (www.meshguides.org) addressing the UN's SDG 4, and with Professor Younie and Ulf Lundin from Sweden, initiated the European SchoolNet in 1995 (www.eun.org). She is an elected board member of the Council for Subject Associations and the Technology Pedagogy and Education Association. She has previously held elected roles on the British Educational Research Association national council and the national council Universities Council for the Education of Teachers.

Sarah Younie is Professor of Education Innovation and previous Director of the Institute for Education Futures at De Montfort University. She sits on ICET (International Council on Education for Teaching) and is the UK BERA (British Education Research Association) Convenor for Educational Research and Policy Making Special Interest Group. She is a Trustee and founder member of the Education Futures Collaboration (EFC) charity and MESH (Mapping Education Specialist knowHow) project, which provides research evidence to inform teachers' professional practice, and represents MESH on the UNESCO International Teacher Task Force panel. MESH contributes to UN SDG4. She has been involved in international research on technologies in education for UNESCO, EU, UK Government Agencies, Local Authorities and educational charities. As the UK Chair of the National Subject Association of IT in Teacher Education (ITTE) she has submitted evidence for Parliamentary Select Committees. Professor Younie is currently the Editor-in-Chief for the international *Journal of Technology, Pedagogy and Education*.

EDUCATION SYSTEM DESIGN

Foundations, Policy Options and Consequences

Edited by Brian Hudson, Marilyn Leask and Sarah Younie

LONDON AND NEW YORK

First published 2021
by Routledge
2 Park Square, Milton Park, Abingdon, Oxon OX14 4RN

and by Routledge
52 Vanderbilt Avenue, New York, NY 10017

Routledge is an imprint of the Taylor & Francis Group, an informa business

British Library Cataloguing-in-Publication Data
A catalogue record for this book is available from the British Library

Library of Congress Cataloging-in-Publication Data
Names: Hudson, Brian, 1951– editor. | Leask, Marilyn, 1950– editor. |
    Younie, Sarah, 1967– editor.
Title: Education system design : foundations, policy options and
    consequences / edited by Brian Hudson, Marilyn Leask and Sarah
    Younie.
Description: Abingdon, Oxon ; New York, NY : Routledge, 2021. |
    Includes bibliographical references and index.
Identifiers: LCCN 2020023449 (print) | LCCN 2020023450 (ebook) |
    ISBN 9780367203801 (hardback) | ISBN 9780367203771 (paperback) |
    ISBN 9780429261190 (ebook)
Subjects: LCSH: Instructional systems—Design. | Curriculum planning. |
    Educational planning. | Education and state.
Classification: LCC LB1028.38 .E327 2021 (print) | LCC LB1028.38
    (ebook) | DDC 371.33—dc23
LC record available at https://lccn.loc.gov/2020023449
LC ebook record available at https://lccn.loc.gov/2020023450

ISBN: 978-0-367-20380-1 (hbk)
ISBN: 978-0-367-20377-1 (pbk)
ISBN: 978-0-429-26119-0 (ebk)

Typeset in Bembo
by Apex CoVantage, LLC

This book is dedicated to all teachers, with particular recognition of long-serving teachers and head teachers around the world, who work within challenging political contexts, but who manage to put the learning and wellbeing of their students first.

The book is also dedicated to those policy makers who are able to step aside from party politics and consult with communities, businesses, parents/carers and learners to create the best education system possible providing pathways to self-realisation, lifelong personal fulfilment and community wellbeing.

We also dedicate this book to all those training to be teachers now and welcome them to this rewarding profession.

CONTENTS

SECTION 6
Policy options and consequences   251

FIGURES

TABLES

AUTHORS AND CONTRIBUTORS

Authors

Jon Audain is Senior Lecturer in Primary ICT and Music, University of Winchester. Chair of the Technology, Pedagogy and Education Association.

Sonia Blandford is founder and CEO of award-winning school improvement charity, Achievement for All. Prolific author and international speaker on social mobility, special educational needs and leadership. Former pro-vice chancellor (Canterbury Christ Church University), Teach First director and school senior leader, 2016 *Sunday Times* Most Influential (Education) and 2018 Social Mobility Award finalist (Outstanding Individual).

Nikki Booth is Head of Assessment and teacher of music, Spanish, and mathematics at Wolgarston High School, Staffordshire, as well as PhD researcher at Birmingham City University. Alongside his passion for music education, he also has a deep interest in educational assessment and how it can be used effectively to enhance teaching and learning.

Tim Brighouse retired from the post of London Commissioner for Schools in 2007 after five years of leading the London Challenge. Before that he spent 10 Years as Chief Education Officer in Birmingham and 10 years also as CEO in Oxfordshire separated by four years as Professor of Education in Keele University.

Sharon Clancy is Senior Research Fellow in adult education/lifelong learning at the University of Nottingham. Her writing focusses on education, class and culture, alongside cognitive and social justice issues. A voluntary sector leader before entering academia, Sharon is Chair of the Raymond Williams Foundation and was Head of Community Partnerships at the University of Nottingham (2007–2013).

Steven J. Courtney is a senior lecturer at the University of Manchester. His research interests focus on who educational leaders are, what they do, why they do it and how that might be understood in relation to education policy.

Graham Donaldson is the former head of Her Majesty's Inspectorate of Education in Scotland. In addition to international consultancy, he is currently an Honorary Professor at the University of Glasgow and professional advisor to the Scottish and Welsh Governments. His particular research interests relate to system change with a focus on curriculum, professional learning and accountability.

Hugh Greenway is CEO of the Elliot Foundation and sits on the education advisory board to the British Council. His interests include behavioural change and organisational design.

Helen M. Gunter is professor of education policy at University of Manchester.

Stephen Hall is a lecturer in education at Staffordshire University and previously a primary headteacher.

Moira Hulme is Professor of Teacher Education at Manchester Metropolitan University. Her research addresses teacher education policy from an international, comparative and historical perspective.

Helen Knowler is a Lecturer in the Graduate School of Education at the University of Exeter. Her research interests relate broadly to Inclusive Education, but she focuses on the prevention of permanent exclusion from school and the inclusion of pupils with SEMH in mainstream settings. Helen is a fully qualified teacher and worked as a teacher and advisory teacher supporting pupils with SEMH before becoming a researcher in HE.

Linda la Velle is Professor of Education at Bath Spa University.

Jari Lavonen is a Professor of Physics and Chemistry Education at the University of Helsinki, Finland. He is a director of National Teacher Education Forum and member of the steering committee of the Finnish Education Evaluation Centre. His main research interests are science and technology teaching and learning, curriculum development, teacher education and use of ICT in education.

Brian Matthews taught science in London schools, then trained science teachers on the PGCE at Goldsmiths, and now at King's College. He has researched ways of developing emotional literacy and equity in science classrooms and has published *Engaging Education*.

Karen Meanwell, Associate Head of School of Teacher Education, Manchester Metropolitan University. Karen's research interests include mentor training and the development of subject knowledge within school settings.

Hannele Niemi is Emerita Professor of Education and Director of Research at the Faculty of Educational Sciences, University of Helsinki. Her main research interest areas are teachers' professional development, moral education and technology-based learning environments.

Christina Preston, Founder of MirandaNet and Associate Professor at De Montfort University, has won five international awards for her contribution to education innovation and community of practice development. Her research and practice focus on the role of education technology in teaching and learning and on ways of helping the teaching profession to adopt effective policies and practices in a fast change field.

Richard Procter is a Lecturer at De Montfort University. His particular research interests are in how technology can be leveraged to improve the use of research by the teaching profession and thus improve outcomes for learners. He has worked on a number of projects exploring the use of technology in the field of education. He is MESHGuides Chief Editor.

Rosie Raffety is Founding CEO of The Academy for Innovation Consultancy, UK. She has held Associate Professor roles at the Claude Littner Business School, University of West London; Bedfordshire University; and St Mary's University, Twickenham, London. She is a founder member of MESHGuides and former Senior Consultant with the Innovation Unit, UK and National College for School Leadership. Her Ph.D. research (University of Exeter, 1999) was in the micropolitics of change in schools. Her expertise is in organisational innovation, leadership and pedagogy.

Emilee Rauschenberger is Postdoctoral Research Fellow at Manchester Metropolitan University. Her current work examines the spread and impact of fast-track teacher training programmes.

Kate Reynolds is Director of Education at Brighter Futures for Children and Emeritus Professor at Bath Spa University. Her research interests include policy, equalities and social justice and all things education.

Sana Rizvi is a Lecturer in the Graduate School of Education at the University of Exeter. Her research interests relate to minoritised communities' experiences of education at the intersections of disability, race, gender and immigration trajectory.

Chris Shelton is Head of Education at the University of Chichester. His particular research interests are technology, computing and digital literacy in schools and universities.

Carl Smith is Principal of Casterton College Rutland, shortlisted for Secondary School of the Year 2019. Smith was England's first Advanced Skills Teacher of History in 1997.

Mick Waters was Director of Curriculum at the Qualification and Curriculum Authority, having previously held senior posts in schools and Local Education Authorities. Currently he works with schools across the country and at policy levels with governments internationally.

Caroline Whalley CBE is founder of The Elliot Foundation and has held executive positions in public, private and charity sectors. She researches connections across knowledge boundaries to enrich understanding of how and why to educate.

Contributors

The following colleagues were part of the workshops conducted during the development of this book and/or were consulted with respect to the content of the chapters.

Björn Åstrand is Senior Lecturer at Umeå University and former Dean of Teacher Education and Educational Sciences at Karlstad University (2014–2017), Sweden. His research interests are focussed on educational history, comparative education, democracy and values and teacher education.

Chris Boothroyd is a retired headteacher and member of OFSTIN.

Francesca Caena is a Lecturer at the Università Ca' Foscari Venezia, Italy who is currently working as a researcher at the EC Joint Research Centre in Seville. Her most recent research interests focus on aligning teacher competence frameworks to 21st century challenges and in particular to the European Digital Competence Framework for Educators.

Davinder Dosanjh is Executive Director of the Leicestershire Secondary SCITT at The Mead Educational Trust. A senior leader involved in teacher education and a former Her Majesty's Inspection with Ofsted. She is Challenge Partner Reviewer, External Examiner for Intitial Teacher Education programmes working with a range of routes into teaching.

Eve Eisenschmidt is Professor of Education Policy and Management in the School of Educational Sciences at the University of Tallinn, Estonia. Her most recent research focusses on exploring the shaping of teacher identities through student teachers' narratives.

Nansi Ellis is Assistant General Secretary of the National Education Union.

John Fowler commissions and writes the Local Government information Unit's education, children's services and skills briefings. He has over 30 years' experience in local government in management, performance and policy roles for seven local authorities in London and the south east.

Brian Lightman's career in education spanning 40 years included two secondary headships and a national role as General Secretary of the Association of School and College Leaders. Continuing to remain strongly engaged with education policy he works as an independent school leadership consultant. www.lightmanconsulting. co.uk @brianlightman

Erika Löfström is Professor in the Department of Education at the University of Helsinki, Finland. Her research interests include research ethics and integrity; academic writing and plagiarism; ethics of supervision; academic teacher development; teacher education; teacher identity; and teacher beliefs.

Joanna Madalińska-Michalak is Professor of Social Science within the field of educational research at the University of Warsaw, Poland. Her research focuses on teachers' professionalism and ethics, educational leadership and school development, and teacher education and teacher education policies in Europe.

Philip Moriarty is professor of physics at the University of Nottingham, a father of three, and served as governor for a number of years for his children's primary school. He writes regularly for the Times Higher Education and has been a frequent critic of the pseudostatistics and faux-quantitative metrics that underpin the primary, secondary, and higher education sectors. He blogs at muircheartblog. wordpress.com.

Deborah Outhwaite is Director of the Derby Teaching Schools Alliance. Her research interests are in leadership preparation and development with cross-phase school leaders and teachers

Rachel Peckover is Deputy Headteacher at Burbage Junior School and a Doctoral Researcher at De Montfort University. Her research interests are Primary School Leadership and Initial Teacher Education.

Jens Rasmussen is Professor in the Danish School of Education at Aarhus University. His research interests focus on the reform of teacher education and teacher educator competences.

Marco Snoek is Lector of applied research at the Centre of Applied Research in Education at the Amsterdam University of Applied Sciences. His research interests are in the development of teacher education curricula, induction programmes and Master's programmes for teacher leaders in the Netherlands.

David Wolfe is a QC with Matrix Chambers, London.

Pavel Zgaga is Professor of Philosophy of Education at the Faculty of Education, University of Ljubljana, Slovenia. His primary research interest is in higher education studies.

FOREWORD

It has always seemed strange to me that big bookshops carry so few books on education. There is usually a small section of shelving dominated by books full of practice tests and exam study guides for parents to buy to use with their children. Sometimes there are a few titles clearly targeting teachers but virtually nothing for the 'general public' about education policy, provision or oversight. There are plenty of books on law, health and politics. It is as if the education of our children is not a matter for public discourse. Schooling is a service, and the job of parents is to get their own children into the best school they can and support them while they are there. Politicians decide the structures and the professionals do the best they can. The bigger picture is not of public concern and they need not think about it.

This is a book that should be read by people within and without the world of schooling. It is a wide-ranging and thoughtful book. It is wide ranging in three ways. First, it moves around the inside of the English education system, offering insights into why things are as they are today. Second it ranges around the world looking at the way different nations have developed their approach to the learning of their young, often mirroring the developments in the UK. Third, it looks forward and proposes some steps that could lift our ambition, improve effectiveness and help future generations build a better world.

The analysis of the evolution of policy and practice in education systems is thorough. From the beginnings of state schooling for all in 1870, the book traces the policy directions and their effect on the professionalism of the teachers upon whom the system ultimately depends. Efforts to improve the effectiveness of teachers, through initial training and the various stages of what is now referred to as professional learning, are detailed. The steps to shape the curriculum for young people while at the same time ensuring standards through examination are retraced. The gradual inclusions and exclusions of pupils with additional needs or particular challenges are exposed with the reasons for them underlined. The assertion that society's unfairness is perpetuated through many of the ways the system works is balanced with suggestions of how this might be addressed. The purpose and value of our assessment and examination system is tested. The growth of the accountability and its impact upon the system is charted. The rise in international comparison and the impact of it is considered. The current multi-layered fragmentation of the system is argued to be uneconomic and over-complex in terms of the needs of young people. There are calls for an outlook of continuous improvement as opposed to the traditional deficit model of effectiveness. All of this constantly leads to the question of our central purpose in education.

Running through the book is the thread about where the decisions about policy are best taken. The extent to which central government has exerted increasing control over the last thirty years is revealed along with the reasons, benefits and flaws. The influence of the Secretary of State is a crucial element. While regular cabinet re-shuffles mean that the post is rarely held for long, the dramatic and lasting influence of three particular individual Secretaries of State since 1980 is analysed along with their effect on the schools of today. Whatever the motives, powerful politicians driving reform on top of reform create a switchback of practice that often leaves even the most hardened educational traveller with motion sickness.

The book questions whether there could be other ways to structure education policy and visits systems across the globe to look at alternatives and consider their merit. There are fundamental questions about whether the world into which children are now being born is changing so fast that we need a different form of schooling altogether. The influences of the shift of populations across the world, the rise of new super-powers, concern for environmental sustainability and the place of artificial intelligence in learning all raise questions about whether schooling should be re-conceptualised. While some argue that we risk our children's futures by changing our traditional approaches, others would question whether we might risk their futures more if we continue as we are. As we move forward, where should the decision making lie?

At the same time as being wide ranging, the book is thoughtful. It is one of those books that could be dipped into for a snapshot of aspects of education over time. Each section and chapter will provoke thoughts about experience, rationale or practice. The resonance between sections will provoke the urge to switch to another section and come at different issues from similar angles.

Just as intriguing would be to read the whole thing from front to back, and enjoy a coherent argument unfolding through the pages of experience and wisdom in print.

The book is unashamedly seeking progress. It recognises good achievements of the last century and a half and at the same time asks whether we can continue to be satisfied with what we have achieved, whether we should want and expect more for our young.

It invites a new form of relationship between state and schools, building consensus rather that grappling with polarities, and calls for a re-consideration of the way decisions are taken, proposing a 'standing national education advisory council'.

The book is not foolhardy, recognising the logistical difficulties of changing the structures that have pertained for so long and the challenge of structuring a new organisational image in a world where there are so many vested interests.

When you have read this book, you might consider whether the argument and premise is one with which you find favour. If you do, then what might you do about it? For the book is a call to people of like mind to influence the system.

Given that the general public does not tend to read books about education policy issues, the challenge would seem to be that of taking the debate to a wider community of interest. You could play your part. Perhaps you could buy a second copy for someone else. A parent or a governor at a local school might be a start. Someone who is influential in business as an employer might find it informative and eye opening.

You might pass this book to a fifteen-year-old student. Young people are touching the nerve of humanity by asserting the influence of their learning upon their society. They are stepping up to be part of the drive in the environmental sustainability debate, they are challenging the gun lobby, building a campaign for the global education of girls. They will have views on the usefulness of their own education. Ask the teenager to pass the book to someone else who he or she thinks should read it . . . and then do something positive about what he or she has read.

If you are a teacher and you find yourself realising why the system is as it is, determine to re-exert professionalism for yourself and colleagues. Join wider communities of educational interest and contribute your own understandings to debates about pedagogy and learning.

If you read the book as a head teacher of a school, take seriously your role in the context of wider system leadership. Influence your own staff and community to consider the bigger picture of education through some of the issues raised in the book.

As a Local Authority officer or influential in a Multi Academy Trust, you could bring forward some of the issues addressed in the book within collective meetings or with officials from the Department for Education. Those within the system have to exert more dynamic influence than is currently the case.

Whoever you are, you could make an appointment at your MP's surgery to talk about the premise of the National Education Advisory Council – why it matters and what it could achieve. If enough people did this nationwide, it would build a groundswell of opinion that something needs to be done, which would register with politicians and possibly see progress.

If you are a politician, national or local, you could consider carefully the notion of a National Education Advisory Council and engage with others about how we can move on from the centralised model of schooling, leave behind polarised politics and build consensus. Similarly, if you are a civil servant or policy director within the system, extending the debate within your community would be fruitful.

If you are what is called the 'general public', feel free to get involved in the world of education in the search for the best system to serve our young people. If reading the book in a nation other than England, raise the appropriate issues within your own context and join international alliances that are focussed upon the future of schooling.

Whatever you do, consider the book through its enthusiasm for the best school system possible. The cumulative experience of the writers is enormous. They have seen the system from so many different perspectives and their insights are fascinating. All of the writers are committed enough to offer their effort through a deep concern for the lasting health of the education system. It is a book well worth reading and it merits serious thought and action. In education we are trying to influence individual opportunity and build life-long habits and prospects so that today's children can make a positive difference to their world. As for the best way to do that, let's make decisions wisely.

Mick Waters

PREFACE

This book is for anyone who cares about education and is intended to help you decide what your views are on the biggest policy and practice issues for education.

It was inspired by a national debate in the UK following a policy proposal from Her Majesty's Opposition in the run-up to the General Election of December 2019 to establish a National Education Service. In part it can be seen as a response to the call by Benn et al. (2019) for contributions to a new conversation about education at a national level, one from which will emerge new ideas, including alternatives to present policies. In reflecting upon the accomplishment of completing this book, the editors see it also as a significant contribution at the international level to the field of 'educational systems design'. The principles of educational system design were articulated in a landmark paper by Reigeluth (1993) in which a model for a fundamental change process is presented which uses the stakeholder approach. The stakeholder approach is based on the recognition that fundamental change is far more difficult than piecemeal 'add-ons' and that such fundamental change is *systemic*. For it to be successful, the change process must result in shared ownership of the new system. This approach is contrasted with the 'expert approach' that is top-down and which entails one or two powerful individuals in planning all aspects of the new system. The stakeholder approach is much more collaborative and requires all stakeholder groups to work together on a new system design being "constantly kept informed by their representatives and allowed to 'buy in' or opt out" (Reigeluth, 1993, p. 118). This model is based largely on the experiences of people well versed in systems design. It was acknowledged at the time that much work was needed to test and improve this process model: "My hope is that this tentative process model will provide a useful springboard, if not foundation, for further development of powerful process models for the fundamental change of our educational system" (Reigeluth, 1993, p. 130). However, it is notable that follow-up work has been very limited during this period of nearly 30 years since this paper was first published. The editors of this book hope that it makes a contribution to changing this situation.

More recently the UN's Sustainable Development Goals (SDGs) are intended to challenge both developed and developing countries to provide the best education possible for all children. The editors hope this book supports the UN's SDGs by helping better decision making by the policy makers who have leadership responsibility in their country's national education service.

Around the world, countries organise the structure of their national education services in similar ways, and the OECD identifies many problems held in common: teacher quality, teacher development, the link between curriculum, assessment and employers and wider needs of society.

We use the word 'service' to emphasise the human element of any national education provision. National education provision depends on the services that individual teachers provide supported by a system of structures. The word 'system' is used to refer to supporting structures.

Each chapter deals with an area which provides a major *foundation for* a national education system and service: such areas include goals, aims, values and principles; curriculum, assessment, leadership (for innovation and development) and accountability; issues of social justice and inclusion (social mobility, selection, segregation, SEND, adult education) initial and continuing teacher development, the concept of professionalism and access to research-based knowledge to underpin practice. A major area not included is the financing of the service as documenting and benchmarking variation between services was beyond the scope of a single chapter in this book. Each chapter ends with *policy options* and the penultimate chapter discusses *consequences* of a range of policy options. *Decisions* of course are influenced by the values of the decision makers.

In a quest for improvement, teachers often find that initiatives developed by one government are copied and applied in other countries, only to be abandoned back in the original country as a new education minister moves on to the next initiative (fad or fashion). In other countries, a more consensual approach can be found with a number of jurisdictions requiring a 'super-majority' in the parliament or relevant governing body, for major changes to be made. In England, the Secretary of State for education, working with politicians from their own party, and without the support of even a simple majority of voters, makes choices about national educational provision based on the ideology of the party that shape society for decades.

Teachers are very aware that the outcomes of their work – the development of the mind and brain, personal well-being and lifelong fulfilment –are very difficult to measure. Teachers are also very aware that politicians would never interfere in medical practices in the way they feel able to alter educational practices.

As authors, we would like to see a situation where top-level and up-to-date summaries and syntheses of research underpinning educational practices are easily accessible to teachers, politicians, parents, learners and inspectors so that change in education could be carefully planned and based on evidence. See Chapter 19 for how 21st century technologies could be cost-effectively used to support universal access to the latest quality assured research-based knowledge in subject content and pedagogy regardless of the country of origin.

This book sets out choices for national leaders of education services and the consequences of choices from the teacher/parent/employer/society and community perspectives.

There are plenty of self styled education gurus eager to provide advice to governments which, as often as not, turns out to be of financial benefit to those espousing the ideas. We recommend consultation with networks of experts who collectively can draw on a wide range of research and evidence across age ranges, contexts and countries.

We hope this book enables those taking decisions at the national level to pause and consider the unintended consequences of their decisions before committing to courses of action.

The book uses the English education service as an example in a number of chapters as it has undergone particularly radical change since a change of government in 2010 and it provides an example of the consequences of a government pursuing a 'small state' agenda which leaves the provision of vital services to the free market.

The book focuses on the 0–18 age group but recognises that access to life-long education is necessary for citizens to keep up with changes in the modern world.

Chapter 20 examines the potential consequences of different types of policy choices driven by different sets of values. The choice of how to act remains with the policy makers, although in Chapter 6, a radical de-coupling of government from complete control of a national education service is proposed, returning decision making power over education to a cross-political party group representing the different political parties in Parliament.

The final chapter (Chapter 21) on *Education in emergencies: pandemic/disaster planning for education sector continuity* was added after the bulk of the work on the book was completed in order to address some of the issues raised by the onset of the pandemic that began in March 2020 as a result of the COVID-19 virus.

Brian Hudson, Marilyn Leask and Sarah Younie, September 2020

References

Benn, M., Fielding, M. and Moss, P. (2019) For a New Public Education in a New Public School, *FORUM*, Vol. 61, No. 2. http://dx.doi.org/10.15730/forum.2019.61.2.147

Reigeluth, C. M. (1993) Principles of Educational Systems Design, *International Journal of Educational Research*, Vol. 19, No. 2, 117–131.

ACKNOWLEDGEMENTS

This book provides an analysis drawing on research and other evidence from many countries and systems.

The editors are particularly grateful to those who gave time to attend workshops where the ideas were discussed and developed and those who gave their time willingly to comment on drafts.

Those who attended shared their knowledge and their experience of positive and negative change in the education service over many decades and from many countries.

We thank the following for granting permission to publish and adapt work for which they hold the copyright:

- Education futures collaboration charity (Chapter 19)
- OECD (Chapters 2 and 13)
- Peter Lang publishers (Chapter 15)

We are very grateful also for the generous support from Karlstad University in helping to finalize the text at the end of the editorial process.

SECTION 1

An education service for the future

Values and principles

The book is divided into five sections, each dealing with a section of an education service, and a sixth, providing a summary and reflections on the previous chapters.

We conceptualise an education service as an ecosystem with interdependent components and foundation elements.

Section 1 Foundations: aims, values, principles

This Section introduces ideas about the fundamental values and principles which underpin the decisions made about the structure and function of any education service.

Chapter 1 introduces the global context for education which affects all countries. By way of example, it introduces the national education system review process adopted in Wales and the outcomes. The chapter raises issues of accountability and engagement of education professionals in decision making.

Chapter 2 introduces the values underpinning the OECD's "Global competence" framework and the international work that is being done to identify 21st-century skills for learners. In light of this international thinking, the author challenges you to identify the values which would underpin any education service that a nation might develop.

Chapter 3 challenges you to identify the principles, arising from these values, which would inform the development and operation of a national education service. The chapter introduces implementation challenges such as the complexity of the system and unintended consequences, which may result during policy implementation or beyond.

Section 2, which follows, examines the application of these ideas in the English context as the structures and processes in the English system which underpin the service to the populace, represent an example of extreme processes creating a system which is an international outlier. The service and professionalism provided by teachers to learners, however, remains similar to that of other countries.

1

TOWARDS A LEARNING EDUCATION SYSTEM?

Globalisation, change, improvement and accountability in uncertain times

Graham Donaldson

Introduction

The role of school education in promoting the learning and wellbeing of young people has never been more important, yet our understanding of how best to achieve these goals seems to be becoming increasingly tenuous.

> Change is the only constant.
>
> *Heraclitus, the Greek philosopher, around 500 BC*

> A crucial policy issue is ' . . . how to deliver high quality, efficient, equitable and innovative education in increasingly complex education systems.' . . . [T]he challenge is to ' . . . balance responsiveness to local diversity with the ability to ensure national objectives.'
>
> *(OECD, 2016)*

In the face of dramatic and accelerating changes to how we live and work, the role of school education and the nature of the curriculum has become highly contested. At the same time, evidence that established approaches to education reform have had limited effectiveness suggests that there will be a need for fresh thinking about educational governance and approaches to change if schools are to keep pace with a rapidly transforming external environment.

What then should be the role of school education in face of the growing fragility of many current assumptions about its enduring relevance to the future? How can we be confident about what learning matters most and ensure high standards as external expectations change? How can we balance apparent tensions between pressure to raise standards and student and teacher wellbeing? How can schools best address inequalities and meet the diverse needs of all their learners? Can school systems reform in ways and at a pace that reflect an increasingly febrile and complex world? What might be the key characteristics of a learning education system that can meet these challenges?

The change imperative

History bears witness to the capacity of human beings to adapt and even thrive in face of the inevitability of change. New baselines are constantly emerging upon which successive generations then build. Advances in technology, for example, such as the invention of the printing press, the harnessing of steam power or the advent of electricity have each transformed how people have lived and worked and how societies and economies have functioned. However, developments in science and technology feeding globalisation and allied to climate change have introduced changes over at least the last thirty years that impact how we live and work on a scale and at a pace that bear little comparison to those experienced by previous generations. The significance of the current context is summed up by Friedman (2019), who argues that we are 'living through one of the greatest inflection points in history'. Similarly, Andreas Schleicher, the Director for Education and Skills at the Organisation for Economic Development and Cooperation (OECD), points to the interaction between technology and globalisation as making, 'the world more volatile, complex and uncertain' (Schleicher, 2018a). While we cannot be sure about the longer-term impact of the coronavirus pandemic, it seems likely that it will have a catalytic effect on pre-existing forces and tensions. For example, questions about how to determine an appropriate balance between digital and face-to-face learning or how to address growing national and international inequalities have already been thrown into stark relief by the exigencies of the pandemic.

Perhaps the strongest underlying pressure to change has stemmed from developments in technology. From the second half of the 20th century we have seen an accelerating process of technological change, from the earliest computers to contemporary developments in artificial intelligence, big data, biotechnology, quantum physics, robotics and miniaturisation. Since the earliest computers and the development of the World Wide Web in 1989, the world has seen the power of algorithms and accelerated connectivity transform how we live, relate and work.

Technological development is already significantly affecting the nature of employment with the displacement of established career paths and the demand for particular and new skill sets. While it is not possible to predict the shape of the emerging job market with any certainty, it is clear that the availability of occupations that are open to digitisation will diminish while those that complement and make use of the digital world will grow (Cowan, 2014). Experience suggests that while innovation displaces existing jobs, it also creates new occupations, making fears about longer-term mass unemployment less compelling. However, even if such an optimistic assumption proves correct, there will be an inevitable gap between displacement and replacement with major implications for those affected.

Frey (2019) highlights the risks to society and even democracy associated with 'the increasing divide between winners and losers from automation' (page 343). We need to explore the extent to which education can help to mitigate these short-term effects. If we cannot predict the requirements of future jobs, can we nonetheless help young people to understand the processes that are shaping their lives and promote their capacity to engage positively with change?

The term 'globalisation' captures the competing pressures of a world that is increasingly interdependent and interconnected and yet at the same time highly competitive. Individual countries can no longer feel insulated from developments elsewhere in the world; one country's energy consumption, for example, has consequences far beyond its own borders. Global companies have maximised value by creating international supply chains, drawing on assets of labour and expertise wherever they can contribute most efficiently. For countries the result is constant pressure to compete for investment while for individuals sources of employment become increasingly transient. Long-term careers in a single company or particular line of work are being overtaken to an increasing extent by the 'gig economy'. The prize lies in high value occupations requiring personal and collective investment in innovation, creativity and learning.

At the same time, we are seeing changing patterns of migration, partly reflecting the mobility of expertise, partly movement to accessible and more attractive sources of employment and partly displacement of people in the face of disruptive elements such as conflict or compromised availability of basic natural resources. Education systems are struggling to respond quickly to an increasingly multi-cultural society and shifting demands for expertise.

These twin pressures of globalisation and technological development, further accentuated by the current pandemic, introduce unprecedented levels of uncertainty about how today's young people will earn a living. But increased connectivity also introduces further pressures on our lives individually, socially and as citizens. Digital social media expand opportunities, removing barriers of geography and time in human interaction, but they also introduce fresh concerns about privacy, bullying abuse, exploitation and mental health.

Digital connectivity will make more participatory forms of democracy more possible or even more likely, giving rise to important questions about systems of governance, political cultures and the nature of citizenship in the future. For example, the issue of sustainability in the face of resource depletion and climate change has major ethical and value implications requiring measured consideration of often competing priorities. Autocracy thrives by providing simplistic answers to complex questions. Access to information and opportunities to voice opinions are limitless but tests of truth are much more elusive.

Taken together, these and other engines of disruptive change pose questions about the role of education in helping young people to navigate and contribute to an increasingly uncertain world. How far will today's assumptions about schooling continue to hold firm in a world characterised by volatility, complexity and unpredictability? Should we see schools as islands of stability, passing on established cultures and ways of thinking through a curriculum that has been in place for decades? Or should schools be incubators of creativity that foster abilities associated with connecting and applying knowledge and discernment in identifying and evaluating its integrity? In reality, they must be all of these things. What is needed is open and informed debate about the purposes of schooling and a determination to keep reflecting and learning if schools are to continue to serve the long-term interests of our young people.

Revisiting the purposes of schooling – the UK context

In the UK, the period from 1870 through to the mid-1970s saw an almost unquestioned faith in the power of education to drive personal, societal and economic wellbeing. The developing political goal throughout that period envisaged as many young people as possible spending longer in school and moving into tertiary education. In the United Kingdom, the school leaving age became 15 in 1947 and 16 in 1972, with participation in education in England to age 18 now mandatory. At the same time, the period since the mid-1960s has also seen a greater policy focus on the role of education in mitigating inequality. The philosophy of the Butler Education Act of 1944 with its tri-partite school structure has increasingly but not entirely given way to a comprehensive school system within which the purposes of education are seen as a common entitlement. The introduction of a national curriculum in 1988, for example, was in part driven by the pursuit of greater equity. The importance of pursuing both equity and excellence in school education is now professed as one of the key drivers of education policy across the UK.

Until the 1970s the fundamental purposes of schooling were not the prime focus of political attention; what was taught remained largely the preserve of educational professionals. Fred Jarvis, who was general secretary of the National Union of Teachers (NUT) at that time, commented in a *Guardian* article in 2001 that 'the whole tradition was that what the schools actually taught was not the concern in terms of responsibility of the government or ministers. Whenever questions were asked in the House, it was always "those were matters for the teaching profession"' (Woodward, 2001).

Arguably a 1976 speech in Ruskin College, Oxford, by the then British Prime Minister signalled the start of a trend towards reduced faith in professional educators and increased interest from politicians and 'think tanks' about the content of education. Three quotations from Callaghan's speech illustrate the nature of the growing concerns.

> The goals of our education . . . are to equip children to the best of their ability for a lively, constructive place in society and also to fit them to do a job of work. Not one or the other, but both. . . . [T]here is no virtue in producing socially well-adjusted members of society who are unemployed because they do not have the skills.

In today's world higher standards are demanded than were required yesterday and there are simply fewer jobs for those without skill. Therefore we demand more from our schools than did our grandparents.

It is almost as though some people would wish that the subject matter and purpose of education should not have public attention focused on it; nor that profane hands should be allowed to touch it. I cannot believe that this is a considered reaction. . . . Public interest is strong and legitimate and will be satisfied. We spend £6bn a year on education, so there will be discussion.

The UK Conservative Government in the 1980s became increasingly active in its attempts to influence school education, culminating in the 1988 Education Reform Act. That Act, which did not apply in Scotland, represented a radically different view of the relationship between the state and schools. It introduced a national curriculum whose purposes, as defined in the Act, were that it should promote the spiritual, moral, cultural, mental and physical development of pupils at the school and of society and that it should prepare such pupils for the opportunities, responsibilities and experiences of adult life. The Act then required prescribed programmes of study in core and foundation subjects, attainment targets at 'Key Stages' and national tests of performance. This prescription, through statute, of the content of what was to be taught in local authority schools in England has remained fundamentally unchanged since then. Changes to the content of the curriculum and the nature of external examinations introduced after 2010 re-emphasised the importance of content and strengthened perceptions of a hierarchy of subjects.

Beyond England, there have been moves internationally to define or redefine the purposes of education and reflect these purposes through reforms in the curriculum. For example, Sinnema and Aitken (2013) identify an international trend in curriculum development towards future-focused goals that promote equity and coherence and relate more directly to the development of competencies. While the internal emphases varied, developments such as Singapore's Teach Less Learn More (2004), Scotland's Curriculum for Excellence (2004), Australia's Melbourne Declaration (2007) and New Zealand's National Curriculum (2007) all reflected a shift towards the promotion of capacities or broad competencies that were seen as a better preparation for a less predictable future for all students. More recently, Wales's Curriculum for Wales is based on four purposes relating to lifelong learning, creativity, citizenship and wellbeing.

Some countries that have performed highly on the Organisation for Economic Cooperation and Development's (OECD) Programme for International Student Assessment (PISA) are also rethinking the purposes of schooling. Finland, for example, has undertaken radical curriculum reform. Sanni Grahn-Laasonen (2017) explained the direction of Finland's curriculum policy by commenting that

We live in a world where everything is changing at an ever faster pace. I believe that learning to learn, being able to acquire new skills, and thinking critically and creatively are some of the key factors for the education

of tomorrow. Equal opportunity for everyone is an important value. . . .
A school system is never finished, and teachers are the change makers.

(Grahn-Laasonen, 2017)

Biesta and Priestley (2013) detected three major curriculum trends: a return
to child-centred and constructivist learning; a reassertion of teacher agency; and
a focus on competencies or capacities. They identify a trend in curriculum policy
'where the purposes of education are no longer articulated in terms of what
students should learn but in terms of what they should become' (Biesta and
Priestley, 2013).

Developments in England, where there remains a more explicit commitment
to traditional structures with core and foundation subjects, have also introduced
requirements to teach broader components such as citizenship and relationships.

Taken as a whole, it is clear that the purpose of school education as reflected
in national curricular expectations is becoming increasingly contested. The current trend appears to be towards more holistic purposes and competence-based
approaches. Purposes must then be reflected in a structure through which the
intentions of the curriculum can be expressed. Recent international developments
generally retain subject knowledge as a key curriculum building block but use
curriculum frameworks to establish a broader definition of desirable knowledge
that includes connections between subjects. Traditional subjects may be subsumed
under broader areas of learning such as the arts or humanities with a greater emphasis on instrumental goals associated with authenticity, application and creativity.
However, such structures generally have in common a belief in the importance of
subject knowledge.

A further factor influencing these curriculum reforms has been the recognition
that teaching and learning approaches need to be carefully matched to the purposes
of learning leading to a stronger emphasis on pedagogy and teacher professionalism.
Teaching becomes more than instruction as the relationship between what is to be
learned and the context and experience of learning itself becomes more significant.
Holistic purposes do not lend themselves to tightly defined, single-track instructional approaches.

The effective translation of competencies into a curriculum framework and
from there to children and young people's experiences in the classroom is complex.
There are clear risks associated with too little or too much specification, insufficient attention to fundamental disciplinary knowledge and a possible disconnect
between curricular goals, teacher beliefs and skills and parental expectations.

The policy challenges associated with the determination of purposes and the
creation of related curriculum frameworks are both complicated and complex. The
conditions and demands of the present constrain longer-term strategic action. (See
the proposal for Education England as an example of a long-term strategy in Chapter 6.) However, the need to resolve such challenges is inescapable. In the absence
of such reform the risk is that educational systems pursue effectiveness in relation
to outcomes that are increasingly irrelevant.

The improvement paradox and accountability

High stakes accountability systems can

> divert attention from meeting the needs of young people as individuals. . . .
> At its worst it can inculcate a culture of fear, inhibiting creativity and genuine
> professional analysis and discussion. Pupils can come to serve the reputation
> of a school rather than the school serving the needs of the pupil.
>
> *(Donaldson, 2018, p. 23)*

The search for greater school effectiveness has been central to educational policy for over 50 years. While debate about the nature of the curriculum has grown recently, the focus of policy has been dominated by pressure to raise 'standards', increasing intervention in the ways schools are governed and even in classroom practice itself.

In particular, tight and often statutory specification of content and standards; measurement and inter-school comparison of outcomes; competition; external scrutiny; and greater control of the teaching workforce have all featured as key aspects in the pursuit of effectiveness.

The drive for greater effectiveness has mainly been a top-down, centre-periphery strategy within which schools and teachers have largely been seen as implementers or deliverers of externally set expectations. In contrast to earlier freedom and trust in schools and teachers, the curriculum in many countries has been specified in statute, creating a clear set of expectations for schools to meet. Such an approach was partly designed to establish curriculum entitlement for all pupils as opposed to the variability in provision that can be created by local circumstances and beliefs and partly to ensure a more direct relationship to perceived economic and societal imperatives.

Where national expectations are set in legislation, there is a requirement to ensure that such expectations are understood and followed across a country. The tendency has been to adopt a linear model of change whereby attention is focused on communication chains, provision of exemplar resources and cascade approaches to training, together with feedback and accountability mechanisms to evaluate how effectively expectations are being met. Managerial and technocratic processes at least partially replace professional values, knowledge, skills and judgement. Teacher agency, the capacity and opportunity to initiate professional action, is circum-scribed by central prescription and the demands of external accountabilities (Priest-ley et al., 2015). In England, for example, the freedom of self-governing academies to determine their own curriculum is subject to the ultimate test of the approval of the national inspectorate, the Office for Standards in Education (Ofsted). National literacy and numeracy strategies established by the Labour Government in 1998 defined both 'the what' and 'the how' of teaching. Equally, significant responsi-bility for the formation of teachers has moved progressively from universities to schools, now reflecting more of a quasi-apprenticeship or craft model with much less emphasis on the theoretical underpinnings of learning and the teacher's role.

High-stakes accountability has also been used as a key driving force of improvement. The publication of the results of tests and examinations in relation to national targets creates direct pressure on schools to raise standards as defined by the tests and the targets. At the same time, external inspection of schools leading to public reports that grade the school provide a further dimension of high-stakes accountability.

Evidence of the impact of centrally driven reform is at best mixed. While political rhetoric can highlight improved test and inspection results, research evidence of success is much more qualified. Hoyle and Wallace (2005) found that

> there is strong evidence from a variety of sources that two decades of reform have not led to anticipated levels of educational improvement, and certainly not commensurate with levels of investment in education, but have led to widespread teacher and headteacher dissatisfaction.

Similarly, Kerr and West (2007) comment that the impact of policies has been, at best, mixed. They suggest that neither general nor targeted interventions have, thus far, demonstrated substantial sustained improvements that can be spread widely. Perhaps the following quote from Hattie (2009, p. 254) best sums up the thrust of research evidence: 'We have in education a long history of innovation but it rarely touches but a chosen few'. Hattie's observation is further reinforced by the finding of Tymms and Merrell (2010, p. 456) that '[f]ive hundred million pounds was spent on the National Literacy Strategy with almost no impact on reading levels'.

If the impact of centrally driven reform is limited, there is also evidence that high-stakes accountability systems can lead to significant, negative unintended consequences. Donaldson (2018, p. 23) in his review of the Welsh education inspectorate, Estyn, found that:

> In addition to the stress that these systems inevitably place on schools and their pupils, such cultures can divert attention from meeting the needs of young people as individuals as schools seek to disguise weaknesses and present themselves in as good a light as possible. Undue attention may be given to those pupils whose marginal improvement will affect performance figures or attempts may be made to select the school population at the expense of young people with the greatest needs. At its worst it can inculcate a culture of fear, inhibiting creativity and genuine professional analysis and discussion. Pupils can come to serve the reputation of a school rather than the school serving the needs of the pupil.

The drive to raise standards through testing and inspection has focused almost exclusively on outcomes in literacy and numeracy and performance in national examinations, supplemented by the three yearly results of PISA. This relatively narrow definition of standards has resulted in reduced breadth in pupils' curriculum experience. Such concerns led the head of Ofsted, Amanda Spielman, to observe at the 2017 Festival of Education,

> all managers are responsible for making sure teachers' time is spent on what matters most. This means concentrating on the curriculum and the substance of education, not preparing your pupils to jump through a series of account-ability hoops. . . . [T]o reduce education down to this kind of functionalist level is rather wretched.
>
> *(Spielman, 2017)*

The need to raise standards and improve equity in performance are likely to remain as the central requirements of modern education systems. However, a strategy that relies on central prescription, marketisation and high-stakes accountability has a number of problematic consequences. While such approaches may lead to more schools that can be regarded as satisfactory and some that are rated excellent, these relatively modest results are achieved at significant costs. Compliance, gaming and risk avoidance are natural responses to external accountability and are inconsistent with the flexibility and creativity that are needed in a context characterised by innovation, uncertainty and ethical complexity. Markets create losers as well as winners and can accentuate inequality. Leadership can become directed towards impression management, disguising weakness rather than working openly and collaboratively to secure real improvement. Teacher agency with its sense of professional responsibility is reduced to mechanistic implementation within narrowly defined parameters and expectations. Students are trained to perform in tests and examinations with only limited opportunities to develop as rounded individuals and develop their creativity.

The policy debate in many countries has been dominated by trying to achieve improvement by doubling down on the mechanisms of external specification and control. At the same time, trends in governance have been towards more local freedom within which schools have greater control over key decisions including staffing and resources. Such freedom, however, is heavily constrained by the impact of funding restrictions, accountability pressures and the need to compete for students. The consequence is a complex mosaic that can restrict professional agency and inhibit the scope for strategic responses to the longer-term needs of young people.

Towards a learning education system?

Looking across recent developments, there is an emerging view that real and sustained educational improvement requires:

- clarity of long-term purpose, encompassing equity, excellence and wellbeing
- a curriculum that balances national guidance with local creativity
- the creative engagement of teachers, individually and collectively, in decisions that affect learning

- professional capacity building
- re-imagined leadership and
- much more constructive accountability

In other words, it requires a system that serves the long-term needs of young people through a constant and pervasive process of reflection and exploration: a learning education system.

In contrast to centrally directed reform, a learning system is founded on the principle that increased complexity requires a breadth of vision, a degree of humility and a belief in collaboration. It also recognises the importance of context to real and sustained improvements in quality. Linear change models depend on sequential, usually top-down implementation approaches but in such approaches translation and interpretation of the original intentions can mean that classroom reality may bear little relationship to those intentions. Complexities associated with an increasingly febrile external environment, more pluralistic governance arrangements and empowered and demanding stakeholders require networked and agile systems that learn and adapt.

Both the OECD and the European Union (EU) have been exploring new ways to approach change. The OECD's work on schools as learning organisations points to the difficulties of the education sector in innovating. It refers to teachers' professional expertise extending beyond the classroom to becoming 'knowledge workers' in response to the need for greater agility in a rapidly changing environment (OECD, 2018). Countries have been trying to accommodate their increasingly complex education systems to the changing times, but the education sector does not always have a good track record of successful innovation. Equally, an EU working group has stressed the need for shared goals, less hierarchical structures and participative, 'critical friend' processes. It sees the need for career-long professional development and for the provision of 'the space, time and trust to encourage school leaders and teachers to innovate' (ET2020).

The emerging main features of such a learning system are consistent values, clarity of purpose, a commitment to subsidiarity, a culture of collaboration, investment in career-long professional learning, ethical and distributive leadership and constructive accountability.

Particularly in periods of rapid and deep change, clarity about agreed fundamental purposes is essential if the curriculum is not to become overloaded and potentially obsolete. Debate about what those purposes should be is therefore essential. The challenge is to establish a long-term strategic direction that goes beyond short-term effectiveness as the only measure of success. A focus on effectiveness and improvement should reflect agreement on the purposes that these processes should serve.

As described earlier, the international debate seems to be moving towards purposes that describe the competences required to engage positively with uncertainty. In Australia, Scotland and Singapore, for example, purposes relate to areas such as lifelong learning, creativity, citizenship and wellbeing. The OECD

(2018) in its '2030 Project' refers to the small world of the curriculum and the big world of learning. It sees competency as being more than just the acquisition of knowledge and skills, involving 'the mobilisation of knowledge, skills, attitudes and values to meet complex demands'. Schleicher goes on to argue that, 'Education can equip learners with agency and a sense of purpose, and the competencies they need to shape their own lives and contribute to the lives of others' (Schleicher, 2018b).

However the purposes of school education are framed, they should address the need to equip young people to engage successfully with their future lives. The unpredictability of that future means that the school curriculum must go beyond the acquisition of content to a focus on deep knowledge and, critically, the capacity to apply that knowledge creatively. Deep learning is not simply how much knowledge has been acquired but real understanding of the knowledge that matters most in relation to fundamental educational purposes and the capacity to apply that learning in different contexts.

A governance culture based on subsidiarity recognises that hierarchies and lockstep management approaches are ill suited to the complexity of the challenges facing education. A wide-ranging 2016 OECD report identifies a crucial policy issue as being 'how to deliver high quality, efficient, equitable and innovative education in increasingly complex education systems' (p. 3). It concludes that the challenge is to 'balance responsiveness to local diversity with the ability to ensure national objectives' (OECD, 2016, p. 11). Interdependence, self-regulation and fluid relationships characterise emerging governance models.

Subsidiarity requires scope for significant decision making at successive levels in the education system. Decisions are not passed down as requirements to be delivered but flow from a clear understanding of respective roles and responsibilities throughout. Collaboration and respect are key features of subsidiarity in a learning system.

More specifically, a commitment to subsidiarity requires a policy process that secures engagement in and commitment to the strategic direction while leaving genuine scope at the local and school levels to determine the ways in which national objectives will be realised. The implication is that legislation should specify purposes, duties and processes but not the detailed content of the curriculum. Boundaries and degrees of specificity should be determined through a collaborative process involving honest and careful analysis of respective views and strengths. The objective is that young people in schools should experience relevant education in ways that engage and challenge them and that schools and teachers should be central to achieving that end.

A learning system is founded on the ability of schools, teachers and other practitioners to play a direct and creative part in shaping and realising the curriculum. That implies a different and in many ways deeper form of professionalism than one that is focused on delivery or implementation. Real agency, career-long professional learning and re-imagined leadership are all integral to a learning education system committed to subsidiarity.

The International Alliance of Leading Educational Institutes (National Institute of Education, 2008), described a redefined professionalism embodying a commitment to lifelong learning and reflection. Similarly, Donaldson (2011) in his review of teacher education in Scotland highlighted the need for extended professionalism if teachers and school leaders are to be 'prime agents in the change process.' And OECD Secretary General Angel Gurría in his Foreword to a 2011 report (Schleicher, 2011) recognised that teachers will increasingly need 'not just to improve educational outcomes in classrooms, but to be at the centre of the improvement efforts themselves and to embrace and lead reform'. Since 2011, a series of international OECD-led summits on the teaching profession have consistently stressed the need for greater investment in teachers' professional growth.

A learning education system must therefore embody reinvigorated and reconceptualised approaches to teacher professionalism. Equally, new thinking about leadership is required if the right conditions are to be created for teachers to exercise their widened professional responsibilities. Leadership that focuses on the school's competitive performance or on its place in league tables is unlikely to create such conditions. Competition is difficult to reconcile with a collaborative culture that harnesses collective professional capital in the pursuit of better learning and improved outcomes for young people. If broad purposes, creativity, collegiality and local context are to be central to the educational culture, then leadership needs to give them significant priority in key decisions. The fundamental goal remains to maximise the quality of all young people's learning and to foster both their and the staff's wellbeing.

External, mainly summative, evaluation directed towards accountability has assumed an increasing place in policy and practice over at least the last 30 years. However, accountability systems that focus narrowly on outcomes without sufficient attention to supporting improvement or to understanding of context are inconsistent with a learning education system. A major OECD review (2013) of evaluation and assessment calls for such systems to support improvement in the classroom and for the engagement of schools and teachers in the process. External evaluation mechanisms that focus on compliance can lead to the curriculum and pedagogy becoming narrow and mechanistic.

Accountability remains important in a learning education system but must reflect the breadth of purpose underpinning school education. It should encourage and complement self-evaluation, providing a vital external perspective in securing improvement. If improvement is to be driven by learning, then there needs to be trust that the identification of areas for improvement is not then used to downgrade the school. Indeed, inspections that focus on high stakes gradings are in many ways antithetical to an open, learning culture.

Lessons from a small country – Wales

Many of the features of a learning education system described previously are present to varying degrees in countries across the world. Wales, in particular, provides a developing example of a comprehensive approach to embedding these features in both policy and practice.

Since devolution in 1999, Wales has had responsibility for almost all aspects of school education including most recently teachers' terms and conditions. Its hitherto close alignment to English education has changed progressively from that date.

Confidence in the performance of Welsh schools diminished following a series of poor PISA results dating from 2009. In response to this growing concern, the Welsh Government instituted a number of policy initiatives designed to secure improvement, partly by challenging assumed complacency in the system. Testing of students, appraisals of teachers and colour-coded banding of schools were among the measures introduced. The result was a high-stakes accountability culture that an OECD review in 2014 suggested had failed to strike the right balance between accountability and improvement. At the same time, pressure on the national curriculum was growing and Graham Donaldson (author of this chapter) was asked to undertake a review of national curriculum and assessment arrangements. His report, "Successful Futures" (Donaldson, 2015) made a set of recommendations covering curriculum, assessment, governance, professional learning, leadership and accountability. Following national consultation all 68 recommendations were accepted and a major reform programme was set in train.

The Welsh reforms are described in a national mission statement (Welsh Government, 2017). The central objective is the development of a new Curriculum for Wales supported by a number of enabling objectives covering:

- developing a high-quality education profession
- inspirational leaders working collaboratively to raise standards
- strong and inclusive schools committed to excellence, equity and wellbeing
- robust assessment, evaluation and accountability arrangements supporting a self-improving system

In addition, Wales is working with the OECD to develop its schools as learning organisations (OECD, 2018). Taken as a whole, Wales is committed to establishing many of the features of the kind of learning education system described in this chapter.

The curriculum in Wales is now founded on four broad purposes: to develop young people as: successful, capable learners; ethical, informed citizens; enterprising, creative contributors; and healthy, confident individuals. These purposes are more than simply statements of intent but are explicit expectations that will drive decisions about content, pedagogy and assessment.

A unique feature of the Welsh approach is its commitment to the kind of subsidiarity recommended by the Successful Futures report. The Welsh Government's approach to subsidiarity involved a co-constructive approach to the development of the curriculum. While Successful Futures set the strategic direction, around 170 'pioneer' schools drawn from across Wales undertook the development of the national curriculum framework. Co-construction as applied in Wales involved striking a balance between creating consistent national expectations based on the four purposes of Successful Futures and placing duties on those responsible for the realisation of those expectations. The interpretation and elaboration of the framework gave a leading role to the profession working with academics, officials and experienced developers from within Wales and beyond. The final aspect of co-construction in Wales is the realisation of the curriculum in the classroom through giving schools and teachers significant scope to elaborate the curriculum in ways that respond to the local context.

In governance terms, the Welsh Government retains the key leadership role but is discharging that role through more emphasis on facilitation and support rather than direction and control. Its Education Directorate has itself adopted a learning organisation approach (Santos, 2019) and is working with the OECD to adapt its own approaches to reflect the advice it is giving to schools about the value of becoming a learning organisation. Similarly, there is also a change of role for Wales's four regional consortia with a move from an emphasis on challenge to one of support.

The other elements of a learning system are also central to the reform programme. Professor John Furlong undertook a review of teacher education and his report, 'Teaching Tomorrow's Teachers' (Furlong, 2017), is in process of being implemented. In addition, Professor Mick Waters orchestrated the development of new teaching and leadership standards that articulated directly with the new curriculum and the focus on greater teacher agency. A new national professional learning model has also been developed, based on greater collaboration amongst the key providers, including the universities. A further piece in the reform jigsaw was the establishment of a National Leadership Academy, again in recognition of the need to rethink and strengthen leadership in the new context.

One of the most challenging aspects of the reform lies in winning support for necessary changes to accountability. The 'high-stakes' culture developed in the period after the 2009 PISA results was seen as incompatible with a reform programme based on co-construction and subsidiarity. In line with recommendations from OECD Reviews (OECD, 2017, 2018) that evaluation and accountability should focus on learning and improvement, the Welsh Government is reviewing its evaluation and accountability arrangements. The education inspectorate, Estyn, also instituted a review of its role (Donaldson, 2018) and is moving to an approach to inspection based more strongly on self-evaluation, without gradings in inspection reports and with an explicit commitment to improvement and capacity building.

Taken as a whole, the reforms being undertaken in Wales reflect many of the features of a learning education system described in this chapter. The development programme is currently planned to run through to 2022 followed by a phased introduction with full realisation by 2025.

Reflections

The world is in a period of deep and transformative change and uncertainty. The nature, scope and pace of that change remains impossible to predict. However, its implications inevitably challenge our understanding of how best our education systems can help prepare future generations to shape societies and economies and to thrive through uncertainty.

Climate change is already posing existential threats to countries across the globe and its implications will exercise the minds and the values of future citizens. Technology has transformed how we live and work but the future impact of artificial intelligence, robotics and new forms of connectivity will undoubtedly present new opportunities and pose fresh challenges. At the same time, access to technology is also accentuating inequities in young people's capacity to learn in both conventional instruction and the development of the habits and skills of independent learning. The coronavirus pandemic has highlighted underlying tensions and energised creativity in ways that may transform the future social, economic and educational landscape. We need a school curriculum that can help young people to understand those challenges and help equip each one of them to seize the opportunities offered.

Debate about how best to proceed spans a broad spectrum of possibilities. At one end lies the belief that the fundamentals of knowledge are timeless and that the school curriculum should continue to be built around established subjects and centrally defined content. At the other end there is a view that sees the need to devote greater attention to building capacities in our young people that will help equip them to meet as yet unknown future challenges. Arguments can polarise around one or other of these extremes but the way forward is likely to be found in balancing elements from each. Achieving that balance will require openness to ideas and evidence and recognition that the forces that will shape the remainder of the twenty-first century are very different from those of the past.

Whatever decisions are taken about the nature of the curriculum, our approaches to education reform need to reach into every classroom and every community in order to address fundamental issues of equity and relevance. We need to be both agile and discriminating in what and how we teach. That will require a much greater focus on purpose and context, striking a judicious balance between an agreed strategic course and the ability of those who are directly engaged in the learning process to shape the reality of the classroom experience. An OECD discussion paper, looking specifically at Wales, has highlighted the need to adopt more sophisticated governance and change strategies in the face of an increasingly complex landscape:

> [T]he age of incremental evolution and piecemeal policy approaches is ending. The rate of change in the world is exponential and what tomorrow looks like for today's children eludes accurate prediction. This means that education systems need to have deep reflections on how they are adapting and frank conversations about why some of their reforms truly transform learning and lives . . . and others stumble out of the starting block.
>
> *(Santos, 2019)*

We will need to raise 'standards', but we need to be sure that we have a definition of standards that embodies what matters most for our young people and their futures. We will need to address issues of equity and wellbeing and that means eschewing simplistic command and control policies if teachers are to meet the diverse needs of their pupils. We will need to invest in the professional growth of our educators and leaders if they are to exercise real agency. We will need to establish forms of accountability that give necessary assurance without reducing learning and teaching to mechanistic compliance. We will need an approach to innovation and improvement based on a culture of continuous learning.

The previous discussion suggests three broad policy options. The choices made will be influenced by context, values and beliefs about the appropriate role for professionals in contributing to policy as well as practice in increasingly complex global, national and local environments.

Policy options

The issues raised in this chapter lead to a number of policy options:

Policy option 1 (accountability through scrutiny and pressure): adopt a high-stakes approach to accountability that defines specific expectations supported by strong, compliance-based external scrutiny.

Policy option 2 (accountability focused on improvement): create an expectation that self-evaluation will complement external scrutiny, both having a strong focus on improvement.

Policy option 3 (accountability within a learning system): establish self-evaluation and external scrutiny as part of a wider culture of policy and professional learning that recognises the need for constant reflection on both the what and the how of education and for schools to have the confidence and capacity to innovate.

References

Biesta, G. and Priestley, M. (2013), 'Capacities and the Curriculum', in M. Priestley and G. Biesta (eds), *Reinventing the Curriculum*, Bloomsbury, London.
Cowan, T. (2014), *Average is Over*, Plume Penguin Books, New York.
Donaldson, G. (2011), *Teaching Scotland's Future*, Scottish Government, Edinburgh.
Donaldson, G. (2015), *Successful Futures*, Welsh Government, Cardiff.
Donaldson, G. (2018), *A Learning Inspectorate*, Welsh Government, Cardiff.
ET2020 Working Group Schools 2016–18 (2018), *Teachers and School Leaders in Schools as Learning Organisations Guiding Principles for Policy Development in School Education*, EU.
Friedman, T. (2019), *Thank You for Being Late*, Penguin Books, Random House UK.
Frey, C. B. (2019), *The Technology Trap*, Princeton University Press, Princeton.
Furlong, J. (2017), *Teaching Tomorrow's Teachers*, Welsh Government, Cardiff.
Grahn-Laasonen, S. (2017), *The Global Search for Education: Meet the Minister – From Finland* – C. M. Rubin Blog Post February 8.
Hattie, J. (2009), *Visible Learning*, p. 254, Routledge, London.
Hoyle, E. and Wallace, M. (2005), *Educational Leadership: Ambiguity, Professionals and Managerialism*, pp. 4–5.

Kerr, K. and West, M. (2007), *Insight 2 Social Inequality: Can Schools Narrow the Gap?* London: British Educational Research Association.

OECD (2013), *Synergies for Better Learning*, OECD Publishing, Paris.

OECD (2014), *Improving Schools in Wales*, OECD Publishing, Paris.

OECD (2016), *Governing Education in a Complex World*, Educational Research and Innovation, OECD Publishing, Paris.

OECD (2017), *The Welsh Education Reform Journey: A Rapid Policy Assessment*, OECD Publishing, Paris.

OECD (2018), *Developing Schools as Learning Organisations in Wales*, OECD Publishing, Paris.

Priestley, M., Biesta, G. and Robinson, S. (2015), *Teacher Agency an Ecological Approach*, Bloomsbury, London.

Santos, R. (2019), 'Walking the Walk': Welsh Education Directorate becomes a 'Learning Organisation' https://oecd-opsi.org/walking-the-walk-welsh-education-directorate-becomes-a-learning-organisation/

Schleicher, A. (2011), *Building a High-Quality Teaching Profession*, OECD Publishing, Paris.

Schleicher, A. (2018a), *World-class: How to Build a 21st-century School System, Strong Performers and Successful Reformers in Education*, OECD Publishing, Paris.

Schleicher, A. (2018b), *The Future of Education and Skills Education 2030*, OECD Publishing, Paris.

Sinnema, C. and Aitken, G. (2013), 'Emerging International Trends in Curriculum', in M. Priestley and G. Biesta (eds), *Reinventing the Curriculum*, Bloomsbury, London.

Spielman, A. (2017), *Enriching the Fabric of Education*, OFSTED, London.

Tymms, P. and Merrell, C. (2010), 'Standards and Quality in English Primary Schools over Time', p. 56 in Alexander et al. (eds), *The Cambridge Primary Review Research Surveys*, Routledge, London.

Welsh Government (2017) *Education in Wales: Our National Mission Action Plan 2017–21*, Welsh Government, Cardiff.

Woodward (2001), 'What's New', *Guardian Newspapers*.

2

AIMS AND VALUES

Direction with purpose

Brian Matthews

Introduction

Following the issues raised about globalisation and values guiding an education service in Chapter 1, in this chapter we consider how to produce a set of aims and values to give direction and purpose to an education service, using England as a case study. First we ask you to consider your values:

> Values are principles and fundamental convictions which act as general guides to behaviour; enduring beliefs about what is worthwhile; ideals for which one strives; broad standards by which particular beliefs and actions are judged to be good, right, desirable or worthy of respect.
>
> *(Halstead & Taylor, 2000, p. 3)*

There are many questions that can be asked about an education service, such as, How should the teachers be trained? What is their role? How much should young people be involved? However, a key question is: What is the purpose of having an education service? The answer is crucial to the way the service is organised.

If the aim of your education service is mainly for pupils to learn the important facts in discrete subjects, there will be a curriculum, pedagogy and assessment system to support that. If you think education is about developing individuals able to think for themselves (Postman & Weingartner, 1971), then your service will have a very different curriculum, assessment and pedagogy.

Each of these perspectives has different values underlying them.

This chapter argues for clear specification of the values guiding decisions and for informing policy directions.

In order to uncover some possibilities, I start at the global level, looking at international studies which indicate what pupils should learn in the 21st century.

The next section considers predictions for future employment, then broadens out to look beyond employment to include the views of parents, before considering which values are important. As you read, I suggest you identify the values important to you.

What young people need for the predicted future – 21st century skills

International studies have looked at the way that employment is changing and how this might affect people's lives. Studies have found that technology is changing the workplace and there is an increase in the 'gig economy' (Brinkley, 2016; Tait, 2016) with short term contracts and self-employed work. In the 'gig' economy, like jazz performers doing a 'gig', people get paid for the piece of work they do. On one hand this can be seen as a positive as people have flexibility and can organise their work around their lives. On the other hand, it can be exploitative with little work-place protection and employers only having to pay when work is available (TUC, 2016). As a result, workers may not be paid the minimum wage, nor have sickness benefits or holiday pay. Also, the increasing use of robotics/automation is predicted to replace up to 30% of present jobs with either low paid or high paid jobs (Man-yika, Lund, Bughin, & Mischke, 2016). A major implication of the gig economy is that people are likely to have a large range of jobs during their lifetime. Accom-panying this is a rapidly changing workplace society where knowledge quickly becomes out-of-date, and 'schools have to prepare students for jobs that have not yet been created, technologies that have not yet been invented and problems that we don't yet know will arise' (Schleicher, 2010, p. 1).

While there are many disagreements about just how the changes will affect people, it is possible that more people will feel insecure, and that society and employment will be more fractured (Tait, 2016). These trends will place social and emotional pressures on people. Hence, pupils will benefit if they develop emo-tional resilience and collaboration with others.

Indeed, international studies have stressed the need for people and pupils to develop what is called the 4Cs – Collaboration, Communication, Critical thinking and Creativity (European Commission, 2016; Jayaram, 2012; O'Sullivan, 1999; Pellegrino & Hilton, 2012; Voogt & Roblin, 2013). These are often expressed in different ways, for example the Confederation of British Industry (CBI) argues that the curriculum is too narrow, that attitudes are important and that elements such as teamwork, self-management and problem solving should be taught in schools (CBI, 2010a, 2010b, 2012).

A fuller set of these skills, often called the 21st Century skills, is listed in Table 2.1.

While these skills are often expressed in different ways, the emphases are all in the same direction, namely, the development of social and emotional skills along-side cognitive development. These skills are, of course, not new. They are in the same tradition as the Whole Child movement from the 1960s and the *Soul of Education* (Abbott, 2014). The development of these skills are seen to help with wellbeing and mental health central to young people's ability to be employed and function in a changing society.

TABLE 2.1 21st century skills

21st Century skills
21st Century skills include:
- Critical thinking, problem solving, reasoning, analysis, interpretation, synthesising information
- Creativity, artistry, curiosity, imagination, innovation, personal expression
- Perseverance, self-direction, planning, self-discipline, adaptability, initiative
- Leadership, teamwork, collaboration, cooperation, facility in using virtual workspaces
- Information and communication technology (ICT) literacy, media and internet literacy, data interpretation and analysis, computer programming
- Civic, ethical, and social-justice literacy
- Economic and financial literacy, entrepreneurialism
- Global awareness, multicultural literacy, humanitarianism
- Scientific literacy and reasoning, the scientific method
- Environmental and conservation literacy, ecosystems understanding
- Health and wellness literacy, including nutrition, diet, exercise, and public health and safety (Great Schools Partnership, 2018)

Education and global competences – about more than employment

Education is much more than preparing pupils for employment, as indicated by the movement to educate the whole child. An example of a change in emphasis internationally is provided by the Organisation for Economic Co-operation and Development (OECD) and PISA deciding to produce a global competency framework which also calls for a new concept of growth (Piacentini, Barrett, Mansilla, Deardorff, & Lee, 2018):

> Global Competence includes the acquisition of in-depth knowledge and understanding of global and intercultural issues; the ability to learn from and live with people from diverse backgrounds; and the attitudes and values necessary to interact respectfully with others. . . . [C]ross-cultural engagement should balance clear communication with sensitivity to multiple perspectives and . . . equip young people not just to understand but to act. . . . The greatest of these is the need to find a new concept of growth. This may not be a quantifiable concept, based solely on maximising economic gains, but a multidimensional concept that includes care for the environment and social harmony, as well as acceptable levels of security, health, and education. It will cover . . . subjective well-being and quality jobs. It will ensure that the benefits of growth are fairly shared across society.
>
> *(Ramos & Schleicher, 2016, p. 3)*

The OECD (Ramos & Schleicher, 2016, p. 2) sees the strands of provision in an education service, including values, as being interwoven, see Figure 2.1.

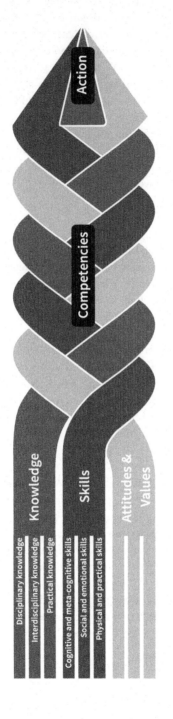

FIGURE 2.1 Strands of provision in an education service including values

Note the inclusion of practical and physical skills, which are often undervalued. The previous material illustrates the importance of the 21st century values to education, as the world becomes more internationalised, partly because of technology. Pupils, in order to gain global competency, need to develop such attributes as tolerance, resilience, being able to handle uncertainty, self- and critical-reflection, as well as empathy. Learning from mistakes and being able to deal with uncertainty and confusion is a crucial part of learning. Failure should be celebrated, provided it is followed with effort and seen as an opportunity for reflection and growth.

There are many other reasons for pupils developing social and emotional skills, such as: being able to contribute to society; take part in a democracy; forge non-sexual and sexual relationships; develop caring skills, including parenting skills; have good mental health and work for social justice.

Parental views

Parents are also concerned that their children develop social and emotional skills. Research has shown that parents' concerns that their children perform well at exams and qualifications are closely followed by concerns about bullying (Adams, 2016). There are many concerns parents have both in choosing a school and what they want from education (Millar & Wood, 2012). Academic success is often a main one, however:

> There was a clear consensus that academic success should be accompanied by a range of other skills; life skills, practical and social skills, communication skills, ICT and problem solving skills were valued alongside academic qualifications. Many parents talked about the need for young people entering adulthood to be polite, well mannered, have confidence, self-esteem, common sense and respect for others.
>
> *(Millar & Wood, 2012, p. 10)*

In 2018 a survey of 1,500 parents found that the top three characteristics of a successful school were happiness (55%), enjoying learning (44%) and gaining behaviours like resilience and self-confidence (41%) (Parentkind, 2018). These were well above factors such as, in England, the Ofsted ratings (24%). Emotional wellbeing and mental health were a concern of 60% of parents (Parentkind, 2018, p. 5).

Hence, we can see that parents, from a different perspective to that of the OECD, also want pupils who are happy, develop social and emotional skills, and have good mental health. Also, developing such skills ties in with other aims, such as preparing pupils to take place in a democratic society; for example, Bazalgette (2017) argues that developing empathy is related to having a civil society.

Values

It is now pertinent to look at values and education. It was, of course, possible to start with values but firstly we needed to consider a basis for selecting values.

There are many discussions about values, and their relation to attributes, ethics and virtues, but I am going to use the definition from Halstead and Taylor (Halstead & Taylor, 2000, p. 38):

> Values are principles and fundamental convictions which act as general guides to behaviour; enduring beliefs about what is worthwhile; ideals for which one strives; broad standards by which particular beliefs and actions are judged to be good, right, desirable or worthy of respect.

The attitudes and values from the OECD report are outlined as shown in Figure 2.2. (Ramos & Schleicher, 2016, p. 6).

This chart is useful in that it indicates common international issues. (There are 34 countries in the OECD. Albeit that these are advanced countries [ACs], the concerns of middle and low-income developing countries [LIDCs] are also relevant, particularly as LIDCs may look to ACs for knowledge transfer and system developments, including Education. This is why arguably the UN SDGs [4 for Education] are relevant for all countries).

The values that emerge from the previous discussion, along with associated ideas, include:

1   Collaboration, cohesion
2   Equality and social justice, gender/trans/diversity/equality
3   Happiness
4   Concern for others, (interconnectedness) cohesion, be willing to adapt
5   Valuing cultural diversity, integration
6   Critical thinking, open-mindedness and problem solving
7   Creativity
8   Emancipation and empowerment, with the belief that that everyone can grow and generate ideas

Arguing that collaboration should be a core value does not mean that there is no competition. One does not exclude the other; the emphasis is to promote collaboration more than competition. Similarly, with the other values. Nearly all of the skills involve social and emotional development along with attention to gender and sexuality.

The values listed previously imply many aspects of the 21st century skills mentioned earlier, and it is worth unpicking *collaboration*. This includes cooperation and being communal – even developing community – and this emphasis would stand in stark contrast to the present stress on individualism in education in England.

The values underpinning any national education system and service must be explicit so that the service will be coherent. There are many diverse views on education and the challenge is to see how these can be accommodated but still to have a service that is responsive to educational research and knowledge (Fabian Society Education Policy Group, 2020).

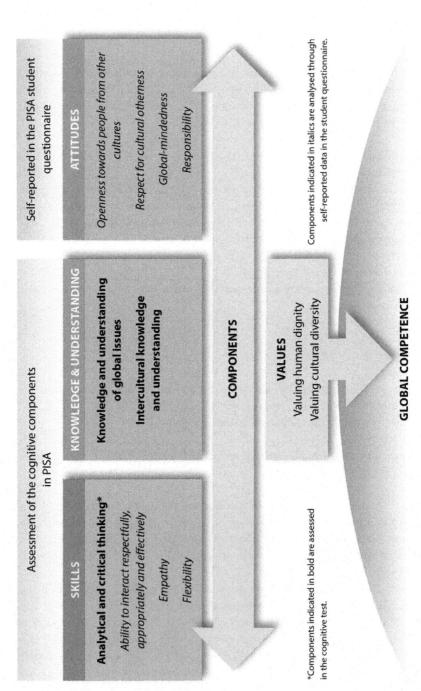

Assessment of the cognitive components in PISA

Self-reported in the PISA student questionnaire

SKILLS

Analytical and critical thinking*

Ability to interact respectfully, appropriately and effectively

Empathy

Flexibility

KNOWLEDGE & UNDERSTANDING

Knowledge and understanding of global issues

Intercultural knowledge and understanding

ATTITUDES

Openness towards people from other cultures

Respect for cultural otherness

Global-mindedness

Responsibility

COMPONENTS

VALUES

Valuing human dignity
Valuing cultural diversity

Components indicated in italics are analysed through self-reported data in the student questionnaire.

*Components indicated in bold are assessed in the cognitive test.

GLOBAL COMPETENCE

FIGURE 2.2 Global competences

The values indicated previously are those that are focused on education. However, there are also a wider set of values concerning society. The Fabian Society values provide an interesting starting point. The Fabian Society is a UK think tank which started in 1884, but their stated values seem to fit well with the concept of the values underpinning democratic society and its national education system and service, and perhaps provide a starting point for debate:

- greater equality of power, wealth and opportunity
- the value of collective action and public service
- an accountable, tolerant and active democracy
- citizenship, liberty and human rights
- sustainable development
- multilateral international cooperation (Fabian Society, 2020)

A national education system and service could be established to provide education for these values, which are not dissimilar to the 2008 English National Curriculum (Qualifications and Curriculum Development Agency, 2010), although this curriculum has been totally altered by successive Governments since 2010.

So far there has not been a discussion of subject learning. Clearly skills can only be learnt with cognitive learning. Subject knowledge and understanding are essential, but what is coming out of studies is that the present emphasis on cognitive learning is to the detriment of the development of skills and there needs to be a re-balancing. An essential part of this I suggest is to integrate feeling and learning.

Taking a values approach has led to us constructing a vision for education that can be transformative. Values are a theme that runs through the rest of the book. Each chapter is explicit about the values underpinning choices. This gives direction and purpose to the ideas, and a coherence to a transformative vision that is sadly lacking in the present English education service.

Implications of not responding to the changing world

The implications for education and society of incorporating these suggested changes, or not doing so, are great. If we do not respond to the challenges that exist because of a changing world and the influence of technology, we are likely to be left behind economically, industrially and also socially. This is because we will not be preparing young people for the world they will grow up in.

It is also important to emphasise that most of the values and skills identified previously have a social and emotional base. These are important in the workplace where increasingly people have to collaborate. People come with different specialisms, cultures and attitudes which can all contribute to solving problems and completing tasks.

Additionally, skills and values improve social relationships and cohesion. To have, for example, positive relationships between genders, both sexual and non-sexual, is important for society. There has been much in the news about the sexual harassment of women in the workplace, and this affects both genders negatively and can undermine many relationships.

It is possible to start in schools to enable young people to develop emotional habits where they discuss feelings about each other while learning, which include intersectionality and promote inclusion across gender, ethnicity, disability divides. Matthews (the author of this chapter) undertook research in schools (2006, 2015) on developing the skills required for a simple form of deliberative democracy. Boys and girls from different ethnic backgrounds worked in groups on a collaborative task, initially with an observer. After this the pupils individually reflected on what he or she felt occurred, and then, in a group, collectively analysed the cognitive, social and emotional aspects of their work together. The process involves collaborative group work, rather than just working in a group, because of the nature of the tasks and the structure for the reflection. The discussions involved voices of representation across gender and ethnicity.

The findings have shown that the boys and girls did not find it easy, but they learnt to understand each other across diversity (Matthews, 2006). In principle, young people can develop habits of mind where they discuss *both* logic and emotion together and as a result can come to an understanding of difference. This in turn can help girls and boys to accept each other as people and not be threatened by difference because of lack of understanding.

Such activities promote inclusion and provide an example of how schools can cultivate ways of developing the skills and values young people need for the next century.

Reflections

All education services are based on underlying values and these are transmitted to young people.

The values that are decided on exert a strong influence on the way an education service is organised. These values can be arrived at in many ways and in this chapter the starting point has been based on research from international studies to parental views. The similarities between these have drawn out.

If an education service is based on positive, well-considered values, then this will aid young people and society. To give an example, if equality is valued, then young people should develop an understanding that we are living in an increasingly diverse world with gender, 'race', cultural and religious variations. For example, gender equality is seen as important. Defining one's sexuality is increasingly seen as crucial, and LGBT views are progressively more being understood.

Often individualism is accepted as being important. However, for equality across sexualities and cultural differences, individualism should be tempered with accepting that the individual only exists within a community, and so forms his or her identity as an individual-in-group. At the root of this is the development of factors such as empathy, self-reflection with others, consideration and resilience.

Policy options

The issues raised in this chapter lead to a number of policy options, for example:

Policy Option 1: A over-emphasis on educating pupils simply to learn facts
Policy Option 2: Preparation for employment with attention to 21st-century skills
Policy Option 3: Developing as a person beyond work, including social and emotional development.

Chapter 21 provides further reflections and an executive summary of options, consequences and cautionary tales arising from each of these options.

References

Abbott, J. (2014) *Battling for the soul of education. Moving beyond school reform to educational transformation*. Retrieved from www.battlingforthesoulofeducation.org/: Education 2000/ The 21st Century Learning Initiative/ Born to Learn.

Adams, R. (2016) Parents more concerned about results than child's happiness. *The Guardian*. Retrieved from www.theguardian.com/education/2016/sep/02/parents-concerned-about-results-than-childs-happiness-says-survey

Bazalgette, P. (2017) *The empathy instinct. How to create a more civil society*. London: John Murray.

Brinkley, I. (2016) *In search of the gig economy*. Lancaster University, Lancaster, UK. Retrieved August 2020, from https://www.lancaster.ac.uk/media/lancaster-university/content-assets/documents/lums/work-foundation/Insearchofthegigeconomy.pdf

CBI. (2010a) *Fulfilling potential. The business role in education*. London: Confederation of British Industry.

CBI. (2010b) *Ready to grow: Business priorities for education and skills. Education and skills survey 2010*. London: Confederation of British Industry.

CBI. (2012) *First steps. A new approach for our schools*. London: Confederation of British Industry.

European Commission. (2016) *Competence frameworks: The European approach to teach and learn 21st century skills*. Retrieved February 2017, from https://ec.europa.eu/jrc/en/news/competence-frameworks-european-approach-teach-and-learn-21st-century-skills

Fabian Society. (2020) *About Us*. Retrieved August 2020, from https://fabians.org.uk/about-us

Fabian Society Education Policy Group. (2020) *Blogs*. Retrieved August 2020, from https://fabians4education.edublogs.org

Great Schools Partnership. (2018) *Glossary of education reform*. Retrieved November 2018, from http://edglossary.org/21st-century-skills/

Halstead, J. M., & Taylor, M., J. (2000) Learning and teaching about values: A review of recent research. *Cambridge Journal of Education, 30*(2), 169–2002.

Jayaram, S. (2012) *Skills for employability: The need for 21st century skills*. Washington, DC: Results for Development Institute.

Manyika, J., Lund, S., Bughin, J., & Mischke, J. (2016) *Independent work: Choice, necessity, and the gig economy*. Retrieved from www.mckinsey.com/global-themes/employment-and-growth/independent-work-choice-necessity-and-the-gig-economy

Matthews, B. (2006) *Engaging education. Developing emotional literacy, equity and co-education.* Buckingham: McGraw-Hill/Open University Press.

Matthews, B. (2015) The Elephant in the room: Emotional literacy/intelligence, science education, and gender. In D. Corrigan, J. Dillon, R. Gunstone & A. Jones (Eds.), *The future in learning science: What's in it for the learner?* Dordrecht: Springer.

Millar, F., & Wood, G. (2012) *A new conversation with parents: Family matters.* Cambridge, UK: Pearson.

O'Sullivan, E. (1999) *Transformative learning: Educational vision for the 21st century.* London: Zed Books.

Parentkind. (2018) *Findings from the 2018 Annual parent survey: Children's mental health and wellbeing.* Tonbridge, Kent. Retrieved from www.parentkind.org.uk/Research – Policy/Research/Annual-Parent-Survey-2018.

Pellegrino, J. W., & Hilton, M. (2012) *Education for life and work: Developing transferable knowledge and skills in the 21st century.* Washington, DC: National Academies Press.

Piacentini, M., Barrett, M., Mansilla, V. B., Deardorff, D., & Lee, H.-W. (2018) *Preparing our youth for an inclusive and sustainable world.* Paris: OECD Publishing.

Postman, N., & Weingartner, C. (1971) *Teaching as a subversive activity.* London: Penguin Books.

Qualifications and Curriculum Development Agency. (2010) *Big picture.* Retrieved February 4, 2019, from http://webfronter.com/camden/learning/mnu2/Curriculum_Design/Curriculum_home.html

Ramos, G., & Schleicher, A. (2016) *Global competency for an inclusive world.* Retrieved from www.oecd.org/education/Global-competency-for-an-inclusive-world.pdf

Schleicher, A. (2010) *The case for 21st century learning.* Retrieved March 2011, from www.oecd.org/document/2/0,3746,en_2649_201185_46846594_1_1_1_1,00.html

Tait, C. (2016) *A good day's work. What workers think about work, and how politics should respond.* London: Fabian Society.

TUC. (2016) Living on the edge: The rise of job insecurity in modern Britain. *Economic Report Series.* Retrieved from www.tuc.org.uk/sites/default/files/Living%20on%20the%20Edge%202016.pdf

Voogt, J., & Roblin, N. P. (2013) *21st century skills.* Netherlands: University of Twente.

3

DEVELOPING *YOUR* VISION

Principles and implementation challenges

Brian Hudson, Marilyn Leask and Sarah Younie

Introduction

Chapter 1 introduced international thinking about the kind of education necessary to prepare young people for an uncertain future. Chapter 2 introduced international thinking about how the aims, values and beliefs of policy makers influence the focus, form, operation and outputs of an education service. Chapter 3 has been designed to help you to clarify the principles which follow from your values.[1] Through this chapter we explore choices and potential consequences of your choices.

The intention of these chapters is to challenge you to be explicit about the values and priorities which underpin your choices. National leadership is a challenging task – there are competing priorities, diverse viewpoints to be reconciled, resource allocation decisions to be made. It can be easy within the day-to-day pressures of the political environment to lose sight of the fact that decisions taken at the national leadership level embody the values that will educate the citizens responsible for the society of tomorrow. Consider Kerslake's analysis here:

> In his introduction to the UK2070 Commission Report (2019), Lord Kerslake asserts that deep-rooted regional inequalities across the UK demand "long term thinking and a special economic plan to tackle them". The report concludes that inequalities are exacerbated by "underpowered 'pea-shooter' and 'sticking-plaster' policies". A case is made for future policy to be "structural, generational, interlocking and at scale". Within advanced economies poverty and inequality have emerged as political flash points (G-7 summit, Biarritz, 2019).
>
> *(Raffety, Chapter 14)*

We start this chapter with three premises with which may or may not fit with your values:

- that a nation's education service provides the foundation for development of a society: that a government creates, shapes or denies, opportunities for society's development, economic prosperity and citizens' wellbeing through its leadership of the national education service
- that civil unrest is a threat to democracies as governments rule by popular mandate and that the chance of civil unrest can be minimised through an education service overtly supporting values of community and social cohesion, tolerance of difference and advancement on merit
- that high quality motivated teachers are the single most important factor in improving educational outcomes and that system stability with managed change, innovative CPD using 21st century technologies together with stakeholder consensus is most likely to achieve this

For the UK, the BREXIT issues divided society. A new focus on education, based on explicit shared values focused on shaping the society of tomorrow, may bring the opportunity to energise communities and bring them together. Other fractured societies may consider how consultation on the values and principles for a national education system and service could help overcome similar challenges.

Foundation principles and the choices they lead to

What principles provide the foundations for the national education service you envisage? Table 3.1 provides some choices. The authors in this book are all

TABLE 3.1 Principles underpinning an education service

Principles inform the underpinning philosophy of any national education service. Here are some examples of principles:
- Education is a fundamental entitlement for all citizens.
- Education of certain types should be restricted to an elite so that they can consolidate and hold power over the rest of society.
- Education 0–18 should be free at the point of use and paid for through universal taxation for the common good.
- Education provision 0–18 should normally be non-selective by ability/aptitude, faith or wealth. Special provision for gifted and talented children, children in care and children with SEND may be required.
- Adult education services provide a foundation for national growth.
- The education service has to prepare children to address global challenges
- The curriculum should be restricted to control the population; e.g. in Franco's Spain, the teaching of foreign languages was restricted so as to isolate the population; under apartheid in South Africa the teaching of higher-level mathematics was denied to children attending black only schools.

- Education can provide a binding force for society supporting integration and social cohesion if children are given positive exposure to the rich cultural diversity and heritage of the society in which they live along with the values of tolerance and an appreciation of difference.
- Education provision in a society is a community responsibility.
- The encouragement of tolerance of differences leading to self-determination is an essential component in a national education service.
- Education resources are a "common good" and knowledge essential to high quality teaching and successful communities should be free at the point of use.
- Making online resources freely available may support improved teaching in poorer nations and support peace and stability.

teachers, and the choices here reflect the knowledge gained through our experiences, nationally and internationally, and our research in education.

Your choice of principles will help engender and lead to a society which is either a

- meritocratic society, where members of society see they have a chance to develop their talents and contribute, or;
- an elitist society where wealth determines opportunities and the majority of the population see they are excluded and disenfranchised, or;
- a society with elements of both of the principles existing side by side, of which the balance may fluctuate over time.

If you have chosen the elitist option, then you may agree with these statements:

- It is possible to predict children's potential and in what they will be successful in life
- intelligence is fixed
- children from wealthy families are innately more able to learn from birth

If you opted for a meritocratic society then you may agree with these statements:

- no one can predict what a child might do in life
- the brain has the capacity to learn throughout life and intelligence is not fixed (neuroscience research shows this)
- the fairest and most productive way to organise society is through recognition of merit – a meritocracy
- young people have the right to access a publicly funded education.

We suggest you make a list of the values and principles that you support as these will guide your decisions in all the key areas of education which are covered in the following chapters.

Policy implementation: stakeholders and levers for change

In any society there will be a range of stakeholders with long-term interest in the operation and focus of the national education service (see Table 3.2). Do you value their input? These stakeholders can provide powerful levers for or barriers to the implementing of your policies. If a policy maker is not able to convince these groups to support proposed changes then this is a good indication that there will be serious resistance across society leading potentially to disruption that politicians may rather avoid. How to minimise potential backlash and non-cooperation against desired change is one of the decisions policy makers must make.

Learning from the past and drawing on expert network knowledge

In the UK there are extensive records documenting past educational policies and practices stretching back over 400 years, and Smith (2016) gives an excellent overview in his book *Key Questions in Education*. Much as politicians might want to make their mark, they are hard put to find something that hasn't been tried and found wanting before. Secretary of State for England. Michael Gove, for example, was ridiculed following a TV interview where he suggested, as though they were new ideas, ideas about discipline and classroom management which Smith tracks back to the 1600s.

A brief meeting with educational historians may be time well spent as with notice, they should be able to provide an overview of the history of particular policy developments in your country: the successes, the failures and the rationale for current structures and practices. Due to the extensive nature of educational knowledge, we suggest you work with groups of experts through their professional networks rather than individuals who – given the scope of the field – necessarily

TABLE 3.2 Stakeholders: potential policy supporters or detractors

Political parties: is cross-party consensus possible? In some jurisdictions, major changes to the education service require a super-majority in parliament.

Industry and business

Parents and carers

School managers/governors, regional or local administrators

Examination boards

University and Further Education/vocational colleges

Professional associations/unions: for headteachers and nursery/school/vocational teachers, universities, teacher training organisations, learned and subject specialist societies

Other specialist groups e.g. NGOs for learners with particular needs such as sight or hearing impairment, physical disability

Specialist research units

The media/commercial publishers

will have limited knowledge. Chapter 19 sets out a vision for a knowledge service supporting the education sector – teachers and policy makers, which makes this knowledge about effective practices in different pedagogic and subject specialist areas easily accessible and open to all.

Interdependencies in the education ecosystem

The education sector is like an ecosystem: there are inter-dependencies between different elements of the service, which outsiders to the service have little chance of identifying, but if these links are cut, elements of the service collapse and can set off a chain reaction leading to unintended consequences.

For example:

- Leaders of tomorrow: Put in place an onerous accountability system and you may find that your young teachers, your leaders of tomorrow in the education service leave to take up jobs outside the profession. So you soon have a shortage of applications for headteachers, leading to the promotion of less expert teachers and a potential consequence of lower quality education for learners over decades. There is then the potential failure to build leadership capacity and expertise in the service to ensure quality.
- Research, publishing and professional development: Educational research, textbook writing and research-based professional development to teachers for example is normally undertaken by university staff, whose time is paid for by income generated through their training of teachers. If you remove teacher training from universities, those jobs are lost and you take out of the service research capacity, textbook writing capacity and specialist continuing professional development programmes. Any replacement service is likely to be less specialist with a potential consequence of lower quality education for learners over decades.

In dismantling current structures because they are in your view imperfect, you may just be returning the education sector to a situation which 50 or 60 years or 400 years ago was found to be unsatisfactory.

Making major policy decisions: balancing idealism with practicalities

The values of the government of the day are likely to be set out in the manifesto which led to them being elected and which a large percentage of the electorate voted for.

However, the risk of imposing ideological change on an education service just because you have a mandate from some of the electorate is that those whom the government expects to carry out the changes – the teachers – simply leave the education service.

To maintain stability in democratic societies as well as to maximise chances of re-election, a government may be wise to see their role as governing on behalf of all the people, not just those who elected them. To this end, engaging the range of different stakeholders in education, including teachers and their representative organisations, would engender greater democratic governing, along the lines of deliberative democracy outlined by Fishkin (2018). Chapter 6 presents a worked-through example for England.

In any case, making major policy decisions not on party political grounds but on evidence and research-based grounds in consultation with stakeholders in education we argue is more likely to bring the long lasting change you want without damaging what is already working well in a service. This incremental change approach which we recommend may not suit political needs for rapid radical change, but the risks associated with quick ideological change can be high, as Chapter 5 outlines.

Service complexity

A common belief held by many who have not been involved in teaching is that teaching is simple: the teacher stands at the front and talks, the children write down what is said and they are tested on that. UK records show that as far back as the 1600s this approach was dismissed as not creating educated citizens (Smith, 2016). Table 3.3 lists the forms of knowledge a qualified teacher will be

TABLE 3.3 Forms of knowledge for teaching (summarised from Shulman 1987 in Capel, Leask and Younie, 2019)

General Pedagogic Knowledge	i.e. the broad principles and strategies of classroom management and organisation that apply irrespective of the subject.
Subject Content Knowledge	i.e. research based knowledge generated by specialist research units in genetics, literature etc.
Subject Pedagogic Knowledge	i.e. the knowledge of what makes for effective teaching and deep learning of concepts in specific subjects at specific ages for particular learners.
Technology Pedagogic Knowledge	i.e. general and subject specific pedagogic knowledge about how to deploy technologies to support learning of concepts in specific subjects at specific ages for particular learners.
Curriculum Knowledge	i.e. the materials and the programmes that serve as 'tools of the trade' for teachers and which ensure progression in learning over the years.
Knowledge of Learners and their Characteristics	i.e. knowledge of child development from psychology, sociology, and neuroscience.
Knowledge of Educational Contexts	i.e. cultural knowledge which impacts on schooling.
Knowledge of Educational Ends	i.e. purposes, values and philosophical and historical influences: both short- and long-term goals of education and of a subject.

drawing on regularly. We estimate there are at least 60,000 specific concepts in the range of knowledge primary and secondary teachers draw on in their teaching. OECD research (TALIS, 2009, 3) confirms that the knowledge base for teaching is disorganised and that this is limiting improvements in the quality of teaching in developed and in developing countries. Similarly, the OECD has found the provision of, access to and the quality of professional development to be patchy (OECD, 2009).

Managing complexity

The following sections in this book (Section 3 on Social Justice and Inclusion, 4 on Teaching and 5 on Teacher Education) provide details of the complexity of the foundations of any education service and the co-dependencies of seemingly separate elements. This complexity means policy makers face a dilemma in making sound decisions. Who is best placed to advise and counsel? Civil servants are usually moved every few years between departments and so really do not have time to develop deep expertise in any area. Even if the policy maker/politician has had a role in education, their knowledge will rarely extend beyond one or two specialist areas.

So how can sound decisions be made?

Policy makers may plough on regardless, perhaps with the help of a few expert 'lone ranger' advisers, or they can decide to work in partnership with the educators who spend their whole lives working on specific areas to develop deep expertise in the previous topics. The danger of the 'lone ranger' expert adviser is obvious given the complexity outlined previously. If your goal is to improve education, through policies based on research and evidence, which should be explicit enough for you to understand and challenge, we recommend the alternative approach – of accessing professional networks/specialist associations which bring together people with a range of deep knowledge in a single specialist topic, then working in partnership with the range of stakeholders whose commitment and expertise to education is an asset to be utilised. We propose from our previous analysis the establishment of a national education board, the aim of which is to bring coherence, consistency and stability to a service that is currently deeply fragmented and highly variable in the quality of the education that it is delivering.

Such a proposal for a national education board recognises that plural values from different stakeholders can create tensions and policy differences; however, a partnership approach, working with an appreciation of deliberative democracy (Fishkin, 2018), can create an alternative.

Similarly, in an analysis of SEND policy development (following on from the influential Warnock report of 1978), Norwich (2019) identifies the need for a more coherent approach to policy making. Norwich (2019, p. 1) proposes an Education Framework Commission to set policy priorities and 'to reconcile plural and sometimes contrary value positions. The Commission would aim to design a 10-year consensual education policy framework, within which political parties and governments will work'.

Reflections

We have assumed you want your policies to lead to a stronger, better educated society through planned and evidence-based improvement (and to avoid public disgrace and wastage of resources). Our recommendation is the establishing of a national education board (or commission, Norwich, 2019) working through cross-party consensus and with stakeholder representatives who can provide independent review of proposals and then back up ministerial pronouncements. This system operates in some countries and has previously operated in England in different forms. Chapter 6 provides a detailed example of how such a national education board may work for England. England has experienced particularly chaotic change since 2010 as Chapters 4 and 5 explain. Chapter 5 provides insights from the point of view of those running schools in the new service since 2010 and Chapter 4 provides an historical route map of the journey to this service.

Policy options

The issues raised in this chapter lead to a number of policy options:

Policy Option 1: develop an unashamedly elitist service
Policy Option 2: develop a service based on meritocracy
Policy Option 3: abdicate any responsibility for national leadership of the service, let the market have a free hand in determining what education is provided, and use minimal state funds to provide provision of no interest to the market

The consequences of these options are discussed in Chapter 20.

Note

1 For example, one of your values might be equality. A principle that demonstrates how this value is operationalized might include the principle that boys and girls have equal access to education. (This is not the case in all countries and it is not so long in the UK since certain subjects were closed to girls or boys.) This may then lead to a need to gather data to demonstrate the value of equality is being upheld by the system and the service.

References

Capel, S., Leask, M. and Younie, S. (eds.) (2019) *Learning to Teach in the Secondary School: A Companion to School Experience*, 8th edn, Abingdon: Routledge.

Fishkin, J. (2018) Random Assemblies for Law Making? Prospects and Limits. *Political Sociology* 46, 359–379. doi: 10.1177/0032329218789889

Norwich, B. (2019) From the Warnock Report (1978) to an Education Framework Commission: A Novel Contemporary Approach to Educational Policy Making for Pupils with Special Educational Needs/Disabilities. *Frontline Education* 4, 72. doi: 10.3389/feduc.2019.00072

OECD (2009) *Creating Effective Teaching and Learning Environments: The First Results from the TALIS Survey,* Paris: OECD Publishing. www.oecd.org/edu/school/43023606.pdf

Smith, J.T. (2016) *Key Questions in Education: Historical and Contemporary Perspectives,* London: Bloomsbury.

SECTION 2

England

A case study, a vision and a cautionary tale

In Section 1, Chapters 1, 2, and 3 introduced international views on what makes effective education systems together with Policy Options around the values and principles which provide the foundations for any national provision.

Section 2 focuses specifically on England as, following an intense period of deregulation and marketisation of the school system and teacher training since 2010, practices in the education sector have become an international outlier. As ministers of education often like to copy what they think is effective practice in other countries, the focus on England section provides a cautionary tale about how overzealous interventions by politicians has caused fragmentation and a loss of coherence in what was a successful system.

Chapter 4 charts the history of the development of education policy in England over the previous 100 years to show the influences leading to policies and how lack of coherence has crept into the system

Chapter 5 provides a case study of the new organisations of schools in England which replaced Local Education Authorities and which are called Multi-Academy Trusts (MATs). The authors, who run a successful MAT, say the new system at a national level is 'unmanageable' and 'unworkable'.

Chapter 6 outlines the way forward for England to return to a coherent and stable education system with managed innovation, high quality CPD and teacher training, and a leading edge curriculum preparing learners for the 21st century. The proposal is for the setting up of a National Board, called provisionally Education England, with decisions arrived at through decision making through consensus between the major political parties, educational stakeholders and others. The chapter introduces the legislative process necessary to establish Education England as an independent body protected through legislation and requiring a supermajority in parliamentary vote to change its method of operation.

The cautionary tale is that there is no point in making top-down radical change if you do not consider the impact on the system as a whole, in particular the inter-dependencies of the whole system. For example, the high stakes accountability system in England which values high grades of pupils and high Ofsted grades as an indicator of a successful school has led to 'gaming' the system. According to the Education Policy Institute,[1] over 50,000 pupils have gone missing from the education system as schools seem to take off their roll those not likely to achieve high grades (see the data presented in Chapters 6 and 16). Chapter 18 provides data about the loss of teachers and the recruitment crisis which have followed these radical changes.

Note

1 Staufenberg, J. (April 18, 2019) EPI: 50,000 pupils 'pushed around the system' in 'unexplained moves'. *Schools Week*.

4

A 'NATIONAL EDUCATION SERVICE'

What can we learn from the past?

Tim Brighouse

Introduction

> Education of the lower classes should be just sufficient to give them that sense of
> awe of higher education which the leaders of the nation demand.
>
> *Robert Lowe MP in discussions related to the 1870 Education Act*

> A sense of powerlessness is the enemy of democracy and arrangements which
> are so centralised run that risk, especially in a service – schools – where one
> of the main purposes is to create future citizens. Wherever you look in West-
> ern Democracies except England there is a powerful role for local government
> whether at the school and 'district' levels and/or regionally.

The English have shown an ambivalent attitude to state funded education and came
to it rather reluctantly and relatively recently. As long ago as 1803 the Bishop of
London declared that 'Men of considerable ability say that it is safest for both the
Government and the religion of the country to let the lower classes remain in that
state of ignorance in which nature has originally placed them' (Leese, 1950). Of
course he put himself outside such company by adding

> It is not proposed that the children of the poor be educated in an expensive
> manner, or even taught to write or cypher. . . . There is a risk of elevating
> by indiscriminate education, the minds of those doomed to the drudgery
> of daily labour above their condition and thereby render them discontented
> with their lot.
>
> *(Leese, ibid.)*

It was the Church which preceded the state in providing education for the poor,
while the rich and the upper classes relied on governesses and public independent

schools for the education of their offspring. In short, the ruling classes then regarded state education as something which would not concern them directly. It can be argued that the same views prevail today and that a 'national education service' should be founded with due regard to that continuing weakness.

The first forays into education legislatively came under the Factory Acts and the limitation of child labour and the remit to the Duke of Newcastle's Commission on elementary schooling in 1858, which emphasised the need for 'what measures, if any, are required for the extension of sound and cheap elementary instruction to all classes of the poor'.

The first explicitly educational legislation was that of Forster of 1870, when Robert Lowe, the architect of the notorious Revised Code, asserted that the 'education of the lower classes should be just sufficient to give them that sense of awe of higher education which the leaders of the nation demand'.

It's important to remember these views, intertwined as they were with the philosophies of both main political parties of the Victorian era, that it was for the individual to survive through his or her own best efforts and that the state should intervene only as the provider of last resort. It coloured the approach which the state and political parties took to the provision of state education until recent times and still lingers within the unspoken assumptions of many despite the present cross-party agreement about the desirability of 'equal opportunity' and 'social mobility'.

A national education service locally delivered

Our modern story however, begins with the end of the Second World War and can be divided into three periods: an age of 'Optimism and Trust' which lasted until 1968; then a brief second age of 'Doubt and Disillusion'; and, finally, a third of 'Markets and Managerialism'. This third era may now have run its course and should give way within any 'national education service' to one of 'Hope, Ambition and Partnership' which might draw some lessons from the earlier ages both of 'what to do' and of 'what not to do'.[1]

Such a third age will be an English-only[2] 'National Education Service' and perhaps, if it is to have a distinctive identity, needs to be marked by a defining Education Act, just as those of 1944 and 1988 defined the first and the third post-war ages. If it were planned for 2020 it would neatly act as punctuation of the 150th anniversary of the Forster Act.

First however some broad-brush history of those three post-war ages.

It was in Lowestoft in 1955 that I first heard about the importance of Butler's 1944 Education Act. It clearly stirred the imagination of my sixth form History teacher at that time who, like most of his staff colleagues having fought in the Second World War, was determined to build a better society than that which we learned about in his mesmerisingly formative lessons.

Later in the early 1960s as a young administrator in a Local Education Authority (LEA), Monmouthshire, I learned much more about the significance of 1944. 'The schooling system was', so my senior Welsh colleague mentors told me,

'a "national education service locally administered"'. The nature of these arrangements involved the Minister of Education suggesting a few strictly limited general
policies within the aims stated in the 1944 Education Act. It was then up to each
LEA to decide whether to accept the Minister's suggestions. When, for example, Anthony Crossland wanted England and Wales to reorganise their secondary
schools along comprehensive lines, he issued his famous Circular 10/65 which did
not 'require' but merely 'requested' LEAs to submit plans. Some politely declined
to do so.

The age of optimism and trust: central and local government roles

The extent of the Minister's powers over schools, as opposed to those over the provision of Further and Higher Education, was confined to discharging three main
duties and responsibilities – 'securing a sufficient supply of suitably qualified teachers'; approving or not any proposal from an LEA or the governors of a Voluntary
Aided school to remove an air-raid shelter; and approving LEA proposals for the
opening or closure of schools and any loan consents required to pay for new or
extended school buildings.

The main engine of action lay in the LEAs.

Butler's Act and the Physical Education and Recreation Acts of the 1930s urged
LEAs to promote the physical, mental and spiritual well-being of their communities. LEAs were therefore busy in the 25 years which followed, not simply in supporting schools directly but also in setting a generally positive educational climate
in the communities which they and their schools served. In discharging the first set
of these responsibilities, LEAs built new schools for the growing post-war population and to accommodate more pupils as the school leaving age was raised on
two occasions.[3] They also created and expanded advisory and inspection services
to support schools and their teachers and established a set of support services for
schools such as Education Welfare Officers, Education Psychologists and Youth
Employment Officer (Careers) teams. In interpreting their wider role, LEAs created Youth Services, extended their pre-war network of adult education courses,
bought Outdoor Pursuits and other residential centres, built new (and extended
existing) Colleges of Further Education and were trusted to oversee the governance and management of a new network of Teacher Training Colleges and Colleges of Advanced Technology, some of which subsequently became Polytechnics
and then Universities.

In this first age of 'Optimism and Trust' there were three main players: central government through the Minister and civil servants in the Ministry – later Department –
of Education; local government through LEAs and their councillors and officers;
and schools through their teachers and headteachers. The main power as we
have seen lay with the middle tier in local government, although the curriculum
and how it was taught was left very much to the schools and individual teachers.
National pay-scales for teachers and headteachers were determined in the Burnham

Committee, where the protagonists were the teachers led by Ronald Gould, General Secretary of the National Union of Teachers (NUT), and William Alexander of the Association of Education Committees (AEC) with the Ministry of Education having simply an observer status – albeit a strong one, since convention demanded that the overall envelope of teachers' salaries should be contained within what the Treasury determined the nation could afford. How much was spent each year on schools was an LEA matter where the Chief Education Officer and the Education Committee argued with other services about how much should be spent and therefore how much the local rates should be raised (since rates supplemented by central government rate support grants were the origin of public funding for schools).

That age of 'Optimism and Trust' within an agreed common purpose thus involved a partnership of central and local government and schools, which was characterised by trust that each would play their part in 'building a new Jerusalem'[4] during years in which there was a general acceptance that 'education was an unquestioned good thing'.

The age of doubt and disillusion: shifting power from local to of central government

'Optimism and Trust', however, gave way to another shorter period of 'Doubt and Disillusion'. It is difficult to determine when exactly this happened, although student unrest in 1968 had caused an unhappy Prime Minister to summon Vice Chancellors to a meeting in Downing Street to explain the causes of campus unrest. An oil crisis soon followed and there was a series of Black Paper publications, popularised by the media, which suggested that the basics were not being given sufficient attention by the schools.

Doubt and Disillusion were epitomised in Prime Minister Callaghan's Ruskin speech of 1976, which launched what was called a 'Great Debate' on education, which referred to an earlier Conservative minister's description of the 'secret garden' of the curriculum, and Callaghan implied it should no longer be secret. During these years too, the reliable middle-tier engine room of change and development, the LEA, lost its trusted status. Local Government re-organisation in 1974 meant the side-lining and eventual demise of the Association of Education Committees (AEC) as new 'corporate management' took hold of local government, locally and in its representative bodies – the Associations of Metropolitan Authorities and County Councils (AMA and ACC). This meant that education, long regarded as the cuckoo in local government's nest, was more exposed and vulnerable in budget discussions locally. In short, the civil service felt it could no longer rely on local government to reflect, through its actions, national government's general wishes.

The age of markets and managerialism – centralising power

In its turn therefore, this second post-war educational age gave way to a third of 'Markets and Managerialism' which might fairly be associated with Margaret

Thatcher's access to the Premiership after the 1979 General Election. Sometimes dubbed as being an example of neo-liberalism, her government's educational White Papers were peppered with what appeared to be mantra words such as 'choice', 'autonomy', 'diversity', 'excellence' and 'accountability'. These were promoted by measures enshrined in legislation. 'Choice' implied that parents needed choice of school, although they were arguably misled since clearly absolute choice could not be guaranteed because school size is not without a limit and in rural areas transport and geography limit choice. In reality the most which successive Education Acts have given parents is the ability to express a 'preference' of school for their child to attend. 'Choice', however, in those early days of 'Markets' did not extend to pupils or schools having choice in the curriculum which was prescribed nationally through what was described as 'broad and balanced', but, being prescriptive and nationally assessed, enabled comparisons to be made of different schools' performance. 'Autonomy' referred to the autonomy of individual schools which was encouraged by legal imperatives such as delegation of decision making over budgets, called initially LMS (Local Management of Schools). A recurring theme has been the wish to discourage schools from being dependent on their maintaining local authorities. 'Diversity' over the years has been encouraged through establishing different types of schools. Part of the 1944 Education Act had been a 'settlement' of the respective roles of the state though local education authorities and the voluntary sector mainly in the form of the churches and other faiths which have run Voluntary Aided schools complementing 'county', later designated 'community', schools. As the need for more diversity was encouraged however, new forms of difference in the provision of schools were devised. First there was 'Grant Maintained' status.[5] Then there were 'Specialist', 'Foundation' and 'Trust' schools. More recently there have emerged 'Academies' and 'Free Schools', both in effect revivals of the 'Grant Maintained' model. By such diversity in schooling backed by each school's autonomy in the context of increased parental choice and the publication of school outcomes, a quasi-market in schooling has been created. Competition among and between schools is thereby encouraged as their results are published and the parent, as consumer, makes choices among an array of schools following roughly the same curriculum.

The case for adding the word 'Managerialism' to 'Markets' as an apt descriptor of the 'Age' rests on two factors. Firstly there is the need for regulation and action when either compliance is required in a marketplace or the purposes of education need to alter to reflect changed circumstances. The temptation to do more than that and try directly to promote changed practice in schools has proved irresistible. In this case it was Sir Keith Joseph, ironically the politician credited with being the instigator of neo-liberal ideas supporting a social market economy as well as believing that the 'market itself will find the solution', who first introduced the idea that central government should directly fund what he deemed desirable changes in schools. He announced his intention to do so at the Council of Local Education Authorities (CLEA) Conference in 1982 where, to a surprised audience,[6] he stipulated that central government through specific grant would spend up to 0.5% of the schools' budget on projects to enable schools and their local authorities to address issues which required attention as a result of changes in society. Joseph's first two priorities in this form of specific as opposed to general grant, were the Low Attainers Project (LAP) and the Technical and Vocational Education Initiative (TVEI), managed through, controversially, not the DFE but the Manpower Service Commission (MSC) as part of the Department of Business while simultaneously introducing the first computers into schools.

The second need for intervention in a competitive market arises when inevitably some schools fail as others are seen to succeed. The consequent need to make arrangements for pupils in such 'failing' schools is obvious. This task was initially left to local authorities but the emergence of academies has increasingly involved central government, through a set of Regional Commissioners, having a role in clearing up the mess involved in failing individual academies or Multi-Academy Trusts (MATs): a prescriptive hands-on management occurs in these cases. It could be argued that management does not necessarily imply managerialism. Over the years however the product of so much legislation – there were just two Education Acts of Parliament between 1944 and 1980 and there have been almost 50 since – has been to centralise power at the expense of local government and, in some important respects, the schools. Successive Secretaries of State in consequence, empowered by so many Education Acts, have not been able to resist meddling in what schools do. They have pronounced not just on the curriculum and what is taught but on how it is taught.[7] They were aided in doing so by Joseph's trail-blazing initiatives with LAP and TVEI.

The legacy of successive Secretaries of State – 'unnecessary and unwarranted interference'

It is tempting for a Secretary of State to want to make a mark not just for reasons of legacy but sometimes as a means of political advancement and occasionally as a personal whim. Almost all incumbents of the post since the Education Act of 1988 have been guilty of unnecessary and unwarranted interference in matters formerly left to local decision whether by the schools themselves or local authorities.[8]

Local Authorities have progressively been stripped of educational powers and responsibilities during the period of 'Markets and Managerialism'. First the Colleges of Further Education were removed from their influence along with the Colleges of Advanced Technologies, Polytechnics and Colleges of Education. Successive iterations of the rules of local financial management of schools, as a means of distributing money for schools' budgets, then stripped LEAs of the capacity to have their own priorities for education. Since 2010 and the imposition of austerity measures and the simultaneous encouragement of schools to seek academy status, local democratic influence has diminished further as shrinking local authorities have been stripped of powers and cash by cuts in government grant and centrally imposed limits on their capacity to increase revenue via household and business rates. In schools the perverse outcome is that those which have acted on central government's encouragement to become Academies or Free Schools are no longer dependent on (and controlled by) local authorities but have ended up being *more* dependent on (and controlled by) a distant but nevertheless interfering national government in the form of the DFE and the Education Skills and Funding Agency (ESFA) through whom they have a contract directly with the Secretary of State. In doing so, this group of Academies – about a third of state-maintained schools in 2018 – are obliged to become in effect a hybrid of a private limited company and charitable body.

It is difficult to overstate the huge change in the relative importance of the main players beyond the school. Local Authorities – the word 'education' was symbolically removed through legislation in 2006 – have only residual powers left. The Secretary of State and his/her appointed officers in the civil service in the DFE and its agencies, however, have enormous power. Meanwhile the schools themselves have exchanged power in curriculum which in the first post-war age was left almost entirely to them, for almost complete power over how they spend their budgets.

If that broadly describes what has happened in the two educational ages which sandwiched the last period of 'doubt and disillusion', it is perhaps appropriate to draw up a balance sheet of successful and less successful interventions and characteristics of the two periods as well as why efforts to effect change were more – or less – successful.

1945–2018: an attempt at a balance sheet of what worked and what was less successful

I choose to analyse comparative success under the following four headings: governance structures; finance; accountability arrangements, examinations and testing, school improvement and the curriculum; and the supply and retention of teachers.

The list is not entirely unjustified since in each of these four issues there is a choice to be made beyond the school itself about whether responsibility should lie with central government or some democratic body between the school and the state nationally.

Governance structures

At present governance structures exist at three levels: national, middle tier and school. In the relatively settled consensus years following the 1944 Education Act, we have already described the key role of the middle tier exercised by the LEA. Its relationship with individual schools came to be represented as one of undue 'control' on its part and 'dependence' on the other. This however masks subtle regional variations. Some LEAS – mainly counties – ensured each school had individual governing bodies[9] mostly consisting of local 'worthies' and inevitably with limited powers although always playing a strong – sometimes too strong – role in appointing headteachers and other staff. Other LEAS – mainly urban – made a token effort in discharging their obligations to have individual governing bodies by including within the remit of their Schools' Sub-Committees the 'school governing body' role and received reports, one after the other, from individual primary headteachers in long sessions on a termly basis.[10] An Act of 1986 following the Taylor report ensured that every school had its own governing body with prescribed rules for composition to ensure fair representation of various stakeholders such as the local community, parents, staff and the LEA. One of the details of the 1986 Act arguably had a large and positive impact on school improvement – a topic which was receiving attention for the first time in some LEAs.[11] There was a nationally prescribed method of appointing headteachers the detail of which – three governors and an equal number of LEA councillors – went some way to ensure that the best person was appointed to headship. Such an arrangement, which minimised the chances of either the LEA or the school governing body having undue and perhaps improper influence, was abandoned after the reforms of 1988 which pushed the pendulum in favour of the school making the appointments without reference to the wider view which had been provided by the LEA. With the emergence of Academies, a more complex position of local governance has arisen. On the one hand in self-standing academies, there is the danger that headteacher appointments are made without a wider perspective. On the other, in Multi-Academy Trusts (MATs) with whom the DFE has a direct contract and to whom the budgets of all the academies with the MAT are disbursed, there is the danger that school autonomy is negated and MATs behave in a controlling way similar to that which characterised the worst LEAs in the first period of 'Optimism and Trust'.

Both Scotland and Wales have retained the balance of governance among the national and local governments and the school with populations of 5 million and 3 million respectively. In the English-speaking world there is nowhere with a more centrally controlled educational system than England with a population of 47 million. A sense of powerlessness is the enemy of democracy and arrangements which are so centralised run that risk, especially in a service – schools – where one of the main purposes is to create future citizens. Wherever you look in Western Democracies except England there is a powerful role for local government whether at the school and 'district' levels and/or regionally.

The first challenge for a national education service is to determine what will be devolved so far as power and responsibility are concerned; what will be decided centrally; and how that arrangement should operate in practice and be protected by statute. Learning from other more successful schooling systems in countries with similar or connected cultures will provide some helpful pointers as will learning from our own history. Retaining such an over-centralised service as that which has emerged in the period of Markets and Managerialism should not be an option. Nor will the National Health Service be a useful guide since its purpose is so different since, unlike the education service, it is not involved in providing the knowledge and shaping the attitudes, habits and skills of our future citizens.

At the extremes of the schooling system the choices are uncontentious; nationally the Secretaries of State, seen to be answerable to Parliament, should have a few broad-brush powers and be able to articulate the broad aims of schooling and the national values which all citizens in England subscribe to as well as being able to promote through specific grants changes discussed in a new 'standing national education advisory council' with representatives of teachers, parents local and regional councillors and school governors. Discussion will be necessary to decide the extent and nature of the powers of Secretaries of State but they should include the duty to secure in different regions of the country a sufficient supply of suitable qualified teachers. Some central control of expenditure on new and extended school buildings is also a key role. And it is uncontentious that national politicians should describe the broad curriculum expectations of the state's future citizens, although it is odd that in the UK that should apply only to the separate parts of the UK. Beyond that the danger of centralisation has become all too apparent in the age of Markets and Managerialism. Locally there is a strong case for school governing bodies with representatives of parents, staff, councillors and the local community including employers: their remit would be largely unchanged from those at present, though they should be expected to have a greater say in curriculum design and decisions and should be liable to less direction from the Secretary of State.

What has fallen into neglect is the role of the middle-tier – in the first period exercised by the Local (Education) Authority. More recently there has been discussion of regional bodies building on the remit of Regional School Commissioners and there is certainly a case for school improvement and special educational needs services to be run at this level, leaving pre-school provision, school admissions, school transport and local accountability for these services and schools to be run by existing Local Authorities.

Finance

Until 2006 the 'financing' of state schools was a matter determined variously by the about150 separate LEAs which used government RSG (Revenue Support Grant) to decide locally how much was spent on schools among their various educational provisions and, having so determined, apply the school funding through a formula originally approved when Local Management of Schools (LMS) was introduced after the 1988 Act. Since funding had diverged over the years after 1944 the post-1988 formulae exposed significant differences in funding of apparently similar schools in different parts of the country. In 2006 the government took school budgets out of local authorities so that it would no longer be a charge on the rates and naturally the question of establishing a fair national schools' formula has assumed greater importance.

Given this history it seems sensible to have a national schools funding formula regarded as a percentage of the total cost of schools – say between 85% and 90% with a variable amount extra being raised and spent locally. The need for some local funding is necessary for two reasons: first there needs to be a democratic local voice and involvement to give voice, as happened until 2006, if there are cuts in funding nationally which ministers and DFE naturally wish to present in the most favourable light. (It is noticeable that now it is simply the teacher unions who are drawing attention to educational cuts affecting schools: in the past it would have been education officers in local authorities.) Secondly however there are services to learners, such as those requiring SEND, which cannot be settled within a school's budget. So Educational Psychologists and other specialist and expert services need to be provided from a wider perspective. These could be funded at a regional level.

When Keith Joseph (mentioned earlier) introduced specific grants to stimulate desirable and urgent change – in his case LAP and TVEI – he was justified in doing so since the speed of change to which society and schools needed to respond was beginning to accelerate. The introduction of computers and their use in schools would not have happened as fairly or comprehensively without the stimulus of government specific grants. How such grants are administered and for how long is important and needs to be known from the outset. These initiatives could be administered through the regional authorities suggested as part of the middle-tier. In effect the London Challenge (2002–2011) was a regional initiative even though administered through the DFE. It involved the closest collaboration with the 32 London Boroughs and the City of London as well as close working with the Greater London Authority and the Mayor. It is generally regarded by Ofsted and researchers as a great success and certainly the school outcomes, where London is now performing better than any other region, would support that. It makes a strong case for regional democratic input. That said it avoids the question of how the funding of regional authorities should be raised. Is this a case where a proportion of the business rate could be held for the activities of the regional authorities with supplementary specific grants from central government when they want attention paid to particular school improvements?

Accountability arrangements, examinations and testing, school improvement and curriculum

The order of the words in the heading is significant. At present accountability is dominant both to facilitate the operation of the market and to identify blame. The easiest way to hold schools to account is to find things that are measurable such as results in externally marked tests and exams where candidates regurgitate memorised knowledge and some easily assessed skills. If the knowledge, skills, attitudes or values are not susceptible to relatively simple uncontested examination, then the school, which gets judged on the published exam and test results, tends to regard them as of second-order importance. School Improvement is important but tends to be assessed by what is measurable, namely exam and/or test results together with data on absence and exclusion. Curriculum takes a back seat.

It is at least arguable that the order in the heading should be reversed. We should start with what knowledge, skills, attitudes and values we want our future citizens to have and then determine the experiences which will give them the greatest chance to acquire them before working out how they are best assessed and validated. Just because something is easily measured does not necessarily mean it is of the highest value. In the first post-war age it was like that: headteachers and teachers were assessed on interview for their posts by reference to their understanding of the aims of schooling and their knowledge of curriculum and good and effective teaching. Accountability was hardly mentioned.[12] It is only in the 1980s that accountability, which was signalled as a concern in Callaghan's Ruskin speech in 1976, started to gain prominence. Oxfordshire in 1979 introduced a systematic School Self-Evaluation process[13] where schools were required to give a four-yearly account of the school's activities involving a self-chosen peer headteacher and reporting outcomes to their governing body and a panel of the Education Committee. It was an initiative taken to head-off more punitive possibilities as the council had decided to require the publication of exam results 'in order that parents could make a better choice of school'.[14] Other LEAs required a more tick-list self-evaluation and yet others renamed their advisory services to schools an 'Inspectorate'. Some LEAs did nothing. At the time HMI (Her Majesty's Inspectors) did not publish inspection reports on schools, which were themselves very rare, since HMI were engaged on survey work which led to publications which, with HMI-run conferences, influenced schools' practice and informed the basis of their advice to Secretaries of State.

Accountability arrangements for schools changed radically in 1992 when Ofsted was created and regular school inspections started (with rankings – at first with seven levels, now with four) and were publicly available. In 1993 school exam and test results were also published nationally in league table form. While at first Ofsted considered broader aspects of school life, they soon focused more narrowly on pupil outcomes. Poor exam or test results in practice correlated to their placement in the Ofsted ratings of 'Outstanding', 'Good', 'Requires Improvement' and 'Inadequate'.

In late 2018 HMCI Amanda Speilman identified Ofsted's role in the distorting and narrowing impact on the curriculum and changed the school inspection framework from September 2019 in order to encourage schools to consider the wider aspects of schools' purposes and to demonstrate their curriculum thinking. While this is to be welcomed, it needs to be complemented by other reforms to examinations and the accepted means of assessment which have always influenced schools' curriculum practice.

If the first post-war age of Optimism and Trust was too relaxed on issues affecting accountability, examinations tests, school improvement and curriculum, the latest period has been too tightly prescriptive.

One of the first tasks of the 'standing national advisory council' to the Secretary of State suggested earlier in this book should be to consider appropriate arrangements for a new curriculum dispensation: how it should be examined and assessed and what arrangements there should be for school inspection and the relative roles of the local authority scrutiny committee the newly established regional educational authorities and Ofsted in them.

The supply and retention of teachers

This final, fourth point is arguably the most important. After all the 'teacher effect' is so much greater than the 'school effect' in improving pupil outcomes. If the school as a whole sets the climate within which learning happens, it is the teacher who makes the daily weather.

Until Michael Gove as Secretary of State gave up his duty 'to secure a sufficient supply of suitably qualified teachers' there had been at least some national attempt to plan and assess the need for teachers based on differing factors such as geography and school populations and estimates of wastage and retirements. In the early years after the 1944 Butler Act there was the most extensive planning arrangement with an Advisory Council for the Supply of Education and Training of Teachers (ACSETT) backed by regional Area Teacher Training Organisations (ATTOs) based on networks of Teacher Training Colleges (later Colleges of Education) and University Departments of Education. As routes into teaching have proliferated (e.g. Schools Direct, Teach First) there is no going back to a nationally planned system, although it should be a ministerial responsibility to ensure there is a sufficient supply of suitably qualified teachers.

And it is surely a legitimate matter for the suggested 'standing advisory education council' to consider in partnership with whatever middle tier/regional democratic body is established.

Finally, there is the question of teacher retention and their continuous professional development. This has been a running sore since the Second World War and relatively neglected when compared with other school-related issues. This too will need to be high on any future agenda.

Reflections and disclaimer

As the reader will have noted I have not attempted to cover individual provisions such as Pre-school and Early Years, Careers Advice, Youth Services, Special Educational Need and Disability Services (and particularly those which overlap with NHS provided specialisms) or the myriad of other services such as those for music, drama and opportunity for residential experiences. It is not that they or Adult Education opportunities or Colleges of Further Education or Universities are unimportant (indeed they are vital) or that there are not lessons to be learned from our differing experiences of their successes and failures over the 74 years since the 1944 Act. It is simply that if the main lessons dealt with here are heeded by the creation of democratic regionally based bodies to fill the middle-tier deficit which has grown since 1988, their healthy revival or sustenance can be determined by a combination of national and regional actions with prompting from the newly established 'standing national education advisory council' recommended earlier.

Policy options

Following this analysis of the different models of political control between central and local government in England over 100 years, we suggest there are four policy options open to policy makers:

Policy Option 1: Power over educational matters is largely devolved to local government (The age of Optimism and Trust)

Policy Option 2: Central government assumes some powers over particular priorities (The age of Doubt and Disillusion)

Policy Option 3: Central government assumes total control in most areas (The age of Markets and Managerialism)

Policy Option 4: Central government takes a strategic leadership role finding consensus in partnership with major political parties, education stakeholders, local and regional bodies (The proposed age of Hope, Ambition and Partnership – as outlined in Chapter 6 as Education England, a form of standing national advisory council)

The consequences of these Policy Options are discussed in Chapter 20.

Notes

1 For a more extensive description of the three ages see Brighouse in Tse et al. 2018.
2 In 1998 devolution to Stormont, Holyrood and the Welsh Assembly has meant that the four UK education systems have diverged in ways that they did not before.
3 The school Leaving Age was raised in 1947 and 1971 to age 15 and age 16 respectively across the UK.
4 (Bew, 2016).
5 Grant Maintained Schools were expected to become widespread and popular. Schools however were mostly busy enjoying the fruits of Local Management of their budgets too much to feel the necessity to take the next step of divorcing themselves from the safety of the LEA umbrella.
6 As CEO for Oxfordshire I attended the conference and agreed with my counterpart in Somerset on the return journey a joint – and as it turned out successful – bid for the Low Attainers Project (LAP).
7 One example illustrates the point: the introduction of prescribed methods of teaching reading through synthetic phonics backed by testing of phonics at the end of Year 1.
8 The most obvious, if trivial example, is Michael Gove's decision to send a copy of the Kings James bible to every school soon after becoming Secretary of State in 2010.
9 I use the word 'Governing' body although prior to 1986 only secondary schools had Governing bodies while primary schools had 'Managers'. I use the word 'Governors' throughout the chapter.
10 Even in these authorities there were individual governing bodies for secondary schools.
11 Until Rutter, M. (et al.) *Fifteen Thousand Hours: Secondary Schools and their Effects on Children* (Harvard, 1979) there had been no school effectiveness research and consequently no attention paid to the individual school effect.
12 It should be emphasised that in financial matters there was strong accountability through internal and external audit.
13 The Oxfordshire scheme was based on a booklet from the ILEA called 'Keeping the school under review'.
14 See Report of Oxfordshire County Council meeting July 1978.

References

Bew, J. (2016) *Citizen Clem; a Biography of Attlee*. London: Quercus.
Brighouse, T. (2018) School Buildings in Tse, H.M., Daniels, H., Stables, A. and Cox, S. (eds) *Designing Buildings for the Future of Schooling: Contemporary Visions for Education*. Abingdon: Routledge.
Leese, J. (1950) *Personalities and Power in English Education 'Politics and Power'*. Leeds: E.J. Arnold.

5

POLITICS ASIDE

From fragmentation to coherence

Caroline Whalley and Hugh Greenway

This chapter is written by Caroline Whalley and Hugh Greenway, who are the Chair and CEO of what in Ofsted terms is a successful Multi-Academy Trust (MAT) in England. Whalley was previously Director of Children Services in a London Local Authority.

Multi Academy Trusts (MATs) were initially created to address underperforming secondary schools. This remit was expanded by the UK Coalition Government in 2010 to include free schools, converter and underperforming primary schools. This rapid, reactive and often chaotic growth has led to some success in both tightly defined local cluster and cross regional Trusts. However, all MATs lack the scale, infrastructure and geographical raison d'être of a Local Authority. The current national picture lacks coherence and strategic direction.

The problem with the English state education sector is not a lack of grip. There is too much grip from too many agencies without any vision, direction or control. This chaotic and contradictory approach is stifling a world-renowned system and preventing teachers and school leaders from acting in the interests of their children.

DfE Tops list of concern

In June 2019 the UK Government Public Accounts Committee identified the Department for Education as topping a list of 'concerns'. In her Annual Report to Parliament, Committee Chair Meg Hillier MP highlighted the 'lack of grip' over the academies' system, a lack of transparency and the DfE and Ofsted's failure to 'take up the baton' over funding squeezes.[1] This may be the right conclusion, but for entirely the wrong reasons.

It is unclear whether the Public Accounts Committee has been poorly briefed, genuinely believes what it is advocating or is playing politics. But it has got hold of the wrong end of the stick. The interests of children in academies will not be served by even more oversight. Conversely, as Academies Minister, Lord Agnew, explained, the DfE is actually consulting on raising the level of oversight in the LA maintained sector to bring it up to the level of academy trusts.[2]

The problem with the English state education sector is not a lack of grip. There is too much grip from too many agencies without any vision, direction or control. This chaotic and contradictory approach is stifling a world-renowned system and preventing teachers and school leaders from acting in the interests of their children.

Current status of English state education – the problem

At the time of writing our state education sector is in flux and appears to lack any substantive vision.[3] We have a partially reformed and therefore massively fragmented system comprising 152 Local Education Authorities (LAs), 740 Multi-Academy Trusts (MATs) and 1,651 Single Academy Trusts (SATs – which include Free Schools).[4] This is a multi-provider, multi-agency system where the biggest MAT is smaller than the smallest LA. The average size of schools that are not academies (most of which are one form entry primary schools) is 279 pupils. The majority of schools that are not academies are faith-based primary schools and they average 189 pupils.[5]

The impact of the problem – pressure on the system

1   *The absence of any big vision means there is no strategic direction*
    Multiple agencies are stakeholders but all operate differently[6] (LA, government department, government agency, charitable trust etc.). All broadly attempt to operate in the interests of children but because they are forced to compete for scraps in a fragmented system, they often waste time and money fighting with each other, duplicating effort and placing greater workload on schools.

2   *In its current format the 'system' is unsustainable*
    Multi-Academy Trusts aren't big enough to survive because they lack the scale to provide sustainable support to their schools and to absorb operational risks. Local Authorities (and the Church) are left with the smallest, least viable schools. Thus, despite still being bigger organisations than MATs, the drain on their remaining resources is more acute. Consequently, without action on funding or drastic cost cutting, all will get weaker and many will go to the wall.[7]

3   *In its current format the "system" is unmanageable*
    The eight Regional Schools Commissioners have an impossible job. They are expected to have oversight and influence over an average of 90 MATs, 200 SATs, and almost 20 LAs each.[8] They simply do not have the resources to have an impact when they are stretched this thin.

4   *In its current format the 'system' is unknowable*
    Over the last 10 years one of the biggest consequences of structural reform has been the loss of tacit knowledge of schools and of children.[9] There are

only 190 days in the school year and from the previous numbers this means that RSCs have little more than half a day a year to seek to understand each of organisations over which they have authority. Ofsted is also being forced to cut its cloth in line with its budget, which will have significant risks to the validity of its judgements.

5   *In its current format the 'system' may be unfixable*

Due to the pressures outlined previously most LAs and MATs have declining school improvement capacity. Moreover, the bureaucracy that has grown like a fungus in the cracks of fragmentation almost always clogs up the system by acting defensively, seeking to prevent the inevitable PR problems rather than looking forward to improve the system. This blame and scapegoat approach adds delay and indecision, which compounds the problems mentioned previously.

6   *The current situation is likely to get worse before it gets better*

The fragmentation of the system from 152 LAs to 2,500+ providers of different types has led to entirely predictable inflationary pressures at the same time as funding becomes more constrained. These cost increases not just in executive pay[10] but in everyday procurement from utilities though to IT have occurred through the lower purchasing power of smaller entities. The only way to balance these two pressures across the system has been an increase in the level of risk accepted by all provider types.

These problems may be invisible to policy makers

Just because the top line performance indicators are not currently going in the wrong direction does not mean that the what we've said above isn't true. It is our view that the system is currently being held together by a handful of hyper-productive individuals in small organisations who do not have the time or inclination to succession plan. When they retire exhausted or trip up inadvertently through overstretch, their organisations often fail behind them.

Possible tactical solutions

A   *Reduce the number of points of failure*

Increase the average number of pupils per organisation to 20,000+ by incremental measures, whether by turning LAs into MATs, giving MATs to LAs, merging MATs, merging LAs, aggregating SATs, creating hybrids or inventing a new vehicle entirely. The total number of organisations must be reduced so that system leaders have a chance of making an impact. There is too much pressure on those leading the smallest organisations and too much expected on those above them.

B   *Educate politicians, civil servants and system leaders about the difference between regulation, management and oversight*

Presently there appears to be a misunderstanding of regulation as a process. The structural reforms of the English education system over the last decade have been sold on the basis of their 'freedoms' when in fact they have led to the exact opposite. There has been a massive drawing in of power to central government that has set itself up as judge and jury despite, for the reasons set out previously, not being able to perform this role properly.

Regulators are *not* responsible for failure in a system. They are responsible for finding failure and prosecuting it where appropriate.[11] Finding failure in a manner that the Chair of the PAC highlights in her report is, therefore, evidence of success, not failure.[12] There is more transparency about the management and funding of schools than there has ever been. The sure and certain knowledge that, should you break the rules, you will be caught and punished is what keeps those who are actually responsible for failure on their toes.

The regulator cannot and must not manage. For the system to work there must be clear separation of powers.

C   *Separate funding from oversight and oversight from audit*

The ESFA is both a funder and a regulator and increasingly steps into the role of direct management.[13] If we are to create a successful, self-improving system, we need to incentivise self-reporting and self-criticism particularly when it is clear that there is nowhere near enough money to run the system directly from Whitehall. The ESFA should be the accountant and paymaster for the system, not also the auditor and senior manager.

D   *Change the legal status of Academy Trusts*

All academy trusts, whether single or multi-school, are annually audited as companies and charities as well as answering to the ESFA, DfE and Ofsted. There is a surfeit and overlap of accountability and regulation with emphasis on the financial aspects. Primary legislation to change the legal status of academy trusts would enable their regulation to be simplified, thus reducing costs and also significantly reducing the opportunity cost burden on Trusts that is required to service the multiple regulatory bodies which have grown significantly in recent years.[14,15] Letting a framework contract for audit for entire RSC regions would increase the tacit knowledge of the regions and improve the effectiveness of the RSCs.

Houston, we have a bigger problem

However, the much larger issue is that our globally respected education system is so fragmented and fractured that it is on the verge of a breaking point. The issue isn't solely school budgets, although that is where it has broken through to the public consciousness. The issue is that government no longer thinks about the system costs of education. Indeed there is scant evidence that government thinks about education as a system at all.

We are now stuck with a multi-provider system because no political party has a credible joined-up plan. There is no government money left to pay for remedial action or political leadership able to rationalise and re-distribute existing resources.

Labour's 'National Education Service'[16] will fail in its current format because there is no longer the capacity to run schools through their reimagined LAs nor the money to roll the academy project back. The Conservative approach appears to be the pursuit of platitudes. Publicly they say, "Everything's all right" whilst privately overregulating to ensure that there's always someone else to blame for failure. The centrist politicians have no stated education position.

The big idea – separation of power between education delivery, oversight and politics

Why?

1 Politicians are social engineers, or at least they aspire to be. Most, if not all, enter politics with a desire to make the world a better place. But this urge to improve needs counterbalancing forces to prevent it from unintentionally doing harm. In the past elected governments proposed, created and implemented the legislation in tandem with a knowledgeable civil service. "Civil servants support the Government in power but they are employees of the Crown and not Parliament. In order to keep their independence from the politics and the parties in power, civil servants are protected from them by their roles and responsibilities".[17]

2 Increasingly over the last two decades, rather than working with regulated civil servants[18] to support their activity, Ministers have employed SpAds.[19] Special Advisors have no formal democratic mandate and are, in effect, temporary civil servants unbound by any rules of engagement or code of conduct. They are loosely accountable and only regulated indirectly. SpAds don't have to listen to stakeholders or even understand the systems with which they tinker. The history of living with the unintended consequences of their policy decisions suggests that SpAd policy theorists conduct few, if any, thought experiments nor use appropriate research. Worse they rarely consult stakeholders to better understand the systems they redesign. This apparent indifference breeds mistrust in the sector which then fails to speak to power in a mature fashion when it is consulted.

3 The loss of tacit knowledge in the civil service and in local authorities has allowed government policy to be pushed through into legislation without effective moderating influence. When this policy changes the structure of the sector itself, the imbalance is compounded. Government is now too powerful and unchecked by dialogue with practitioners and system-leaders. Had this structural reform led to significant improvements for all children, then the experimental risks might have been justified but it hasn't.[20,21] Taxpayers' school improvement money has been spent dismantling the power bases of those who opposed government policy. The result of which has been the overall weakening of our educational institution. We have created a system that cannot entirely function. In a digital era when opinion voiced loudly can crowd out fact, this makes our schools and children more vulnerable than they have ever been.

4   Subsidiarity is not a fashionable term at present. But in education, decisions need to be made as close as practicable to the children that they affect for the reason that education is hard to scale. Classical and neo-classical management approaches tend not to work across the whole system. Our approach needs to be better tuned to context and complexity. On the rare occasions when there is undisputed, evidence-based, 'best practice', then it can be rolled out in volume. But where doubt increases, a more modest approach of enquiry and reflection is required.

5   Most LAs are little more than empty shells and the RSCs have neither the time nor the money to step into the vacuum left behind by LA decline. MATs are far too small and mostly lack the skills required. The ESFA and the DfE mistake their power for control over the system.

Reflections

Nationally, we need to reimagine the system of school oversight and move away from the deficit model. The neo-Victorian view that without rigorous oversight, schools like children are likely to misbehave and perform poorly, should be shelved in favour of a presumption of continuous improvement. School leaders and teachers on the whole strive to improve outcomes for all children. Although present in most secretary of state speeches in the last decade, this idea should be given more than lip-service and be allowed to work in practice. The improvement of schools takes time to work and sustaining that improvement requires policy that prioritises it rather than school shaming.

Structural reform in education was mis-sold. It continues to be sold as being about the balance between 'academy freedoms' and 'accountability'. The reality is very little, if any freedom but much more control.

Policy options

The issues raised in this chapter lead to a number of policy options:

Policy option 1 – Status Quo remains

This will lead over time to further inequalities and diseconomies. The system will remain fragmented and meaningful improvements to the picture nationally will not occur.

Policy option 2 – All schools in one diverse but resilient system

A national framework of 20 Regional Schools Commissioners overseeing roughly 1,000 schools each and with these schools distributed evenly between 20 organisations (LAs, MATs, Diocesan bodies, hybrids of all three) would be much more resilient. At the same time, no organisation or agent in the system would be too powerful to put itself before the interests of children and none would be too weak to function. This structure, National Schools Commissioner and the RSCs, could be overseen by a cross-party group which sets up and directs a stable national framework for educating our population. System coherence takes time to build as does system improvement. Sustaining that improvement requires policy stability that prioritises national outcomes rather than political dogma. Shaping and taking longer term educational decisions for the greater benefit of all, brings freedom from direct political activity, its change and constraints.

Policy option 3 – Separation of powers

This option could work alongside options 1 and 2 or work as option 3 independently.

The ESFA should be separated from its oversight function. Instead, it should focus solely on fiscal responsibilities including determination of funding formulas, funding delegation and distribution of funding. The ESFA would then be in a better position to support longer range financial planning and resource geographic, phase and curriculum areas more flexibly. Procuring and letting regional contracts to audit firms, with directional oversight provided from the National Audit Office, would also create savings through economies of scale as well as growing the system knowledge available to RSCs.

A body – for example, Ofsted – is given the overview role of all organisations in relation to performance, governance and value for money and would report to RSCs. RSCs would use and share this information for impartial educational and governance system improving.

In the interests of all of our children and all of our futures, isn't it time to redress the imbalance between politics, government and the profession in our education system?

Chapter 20 provides further reflections and an executive summary of options, consequences and cautionary tales.[22,23]

Notes

1 Fourth Annual Report of the Chair of the Committee of Public Accounts – pp. 6–7 www.parliament.uk/documents/commons-committees/public-accounts/2370.pdf
2 https://schoolsweek.co.uk/dfe-to-consult-on-bringing-la-school-transparency-in-line-with-academies/
3 This is not to suggest that vision was previously lacking. One could argue that we have had a surfeit of green & white papers over the last decade from 2009 'Your child, your schools, our future', the revolutionary 2010 'The Importance of Teaching', through to the alliterative but oxymoronic 2016 'Education Excellence Everywhere' and the retrograde 2016 'Schools that work for everyone'. But all have quietly fizzled away after several years of weak government.
4 www.compare-school-performance.service.gov.uk/ – Data download 2017–18.
5 Ibid.
6 House of Commons Library, 'FAQs Academies and Free Schools 07059', June 2019 https://researchbriefings.parliament.uk/ResearchBriefing/Summary/SN07059#fullreport

7   Kreston Reeves, 'Academies Benchmark Report 2019' – 'We commend the work academies have made in delivering savings but the Benchmark Report offers a warning that further spending reductions will be hard to achieve, and Trusts cannot rely on their reserves forever. They will run out in 5 to 6 years without any changes'. www.krestonreeves. com/news-and-events/31/01/2019/academies-benchmark-report-2019-released

8   House of Commons Library, 'Academies and free schools Briefing Paper 07059' June 2019 – Numbers of Multi-Academy Trust and Free Schools

9   House of Commons Library, 'Education spending in the UK Briefing Paper 1078' July 2019 – pp. 6. Decline in Education spending since 2010 is between 16% or 25% depending on the method of calculation. Given that 75%+ of education budget is spent on staff cost this is a huge loss of tacit knowledge

10 https://schoolsweek.co.uk/more-trusts-in-deficit-plus-4-more-academy-sector-accounts-findings/

11 We exclude Ofsted from this criticism. Our experience of them as a regulator is of one very aware of their role: equally reflective and self-critical

12 It more accurately highlights the lack of oversight in the LA maintained sector https:// schoolsweek.co.uk/dfe-to-consult-on-bringing-la-school-transparency-in-line-with-academies/

13 The Academies Finance Handbook, which is effectively a schedule to the contract between government and academy trusts and has expanded from 27 pages in 2012 to 66 pages in 2019, clearly evinces this creeping control.

14 In addition to the growth in regulations outlined in note 13 immediately preceding there is also the Charity Commission's Handbook 'The Essential Trustee' and the DfE's 138 page 'Governance Handbook'.

15 Indeed the burden has grown again since writing this article with more guidance and requirements added to the pile www.gov.uk/government/publications/academy-trust-financial-management-good-practice-guides?utm_source=ESFA%20update%20 31%2F07%2F2019

16 https://labour.org.uk/manifesto/education/

17 www.civilservicecommission.org.uk/

18 Civil Service Vision 2015 to 2020. 'A brilliant Civil Service that helps to keep the United Kingdom prosperous and secure, supporting the governments we serve in implementing their commitments and delivering high quality services for the public'.

19 www.civilservant.org.uk/spads-statistics.html

20 www.suttontrust.com/research-paper/chain-effects-2018-academy-chains/

21 https://epi.org.uk/publications-and-research/quantitative-analysis-characteristics-performance-multi-academy-trusts/

22 The ESFA brings together the former responsibilities of the Education Funding Agency (EFA) and Skills Funding Agency (SFA) to create a single agency accountable for funding education and skills for children, young people and adults.

23 https://www.gov.uk/education/academy-and-academy-trust-finance-and-reporting# guidance_and_regulation

6

EDUCATION ENGLAND

From chaos to consensus?

Sarah Younie, Brian Hudson and Marilyn Leask

Introduction

The problem addressed in this chapter concerns the number of changes to the education system that have occurred, meaning that:

> Reforms to the English education system are unsustainable and have left it "unknowable" "unmanageable" and in its current form "unfixable". . . . These problems may be invisible to policy makers.
>
> *(Whalley and Greenway, Chapter 5)*

> The questioning of democracy is unprecedented in my lifetime.
>
> *(Fishkin, 2018)*

British society is at a cross-roads. At the time of writing it is uncertain whether the 'United Kingdom' will survive because of the BREXIT divisions. Independence movements in Northern Ireland, Wales and Scotland are growing. The 'post-war' cross-party consensus on how to run our parliamentary democracy and the shared vision of achieving a meritocratic society through free education to degree level, free healthcare at the time of need and high quality council housing for those on low incomes and legal aid to allow citizens redress through the courts, has been shattered.

The heavily cross-referenced Wikipedia entry[1] on the United Kingdom's Austerity Programme starting in 2010 makes grim reading with references to over a quarter of a million early deaths[2] and with financial cutbacks principally affecting the living standards of disabled people, children, women and particularly women of colour. This is mentioned here as many teachers work in the poorer communities which have felt the burden of cutbacks acutely. Class divisions and wealth inequalities are sharp and a rising tide of discontent has been provoked through policies such as tuition fees, elitism entrenched through spurious league tables of schools and universities, privatisation of council housing and policies which have led to charitable food banks[3] becoming widespread.

There is widespread dissatisfaction with the provision of education, from 0–18 years, with concerns being expressed by all political and professional stakeholders apart from the government in office.

> In June 2019 the Public Accounts Committee identified the Department for Education as topping a list of "concern". In her Annual Report to Parliament, Committee Chair, Meg Hillier MP, highlighted the "lack of grip" over the academies' system, a lack of transparency and the DfE and Ofsted's failure to "take up the baton" over funding squeezes.[4]
>
> *(Whalley and Greenway, Chapter 5)*

The Confederation of British Industries say the curriculum is too narrow (CBI, 2010a, 2010b, 2012), Teacher recruitment goals are not met by the DFE and retention is poor; their own research shows over 20% of new teachers leave the profession within the first two years of teaching, and 33% leave within their first five years[5] (DFE, 2019).

An education system that is described as "unknowable", "unmanageable" and in its current form "unfixable" (Whalley and Greenway, Chapter 5) cannot be called a system. The chaos that has ensued from a plethora of radical reforms in England since 2010 has led to this book in which the intention is to support better policy making by making explicit the options that policy makers face and the potential positive and negative consequences of their choices (see Chapter 20).

In this chapter we examine a way out of the chaos in the current English education system.

How a society's young people are educated and the opportunities for lifelong education shape the society. Missed educational chances result through a restricted curriculum, through poor teaching, through lack of access to education impact on an individual, their family and society for the whole of that person's life.

Our proposal: Education England

We propose that:

- the government establishes a new body, governed by a national representative council to oversee education 0–18 with the provisional name of Education England (EE). The EE Council would oversee development of the English education system and be accountable to Parliament.
- The EE Council would have balanced political representation from major parties (in proportion to the votes cast in the most recent election) and equal representation from specialist subject/professional associations, research units

TABLE 6.1 Provisional list giving the philosophy, values and principles underpinning a new national education system

---

- Education is a fundamental entitlement for all citizens
- The Education system has the knowledge and power within the system to self-improve and self-monitor and needs supportive national structures to enable that to happen (based on trust and critical partnership and not punitive)
- Education of our society's young people is a community responsibility (0–18 yrs)
- Education resources are a local/community, regional and national, international (force for peace and stability) resource to be deployed for the common good (knowledge for public good to be sharable – being free and accessible to all)
- Education can provide a binding force for society supporting integration and social cohesion if children are given positive exposure to the rich cultural diversity and heritage of the society in which they live along with the values of tolerance and an appreciation of difference
- Education provision 0–18 should normally be non-selective by ability/aptitude, faith or wealth. Special provision for gifted and talented children, children in care and children with SEND may be required
- Adult education services provide a foundation for national growth
- Education resources are a "common good" and knowledge essential to high quality teaching and successful communities should be free at the point of use
- Making online resources freely available may support improved teaching not just in England but also in poorer nations and support international peace and stability
- Education 0–18 should be free at the point of use and paid for through universal taxation for the common good
- The education system has to prepare children and young people for living and working in civil democratic society and also to address global challenges facing the society

---

across all disciplines, businesses and commercial knowledge services. The chair would be a politically neutral position.
- The roles to be covered by Education England are covered in Table 6.1.

Expected benefits

- Restoration of stability, consistency, coherence and high standards across the English education eco-system.
- A coherent strategy covering recruitment, initial education and continuing professional development of teachers.
- Alignment between initial teacher education and CPD, the curriculum, examinations and teaching approaches.
- Education policy affecting English schools would be made on the basis of evidence, predicted long term economic interests, promotion of individual wellbeing and societal cohesion.
- Digital tools would be used for the maximum benefit of all aspects of the service[6]
- A new vision, developed through consultation, for a truly nationally coherent education service and system providing high quality education which takes account of the needs and aspirations of users may help heal Brexit divisions.

Understandings fundamental to the proposal

- Policies are more likely to be effective in improving learners' potential to contribute to and build a stable and economically resilient society if developed through consensus.
- Policies based on individual beliefs, party political ideology, quick fixes, fads and fashions lead to inadequate long-term thinking, instability in the supply and availability of experienced teachers with subsequent damage to our economic growth.
- Digital tools[7] support new inclusive ways of working at lower cost. For example, representative samples of teachers in different specialisms can be easily brought together in a one-hour video conference at the end of the school day to 'sense test' proposals; national state-of-the-nation surveys with representative samples of heads or subject specialists can be surveyed about issues, about potential impact and unintended consequences of policies.
- Knowledge for effective teaching is complex.[8]

Education England – foundation values

The vision for Education England outlined here is built on the values[9] identified by the OECD (Saussois, 2003; Ramos & Schleicher, 2016, p. 6, see also Chapter 2) of equal entitlement and valuing the individual regardless of his or her background and location in the country. Choosing different values would lead to a different structure and different decisions over the deployment of resources (See Chapter 2).

Table 6.1 provides the starting point for the values and principles underpinning a new coordinated national education system overseen by education England (EE).

The Govian/Cummings/Gibb values legacy (2010 onwards)

The Gove, Cummings and Gibb's radical reforms from 2010[10] in England appear to have led to a values shift in the management of some schools and school "chains". "Gaming" the system (Ing, 2018) by removing children from the school roll[11] to appear high in national league tables rather than on educating the child has been identified as an unintended consequence. Another is that the DfE has not been able to control salaries and deployment of funds so that salaries for leading roles in MATs for example, calculated on a group of schools basis, when compared with local government, can be 10 times what a Director of Children's Services earned. Lord Storey is quoted in Hansard as saying:

> the chief executive of one of our multi-academy trusts [MAT] is on a salary of £440,000 – nearly three times the salary of our Prime Minister. At a time when schools are having to make cuts and struggling with their budgets, does the Minister not agree that this issue needs to be properly addressed?
>
> *(Hansard, 14 February, 2019)*

MATs are smaller than LAs and on a like-for-like basis, this salary is around nine times what a Director of Children's Services for a Local Education Authority on a salary of £100,000 was paid.[12] As teacher salaries are the main cost to an education system, these high salaries represent teachers and materials not being available to children. (In this case, the excessive salary could have paid for 20 more teachers.)

This deregulation has led to a hidden scandal of a lost generation of young people[13]:

- Education DataLab looked at pupils – from year 7 to year 11. This report[14] found that, in 2017, 22,000 pupils between year 7 and year 11 had left their school but were not attending any other state school[15]. The UK Government (2019) Timpson Report found that schools were pressuring parents to remove their children without protecting their right to education by following due process;
- Nearly 50,000 students at the most critical time of their study 'have left school rolls in England, moving to a different school or leaving the state school system completely, for entirely unknown reasons. . . [for] those expected to have completed year 11 in 2017. . . as many as 8.1 per cent of the entire pupil population were subject to moves that *cannot be accounted for* (with over 55,300 exits by 49,100 pupils).[16]
- off-rolling and possible links to crime: "off-rolling, may increase the risk factors a child has of being drawn into crime" (UK Government, 2019, p. 104).

> Ofsted has conducted analysis to assess the scale of pupil moves and what should be considered exceptional levels that should give rise to questions about off-rolling. Looking at a Year 10 cohort, they found over 19,000 pupils did not progress to Year 11. Many of these will be for good and lawful reasons, but a small number of schools lost a large proportion of their cohort for at least two years in a row. While we cannot quantify the scale of this issue, there is emerging evidence that supports what this review has heard. A survey of teachers conducted by YouGov for Ofsted found that 66% of teachers reported being aware of children being taken off roll as a means of improving their results – 21% of whom had seen it at a school they currently or previously worked in.
>
> *(UK Government, 2019)*

- Students being prevented from staying on into sixth forms[17] and so accessing high level qualifications:[18] "at present, schools, LAs and others report there may be perverse incentives to exclude or off-roll children who might not positively contribute to a school's performance or finances" UK Government (2019).
- Downgrading teacher training:[19] Secretary of State for Education Michael Gove established a culture of denigration of expertise calling those who questioned his policies "the blob[20] and enemies of promise"[21] at the same time as

excessively funding elitist accelerated routes (Teach First[22]) and encouraging schools to employ unqualified teachers.[23]

- Heads have reported confidentially to us that students and parents, typically those with less power in the system, are dissuaded from even applying to their local school by not being given the full tour, by being told of demands for funding and resources required.
- Severe shortages of qualified teachers.[24]
- "98,779 (18%) of pupils in England in 2018 had failed to gain five GCSEs at grade C or higher or the equivalent technical qualifications. . . . Of pupils who qualified for free school meals, about 28,225 (37%) did not achieve this level of attainment"[25] Children's Commissioner (2019).
- Parents have taken to the streets to protest against moving their schools from local control to unknown multi-academy chains.[26]

See Chapters 5 and 16 also for a list of data sources for the these shortcomings and more.

As Whalley and Greenway argue in Chapter 5, "at the time of writing our state education sector is in flux and appears to lack any substantive vision.[27] We have a partially deregulated and therefore massively fragmented system and service comprising 152 Local Education Authorities (LAs), 740 Multi-Academy Trusts (MATs) and 1,651 Single Academy Trusts (SATs – which include Free Schools).[28] This is a multi-provider, multi-agency system where the biggest MAT is smaller than the smallest LA. The average size of schools that are not academies (most of which are one form entry primary schools) is 279 pupils. The majority of schools that are not academies are faith-based primary schools and they average 189 pupils."[29]

The last decade in the English education system has seen immense waste of resources in the order of hundreds of millions of pounds, as resources developed over the first 10 years of the Internet in education were scrapped on ideological grounds by an incoming government.[30] Clearly this level of waste of resource every time there is a change of government is not an approach that is going to take a country forward in the international competition for the best education system. Based on the impact of the ideologically driven change experienced in England since 2010, we propose cross-party consensus is sought to achieve stability in the system going forward.

So-called leadership of the education sector by successive Secretaries of State has led to this situation and a radical remedy is needed which tempers political power with common sense and practical expert knowledge.

Education England – governance and accountability

We propose that Education England be developed to be such an organisation, independent but accountable to Parliament through its governance structure with the remit to oversee and lead the National Education system and service for England.

EE would:

- have its strategy set by its independent Council with members representing major political parties and subject/professional associations
- be developed with sustainability in mind and so require cross-party consensus in Parliament for its closure
- oversee and lead where appropriate (through consensus) the national strategy for primary, special, secondary and FE education in the following areas:

  - setting aims, values and principles
  - regional provision and equitable access to provision
  - curriculum, assessment, leadership and accountability
  - inclusion, selection, social mobility
  - education knowledge services
  - initial teacher education and continuing professional development
  - standards and certification including a public register of teachers and their qualifications and, when the Education Knowledge Service (Education Futures Collaboration, 2019; Leask & Younie, 2013) accreditation services makes updating in subject and pedagogic knowledge easy, manage the regular licensing of teachers via a CPD points scheme in line with longstanding health profession requirements and practices (Royal College of Surgeons, 2018)
  - ensure supply of qualified teachers.

Here are some of the features to be expected of a national education service:

- Annual advisory remit letter from cross-party political group led by Government with representation from parties gaining over a million votes
- No political interference without two-thirds parliamentary majority
- A school system structure and resourcing to support teacher retention, collaboration not competition, sharing of the human resource of teacher expertise, stability, coherence and equity with extra resources for poorly performing schools/ schools in areas of social disadvantage or with rapid turnover of pupils and staff
- Career structure focused on mastery of subject pedagogy not on leadership and management but on quality of teaching and learning
- System structure of supportive specialist networks (local, regional, national) – sustainable and leading to accumulation of deep knowledge, expertise and leading in innovation and research (Younie et al., 2019)
- Spaces for supporting innovation and risk taking and feeding back outcomes of innovation to the whole service and system e.g. through podcasts/vidcasts
- Local accountability and local, regional and national networking.

With respect to creating a national infrastructure to support Education England, we outline in what follows the organisations that would need to be involved and specify the individual role that should be undertaken by each organisation in the service.

TABLE 6.2 Potential stakeholder roles within a National Education Service

organisation	*role*
GOVERNMENT • Secretary of state and ministers with cross-party nominees • select committees • APPGs	• sets broad strategic policy direction within a 10-year plan (National Education Policy Framework) requiring cross-party consensus: change of direction requires 2/3 majority from Parliament • Issues annual remit letters aligned with 10-year plan • Holds National Education Board (NEB) to account Negotiates funding allocation through national formula taking account of regional and local differences
Department for Education Civil servants with secondees from NEB	• Educations areas not covered below by NEB and social care
NATIONAL EDUCATION BOARD (NEB) (Trustees/ governor level) Possible organisation name: EDUCATION ENGLAND (EdE) • Elected and remunerated roles: expertise in education and national leading roles required for all posts, NAO, leaders from government organisations and major political party representation, non-political chair holds casting vote Nominations from government, political parties, Unions, subject, research/ teacher education professional associations, Regional Boards (see what follows). **Interim NEB member list is available.**	• Approval of annual strategic plan/ remit from Executive Board response to government and oversight of operations • Terms of reference: to decide the specificity of directorates areas (suggestions follow) • Decisions made on the basis of evidence • Nationally set structures • Advises what minimal funding is required – from Govt. (national funding formula) • Teacher supply at national level – formula (responsive to regional & local need) (teacher recruitment and retention) • Teacher standards • Regulation of initial teacher education • Long-term (x10 years review) – decouple from politics, for stability • School admissions (national guidelines but locally implemented) • Sets accountability framework
Executive Board • CEO and Heads of Directorates **Directorates/Agencies** • Appointed officials; seconded teachers/teacher-educator researchers directorate policy development – is subject to external review by Regional Education Board nominees	Executive Board: strategic plan development for Council approval and operational Directorates/Agencies: assessment and curriculum (OFQUAL liaison), teacher supply (R&R), ITE and CPD, Research and knowledge services, and inspection liaison (OFSTED), school governance, EYS and Primary, Secondary/FE/vocational, SEND, equity and inclusion, Digital, Adult Ed., Nat. teachers pay & conditions plus back offices services (finance including contracts, organisational/staff development, HR, comms, premises, IT, evaluation)

(Continued)

TABLE 6.2 (Continued)

organisation	role
REGIONAL EDUCATION BOARD	• Mechanisms to make responsive to local need • Composition of RB – open and transparent • Accountability framework delivered – implemented • Hold local boards to account
LOCAL EDUCATION BOARD **Elected membership:** 75% Reps from each sector of ed – EY/pri/sec/FE; 10% – parents, governors, local business; 15% – non-elected officials	• Education officer roles – non-elected local officials/and elected members • Local network of school-to-school, peer-to-peer support and challenge • Focus primarily on Education with close links with local social and health services for children • Hold schools to account on finance audit value for money
INDIVIDUAL SCHOOLS	• Ofsted's four areas: "effectiveness of leadership and management; quality of teaching, learning and assessment; personal development, behaviour and welfare; outcomes for learners."

We hope this brief introduction has helped you understand the concept of Education England, the values and principles underpinning it and stakeholder roles.

Legislating for stability: to support innovation and development

In Chapter 3 and 19, we discuss the meaning of democracy and the risks to democracy where minority governments impose ideological change on an education service. Professor James Fishkin (2018) from Stanford University outlines risks to countries' stability from current disillusionment with democracy. He cites voter dissatisfaction with "flip-flopping" government: wastage of resources with churn of government policy.

He outlines four ways for democracies to take decisions:

- competitive democracy: party competition (leading to misinformation, partisanship and attacking opponents)
- elite deliberation
- participatory democracy: the use of multiple referenda is an example as in California but with complex issues busy voters may not have time to be fully briefed and so may make decisions manipulated through advertising. Fishkin cites the UK Brexit Leave Campaign's use of a bus with a misleading slogan on it as a prime example of misleading use of advertising[31] in a referendum.
- deliberative democracy: where a stratified sample of the population are brought together, presented with evidence from different perspectives to weigh up and

make decisions. Fishkin has taken this concept of "deliberative democracy" into real political decision making in 28 countries, 109 times.

When we started researching for this book, we knew "competitive democracy" policy-making processes were causing problems for the education and system in England (destruction of resources paid for by taxpayers, disillusionment and alienation of teachers and learners). We did not realise this was a wider problem. As it happens, 2019 has been a year of unrest in many countries with the population taking to the streets over perceived injustices: UK (Brexit), Chile, Hong Kong, Lebanon and worldwide Extinction Rebellion protests. Fishkin mentions Mongolia and the many other countries he has worked with.

To return to the specific focus of this book, education systems, it seems clear to us that decisions taken using "deliberative democratic processes" are more likely to lead to an improved education service and better outcomes for young people than the "competitive democratic process currently being employed". We propose Education England as a concept. Norwich (2019) with his focus on vulnerable children suggests a 10-year plan for education services, supported by an independent-of-government Education Framework Commission which we support. Coffield's (2019) consultation proposes something similar.

The consequences of not addressing the problem could be severe as Professor Madeline Albright spells out in her book *Fascism*. Albright, previously Secretary of State in the United States, has had an active political life spanning the period from when she and her family fled Czechoslovakia at the outbreak of World War II to the early 21st century. During this time she negotiated with major political figures from many countries. She describes how both Hitler and Mussolini, once elected, simply used their mandate to change the rules about how their societies functioned. The UK has been jolted out of its post-war consensus that society should be run for the common good rather than to maximise individual gain by Conservative policies initiated by Thatcher in 1989, who is remembered for saying there is no such thing as society.[32]

For these reasons and to provide a stable working environment for learners and teachers focused on the highest goals, we suggest it is necessary to enshrine in law the structure and operation of an educational service and system which has aims, values, principles gaining cross-party and stakeholder support and provides a governance structure of independent professional, political and business oversight within a framework of accountability to the country and to government.

The model of the relationship the Bank of England has to the financial sector has been suggested as a model the education sector could follow.

David Wolfe, QC provides the following insights into the legislative process necessary: "generally, legal changes are brought about by legislation (Acts of Parliament) passed by a simple majority. That can then be changed later by another Act of Parliament. That is the case for even the biggest constitutional changes, such as establishing the Scottish Parliament and its separate powers, the Human Rights Act and membership of the EU (which, as we know, is potentially to be undone by an

Act of Parliament passed by a simple majority). In other words: legislation enacting a national education service and system could be changed by later legislation.

The rare (and I think unique) exception to that has been the arrangements put in place following the Leveson Inquiry relating to press regulation which were put in place partly using a Royal Charter in a way which means that changes require a two-thirds majority of the UK and Scottish Parliaments. But those were special circumstances (a wish to create a regulatory body whose independence was guaranteed such that it could not be improperly influenced by politicians). And the use of that route (a Royal Charter) was regarded as controversial by some people.

Anyway, what follows is what, while it would in theory be possible to use a mechanism which made future change hard, would be ground breaking and controversial" (Wolfe, 2019).

Reflections

We suggest to avoid wasted resources and to maximise the value for money that legislation is passed requiring a supermajority in parliament for any major changes in the education sector. The next chapter addresses the legislation required.

This step should go some way to providing a secure foundation for the development of a truly National Education Service, allowing schools to do long-term planning secure in the knowledge that any major changes are a result of national consensus about the benefit to learners rather than the result of an ideological fad designed to boost the profile of an ambitious politician.

Beyond the scope of this book is lifelong education which provides a way of improving individual well-being, economic prosperity and community cohesion. Brexit divisions in English society must be healed and a consultation about the education system and service fit for purpose in the 21st century may help citizens focus on the future following Brexit.

Policy options for the English education service

The issues raised in this chapter lead to a number of policy options:

Policy Option 1: status quo – with education ministers unable to manage the quality of the currently centralised service leading to increasing numbers of "off-rolled" children, little CPD for teachers, chaotic organisation of Initial Teacher Education and insufficient numbers of teachers.

Policy Option 2: radical reform – establish Education England and proceed through consultation and consensus to bring coherence and high quality to every element of the sector.

The penultimate chapter of this volume provides further reflections and an executive summary of options, consequences and cautionary tales.

Acknowledgements: with thanks to Hugh Greenway, Brian Matthews, Caroline Whalley, and all the other authors in this book who have contributed ideas.

Notes

1 (https://en.wikipedia.org/wiki/United_Kingdom_government_austerity_programme)
2 A study published in BMJ Open in 2017 linked austerity to 120,000 extra deaths in England, primarily as a result of a reduction in the number of nurses.
3 www.trusselltrust.org/what-we-do/
4 Fourth Annual Report of the Chair of the Committee of Public Accounts – pp 6–7 www.parliament.uk/documents/commons-committees/public-accounts/2370.pdf
5 "Over 20% of new teachers leave the profession within their first 2 years of teaching, and 33% leave within their first 5 years". https://assets.publishing.service.gov.uk/gov ernment/uploads/system/uploads/attachment_data/file/786856/DFE_Teacher_Reten tion_Strategy_Report.pdf
6 See Council for Subject Associations and Technology, Pedagogy and Education Policy Paper 19/1/02 CPD, Knowledge Services and Research: A proposal for applying 21st century digital solutions to the urgent but intractable problem of keeping teachers up-to-date for further details
7 Networking, online collaborative writing, and videoconferencing
8 The knowledge base for teaching includes general and subject specific pedagogy and assessment (e.g. different forms for different purposes), SEND (e.g. 50 plus different types), neuroscience (e.g. learning capacity and brain development), psychology (e.g. motivation), sociology (e.g. understanding the cultural capital of diverse communities), technology (e.g. supporting research as well as brain development through demonstrations, simulations, pattern recognition, prediction, repetitive learning, etc.). See also Chapters 3 and 19.
9 "Values are principles and fundamental convictions which act as general guides to behaviour; enduring beliefs about what is worthwhile; ideals for which one strives; broad standards by which particular beliefs and actions are judged to be good, right, desirable or worthy of respect" (Halstead & Taylor, 2000, p. 3). See Chapter 2.
10 Gove gets a failing grade on education – *The Commentator* www.thecommentator.com/article/7364/gove_gets_a_failing_grade_on_education#.XZiwNyfVn2M.twitter. Accessed 5 October 2019
11 "Evidence seen by the [Timpson Review] review has raised concerns of so-called 'off-rolling', in which children are asked to leave the school permanently without proper processes being followed. There is no official definition for what constitutes off-rolling, but Ofsted has defined it as follows:

> the practice of removing a pupil from the school roll without a formal, permanent exclusion or by encouraging a parent to remove their child from the school roll, when the removal is primarily in the interests of the school rather than in the best interests of the pupil. Off-rolling in these circumstances is a form of 'gaming'."
> UK Government Timpson Review of School Exclusions (2019, p. 100)

12 See government interventions here www.gov.uk/government/news/salaries-of-top-academy-bosses-to-be-fair-proportionate-and-justified; as well as Mansell, W. and Savage, M. (July 2019) Tally of £150,000 school academy bosses jumps by 20%: Six-figure salaries at 988 charitable trusts despite increase in deficits. www.theguardian.com/education/2019/jul/28/number-150000-salary-school-academy-bosses-jumps-20-percent. See also https://schoolsweek.co.uk/ceos-at-tiny-academy-trusts-paid-more-than-big-chain-bosses/ Accessed 5 October 2019

13 "[W]hile the vast majority of schools are motivated by doing the best for all pupils, the current performance and funding system does not incentivise or reward schools for taking responsibility for the needs of all children and using permanent exclusion only when nothing else will do. It cannot be right to have a system where some schools could stand to improve their performance and finances through exclusion, but do not have to bear the cost of expensive non-mainstream provision these children then attend, nor be held accountable for the outcomes of the children they permanently exclude. . . . [There is a] lack of safeguards that protect children against informal exclusion and also off-rolling where this exists that, at its worst, can see some children pushed out of education altogether". UK government Timpson Report on School Exclusions 2019, p. 11

14 https://epi.org.uk/wp-content/uploads/2019/04/EPI_Unexplained-pupil-exits_2019.pdf

15 See the UK Government 2019 Timpson Report for the link between off-rolling and crime.

16 https://epi.org.uk/publications-and-research/unexplained-pupil-exits/

17 www.theguardian.com/education/2017/aug/30/mps-attack-ejection-of-underper forming-sixth-formers

18 https://schoolsweek.co.uk/lawyers-call-for-government-to-close-sixth-form-exclu sions-loophole/

19 Vaughan, R., (2010) Gove serves notice on teacher training. www.tes.com/news/gove-serves-notice-teacher-training. *Times Educational Supplement.* Accessed 5 October 2019

20 Passnotes (2 October 2013) Why does Michael Gove keep referring to the Blob? www.theguardian.com/politics/shortcuts/2013/oct/02/michael-gove-referring-to-the-blob Accessed 1 October 2019

21 Passnotes (2October 2013) Why does Michael Gove keep referring to the Blob?www.theguardian.com/politics/shortcuts/2013/oct/02/michael-gove-referring-to-the-blob Accessed 1 October 2019

22 Teach First (2019) "earn a salary and pay no fees" www.teachfirst.org.uk/training-programme?gclsrc=aw.ds&&gclid=EAIaIQobChMIserd4LKF5QIVCLLtCh3VKARA EAAYASAAEgK3qvD_BwE Accessed 5 October 2019

23 Harrison, A., (2012) Academies told they can hire unqualified teachers. London. BBC news www.bbc.co.uk/news/education-19017544 Accessed 5 October 2019

24 www.epi.org/publication/the-teacher-shortage-is-real-large-and-growing-and-worse-than-we-thought-the-first-report-in-the-perfect-storm-in-the-teacher-labor-market-series/

25 "The research for the children's commissioner (www.childrenscommissioner.gov.uk/wp-content/uploads/2019/09/cco-briefing-children-leaving-school-with-nothing.pdf) was based on analysis of official statistics and found 98,779 (18%) of pupils in England in 2018 had failed to gain five GCSEs at grade C or higher or the equivalent technical qualifications. Of pupils who qualified for free school meals, about 28,225 (37%) did not achieve this level of attainment."

26 www.independent.co.uk/news/education/education-news/primary-school-academy-takeover-protests-parents-local-authority-control-a8925471.html

27 This is not to suggest that vision was previously lacking. One could argue that we have had a surfeit of green and white papers over the last decade from 2009 "Your child, your schools, our future", the revolutionary 2010 "The Importance of Teaching", through to the alliterative but oxymoronic 2016 "Education Excellence Everywhere" and the retrograde 2016 "Schools that work for everyone". But all have quietly fizzled away after several years of weak government.

28 www.compare-school-performance.service.gov.uk/ – Data download 2017–18

29 Ibid.

30 Blamires, M. (2015) Building portals for evidence-informed education: Lessons from the dead. A case study of the development of a national portal intended to enhance evidence informed professionalism in education, *Journal of Education for Teaching*, 41:5, 597–607, DOI: 10.1080/02607476.2015.1105532

31 www.telegraph.co.uk/politics/2019/05/16/350m-brexit-bus-slogan-lie-says-jean-claude-juncker/

32 www.theguardian.com/politics/2013/apr/08/margaret-thatcher-quotes

References

Albright, M. (2018) *Fascism: A Warning*. New York: William Collins.

CBI. (2010a) *Fulfilling Potential. The Business Role in Education*. London: Confederation of British Industry.

CBI. (2010b) *Ready to Grow: Business Priorities for Education and Skills. Education and Skills Survey 2010*. London: Confederation of British Industry.

CBI. (2012) *First steps. A New Approach for Our Schools*. London: Confederation of British Industry.

Children's Commissioner (2019) *Briefing: Children Leaving School with Nothing*. London. https://www.childrenscommissioner.gov.uk/wp-content/uploads/2019/09/cco-briefing-children-leaving-school-with-nothing.pdf. Accessed 1 October 2019.

Coffield, F. (25 September 2019) Ofsted: What Would an Alternative Look Like? *Times Educational Supplement*.

DFE (28 January 2019) *Teacher Recruitment and Retention Strategy Report*. www.gov.uk/government/publications/teacher-recruitment-and-retention-strategy.

Education Futures Collaboration (2019) *Policy Briefing Paper 19/2 Education Knowledge Services*. www.meshguides.org, with the Council for Subject Associations (www.subjectassociations.org.uk) and Technology, Pedagogy and Education Association (www.tpea.ac.uk).

Fishkin, J. (2018) Democracy When the People Are Thinking. *TedX Video*. https://www.youtube.com/watch?v=27tVMj6YUNM. Based on his book: *Democracy When the People Are Thinking: Revitalizing Our Politics Through Public Deliberation*. Oxford University Press. cdd.stanfoed.edu.

Hansard (14 February 2019) Lord Storey's question on MAT CEO salaries. 11.14am Vol795. https://hansard.parliament.uk/Lords/2019-02-14/debates/0EB8139E-6E4F-4887-9ADC-7EF95A7816D8/Multi-AcademyTrustsSalaries?highlight=three%20times%20salary%20prime%20minister#contribution-12B75F7C-E7A3-4F79-BFA9-E03044494550. Accessed 30 September 2020.

Ing, E. (2018) Vocational Qualifications, Progress 8 and 'gaming'. Ing is Regional Director, East Midlands. *Gov.UK OFSTED Blog*. https://educationinspection.blog.gov.uk/2018/09/04/vocational-qualifications-progress-8-and-gaming/. Accessed 5 October 2019.

Leask, M. and Younie, S. (2013) National Models for Continuing Professional Development: The Challenges of Twenty-first-century Knowledge Management. In: *Professional Development in Education*, 39(2): 273–287. DOI: 10.1080/19415257.2012.749801.

Norwich, B. (2019) From the Warnock Report (1978) to an Education Framework Commission: A Novel Contemporary Approach to Educational Policy Making for Pupils with Special Educational Needs/Disabilities. *Frontiers Education,* 4(72). DOI: 10.3389/feduc.2019.00072.

OECD (2009) *Creating Effective Teaching and Learning Environments: The First Results from the TALIS Survey*. Paris: OECD Publishing. www.oecd.org/edu/school/43023606.pdf

Ramos, G. and Schleicher, A. (2016) *Global Competency for an Inclusive World*. www.oecd.org/education/Global-competency-for-an-inclusive-world.pdf. Accessed 16 October 2019.

Royal College of Surgeons (2018) *Reading for CPD: How Our Reflective CPD Form can Help*. London. www.rcseng.ac.uk/library-and-publications/library/blog/reading-for-cpd/. Accessed 17 June 2019.

Saussois, J. (2003) *Reflections on OECD Studies on Knowledge Management and Related Issues: Implications for Schooling for Tomorrow*. Paris: OECD Publishing.

Story, Lord (11.14am 14 February 2019) Multi-Academy Trusts: Salaries. House of Commons. *Hansard*, 795. Accessed 5 October 2019.

UK Government (May 2019) *Timpson Report on School Exclusions.* https://assets.publishing.service.gov.uk/government/uploads/system/uploads/attachment_data/file/807862/Timpson_review.pdf. Accessed 5 October 2019.

Whalley, C. and Greenway, H. (2020) 'Politics Aside: From Fragmentation to Coherence'. Chapter 5 in B. Hudson, M. Leask, and S. Younie (eds) *Education System Design: Foundations, Policy Options and Consequences.* Abingdon: Routledge.

Wolfe, D. (7 January 2019) "Legislation for a National Health Service" Email Exchange with the Authors.

Younie, S., Audain, J., Eloff, I., Leask, M., Procter, R. and Shelton, C. (2019) Mobilising Knowledge through Global Partnerships to Support Research-informed Teaching: Five Models for Translational Research. *Journal of Education for Teaching: International Research and Pedagogy*, Special Issue on 'Perspectives on Evidence-based Knowledge for Teachers: Acquisition, Mobilisation And Utilization'. https://doi.org/10.1080/02607476.2018.1516348. Accessed 17 June 2019.

SECTION 3

Issues of social justice and inclusion

Section 3 focuses on issues and policy options in relation to achievement and equity; selection based on wealth, ability, aptitude and faith; Special Education Needs (SEN) and adult and further education

Chapter 7 addresses the issue of social mobility from a working class perspective. It argues for a coordinated approach across government departments in order to address the issues leading to poverty, lack of self-belief and aspiration.

Chapter 8 considers issues related to school selection based on wealth, ability, aptitude and faith. In relation to policy options it firstly considers the maintenance of a divided system with access to political and economic power restricted to the wealthy with limited opportunities for social mobility. Secondly it considers the establishment of a free and open-to-all system, within a national education service in order to build a meritocratic society, involving phasing out all state support for private education provision.

Chapter 9 presents an overview of segregation in schooling arrangements in England and considers the implications of the *logic of exiting* from the public education system as an integral aspect of the modernizing neoliberal project.

Chapter 10 on SEND addresses the particular options for supporting young people with SEND to achieve. The chapter takes the starting point of the need for inclusive education to be part of a well conceived, adequately resourced and carefully monitored whole-school equal opportunities policy.

Chapter 11 focuses on Adult and Further Education through a study of the negative impact of austerity measures on life chances and societal well-being in England over recent years.

Section 4 which follows examines issues and policy options related to curriculum, assessment, leadership and accountability.

7

SOCIAL MOBILITY

A working class view

Sonia Blandford

Introduction

> If we were to shine a light on every pupil, how many would not be able to make progress?
>
> *Blandford (2011)*[1]

This chapter highlights issues covered in depth in my publications *Born to Fail? A Working Class View* (2017)[2] and *Social Mobility, Chance or Choice?* (2019).[3]

The world, as we would like it to be, is a one where all children know that with passion and focus and hard work, they can be whoever they want to be. Unfortunately, we do not live in that world:

> In a more socially mobile society, everyone should have a choice, be aware of that choice and be able to exercise it. From birth people should have equal opportunities whether at home, school, further education (FE) college, university or in training. . . . Everyone should be recruited on merit no matter which school or university they attended. The old boys' network must no longer be a passport to success. . . . [T]hose from disadvantaged backgrounds should not be held back because they don't fit in.[4]

In 2018, the OECD PISA Equity report, *Equity in Education: Breaking Down Barriers to Social Mobility,*[5] underlined what few would challenge: that every child, every human being, deserves the same opportunities (chance) to gain skills and progress through society regardless of gender, sexuality, disability or socio-economic, ethnic or cultural background (choice). The report makes for sober reading, pointing out in the UK that while educational attainment has increased, inequalities remain entrenched. However, those children and young people that are supported to make progress can accumulate collateral throughout life, both in education and later in the labour market that will drive their future social mobility.

The OECD report also shows that the impact of inequality extends much farther than economic wealth: it ripples out to all aspects of society such as poorer health, in a climate of violence or social unrest (2019, Timpson report).

The context for the discussion in this chapter is England, which has longstanding class divisions.

We used to think that meritocracy – the idea that talent and capacity would overcome socio-economic barriers – was the key. This has been the mantra of successive governments. Meritocracy remains part of the social mobility conversation, but clings to the idea that if you have talent (and I add here that everyone has some talent) – you can improve your circumstances by hard work.

This clearly is no longer true (or is not working). Too many hard-working people now feel left behind or just about managing or worse, and that they have failed and have no value. This includes working-class young people who have played by the rules and worked hard to enter university (the most popular and publicised national test for working-class social mobility) and not been able to manage for a number of reasons.

Those reasons include not having enjoyed the same educational preparation as their better-off peers; not having the same practical or financial support as their peers; or simply not having access to work after graduating from university. This is not likely to get better any time soon. We know millions of young people fail at the point of GCSE assessment (over 30% of our school population, and more than over 50% of pupils on free school meals) and who get stuck in an unproductive cycle of retaking GCSEs. The actual and real talents of these children and young people are too easily and frequently ignored, and possibly never even discovered.[6]

Definition: social mobility

I need to set out my definition of social mobility:

> social mobility is achieving positive change in socio-economic status, and more widely, building better futures for all, in terms of wellbeing, health, and engagement with all that life has to offer.

To support social mobility, we must provide children and young people with real chances and choices: chances and choices that are not determined by class, but by heritage, location and self-efficacy; chances and choices that are respectful of individuals; chances and choices that are non-judgmental, and not defined by movement between classes or location; chances and choices that provide opportunities for everyone to be included, and to belong; chances and choices that prepare the way for everyone to succeed in life, in education, health, employment and housing.

Is equality of opportunity a core British value?

If confronted with a television camera recording their views for broadcast, probably few people in England would say there should not be equal access to education and the most prestigious jobs in the country and the will to act certainly exists in some quarters (see the section: 'Government commissions and the need for action'). So why is progress not being made as explained by the Gini coefficient research (2019)?[7]

Do we, as a society, really care enough about equality of opportunity for all, to change?

Is the traditional national measure of educational achievement – maximised university entrance useful for, or even relevant to, working-class children and young people and children facing disadvantage whose priorities may be supporting themselves with a job and a home? If we are serious about unleashing the talent of all children and young people, regardless of their background, challenges or needs, we must consider new and innovative approaches to post-14 education.

Do we dare to?

Equality of opportunity: a shared responsibility?

In my book *Born to Fail? Social Mobility: A Working Class View*,[8] I argue that all education and business leaders, professionals, practitioners, parents or carers and members of society have a shared responsibility to ensure that our education service (in its widest sense) gives every child and young person a right to real chances and choices and support that maximise their opportunities.

Born into poverty in the late 1950s, I am now one of the country's foremost experts on and champions for improving the aspirations of children from disadvantaged backgrounds. I assert that social mobility is about changing the way people (which people) think, act and engage and crucially, understanding there is an alternative way to live to ensure everyone can succeed. At the heart of this is mutuality.

My story began when children from the estates where I was growing up participated in a study of disadvantaged children (later published in 1973 as *Born to Fail?*) and the enormous inequalities we suffered (health, family circumstances, educational development) were compared to what the authors then called 'ordinary' children.

Shockingly, the findings of the 1973 *Born to Fail* study[9] are as real today as they were in the 1960s and 1970s. Children and young people are still not reaching their full potential because of education, poor housing, poor health outcomes, and a lack of care (see Chapter 6).

Following on from *Born to Fail?*, in consultation with 14 eminent education, business and policy leaders I put forward proposals in *Social Mobility, Chance or Choice?*[10] which are based on a simple central premise: providing better and more meaningful chances and choices for children and young people will increase their future social mobility.

- *By chances*, I mean opportunities in an equal and mutual context where everyone is valued in education, training and the workplace.
- *By choices*, I mean giving children and young people real agency in securing positive options for their future in terms of their: overall life-course; employment/career; and better health, wellbeing, security, happiness, and engagement in society – in short: true social mobility.

I argue that we can only offer real chances and choices through mutuality, where all are valued regardless of their background, challenges or needs.

If we are in a place and at a time when we are embracing new thinking, we must recognise the great things that have been achieved by recent initiatives in health, social care and education but also acknowledge, accept and address what has not worked and what is not working.

Is social mobility about becoming middle class? Re-evaluating how we tackle questions on working class disadvantage and outcomes

In this section, first published in *The Key*,[11] I argue that in England, we need to re-evaluate how we tackle questions on working class disadvantage and outcomes. I question the injustice of the current prevailing view of social mobility, which is that the working class have somehow failed and they should become more like the middle class: that is, pass the required exams to go to university, get a degree or two, buy their own house and live a healthy life, contributing to society and the economy.

What is needed is an alternative way of thinking about social mobility – a way of thinking that crucially *listens to, engages and involves* the working class in determining what their future should be – an alternative way that values partnership, mutuality and collaboration and which, by doing what is right, creates opportunities for all. What would happen if we responded to old questions with new thinking?

Why do working class children not achieve?

The need to understand how and why children can learn is fundamental to pedagogy – how teachers teach. Getting teaching right for the working class remains an ongoing challenge in many schools. An appropriate starting point might be to increase understanding of how working class, disadvantaged children, as well as those with special educational needs and disability (SEND), learn; refocus teacher training and professional training on this; and identify what is needed to prepare children for work. We need to change the mindset of the adults and services around schools to improve outcomes for all children. If you change the attitudes and behaviours of adults, you improve the attitudes and behaviours of the child.

Why isn't school considered relevant by the working class? A curriculum that is not socially and culturally relevant to working class pupils, that presents more barriers than opportunities, will not engage them in learning. The national curriculum in England has been developed based on the knowledge and experience of the middle class. There are solutions to this dilemma that, if implemented, would address the needs of all children.

The first is to break down barriers to learning by providing opportunities for all children to participate in social and cultural activities: sport, the arts, debating, volunteering, wider community-based activities, museum trips and more.

The second requires us to relate the curriculum to the social context of the child and his or her future. All communities have a rich heritage, which can help shape the curriculum.

Thirdly, we should introduce learning about the workplace in primary school, which will raise ambitions, break down barriers and provide relevance to learning.

Increasing access to learning for all children should be the benchmark of a successful school.

Why isn't there the will to stop the growth of disadvantage among the working class? Part of the problem is that the context of UK poverty has changed. Poverty is no longer just an issue for people out of work or living in social housing. It impacts on people with disabilities, people who've become ill and had to give up work, people in work, young people (including some just out of university), people renting from private landlords. The drive for welfare reform has been seen as an answer to the problems of disadvantage, but it's failed to understand this changing context and therefore the necessary solutions: better housing, investment in communities – or reinvestment where cuts have decimated good work – and a continued drive to grow employment and provide good jobs that provide an income on or above a living wage.

Why is working class success only measured by exam results? The annual media frenzy that follows SATs and GCSE exam results only serves to remind the majority of the working-class families that their children are disadvantaged, with private and grammar schools forming the majority at the top of published league tables. The minority of working class students who do meet national performance measures demonstrates that passing exams is a possibility at primary and secondary, but a lack of social and cultural capital makes this harder: recent primary SATs serve to prove the difficulties for those without that capital to respond to questions in the English exam.[12]

The Education Policy Institute (EPI) report, *Closing the Gap* (2017)[13], reminds us that it will take decades to 'close the gap'. A more meaningful assessment at secondary phase would include destination outcomes, measuring students' outcomes by where the examinations take them.

Why is there a lack of ambition for the working class? There is no evidence that the working class cannot achieve – in education, employment, housing and health. There is also no evidence that the working class are any less likely to have a desire for success than others. What there is, though, is a lack of societal ambition outside spurious targets (like university entry) that only concern 50 per cent of the population at best. To increase ambition for the working class there needs to be a mutual understanding of what is available in terms of alternatives, and engagement with the working class about what they actually want. By talking and listening, ambitions can be met – a 'do with' rather than 'do to' approach.

So, are the working class born to fail? Research[14] would indicate that rather than reducing the chances of failure within the working class over the last 40 years, we have increased the possibility of failure in housing, education and social care.

We can change the way we tackle social mobility. Ultimately, it is about taking responsibility, and creating a shared moral purpose, ambition and integrity, owned by the working class, that can provide the opportunities and resources needed for all children and their families to achieve. This is social justice in action, and possibly, social mobility that really works.

Time for a new conversation: equality of choice

I do not wish to go back to a time where it was accepted that the playing field was not level and that as a working-class person you had to work twice as hard (and be pretty lucky) to be in with a chance. That was the time I grew up in, and I do not recommend it. But I am not comfortable with today's reality; when educators talk about levelling the playing field and governments claim that education funding automatically creates opportunity, the reality falls short and betrays those who have signed up to the idea of meritocracy. It betrays everyone.

In my work, I have had the privilege to see and feel the difference social mobility in its best sense can look like, and how everyone can benefit as a result. I have seen employers working with schools to support learning and to showcase the opportunities in their arena. I have seen young people helped into that first job and mentored and supported as they earn and learn and grow. And I have seen universities squaring up to the twin challenges of working-class access to higher education and the numbers of working-class students who drop out of studies.

This kind of thinking is exciting to see and demonstrates mutuality and choice in its finest form.

Mutuality happens when, instead of us thinking about helping children escape the constraints of their class and making judgements about what people from disadvantaged communities need to change, we focus on providing equality of choice. This allows people on all sides of the political spectrum, and from across all classes and cultures, to have their voice heard in the conversation about what happens next, to have a role to play, to value their class and background identities, and own their own change. When we do this, everyone in society benefits.

Equality in education is not about everyone getting the same marks. It is about everyone having access to the same chances providing equal choice, regardless of socio-economic background, learning abilities or talents.

While access to universities improves and apprenticeships embed in the service allowing more people to realise their potential, we should continually question whether we are identifying and meeting the needs of everyone. What happens to those with no obvious talent who find education challenging? What happens to those who face more challenges than most who fail to get the necessary GCSEs? What opportunities can we offer to ensure lifelong learning so there is always a chance to access education and work (see Chapter 11)?

Companies, industry, and employers are already challenging the assumption that statutory exams are a measure of ability (they are seeing that assumption being proved wrong whenever they employ hardworking and effective young people with no qualifications) and now it is time to rethink these assumed tests of work readiness. Should we not rather look at basic skills (be that maths, English, team-work, communication) and a desire to learn and be part of a workforce?

Should we worry less about the different types of schools in the country, and to focus more on how they can work in partnership with each other for their mutual benefit. By doing that we might level the field so all pupils can share in the aspirations and opportunity and sense of entitlement that is experienced in the independent sector.

The question of social mobility

In an interview published in *Social Mobility, Chance or Choice (2019)*[15] Natalie Perera, Executive Director and Head of Research at the Education Policy Institute, says:

> I do think there is a lack of understanding about what social mobility is. . . . The debate around grammar schools has highlighted this. People are confus-ing the idea of getting a few bright children into grammar schools and onto a path that improves social mobility, with a policy that changes the game for the population as a whole. Anecdotal evidence – the 'I was a working-class girl and grammar school and look how well I have done' exacerbates that and gets in the way of what we know from the wider research.

Similarly, in my interview with Mary Bousted, Joint General-Secretary of The National Education Union,[16] she asks:

> Why do we expect poor parents and poor children to be this extraordinary when we do not expect that of anyone else? It is like we are saying if you are lucky and escape the circumstances of your birth and are talented you can make it. . . . But why should we expect poor people to rely on luck and extraordinary talent to make something of their life and benefit from secure housing and health when we do not expect it of the middle classes?

Bousted would go as far to say that social mobility may now be a misguided con-cept, something that happened in the past when there were gateways into public sector jobs. But when we have 46% of graduates doing non-graduate jobs, when opportunities for young people are going down and the public purse is being squeezed, the middle class is holding on tight to what is out there, and the ladder of opportunity is being drawn up.

Like me and so many others now advocating a reappraisal of some very hard-wired assumptions, Bousted challenges the idea that social mobility relies on people escaping their circumstances:

> It says to working-class people that they have to leave their culture, the area they have grown up in, the relationships they have forged there so they can move into socially and economically advantaged roles. . . . Surely we should have a society, a productive society, where we have good jobs in all areas. Regional manufacturing and industrial policies worth their name, and good jobs available in those regions for people when they leave school. Opportunities young people can see in their area to incentivise them.

If we dare to recognise the impact of the ladder of opportunity being drawn up (or that it has a missing first rung for so many who want to climb on), we can look at new ways to ensure real equality of access. At the same time, perhaps we also must dare to recognise that some might not actually want to move up the predetermined economic ladder.

We need to take on board the idea that children and young people, as they are growing up, are seeing there is more to life than money. Research[17] (2017) shows that many young people would rather earn less working for a company that does more good.

Those young people are also looking for security and wellbeing and the chance to make a difference. They are also looking for greater educational, social and economic equality where they learn, live and work. For many young people, economic progression is only part of the story: progression includes improvements in their: community, culture and environment; home life and health; work-life balance and ability to make a difference.

The big question seems to me to be: Do we care enough to listen to the young people we profess to want to help and include them in a meaningful national conversation about the lives they want for their future?

In answering this question, as educators, parents, and members of this society, we will determine whether we resolve to work to bring about real change or whether we simply add to the sad record of failed policies that are out of kilter with the needs and desires of those facing disadvantage and which cost them, and the country, dearly.

Research also shows that failing to offer real chance and choice to children and young people facing disadvantage means that we also pay a more hard-edged price in terms of:

- Denying children and young people facing disadvantage with good prospects for a healthy and (economic and social) productive adult life, and a life expectancy equal to that of their more advantaged peers.[18]
- Lost taxes, additional public service costs and associated impacts such as youth crime and poor health costing Britain in excess of £77 billion a year. This

shocking figure was the conclusion of the Impetus Private Equity Foundation 2014 report: *Make NEETS History* in 2014.[19] This report also concluded that 2014's 13-year-olds who are at risk of becoming NEET . . . collectively stand to lose £6.4 billion in potential (and taxable) earnings over their life course.

Can we choose a better conversation?

We know that there is real strength in diversity, but it takes really striking ideas to bring that strength alive. At the 2018 Cheltenham Festival, the comedian, actor, and writer Sir Lenny Henry spoke eloquently about the dangers of not having real representation round the table; how when he was the lone black person at the BBC table his energy was expended on trying to make a case for how to better represent black people in Britain, rather than simply being part of a representative group.

The education table is just as guilty. Education policies are often shaped and introduced without a real listening to the teachers who know the most about what is happening in schools, or by taking note of evidence from those trying to support them.

The reasons for this are both party political and systemic. The systemic problem, I argue, arises from the traditional response of policy makers to challenge tending to be two-fold: structural or system change and/or short-term policy goals.

These responses are understandable in the context of a UK political cycle that naturally tends towards short-term activity and the reality of education policy makers having a limited number of levers available to achieve change.

Sam Butters, CEO of the Fair Education Alliance, says the number-one priority has to be moving away from one individual sector having to fix this problem: it is going to take collaboration from a range of different sectors and different people with different levers to pull to solve the issue.[20]

Butters's view, and mine, is that the missing group at the table is the public: the parents, the carers, the grandparents, the aunts and uncles, the brothers and sisters; the young people from all walks of life; and the wider community that share a view of wanting change and who can share solutions.

Sam and I have talked about what a challenge this can be. While people are finally understanding the importance of most elements of diversity – such as gender, race, religion (and businesses are stronger as a result), we don't often talk about class. Like me, Sam is a working-class professional and like me she knows that by the time the working class are in business they are almost middle class already and there is a risk of paying lip service to it.

And if we are to do this, we need to see that their understanding will be based on their own experiences. Experiences can and will be very different from those on the other side of the table, and their ambitions for themselves and their families can be very different from policy makers' ambitions for them.

But how have we got to this point?

Government commissions and the need for action

The Race Relations Act 2000;[21] the establishment of the Community Cohesion Unit (2004); the publication of the 2006 Standards of Community Cohesion; the Education and Inspections Act;[22] the Aiming Higher for Young people: 10-year strategy for positive activities (2007);[23] the Equality Act;[24] and the establishment of the Child Poverty Commission (later renamed the Social Mobility Commission by the Welfare Reform Act 2012)[25] all laid the groundwork for what I, and many of my colleagues and peers, felt could be a new dawn for meaningful approaches that would develop social mobility and choices for children and young people from the working class and those facing disadvantage.

Providing choices in education, learning and opportunity, I argue, challenges the tacit and occasionally explicit policy and public assumptions that working-class lives, opportunities and learning dispositions are in some way predetermined.[26]

Providing real and meaningful chances or choices also challenges the assumption that social mobility means working-class children and young people should work to migrate to a different class in order to reach a position that would represent some form of progression; this fails to recognise and value what is good in all classes and all communities.

Social inclusion for social mobility – a new way of thinking

For a moment, consider the gap between the socially and culturally rich and the financially and educationally stuck.[27]

It is time to challenge the injustice of the current prevailing view of social mobility, that the vulnerable and disadvantaged have somehow failed and they should become more middle class, pass the required number of exams followed by university. In contrast we should reflect on the thinking and action needed to change if every child is to be included, regardless of background, challenge or need. As mentioned earlier, I argue that our change-making focus must be upon the following:

- Improving early years provision
- Building a relevant curriculum
- Improving teaching
- Widening our focus to ask why success is only measured by exam results and,
- Future-Aware pedagogies: The World Economic Forum concludes that in many industries and countries, the most in-demand occupations or specialties did not exist 10 or even five years ago, and the pace of change is set to accelerate. By one popular estimate, 65% of children entering primary school today will ultimately end up working in job types that do not yet exist.

The best evidence we have suggests that the most effective support that we can give to young people to meet the challenges of tomorrow is to embed pedagogies and

TABLE 7.1 Future-aware pedagogies

Effective collaboration	Being able to reflect on, and extend knowledge	Creativity and innovation
Research and problem-solving skills	Self-regulation and self-development	Metacognition
Effective use of technology	Communication	Grit and resilience

practice that could be described as future aware. Future-aware pedagogies[28] support young people to develop the mindset, capacities, and characteristics required to meet new challenges as they arise, and on their own terms. These are listed in Table 7.1

These pedagogies underpin the need to build the core strength of every child or young person. Core strength, defined as a future-aware concept, is the confidence and ability to learn, develop and participate in society.

We cannot predict the future that children and young people will live within. We can, however, be future-aware in our pedagogy and practice. We are future-aware when our teaching and engagements with children and young people develop the resilience, resources, skills and capacities they will need to overcome future challenges and live happy and stable future lives.

Reflections

Achievement for All[29] is a programme I developed to respond to the challenges outlined previously, which encourages and promotes an inclusive approach to education. Inclusion acknowledges the impact of the social environment upon children's abilities to learn and develop. It seeks to facilitate diversity and to ensure that all children's needs are viewed equitably and met fairly. Based on international research in inclusive education[30] and other NCSL research,[31] four key elements were identified within the Achievement for All programmes as being central to inclusive leadership – shared vision, commitment, collaboration and communication.

Ultimately, Achievement for All is about us all – educators, policy makers, charities, businesses – taking responsibility, owning a shared moral purpose, a shared ambition and a shared integrity that can provide the chances and choices needed for all children and young people and their families to achieve. And we need to recognise that we all have a part to play that will ensure every child across the country should have a chance and a choice that will secure their future.

As this chapter illustrates, co-ordination across government departments is needed to address the issues leading to poverty, lack of self-belief and aspiration. Departments responsible for education from early years to lifelong learning; housing, health, transport, media, industry and so on all have a part to play in building strong confident communities where young people can stay if they wish and lead fulfilling lives. The German model with small industries to be found in small villages across the countryside, linked to major transport arteries appears to have lessons for the UK context.

Policy options

I draw the specific listed Policy Options, from Every Child Included in Education[32] priorities which are set within the context of the UK government's Social Mobility Action Plan. At Achievement for All, we have created this collaborative campaign to focus activity and embed change for the benefit of every child and young person.

> **Policy option 1:** Respect and pupil well-being: Promote kindness and wellbeing in education, business and third sector settings, where every child and young person is included every day, addressing mental health, character and resilience through culture and mutuality, celebrating tolerance, patience, friendship, creativity and problem solving.
>
> **Policy Option 2:** Focus funding on early years and a relevant curriculum: Increase investment across all phases of education, beginning with the early years that results in a socially and culturally relevant curriculum, increasing attainment in reading, writing and maths, enhancing life chances and culminating in a meaningful destination for every child.
>
> **Policy Option 3:** Teacher training: Put greater focus on teachers as professional learners through recruitment, retention, and professional development that includes an enhanced understanding of the way disadvantaged and vulnerable children learn.
>
> **Policy Option 4:** Inclusion: Reduce children and young people being excluded in education: increase responsibility for children at risk of exclusion through cross-agency collaboration to reduce exclusions and minimise the number of children and young people at risk, and close the gap for SEND, too often the marginalised and forgotten group.
>
> **Policy Option 5:** Community engagement: Increase recognition of parents, carers and wider communities, valuing all parents and carers as crucial partners in the improvement of learning and life chances for every child.

My belief is that this movement can begin to build a foundation for better lives for every child and young person. All of us, as educators, parents and carers, and members of society must contribute to building this foundation and the real structures for change that will follow. No child should be 'Born to Fail'.

The consequences of these policy options are further discussed in Chapter 20.

Notes

1 Blandford, S. (2011), TES Special Educational Needs Conference Keynote, October 2011.
2 Blandford, S. (2017), *Born to Fail? Social Mobility: A Working Class View*, Woodbridge: John Catt Educational.
3 Blandford, S. (2019), *Social Mobility, Chance or Choice?* Woodbridge: John Catt Educational.
4 UK Government's Social Mobility Commission (2019) Strategy 2019. Retrieved August 2020, www.gov.uk/government/publications/social-mobility-commission-strategy-2019
5 www.oecd.org/education/equity-in-education-9789264073234-en.htm

6   Blandford, S. (2019), *Social Mobility, Chance or Choice?* Woodbridge: John Catt Educational.

7   www.investopedia.com/terms/g/gini-index.asp

8   Blandford, S. (2017), *Born to Fail? Social Mobility: A Working Class View*, Woodbridge: John Catt Educational.

9   Wedge, P. and Prosser, H. (1973), *Born to Fail?* London: National Children's Bureau.

10 Blandford, S. (2019), *Social Mobility, Chance or Choice?* Woodbridge: John Catt Educational.

11 https://thekeysupport.com/insights/2017/10/11/born-to-fail/

12 www.tes.com/news/warning-166000-sats-failures-could-be-turned-school

13 https://epi.org.uk/wp-content/uploads/2017/08/Closing-the-Gap_EPI-.pdf

14 www.oecd.org/social/soc/Social-mobility-2018-Overview-MainFindings.pdf

15 Blandford, S. (2019), *Social Mobility, Chance or Choice?* Woodbridge: John Catt Educational.

16 Ibid.

17 www.aatcomment.org.uk/career/millennials-want-to-work-for-employers-with-a-purpose-beyond-profit/

18 Blandford, S. (2019), *Social Mobility, Chance or Choice?* Woodbridge: John Catt Educational

19 Impetus, (2014), *Make NEETs History in 2014,* London: Impetus.

20 Blandford, S. (2019), *Social Mobility, Chance or Choice?* Woodbridge: John Catt Educational

21 www.legislation.gov.uk/ukpga/2000/34/content

22 www.legislation.gov.uk/ukpga/2006/40

23 https://dera.ioe.ac.uk/7758/1/PU214.pdf

24 www.legislation.gov.uk/ukpga/2010/15/contents

25 www.legislation.gov.uk/ukpga/2012/5/contents/enacted

26 Blandford, S. (2019), *Social Mobility, Chance or Choice?* Woodbridge: John Catt Educational

27 www.oecd.org/social/broken-elevator-how-to-promote-social-mobility-978926430 1085-en.htm

28 This term was developed through discussions between Professor Blandford and Leask.

29 www.afaeducation.org

30 European Agency for Special Needs and Inclusive Education, (2018), 'Raising the Achievement of All Learners in Inclusive Education: Final Summary Report', Brussels: European Agency for Special Needs and Inclusive Education

31 National College for School Leadership (2009), 'Achievement for All: Characteristics of Effective Inclusive leadership – A Discussion Document', Nottingham: NCSL

32 https://afaeducation.org/media/1489/afa- manifesto-final-2205.pdf

8

SELECTION BY WEALTH, ABILITY AND APTITUDE AND FAITH

Good for a country or not?

Carl Smith

Introduction

> We have one of the most stratified and segregated education systems in the developed world, perpetuating inequality and holding our nation back.
>
> When a few public schools can scoop up more places at our top universities than the entire population of boys and girls eligible for free school meals, we are clearly wasting talent on an unforgivable scale.
>
> Does anyone really believe the stranglehold of wealthier children on these university places, and the opportunities they bring, reflects the spread of talent in our country? Of course it doesn't. We are still very far from living in the meritocratic society I believe is a moral imperative. As matters rest, children from poorer homes are being denied the opportunity to fulfil themselves, and to contribute to our national renaissance. So matters cannot be allowed to rest.
>
> *(Michael Gove, Conservative Secretary of State for Education, 2014)*
>
> If our international competitors think that the future is comprehensive, why shouldn't we?
>
> *(Sir Michael Wilshaw, former Chief Inspector of Schools, 2016)*

For the first time in a generation, society has woken up to the fact that Britain is a profoundly unequal and unfair society, and the engine of that inequality is our schools, in particular our independent and grammar schools. However, these debates usually tackle each type of school separately, as though they are two unrelated issues, and in some cases critics of one are advocates of the other. I contend in this chapter that this is a profound mistake and that only by addressing them together will reforms be effective. If a new national education system and service is to provide equal opportunity, it must be founded on the principle that all schools within it are both free and open to all, which means no selection by wealth, current ability or aptitude. If we in the UK can do this, I firmly believe we will have a truly world class education system, become a global leader and an engine of meritocracy and create an institution that we will cherish as much as the NHS. However, if in the UK we reform one without the other, we will remain stuck in unfair and unequal society, where ability and hard work count less than position and privilege. This is the choice that we face and this time we need to get it right for the sake of all our futures.

Selection by wealth is both unfair and inefficient

If we accept that meritocracy is both the fairest and most productive way to organise society, as surely we must, then education selection by wealth is incompatible with a new national education system and service. If we also accept that we are born equal and have the right to a publicly funded education, then it follows that all should have an equal right of access to that education.

This is not controversial, partisan or ground-breaking. Every modern democratic leader, British Prime Minister and mainstream political party would agree, as would for example, the vast majority of the British public. Yet currently the UK is a society where this is not the case, the public recognise that it is patently unfair. The impact of this in a democracy is potentially alienating and destabilising.

Like motherhood and apple pie, everyone who is anyone in British politics, likes the *idea* of improving social mobility, yet depending on who, or what, you read, social mobility in Britain has either stagnated or deteriorated since the 1970s (see Chapter 7, Blandford). According to the Equality Trust,[1] Britain's Gini coefficient, the most widely accepted international measure of inequality, rose quickly in the 1980s, peaked in 2009 and has remained more or less the same ever since. Whatever the precise truth, we are certainly not living in a meritocracy, or anything like a meritocracy, and we certainly do not currently give every child an equal education.

Working from the premise that education is a public good but at any given time we have scarce resources, we must maximise the amount of education we can provide by using the resources we do have efficiently as possible. This means obtaining the best education system that public money can buy or, in other words, maximising our educational productivity. It is hardly efficient or productive to use public money to educate a small number of children at great expense while educating a much larger number of children at small expense. That would be a clear waste of public money and a wholly inefficient way of allocating scarce resources. Yet that is exactly what we do.[2]

Instead, public money, raised for the purpose of educating the public, must be used to benefit everyone and be accessible to all. A founding principle of a new national education system and service must be that public money for education should only be used to educate the nation as a whole. At no point should public money be used, as it is at present, to support children to attend schools that select children by wealth.

The right to an equal education must be balanced with the right to freedom of choice and in a liberal democracy, it is probably unfair to deny individuals *the right* to purchase education for the advantage of their own children. To use public money for this purpose is, however, quite a different matter. Public money should never be used for private benefit.

An alternative viewpoint on the purchasing of education put forward by Brian Matthews (chair of the Fabian's Education Policy Group)[3] is as follows:

1   There is no freedom of choice unless it applies to everyone. Only the rich can pay for private education and so it extends privilege.
2   Private schools are not only about an education choice; private education is mainly about access to power, so that power can be reproduced to the detriment of lesser off people.
3   Private schools insulate people from the rest of society, so they have no understanding, empathy with, or recognition of the Other. As a result the working class become a repository of all their fears that they cannot recognise.

Currently, in England a great deal of public money is spent, and income to the state is forgone, in order to support private education. Estimates vary, but most agree that annually something in the region of £3 billion of public money is either spent or forgone in this way. This misuse of public funds takes a variety of forms, some more obvious than others, and it is worth taking a moment to consider a few of these.

One is the direct transfer of funds to educate the children of public servants who are considered special cases because of the nature of their jobs: notably officers of the armed forces and higher ranked members of the diplomatic services. Deployment overseas is a natural part of their work, and they may be required to move frequently. If their families always moved with them, it may damage their children's education since children need stability rather than constant change and so it is considered reasonable for the state to provide them with free boarding education. There is nothing wrong with this, although it is surely unfair that the privilege is only extended to officers and higher ranks. However, in a new national education service and system there is no reason why more state boarding schools couldn't be created specifically for this purpose and probably also for the benefit of certain other highly mobile children, for example looked after children. Parents could also opt for state boarding as they can now. Indeed, existing boarding schools could be converted to offer this service, possessing as they do the necessary infrastructure. What could not, and should not, be allowed is the use of public money to educate these children in *privately* owned institutions because that is expensive, wasteful and patently unfair. In practice of course, the perk of free private education is used as a recruitment incentive to ensure the state attracts applicants, but surely state boarding schools for military or diplomatic children would not be so bad? Where the state can provide a public service and system more cost-effectively than the private sector, it should surely be encouraged to do so.

Public money for education is also sometimes used to send small numbers of disadvantaged children to private schools in the name of improving social mobility. Various schemes have been created for this purpose in the past, such as the assisted places scheme that ran from the 1980s to the 1990s. The assisted places scheme offered children free or subsidised places in fee paying schools if they were able to score in the top 10–15% in the school's entrance exam. In practice, this meant a small number of, often reasonably affluent children, were educated at considerably higher cost than everyone else, in institutions that were neither free nor open to all. The Independent Schools Council and the Sutton Trust have suggested similar schemes, and Green and Kynaston[4] (2019) in their work *Engines of Privilege* conclude that a Fair Access Scheme would be "the most serious and extensive response to Britain's private school problem". It is rarely the most disadvantaged children who benefit from these schemes because they usually need to pass a qualifying test in the first place. Such schemes remove high attaining pupils from the state system. More importantly, most make the mistake of regarding a few children who show early academic promise as more deserving than others. The proposed Fair Access Scheme may take a different line, but in practice it would still mean some children benefited over others. Melissa Benn[5] has suggested the places could be allocated to the most disadvantaged children including looked after children, but that would probably lead to deep resentment amongst parents on modest incomes who still used the state sector. In reality, many of these schemes have been used in the past as a political device to help justify the tax privileges extended to private schools and help them maintain their charitable status. Others, like the Fair Access Scheme, are very well intentioned, but politically unlikely and fraught with unintended consequences.

The classic rebuttal of those who defend giving state subsidies to private schools is that they educate around 600,000 children a year, saving the state an estimated £3.5 billion in the process. It is a disingenuous argument because that is certainly not the motivation of private schools and it certainly does not justify the state returning some of the money it 'saves' back to the private schools. Assuming the state stopped subsidising private schools, they would in turn stop educating children who cannot afford their new fees, but that would *save* the state money because it costs a lot more to educate these children in the private sector in the first place. As for all the other children they teach who could afford the new fees, presumably they would keep on teaching them, so the state would continue to save money by not teaching them. International students also attend private boarding school but again these could be accommodated in a commercial arrangement with state boarding schools or through boarding with families as is already done with some sixth forms in UK. Education provision like this is a major income stream for New Zealand and potentially could benefit any new national education service and system financially.

However, it is probably true the state would not save money, if that were its only object, if private school fees were raised to the point where significant numbers of privately educated children were 'forced' back into the state sector. To take an extreme example, if 100,000 children transferred from the private to the state sector, assuming each child were funded at £5,000 per head, and leaving aside any capital costs, the state would incur an additional annual cost to the education budget of £500 million. This is a considerable amount and at a time of strained budgets it may cause politicians to hesitate before doing anything that would reduce the number of non-state-subsidised children educated in the private sector, especially when that money could be used to improve support for disadvantaged children who need it most. Fortunately, there is a fair and easy solution.

There are two ways the state currently subsidises private education. The first is through direct funding; the second is through the taxation system. Therefore, an obvious solution to the problem of meeting the additional cost of educating children who transfer from the private to the public sector is to transfer resources out of private schools back into state schools. Again there are various ways of doing this, some more politically straightforward than others.

Green and Kynaston suggest the best way forward is a simple but substantial tax on school fees. Such a move avoids the rather complex matter of removing charitable status from the 75% of private schools that currently claim it, justifiable as that would be, and creates a simple mechanism for raising a very considerable sum of money. Such an *education opportunity tax* could be set at around 20–25% of school fees or at least at the current level of value added tax (VAT) and would raise something in the region of £2.5 billion annually. Such an idea was suggested by Andrew Adonis in the House of Lords in 2017[6] and a similar suggestion was made in the Labour election manifesto of the same year, calling for a VAT levy on school fees. According to Green and Kynaston, only 20% of a Populus poll disagreed with the proposition, which means it would also be politically popular. However, it would be important that the proceeds of the tax were directly transferred into the general education pot and not earmarked for any particular scheme, as both Labour and Adonis wanted, in the case of the former, to pay for free school meals for primary schoolchildren and in the case of the latter, a variety of schemes ranging from offering small group tuition for those in danger of not getting English and maths GCSEs, to offering free music and sports tuition to level the playing field with privately educated pupils and provide the disadvantaged with the cultural capital to succeed. These schemes are well meaning but what schools desperately need are a good supply of well-qualified teachers and a considerably higher level of per head funding. This will help the largest number, in the most efficient way possible, and at a local level where it is most needed.

This relatively quick and easy, as well as electorally popular, way of counterbalancing the tax advantages extended to private schools would give a huge boost to the state education budget well in excess of any extra cost incurred by ending state subsidies to private schools, and would get a new national education service and system off to a great start. That should not detract from the much harder task of reforming the law on charitable status, but it would be an excellent first step to a fairer and more efficient system. Experts in charity law have long struggled with the question of charitable status for private schools and they should continue to do so, as it is clearly at odds with any popular understanding of the word 'charity'. Charities do not serve the interests of a privileged elite while excluding their services to almost everyone else. If a charity doesn't exist to provide to those most in need, then plainly it isn't a charity. In the same way, it runs against any sense of common fairness for private schools to qualify for business tax relief while state schools do not. Addressing the latter anomaly would not only be comparatively easy, it would also provide local government with desperately needed funds. Of course, all these changes would most likely lead to an increase in school fees and an according reduction in demand for private school places, but if an education opportunity tax were introduced at the same time, they may actually also give a net funding boost to state education without having to pay a high political price.

Selection by ability or aptitude is both unfair and ineffective

As we have seen, it is not uncommon for opponents of selection by wealth to advocate selection by ability or aptitude instead, on the grounds that selective schools are 'good' schools because they have high academic standards. This also brings us to the 'levelling-up' argument i.e. if only state schools could be made good enough, private schools would simply wither away. In other words, bolster the state sector by creating new grammar schools and the middle classes will return. In political terms, this has argument has much to commend it, because it appeals to a wide cross section of parents who instinctively feel that in a meritocracy, talent should be encouraged rather than dampened down in the name of inclusivity. For some, the words 'comprehensive school' became synonymous with everything that was supposedly wrong with education in the 1970s and 1980s, i.e. low expectations, poor behaviour and even lower academic standards while grammar schools were associated with a golden age of high standards and school discipline. A more sophisticated argument for grammar schools, as put forward by Nick Hillman (2019), director of the Higher Education Policy Institute, is that the needs of the individual are more important than the need to maximise average achievement across society. Hillman (2019) is well aware there is overwhelming evidence that grammar schools lower the overall achievement rate of children in areas where they operate but makes the valid point that people (or voters) do not care particularly about the overall achievement rate because they only care about the achievement of their child. In other words, he sees support for selective schools as a case of my child, as opposed to every child, that matters as far as parents are concerned.

In reality, however, the vast majority of individual children do not benefit from selective schools, even if some politicians and parents believe otherwise. Study after study shows that they have virtually no positive effect on the children who attend them, and for those who struggled to pass the 11+ without significant coaching, they often have a detrimental effect (Rebecca Allen FFT education datalab 2016). Take for example, the very thorough study of half a million children by Gorard and Siddiqui (2018) from the University of Durham that shows that when adjusted for background and prior attainment, grammar school pupils achieve near identical results to similar pupils in comprehensive schools. Supporters of selection have argued that disadvantaged children do better in selective than non-selective schools but Gorard and Siddiqui show this is simply not the case by pointing out that the disadvantaged pupils in grammar schools are usually much better off than those in non-selective schools so comparing the results of each as though they were the same is wholly misleading. Children on Free School Meals take up 2.4% of grammar school places compared to 14% in non-selective schools (Department for Education 2018) and tend to be considerably poorer. This is not surprising since poorer children are less likely to score highly in the 11+ and the few that do tend to be less poor than the rest. Given this, it would be perverse to transfer large numbers of children on free school meals into grammar schools, as some would like to do, because in most cases they wouldn't perform any better than if they attended a comprehensive school and in some cases worse. It hardly needs adding that children with Education, Health and Care (EHC) plans make up minuscule numbers in grammar schools (0.04%) and those with SEND amount to 3.6% compared to 1.7% and 11% for all schools nationally (Bolton, P, Commons Briefing Paper SNO 1398). Taking the results of these tiny sub-sections of pupils in grammar schools and comparing their results with all similar children nationally would be similarly nonsensical because they also tend to come from more affluent backgrounds. It seems the only reason why parents think individual children do better in grammar schools is that the results of these schools are higher but this is nothing more than a reflection of the socio-economic background of the pupils who attend them. Ofsted makes the same mistake, conflating the concept of a good school with a school that admits more able pupils, allowing Theresa May to be able to claim that, "99% of selective schools are outstanding compared with 20% of state schools overall" (Sept 2016).

Good schools are not schools that only admit 'good' students. Good schools are schools that make a difference to all students, changing positively what would otherwise be a child's fate, and enabling children to achieve something they might otherwise have not been able to achieve. It is an incontrovertible that the children of affluent, educated parents are more likely to do well at school than the children of less affluent or educated parents, regardless of the school they attend. It is rare, and therefore worthy of particular praise, if a school helps children to make more progress *beyond that typically made by* children from a similar background elsewhere. Parents may misunderstand this, but that is no excuse for policy makers to do the same, even if Nick Hillman excuses them on the grounds that they are only reflecting the views of those parents. Policy should be made on evidence, not prejudice, even in a democracy.

Less controversial is the point that schools that select children either by ability or aptitude, are highly damaging to the progress of the majority of the children in their area who do not attend them (around 75% of all children in selective areas). Not only are they unfair, consigning many perfectly able children to what they realise is seen as a second class education, but they don't raise overall standards. In fact, they reduce overall standards, create deep social divisions and destroy the aspirations of the children affected. Once again, the reason is not that the schools the other children attend (what used to be called secondary moderns) are necessarily bad, but that they concentrate disadvantaged, as well as disaffected children, in one place, and disproportionately so when compared to their make-up in the local community. This ghetto-effect means these schools can feel overwhelmed by the challenges and consequently find it really difficult to recruit and retain good teachers. Comprehensive schools need a critical mass of currently able and motivated pupils if they are to succeed, but if those children are vastly outnumbered they tend not to do well (Burgess, Crawford & Macmillan, UCL, 2017). Since 70% of the children that pass the 11+ have been coached, and coaching is much more likely for children from affluent backgrounds, it follows that some currently able children who were not coached, probably because their parents couldn't afford it, are consigned to the 'secondary modern' unfairly, while conversely some less currently able but heavily coached children from more affluent backgrounds go to the grammar school. Unfortunately, Ofsted repeated their mistake of conflating a good school with one that admits currently able children, by equating requiring improvement or inadequate with a lack of affluence, and therefore only rating 12% of secondary moderns as outstanding, but if they were right then why would it make sense to send the least able children to the least effective schools? Concentrating the apparently less able, notwithstanding the fact that some of them aren't, in one school is like writing off three-quarters of the population, and in the 21st century, we can do better than that.

Of course, for a significant number of parents these debates are largely irrelevant, either because they live rural or non-selective areas of the country and effectively have no choice but to take what is on offer locally. Those living in rural areas need good local schools within reasonable travelling distance while those in non-selective areas need to know that taxpayers' money is being spent on schools that their children can access and to be spending very significant amounts of money on selective grammar schools that most people can't access is plainly unfair. Choice in the education market is an illusion for these parents and any system based on choice cannot operate effectively in these areas. Put plainly, parents need to know that they have good local comprehensive schools within easy access of where they live.

This leads on to my final point, that there is no reasonable justification for still having selective grammar schools in a few parts of the country while elsewhere comprehensive schools are preferred. What is it about children in Leicestershire that doesn't apply equally as well to children in Kent or Lincolnshire? What possible reason could there be for deciding that a child's education should be determined by a single performance test at the age of 11 in one county but not in another? The only reason of course is historical accident, because at some point in the past parents or politicians in one area expressed a different view to parents in another. This cannot be right for a new national education service and system because children don't learn differently just because they live in a different county. We must proceed from the basis that if a comprehensive system is right for some parts of the country, it is right for all. The present postcode lottery is no more justifiable in education than it is in healthcare and we can, and should, be doing better for our children.

International evidence about the effectiveness of comprehensive education

The international evidence is clear about the effectiveness of comprehensive education. Most of the world's top performing education systems, at least according to the PISA rankings, do not select children by ability or aptitude until the age of 15 or 16. Joanne Bartley surveys the evidence as part of her paper, the case for change (Bartley, 2019). She cites many studies including that by Lavrijsen and Nicaise (2016) that show that comprehensive school systems work better overall as well as just as well "to challenge higher performers to work at a high pace". She also quotes PISA's own 2016 report on selecting students that says "in education systems that separate students into different types of schools, students' expectations are lower than in systems that have a comprehensive approach". Unsurprisingly then, many school systems around the world are moving away from selection. Finland phased out selection in the 1970s in favour of a comprehensive system and is now regarded as having one of the best education systems in the world. Germany, often cited by supporters of selection as an example of a country that used to select children as young as10, is also moving towards a comprehensive approach, with many of its 16 states already phasing out the Haupstchule (lowest secondary school) and introducing comprehensive schools in their place.

Setting and streaming

Even at classroom level, there are serious doubts about the efficacy of selection. The Education Endowment Foundation, set up by the government with the Sutton Trust with the aim of developing evidence based approaches to teaching children, particularly disadvantaged children, has established a teacher toolkit to evaluate the effectiveness and value for money of various teaching approaches including that of setting and streaming. Their conclusion is that "setting or streaming is not an effective way to raise the attainment of most pupils" and that it has "a very small negative impact for low and mid-range attaining learners and a very small positive impact for high attaining learners" which seems consistent with evidence on the impact of selective school systems as a whole. While selection at classroom level is a different matter, and leaving aside certain circumstances or subjects in which setting or streaming has a positive impact on overall attainment, for example in the teaching of secondary maths or when the population of a school has extreme variations in current ability, it is clear that even at this level selection is not usually beneficial. However, just like in their attitude to grammar schools, many parents *believe* setting is the right approach and consequently, policy makers sometimes advocate it, no doubt in the spirit of democracy. As I said before, education policy should not be based on popular prejudice, and our children deserve better than to have a system inflicted upon them that we know to be ineffective just because some parents, as opposed to the Michael Gove, Secretary of State's infamous experts,[7] think it's a good thing. I am sure public health policy would not be made in the same way.

Quite simply, if a new national education service and system is to be free and open to all, there can be no place for the selection of pupils by ability or aptitude at the age of 11. No credible education system can be built on principles that are both unfair and ineffective.

Legislation needed for England

John Fowler has shown that it would be fairly straightforward to phase out the remaining 163 grammar schools simply by passing a law that a new national education service and system should only provide education in schools "where the arrangements for the admission of pupils are not based [wholly or partially] on selection by reference to ability or aptitude" (Fowler, 2019). A 1976 Act stated precisely that but was repealed in 1980 and since then the situation has been further complicated by the emergence of academies and free schools that act as their own admissions authorities. Fowler points out that the 1976 act made the mistake of allowing local authorities five years to submit plans for the process of transition, which meant a change of government came before the plans had been fully implemented. There is no reason to repeat the mistake again. Instead Fowler suggests that plans should be drawn up over two years and then phased in so that existing pupils were not unfairly affected. Of course, this legislation would need to be accompanied by a repeal of the current legislation that only allows new schools to be set up as free schools and instead allow LAs to create new schools once again, as well as expand existing ones, where needed and with the approval of either the Secretary of State or the Schools' Adjudicator and with the assistance of a capital fund designed for the purpose.

Selection by faith

While it is not the remit of this chapter to consider selection by faith, it is at least worth mentioning that in England faith schools have to an extent become another form of backdoor selection and places in faith schools are often sought after, not out of any sense of religious devotion but out of a perception that these schools somehow filter out the 'less desirable' elements of society and are therefore able to offer a higher standard of education. Leaving aside my earlier point that good schools are not necessarily schools that admit good children, this whole issue is wrapped up with a wider debate about the separation of church and state in an apparently secular society, which is why I chose not to tackle it here. Nevertheless, it is still worth making the point that without consideration of this question, even the reforms I suggest would not establish an entirely level playing field in state education.

The English tradition, as opposed to say the French, has been to offer a multiplicity of faith schools rather than ban faith schools altogether, on the grounds that if people want their child to be educated in a particular faith they should have the right to do so. This point is becoming increasingly contentious as so-called British values come against articles of faith which appear to contradict them, particularly in areas such as sexual orientation and gender identity; in other words, has anyone in a liberal democracy got the right to express the view that the basic principles of that liberal democracy are wrong? This is a whole separate discussion but sooner or later it must be addressed because the present muddled approach is an unhelpful exercise in avoiding the question because the answer might not be acceptable to certain sections of the community. Suffice to say that it would be possible at some point in the future for the new national education service and system to also end selection by faith, if it so chose.

In a secular democracy, there's no place for the funding of faith schools from the public purse. Such schools deny choice to local children and parents who find their local school has a bias towards values that are contradictory to their own.

Alternative provision can be made and is made by parents through their faith communities for times after school, on weekends and during school holidays.

That this is a longstanding issue is evidenced by these quotation from the 19th century taken from Smith (2016):

> The 1870 Elementary Education Act made this provision: "it shall not be required as a condition of any child being admitted into or continuing in the school as he shall attend or abstain from attending any Sunday school any place of religious worship or that he shall attend any religious observance or any instruction in religious subjects in the school or elsewhere from which observance of instruction he may be withdrawn by his parents".
>
> The teaching was to be nondenominational: "No religious catechism or religious formulary which is distinctive of any religious denomination shall be taught in the school". Smith goes on to give following example:
>
> "school boards did have the right to forbid all religious instruction in normal school hours, and this was done in Birmingham board schools from 1873 to 1879. . . . Joseph Chamberlain was keen to assert that he was not against the teaching of Christianity per se but was against the sectarian bigotry that had emerged. His aim was that in Birmingham they would uphold 'the great principles of religious freedom and religious equality' that had made the nation strong".
>
> *Smith (2016), p. 53.*

Reflections

It is crucial that state-subsidised selection by wealth and selection by ability or aptitude are removed from a new national education service and system at the same time if it is to be both free and open to all and make the best use of public resources for the education of the nation as a whole. If the former were achieved but not the latter, then grammar schools would become private schools by proxy and overall standards of education would fall. It would be bad for most children, including most currently able children, and particularly so for the most vulnerable or disadvantaged in society. Conversely, if the latter were achieved without the former, then not only would a new national education service be based on hypocrisy and unfairness, but it would also be just as ineffective as the current system. Neither should happen without the other because they are in a symbiotic relationship. Ending selection would not sacrifice effectiveness for fairness, as some critics may claim, and it would not be a vote for mediocrity as the so-called individualists argue. The evidence is clear: selection in all its forms is both unfair and ineffective, and if we are to build a world class new national education service and system that brings our nation together and makes us stronger, then we must introduce legislation within three months of a new parliament so that once and for all our children can hope that their world will be better and fairer than ours.

Policy options

The issues raised in this chapter lead to a number of policy options:

Policy Option 1: Maintain a divided system with access to political and economic power limited to the wealthy with some 'social mobility' allowed. In previous centuries this may have been easier to maintain although the elite in Tsarist Russia in 1917 and in France in 1789–99 did not manage to keep their population compliant with this process. Allow faith schools to continue and to isolate children from their countrymen of many faiths.

Policy Option 2: Establish a free and open to all, a new national education service and system to build a meritocratic society. This would require phasing out all state support for private education including the removal of tax exemptions, grants, subsidies or other privileges which in the UK are currently extended to both private schools and the pupils' parents. Work from the general principle that public money should only be spent on education that is free and open to all regardless of wealth, current ability or aptitude and pass legislation that:

- prohibits the use of public money to support education in schools that require all or most of their pupils to pay fees and
- requires parents to pay an education opportunity tax on school fees at least equal to the value of VAT
- restricts use of public funds for education to schools where the arrangements for the admission of pupils are not based (wholly or partially) on selection by current ability or aptitude, excepting those specifically created for the purpose of providing education for children with special educational needs or disabilities.

- requires local authorities to publish and apply plans for the phasing out of schools that select by current ability or aptitude within a maximum of two years
- repeals current legislation that prohibits the creation of any new schools that are not free schools and creates a capital fund for local authorities to build new schools or expand or redevelop existing ones as required

Further legislation should seek to remove tax privileges for private schools and define them as private businesses rather than charities.

The penultimate chapter in this volume provides further reflections and an executive summary of options, consequences and cautionary tales.

Notes

1 Equality Trust (2019), *How Has Inequality Changed?* www.equalitytrust.org.uk/how-has-inequality-changed Accessed 5 October 2019.
2 Verkiak, R. (2019) *Critics Take Aim at Subsidies Given to Private Schools.* www.theguardian.com/education/2019/feb/05/critics-take-aim-at-subsidies-given-to-private-schools. Accessed 5 October 2019.
3 Matthews, B. (2019) *Towards a National Education Service, workshop,* January, De Montfort University, UK.
4 Green, F. and Kynaston, D. (2019), *Engines of Privilege: Britain's Private School Problem,* London: Bloomsbury.
5 Benn, M. (2018) *Life Lessons: The Case for a National Education Service,* London: Verso Books.
6 Woolcock, N. (2017) Tax Private Schools to Pay State Teachers, says Lord Adonis, *The Times Newspaper.* www.thetimes.co.uk/article/tax-private-schools-to-pay-state-teachers-says-lord-adonis-fh059h7jx. Accessed 5 October 2019.
7 Mance, H. (2016) *Britain Has Had Enough of Experts, says Gove.* www.ft.com/content/3be49734-29cb-11e6-83e4-abc22d5d108c. Accessed 5 October 2019.

References

Allen, R. (2016) *Inequalities in Access to Teachers in Selective Schooling Areas,* FFT: Education Datalab.
Bartley, J. (2019) *Decision Time, A Plan for Phasing out Selection,* London: Comprehensive Future.
Benn, M. (2018) *Life Lessons: The Case for a New National Education Service,* London: Verso Books.
Burgess, S., Crawford, C. and Macmillan, L. (2017) Assessing the role of grammar schools in promoting social mobility, *Dept of Quantitative Social Science Working Paper 17-09,* London: IOE UCL.
Fowler, J. (2019) *Contribution in Towards a New National Education Service Workshop,* January, De Montfort University, UK.
Gorard, S. and Siddiqui, N. (2018) Grammar Schools in England: A New Analysis of Social Segregation Academic Outcomes, *British Journal of Sociology of Education,* 39 (7) 909–924.
Gove, M. (2014) Our Segregated Education System Perpetuates Inequality and Holds Our Nation Back: The Education Secretary Responds to the NS Debate on Public Schools, *New Statesman,* 12 February. www.newstatesman.com/2014/02/gove-michael-our-segregated-education-system.

Green, F. and Kynaston, D. (2019) *Engines of Privilege*, London: Bloomsbury.

Hillman, N. (2019) How to Reignite a Smouldering Fire, *TES*, March.

Lavrijsen, J. and Nicaise, L. (2016) *Secondary Education Regimes and Perceived Equity in Social and Educational Mobility in OECD Countries*, Leuven: Steunpunt Studie-en Schoolloopbanen.

Major, L.E. (2016) *Impact of Selective Education*, London: Sutton Trust, 2016.

Mance, H. (2016) *Britain has had Enough of Experts, says Gove*. www.ft.com/content/3be49734-29cb-11e6-83e4-abc22d5d108c. Accessed 5 October 2019.

Murray, K., et al. (2017) *Life Lessons: A New National Education Service that Leaves No Adult Behind*, Fabian Policy Report, UCU.

Smith, J. (2016) *Key Questions in Education*, London. Bloomsbury.

Verkaik, R. (2019) Critics Take Aim at Subsidies Given to Private Schools, *The Guardian*.

Wilshaw, M. (2016) *Keynote speech Autumn Conference, FASNA*, London. www.gov.uk/government/speeches/sir-michael-wilshaws-speech-at-the-fasna-autumn-conference. Accessed 5 October 2019.

Woolcock, N. (2017) *Tax Private Schools to Pay State Teachers, says Lord Adonis*. www.thetimes.co.uk/article/tax-private-schools-to-pay-state-teachers-says-lord-adonis-fh059h7jx The Times Newspaper. Accessed 5 October 2019.

9

SCHOOL SEGREGATION IN ENGLAND AND THE LOGIC OF EXITING FROM THE PUBLIC EDUCATION SYSTEM

Helen M. Gunter and Steven J. Courtney

Introduction

The provision of and access to school places in England have been subject to radical change from 1988 onwards, and are now primarily based on biopolitical distinctiveness or how we learn relationally what our place is in the superiority-inferiority stakes (Gunter 2018). Calls for choice and diversity are premised on how bodies are individualised and then categorised, and either shamed or acclaimed according to complex but dominant beliefs interplayed with the protection of elite interests. These differences are reflected and reified in school structures, where what had previously been regarded as a 'national' education service 'locally delivered' (see Chapter 5) has become purposively atomised into a range of provision that is not just differentiated, as conceptualised in the quasi-market metaphor (Le Grand 1991), but hierarchised in order to receive children who are worth more or less. Consequently, there are now between 70 and 90 different types of schools in England (Courtney 2015), and while this is presented as modern, in reality it demonstrates the endurance of segregation between and within schools. In this short commentary, following an overview of segregation in schooling arrangements in England, we present and consider the implications of what we call *the logic of exiting*, including how exiting is integral to segregation and to the modernising neoliberal project.

Segregation, segregation, segregation

Segregation is evident and endemic in educational arrangements in England within and beyond schools. For instance, concerning the latter, 'home schooling' involves parents making private provision to educate their children (Ball 2017). For those who take up their entitlement to 'choose' a school place, legalised conviction criteria are used in ways that both structure these choices and also tend to be impervious to research evidence. These criteria produce categories of provision that are predicated on first, biological sex (boys' and girls' schools) (Rivers and Barnett 2011); second, parental wealth and networks (private, fee-paying schools) (Green and Kynaston 2019); third, parental beliefs (faith schools, legally constituted as either academies, voluntary or trust/foundation schools) (Long and Bolton 2017); and fourth, intelligence testing (grammar schools) (Gorard and Siddiqui 2018). While it is illegal to offer school places on the basis of race, it is the case that there are such divides in regard to achievement (Gillborn et al. 2017) and that the quasi-market in education facilitates racially segregated schools through sociological rather than legal mechanisms (Burgess et al. 2005). Within-school segregation can operate on the basis of biology (separate classes for boys and girls), age (year groups), and intelligence (banding and setting).

While choice is premised on the basis of freedom and entitlement to a private good, the processes of segregation through word of mouth, family traditions, and open days are regulated through a complexity of certainty about the human body. As Chitty (2007) argues, there is "a belief in genetic determinism in the area of human intellectual capacity" that we know as eugenics that "grew out of a set of ideas about sustaining and improving the quality of the human race" (p. 6). Hence segregation persists because there is an entrenched regularity in assumptions that shape private decisions. This not only speaks to the child as the object of eugenic measurement to be worthy or not of a school place, but also to parental capability to exercise choice in a responsible, rational way. Notably parents must not depend on the state to provide but must access a place based on a private assessment of both the needs of their own child and also of her potential, where that potential is understood as involving a limit. Importantly, the interplay between notions of 'limit' and 'potential' happens in a space that is susceptible to structuration through class, race and gender. Bourdieu (1977) draws attention to the way in which such spaces can appear free of structure and hence of power to social actors in his concept of *doxa*. This is the self-evident truths about the nature of a given society and its workings, and so *how things are* (including one's position in a social hierarchy) reflects one's impression of *how things should naturally be*. Doxa, considered together with the persistent belief in genetic determinism, enable a clearer understanding of why children with certain bodies, along with blood and inheritance from their parents, might choose provision that is objectively limiting.

The logic of exiting

So far, our discussion has focused on how segregation is produced through practices of access to, or entry into, provision. However, segregated, needs-based entitlement has also intensified discourses and practices regarding *exiting*. Professionals and children can exit (leave) a school and be exited (told to leave) from a school. We have charted and analysed the escalation of such staff and student disposability in relation to staff contract termination (Courtney and Gunter 2015) and the off-rolling of children (Gunter 2018). In these instances, the standards agenda constructs both an ideal teacher (one whose pupils attain undeviatingly high scores in standardised tests and make what is deemed to be at least good progress between them) and an ideal learner (who performs convincingly the role of compliant and successful object of such teaching). Those who fail to embody these constructs are exited from the 'system' where such failure helps to constitute the 'system'.

We want to comment specifically on the idea and reality of consumer choice in a highly segregated 'system' where we want to explore the notion of consumer 'exiting' rather than 'being exited'. This is a complex matter but, following Hirschman (1970), it seems that parents can remain 'loyal' and are still entitled to 'voice' concerns if necessary, but the option and reality of 'exiting' a school is integral to quality. This argument concerning quality applies at micro, meso and macro levels. First, at micro level, an individual may realise his or her potential for embodying quality only through finding appropriate provision and, where necessary, exiting inadequate provision that is unconducive to such self-actualisation. Second, at meso level, the quality of any given school relies on the 'right' consumers identifying it and exiting other provision to locate within it. Third, at macro level, the quality of the 'education system' depends on sufficient numbers of individuals exiting according to this logic. Importantly, the logic of universal *entering* becomes unthinkable and unsayable, where the idea and reality of the local common school for a community is rendered unsound because it is based on risky dependency upon others.

The logic of exiting enables discourses that atomise families: the political construction of tax cuts as a societal good hollows-out and de-legitimises the social-democratic public-good value system. Illuminating the distinction between these two forms of 'good' is the question of whether taxpayers in one family fund school places for *other* people's children, i.e. whether the benefits of education must always be directly related to oneself or to one's family, or whether it is legitimate that they improve societies to the general, but indirect benefit of all. This speaks to wider impulses for self-exclusion through gated communities and tax havens, but is enabled to operate in ordinary ways for less-privileged families through the use of faux-choice processes such as vouchers (see Feintuck and Stevens 2013).

Gunter (2019) has characterised this logic of exiting as 'edu-exit' with five features:

1 **Claims about exceptionalism and freedom as a personal property:** parents are encouraged to claim that their child is incomparable, and so require choice in order to ensure specific requirements, such as what and who they want their child to mix with.
2 **Autonomy and exiting as the solution:** parents are required to accept that *leaving* (threat or actual) is the solution to all problems that may or may not be educational.
3 **Assertions of and lies about the dangers and failure of bureaucracy and elections:** parents are required to act as consumers rather than as citizens, and are encouraged to be anti-political and so replace voting by purchasing.

4   **Ridiculing expertise and evidence:** parents are expected to go with their instincts about what is right for their child and to provide justification based on a combination of what they like and selected data about teachers and the school.

5   **Populist capture:** parents emotionally and practically engage with claims made by school providers about the 'worth' of their child 'deserving' a good school place, and integral to this is not engaging with debates about what happens to other people's children who are disposed of because they are categorised differently.

A restoration project is under way whereby corporate and oligarchic elites are involved in both transparent and stealth-like strategies and tactics in order to enhance their interests, where the major concession is that everyone can 'rise up' if only they can be liberated from public services education (Gunter et al. 2017). We have identified what we call 'corporatised fabrications' that are used to warrant, evidence and imagine the reality of reforms such as 'parental choice' and 'autonomous schools' (Courtney and Gunter 2020). Such lies and myths about new freedoms and innovative potential are audaciously seductive and have impacted on the professional identities necessary to secure the financialisation of educational services (Hughes et al. 2019). While here we are dealing with educational services, Gunter (2019) argues that the experience of edu-exit has readied people in England to engage with the normalities of 'Brexit' or the exit from the European Union.

Reflections

There are many consequences to this analysis: parents become muscular consumers in regard to being afraid to make the wrong choice, and once the choice is made they can adopt the 'switching your provider' culture that is prevalent in the contracting of domestic power supplies or car insurance. Or parents exit from the choice, because in the hierarchisation of children as ranked superior-inferior there can be an acceptance of the place that eugenics has naturally dealt a family (Bourdieu 1977). Biopolitical distinctiveness is what is learned and practiced on the basis of what is *deserved*, or perceived or accepted to be deserved. Hence the objective rules for the allocation of public resources through bureaucratic structures and procedures are replaced by emotional reactions to narratives that construct a warrant for sorting children into hierarchised school places.

There are many questions to raise, but here we would like to conclude by asking: Why are educational professionals being trained and accredited to enable and legitimise segregation? The reason for this may be located in the evidence that rather than children and their parents choosing schools, in fact schools actually choose children, and so professionals have to be trained to secure exclusion (Carrasco and Gunter 2019). Importantly, scholarship and policy briefings in the field – or functionalist knowledge tradition – of school improvement and effectiveness speak the language of equity, but it seems this knowledge is being deployed in order to eliminate, or *exit,* children. Segregation is premised on pre-enlightenment anxieties of how best to preserve social, economic and political structures (divine right of kings, lord of the manor and serfdom), and research is being conducted in order to modernise the presentation but does not tackle the substance of such claims. When research is combined with segregation, then all there is to discuss is tactical implementation, because the strategy is located in underlying purposes of education as reflecting 'natural' biopolitical distinctiveness.

Policy options

Our research and intellectual work have generated a range of questions for policy design and localised enactment by professionals, parents and communities. We are very much aware that different positions can be taken in regard to the trends and analysis we have presented here and can be followed up in our more detailed reports and contributions to debates (e.g. Courtney 2018; Gunter 2018). We suggest taking a critical educational leadership approach to this issue, whereby educational professionals ask questions about social justice and the context in which policy is scoped, framed and enacted (see Courtney et al. 2021). You might begin by mapping the examples of segregation in your system, and then consider: first, the legitimacy of segregation and whether you accept and support, and would want to extend, barriers; and second, how you might challenge segregation and work for a more equitable public system of local in-common schools. There may be other options that you may wish to consider and work on, and we draw to your attention the penultimate chapter, where there are further reflections and an executive summary of options, consequences and cautionary tales arising from these options.

References

Ball, P. (2017) The School of Mum and Dad. *Prospect,* (258) (September), 58–61.
Bourdieu, P. (1977) *Outline of a Theory of Practice.* Cambridge: Cambridge University Press.
Burgess, S., Wilson, D. and Lupton, R. (2005) Parallel Lives? Ethnic Segregation in Schools and Neighbourhoods. *Urban Studies,* 42 (7), 1027–1056.
Carrasco, A. and Gunter, H.M. (2019) The 'Private' in the Privatization of Schools: The Case of Chile. *Educational Review,* 71 (1), 67–80.
Chitty, C. (2007) *Eugenics, Race and Intelligence in Education.* London: Continuum.
Courtney, S.J. (2015) Mapping school Types in England. *Oxford Review of Education,* 41 (6), 799–818.
Courtney, S.J. (2018) Privatising Educational Leadership Through Technology in the Trumpian Era. *Journal of Educational Administration and History,* 50 (1), 23–31.
Courtney, S.J. and Gunter, H.M. (2015) Get off My Bus! School Leaders, Vision Work and the Elimination of Teachers. *International Journal of Leadership in Education,* 18 (4), 395–417.
Courtney, S.J. and Gunter, H.M. (2020) Corporatised Fabrications: The Methodological Challenges of Professional Biographies at a Time of Neoliberalisation. In Lynch, J., Rowlands, J., Gale, T. and Parker, S. (eds) *Practice Methodologies in Education Research.* Abingdon: Taylor & Francis, 27–47.

Courtney, S.J., Gunter, H.M., Niesche, R. and Trujillo, T. (eds) (2021) *Understanding Educational Leadership: Critical Perspectives and Approaches*. London: Bloomsbury.

Feintuck, M. and Stevens, R. (2013) *School Admissions and Accountability*. Bristol: The Policy Press.

Gillborn, D., Demack, S., Rollock, N. and Warmington, P. (2017) Moving the Goalposts: Education Policy and 25 Years of the Black/White Achievement Gap. *British Educational Research Journal,* 43 (5), 848–874.

Gorard, S. and Siddiqui, N. (2018) Grammar Schools in England: A New Analysis of Social Segregation and Academic Outcomes. *British Journal of Sociology of Education,* 39 (7), 909–924.

Green, F. and Kynaston, D. (2019) *Engines of Privilege: Britain's Private School Problem*. London: Bloomsbury.

Gunter, H.M. (2018) *The Politics of Public Education: Reform Ideas and Issues*. Bristol: Policy Press.

Gunter, H.M. (2019) Five Ways in which Edu-Exit was the Test Run for Brexit. *BERA Blog.* www.bera.ac.uk/blog/five-ways-in-which-edu-exit-was-the-test-run-for-brexit

Gunter, H.M., Hall, D. and Apple, M. (eds) (2017) *Corporate Elites and the Reform of Public Education*. Bristol: Policy Press.

Hirschman, A.O. (1970) *Exit, Voice and Loyalty*. Cambridge, MA: Harvard University Press.

Hughes, B., Courtney, S.J. and Gunter, H.M. (2019) Researching Professional Biographies of Educational Professionals in *New* Dark Times. *British Journal of Educational Studies*. DOI: 10.1080/00071005.2019.1673879.

Le Grand, J. (1991) Quasi-markets and Social Policy. *The Economic Journal*, 101, 1256–1267.

Long, R. and Bolton, P. (2017) *Faith Schools in England: FAQs. Briefing Paper Number 06972, 13th March 2017*. London: House of Commons Library.

Rivers, C. and Barnett, R.C. (2011) *The Truth about Girls and Boys: Challenging Toxic Stereotypes about Our Children*. New York: Colombia University Press.

10

SPECIAL EDUCATIONAL NEEDS AND DISABILITIES

Sana Rizvi and Helen Knowler

Introduction

> Inclusive education needs to be part of a whole-school equal opportunities policy. If we are to resist complacency and recognize the degree of struggle still to be engaged with, and if official rhetoric is to be translated into reality in substantive terms in the lives of all pupils, then the question of inclusive education needs to be an integral part of a well-thought-through, adequately resourced and carefully monitored equal opportunities policy.
>
> *(Barton, 1997, p. 234)*

There is a growing emphasis across the globe on making schools more responsive and inclusive to all learners. Despite the divergences in the schooling systems across different countries, the principles underpinning the Salamanca Statement (UNESCO, 1994) and the UN Convention on the Rights of Persons with Disabilities (2006), have strategically shaped how the educational policies of different countries should give due consideration to tackling barriers to discrimination and developing inclusive practices that improve educational outcomes for all learners. In this chapter, we focus on the future of inclusive education policies in the United Kingdom, in particular England and Wales, where the Special Educational Needs and Disabilities (SEND) Code of Practice (DfE and DfH, 2015) has been implemented with similar provisions for learners with different abilities. We hope that policy makers working in similar contexts in other parts of the world can examine the policy options presented here for England and Wales as an example of how schools could become more inclusive in their own contexts. Recent policy reforms in 2014 have been described as moving towards a "more user-led system with reduced local and central government involvement and regulation" by Norwich and Eaton (2015,

p. 119). Some of the issues resulting from the devolving of responsibilities from local and central government with regards to SEND provisions are beginning to be noted in a limited number of small-scale studies (National Autistic Society, 2016; Hellawell, 2019; LGSCO,[1] 2019). These studies report that many learners and their families must wait longer to secure appropriate provisions, adversely affecting their educational experiences.

This chapter presents three future policy scenarios that link education and provisions for learners with different abilities with the broader educational landscape, building on Booth's (1996) idea that meaningful educational inclusion must entail "the process of increasing the participation of pupils within the cultures and curricula of mainstream schools and the process of decreasing exclusionary pressures. To attempt the first without the second is self-defeating" (p. 34). The three policy options discussed in this chapter address these interlinked processes, driven by the general principles that all policies and initiatives should be anchored in inclusion, equity and viewing education as a social good. As academics, we align our own epistemological position with Barton's (1997), that educational policy changes must incorporate a human rights perspective, aiming for democratic participation by all learners.

Policy option 1: consultation processes

Policy option one is concerned with macro-level change that includes education provision for all learners and calls for the establishment of what Norwich (2019) terms the Education Framework Commission (EFC). An independent non-governmental organisation (NGO) will run the Commission to preserve its independence, reconciling contrary educational ideologies; for instance, that Special Education Needs (SEN) is a part of mainstream education, or that SEN is distinct from ordinary education and has its own subsystems, policies and professionals. The Commission will initially bind current and future governments for up to 10 years, so that relevant debates and legislation can occur in a stable environment. Political parties and governments would pursue cross-party education policy and legislation within the framework constructed by the Commission. The Commission would focus on building interdependence between different specialisms, and through consultations with different political parties, individuals and organisations from different sectors will develop effective provisions for learners with different abilities.

Policy option 2: learner experiences

Policy option two is a measure to immediately address the exclusion and off-rolling of learners with different abilities (and learners from other disadvantaged groups), by removing alternative provisions such as pupil referral units (PRU) and other institutional settings that become forced/coerced choices for learners and their families[2] (Knowler and Done, 2019). This policy would mandate that schools increase transparency about how they work with learners with different abilities, and decree that regulating bodies such as Ofsted shift their focus from ranking schools on performance measures to evaluating and supporting schools on becoming effectively more inclusive (Booth and Ainscow, 2011). We see this as essential to ensuring that learners feel included in educational settings, so that they can avail all opportunities provided to all learners within mainstream settings to realise their true potential.

Policy option 3: teacher training

Policy option three is concerned with developing the 'ethical' education professional through collaboration between teacher training providers and university SEND departments. This would entail different partnership models designed to equip all teaching staff with the requisite knowledge about SEN teaching and learning. This policy aims to introduce inclusive and reflexive ways of teaching that are consistent and relevant across all UK educational settings, which all teaching staff must engage with as part of their teacher training programmes and professional development.

Principles for SEND code of practice

In the UK, the term 'Special Education Needs' or 'SEN' was introduced into public discourse in the Warnock Report (1978) to shift from a deficit lens of categorising learners with different abilities as having a 'handicap', towards a focus on protecting resources for learners with different abilities in various educational settings. The Warnock Report pushed for the identification, assessment and proper planning of resources and provisions for learners with SEN, for providing statutory guidance to local authorities on how to work with schools and for including parental views with regards to provisions and placement settings for their children. This emphasis has been carried forward into subsequent legislations and can also be noted in the latest Children and Families Act 2014. However, this is not to say that it has not been problematic to implement legislations to support learners with different abilities with effectively and timely provisions, as well as to ensure that mainstream education is responsive to addressing the goals of inclusion. Divergent teacher training routes and the different ways in which schools are governed affect how learners with different abilities are supported within educational settings (Pulsford and Rizvi, 2019) Previously, local authorities in England had control of pupil services providing schools with access to centralised provisions. However, the last decade has seen a more divergent and market-oriented environment which permits schools increased autonomy, enabling them to procure services from both public and private sources.

The latest SEND Code of Practice (DfE and DfH, 2015) was adopted as a result of the UK government developing a more effective and holistic assessment and delivery of SEN provisions, based on the recommendations of the Lamb Inquiry

(DCSF, 2009) and the Green Paper, 'Support and aspiration: A new approach to special educational needs' (DfE, 2011). The revised Code aims to improve parental confidence in provisions for children and young people, giving more power to frontline professionals and families and introducing a single assessment process for EHC plans. Specifically, the principles underpinning this Code focus on increasing participation, choices and control for learners with different abilities and their parents in decision-making processes, effective early identification of the learner's needs and intervention, a greater collaboration between education, health and social care professionals to enable high quality provisions and a more effective transition into adulthood that includes planning for independent living and employment (DfE and DfH, 2015).

Whilst this Code has been described as a necessary measure to address "serious flaws in the SEN system" (House of Commons Education and Skills Committee, 2006, p. 40), and "a radically different system" (Department for Education [DfE, 2011] to the previous Code [DfES, 2015]), much of the content of this Code builds upon the content of previous guidance and reforms. Commentaries by Norwich (2019), Allan and Youdell (2017) and Lehane (2017), however, suggest that the new Code is ambiguous in terms of outlining specific curriculum and pedagogical practices which contribute to the goals of inclusion, decentre the needs of learners with different abilities by focusing on the roles and responsibilities of third parties, and engage with the procurement and commissioning of services and provisions in technical language.

The terminology of special educational needs

The SEN 'language' used currently in the UK is directly attributable to the Code through its three iterations (1994, 2001, 2015), developed to support transparency and fairness for all learners and their families. The Code outlines the identification, assessment, diagnosis and intervention for learners with SEN, and is a statutory requirement for schools and colleges to follow. The Code sets out guidance regarding working with parents, the role of the SEN Coordinator (SENCO), and partnering with parents and other agencies.

The Code (DfES, 2015) states that a

> child or young person has SEN if they have a learning difficulty or disability which calls for special educational provision to be made for him or her. A child of compulsory school age or a young person has a learning difficulty or disability if he or she has a significantly greater difficulty in learning than the majority of others of the same age, or has a disability which prevents or hinders him or her from making use of facilities of a kind generally provided for others of the same age in mainstream schools or mainstream post-16 institutions.
>
> *(DfES 2015, pp. 15–16)*

The advice then requires class teachers supported by the senior leadership team and the SENCO to make regular assessments for all pupils, focussing on pupils making progress that is "significantly slower than that of their peers starting from the same baseline, fails to match or better the child's previous rate of progress, fails to close the attainment gap between the child and their peers, [or] widens the attainment gap" (DfE and DfH, 2015, p. 95).

The Code is organised into four 'areas of need': Communication and Interaction; Cognition and Learning; Social, Emotional and Mental Health; and Physical/ Sensory Needs (DfE and DfH, 2015). Children can be placed into two categories; the first is 'SEN Support' which is a greater provision than might normally be expected for a pupil of that age to ensure that barriers to learning are removed. If "despite the school having taken relevant and purposeful action to identify, assess and meet the SEN of the child" (DfE and DfH, 2015, p. 104) the child or young person has not made the expected progress, the school or parents can request an EHC needs assessment. However, the term SEN itself is not without controversy. Norwich (1996, 2013) has argued that SEN is a wide-ranging umbrella term or a 'super category' that has produced ambiguity about who is and who is not 'special', as well as confusion about the needs of learners who are categorised with a more general label such as those pupils identified with 'mild learning difficulties'.

There are problematic patterns evident within annual data (DfE, 2019a) collected by the UK Government relating to how children and young people are being designated with SEN. Some groups are more likely to be identified as having SEN; for instance, children from particular ethnic backgrounds, children receiving free school meals (FSM), and boys in general are overrepresented in SEN data. Whilst there is an argument that this reflects population differences in the incidence of SEN, it also raises serious questions about whether learners are identified with SEN due to discriminatory attitudes based on racism, ableism, classism and genderism.

Despite considerable political and socioeconomic analysis of the education of pupils with different abilities, there remains a focus on medicalised conceptions of SEN. Indeed, families often want a medicalised label in order to help their application for specialised support for their child. While some labels remain critiqued within educational research, such as dyslexia (Elliot and Grigorenko, 2014), attention deficit hyperactivity disorder (ADHD) (Graham, 2008), and Social, Emotional and Mental Health (SEMH) needs (Knowler, 2009), the Code largely ignores the idea that labels may be constructed to support professional, parental and political interests (Tomlinson, 2017).

Policy option 1: consultation processes

Against the backdrop of diversification in school governance, and an increasing emphasis on joined-up working within education, health and social care settings, Norwich's proposal for an Education Framework Commission (EFC) appears to be an attractive option for consideration going forward (2019). An EFC would reconcile/accommodate competing value positions within education in general, encompassing special needs education specifically. Norwich's suggestion for an integrated educational policy is influenced by Crouch's (2012) post-democracy political analysis around how citizenship can be re-energised in the midst of rising privatisation, and the blurring of boundaries between public and private owner-ship. Norwich maintains that rather than dismissing how such uncertainties shape educational policies, policy makers should address them directly. Norwich (2019) highlights various competing value positions in his paper, such as identifying a learner with SEN in order to protect provisions against not identifying a learner with SEN so as to avoid negative aspects of labelling. By forming a commission that develops a medium term (e.g. 10 year) national education policy framework, Norwich (2019) suggests that EFC would aim to reconcile such competing posi-tions[3] as far as possible. Under an EFC, key stakeholders including learners, school staff, parents, academics, Ofsted, health and care professionals and representatives from opposing political parties would deliberate about key issues that affect the experiences of all learners including those with different abilities within educational settings.

The Commission is not simply an idealistic goal, as there are similar setups currently in operation to Norwich's proposal. For instance, the Social Metrics Commission (SMC)[4] represents an autonomous and non-partisan organisation that enables the UK government and public to understand the causes and actions neces-sary to challenging poverty. It differs from the proposed Commission in that the SMC does not make any recommendations on current or future policies, and is solely concerned with developing new and effective poverty metrics (SMC 2018 Report).

The Commission would resolve the lack of collaboration currently between various specialisms. For instance, the existing policy for learners with different abilities embraces a piecemeal approach, where the current process of identifica-tion, assessment and intervention of learners with different abilities is not inter-connected with the wider special needs system. Although EHC plans are aimed at providing a holistic and person-centred provision, research has shown that LAs develop EHC plans with a lack of joined-up working from health and social care services (LGSCO, 2019). The Commission would initiate a national dialogue on what statutory support should resemble and how all agencies can be equally involved and held accountable. However, the proposal is not without problems; Norwich (2019) cautions that if membership and governance is not monitored, the Commission could become an elitist organisation that fails to engage and represent the interests and rights of stakeholders.

From our epistemological stance, our concerns are more to do with the Com-mission's mission to reconcile competing value positions. We believe that some of these competing positions are against the values of social justice, equity and demo-cratic participation. For instance, it would be difficult to reconcile the values of choice (preference) versus equity (fairness), since, as Barton (1997) declares, certain choices reproduce ableist structures such as PRUs that disadvantage and exclude learners with different abilities. Barton maintains that the exercise of choice by certain groups with some autonomy and power, such as LAs, may limit the options available for marginalised others. Would it not be more in line with the values of social justice if the EFC first deliberated on the type of "citizenship required in order for the creation of unity without denying autonomy?" (Barton, 1997, p. 240). Whilst Norwich (2019) acknowledges that there will be inevitable trade-offs, he maintains that the EFC should in principle debate what a socially just distribution of opportunity would resemble that is achieved through common agreement.

Policy option 2: learner experiences

This proposal addresses concerns about how some pupils with different abilities are moved in and out of school placements, and the implications for equitable access to education. There is now clear evidence demonstrating that some pupils, once moved out of an educational placement, do not return to complete their education by Year 11. While some pupil movement might be expected due to changes of location or to a more 'specialised' provision, Ofsted reports a noticeable number of pupils who did not complete Year 11 in the placement they started in Year 7 (Bradbury, 2018). Hutchings and Crenna-Jenkins (2019) found that of the 2017 cohort of pupils, 61,123 pupils (10.1 per cent) had at least one unexplained exit from a school. This alarming statistic raises questions about how inclusive secondary schools are. Ofsted also analysed the number of unexplained pupil exits within secondary schools, and found that 340 schools in England were responsible for most of the cases (Bradbury, 2019). The data also demonstrate a disproportionality in relation to these 'missing' learners; the 61,123 children and young people not in a school placement were likely to be already marginalised and potentially vulnerable. As opposed to 'official' permanent school exclusion, these pupils were 'off-rolled', which Ofsted defines as:

> the practice of removing a pupil from the school roll without a formal, permanent exclusion or by encouraging a parent to remove their child from the school roll, when the removal is primarily in the interests of the school rather than in the best interests of the pupil.
>
> *(Ofsted 2019, p. 11)*

Hutchings and Crenna-Jenkins (2019) suggest that several vulnerable pupil groups are particularly likely to leave their school placements for unknown reasons, which cannot be accounted for by changes in care placements or address. Thomson (2019) reports that FFT Education Datalab analysis shows that off-rolling incidents for pupils with SEN Support or EHC plans have increased since 2014. Off-rolling is more problematic when it includes pupils moved to an apparently legitimate placement, but which is not in the pupil's best interests; for instance, moving a pupil with SEN Support to a special school when their educational needs could be met within a mainstream school.

Under Policy Option 2, all pupils would attend one school site; this is not an argument for all learners to attend mainstream schools and scrapping special/specialist provisions. Rather, maintaining community and belongingness is crucial to preventing educational and social exclusion when a pupil is permanently excluded (Gazeley, 2010). We envisage a school site where mainstream and specialist teachers work alongside one another to support all pupils, allowing all pupils to experience flexibility within curriculum provision and accessing appropriate educational experiences. If a pupil finds the 'usual' approach to curriculum delivery problematic, they would access alternative models of provision within the same site, so that they maintain their peer and staff connections. This option would not be unusual or only available to learners with different abilities and could indeed be set out as part of the EFC in Policy Option 1. Crucially, every learner could access some element of specialist or individualised support if required, and it would be expected that some learners would access this specialist provision more than others. We also argue that the unreliable and poor-quality Alternative Provision (AP) ideologically and practically advances the idea that some children can *never* be educated alongside their peers. While research evidence suggests that some AP provides high-quality educational experiences, offering respite for pupils and their schools, many AP providers do not provide high quality educational experiences (Mills and Thomson, 2018). Pupils entering AP become less visible to the wider educational community, and we argue that this 'middle space' between inclusion and exclusion can lead pupils to either transition back into school at best or at worst, into the criminal justice system.

In light of the worrisome statistics outlined previously and the related practice dilemmas for professionals who manage the exclusion process, both formal or less formal in the case of off-rolling (Done and Knowler, forthcoming), we argue for more transparency in relation to the movement of pupils who are at risk of exclusion from school. It is important to state that we are not arguing that the existing SEND system needs to be more efficient in order to promote transparency. Rather, we think that space and place are important factors in preventing permanent and informal exclusions; therefore, keeping pupils visible in school communities is an important dimension of Policy Option 2. We do not advocate for more medicalising or labelling of pupils to generate more resources for problematic pupils, because this is associated with the wider use of specialised/special provision – which encourages the idea that pupils are 'not educable', and could even threaten teacher professionalism because they do not have the 'special' knowledge needed to teach particular pupils (Done et al., 2015).

Policy option 3: teacher training

Policy Option 3 is designed to support teachers from the experienced to newly qualified teachers (NQTs) and everyone in between to become agents of inclusion and social justice (Pantić and Florian, 2015). In line with Booth's positioning stated earlier in this chapter, any future policy agenda with regards to meaningful inclusion must incorporate transforming current teacher practices because they have a considerable impact on the processes of inclusion and exclusion. A proposal to transform teaching practices and to view teachers as agents of change is not new and has been well researched previously (Pantić and Florian, 2015; Hattie, 2009; OECD, 2005) Currently, training opportunities provided to teachers to develop themselves as inclusive educators are inconsistent,[5] and the time, agency and autonomy that are required for teachers to develop inclusive pedagogy have been restricted. This may be due to the increasingly diversified teacher training routes available, a shortfall in the supply of teachers, and an increasing emphasis on school participation in league tables (Done and Murphy, 2018). There are serious concerns about retention rates of NQTs.[6] Although there may be several reasons for this significant dropout rate, it is not unreasonable to assume that teaching the most 'challenging' classes in their first year without proper support could be a significant factor (Lough, 2019).

Policy Option 3 is a proposal to design flexible partnership models between schools with different forms of governance and universities with dedicated SEND research centres. It is not calling for a national teacher training programme to be implemented; rather, it is about creating "a vision of a new democratic professionalism", where social justice and equity are embedded as part of the professional ethos (Anderson and Cohen, 2018, p. 24). Although university led-PGCE programmes tend to adopt a more integrated approach to linking research/scholarship with teaching practices, Initial Teacher Training (ITT) routes often rely on the existing knowledge base of experienced teachers, without reference to the latest scholarship in relation to equipping trainee teachers with the requisite awareness skills of individual pupil needs and how to engage in inclusive pedagogy (Winch et al., 2015). These partnership models will take the strengths and limitations of each individual school into account, as well as a more localised understanding of each school's context, and the demographics of its teaching staff and pupils. These partnership models will incorporate evaluation and catering to the training needs of experienced teachers and former teachers returning to the workforce. Pantić and Florian (2015) posit that for teachers to become agents of change, they require training in how to develop inclusive pedagogy. For Pantić and Florian (2015), engaging in inclusive pedagogy requires an epistemological shift, where teachers reject distinctions between 'most' and 'some' learners, and view the "complexity and diversity of learners as a natural consequence of humanity rather than portraying 'some children' as 'different' thereby creating an unhelpful hierarchy within diversity" (p. 342). It is important to note that this would not be a solitary and individual pursuit resting solely with teachers; rather universities and schools would work collaboratively through the use of mentorship schemes, workshops, lesson plans and reflective exercises to build the capacity of teachers to become inclusive educators. Moreover, this could also be seen as embedded within Policy 1, where democratic professionalism is deliberated and commonly agreed by all stakeholders.

As already stated, this proposal is not new and there are examples of similar practices in an international context. For instance, the Arbeitsstelle für Diversität und Unterrichtsentwicklung – Didaktische Werkstattis[7] supports research in teacher education as well as inclusive pedagogy by providing workshops, counselling sessions and teaching spaces for practicing teachers in the areas of literacy, numeracy and science in an inclusive context, as well as cross-curricular issues such as working with diverse classrooms and the development of individual education plans. Our proposal is similar to Didaktische Werkstattis in terms of support that universities can offer, but our proposed initiative differs in that we intend to include all teaching staff who interact or engage with learners with different abilities rather than just NQTs, because meaningful transformation requires commitment from all stakeholders in the school. This proposal is not without its limitations; firstly, different schools have different time and financial pressures, and it may be difficult to motivate all schools to participate in an initiative like this unless it is supported by wider changes in government policy. Secondly, if we intend to include all teachers and not just NQTs in this initiative, then it will be challenging for universities to provide a consistent level of support to teachers at various stages of their careers and in different educational settings.

Reflections

In this chapter, we have discussed what the future of inclusive education could look like if we consciously adopt a human rights perspective, where democratic participation for all learners is encouraged and valued. We do not offer a particular blueprint for inclusive policies, nor do we suggest that the possible options discussed previously are the most effective solutions to developing inclusive practices. We have, however, stressed that any future inclusive education policies must examine the processes of both inclusion and exclusion that affect the participation, experiences and the outcomes for learners with different abilities.

Policy options

The issues raised in this chapter led to a number of policy options:

Policy 1: this entails an Education Framework Commission (EFC) with a 10-year 'buy in', established and operated independently from government with membership extending to all relevant stakeholders. The EFC should be viewed as a way to facilitate consultation between different political parties on key issues.

Policy 2: this focuses on improving all learners' experiences, introducing the concept of a single-site school for all children including learners with different abilities, varying sensory and/or physical needs, and social, emotional and mental health needs. It incorporates different models of school governance according to the local context.

Policy 3: this focuses on developing teacher capabilities, developing more responsive and flexible partnership models between schools and SEND teams within universities in order to develop teacher education programmes that centre on teacher capacity building in ethics and inclusive pedagogy.

The penultimate chapter provides further reflections and an executive summary of options, consequences and cautionary tales.

Acknowledgements

We would like to thank Professor Brahm Norwich for providing critical feedback which helped in the writing of this chapter.

Notes

1 A recent focus report published by Local Government and Social Care Ombudsman (LGSCO) (LGSCO, 2019) details the experiences of learners with different abilities and their families with the Education, Health and Care (EHC) plan process. The report revealed that nearly nine out of 10 cases (87 per cent) investigated had serious issues, including severe delays in receiving provisions of up to 90 weeks, a lack of strategic partnership working with third parties, a lack of oversight by senior staff, and an inadequate system for funding SEND support (LGSCO, 2019).

2 According to one Ofsted Inspection Report, 5,800 learners with different abilities left school between years 10 and 11, and it is suspected that a significant proportion of them were 'off-rolled' (Knowler and Done, 2019).

3 There are other tensions that Norwich (2019) explores in detail which affect the delivery of SEN provisions, such as the social model of disability versus the medical model of disability, inclusion versus standards agenda, or participation (learner's agency) versus protection (other's agency).

4 Established in 2016, the SMC has a rigorous membership process and includes leading scholars specialising in poverty amelioration from different backgrounds, alongside data and analytical experts and those professionals with experience of supporting people living in poverty.

5 For instance, whilst teachers at maintained schools are all statutorily bound to have Qualified Teacher Status (QTS), academies and free schools are permitted to employ teachers without QTS.

6 Statistics from a government school workforce report in England suggests that 15.3 per cent of NQTs in 2017 were no longer in the workforce in 2018 (DfE, 2019b). In other words, one in seven NQTs drop out in their first year of employment.

7 Didaktische Werkstattis is a collaboration between the Institute for Special Educational Needs and Inclusion, the Institute for Primary Education, and the Ministry of Culture and Education in Hessen, Germany (European Agency for Special Needs and Inclusive Education, 2015).

References

Allan, J. and Youdell, D. (2017) Ghostings, materialisations and flows in Britain's special educational needs and disability assemblage. *Discourse: Studies in the Cultural Politics of Education*, 38(1), pp. 70–82.

Anderson, G.L. and Cohen, M.I. (2018) *The new democratic professional in education: Confronting markets, metrics, and managerialism.* New York: Teachers College Press.

Barton, L. (1997) Inclusive education: Romantic, subversive or realistic? *International Journal of Inclusive Education*, 1(3), pp. 231–242, DOI: 10.1080/1360311970010301.

Booth, T. (1996) Stories of exclusion: Natural and unnatural selection. In Blyth, E. and Milner, J. (eds.), *Exclusion from school: Inter-professional issues for policy and practice*. London: Routledge.

Booth, T. and Ainscow, M. (2011) *Index for inclusion; Developing learning and participation in schools*, 3rd Edition. Bristol: CSIE.

Bradbury, J. (2018, June 26) Off-rolling: Using data to see a fuller picture [blog]. Retrieved from https://educationinspection.blog.gov.uk/2018/06/26/off-rolling-using-data-to-see-a-fuller-picture/

Bradbury, J. (2019, September 9) Off-rolling: An update on recent analysis [blog]. Retrieved from https://educationinspection.blog.gov.uk/2019/09/06/off-rolling-an-update-on-recent-analysis/

Crouch, C. (2012, June 12) There is an alternative to neoliberalism that still understands the markets. *The Guardian*. Retrieved from www.theguardian.com/commentisfree/2012/jun/27/alternative-neoliberalism-still-understands-markets (Accessed October 14, 2019).

Department for Children, Schools and Families (2009) *Lamb inquiry: Special educational needs and parental confidence (Final Report)*. Nottingham: DFCS. Retrieved from http://webarchive.nationalarchives.gov.uk/20130401151715/www.education.gov.uk/publications/standard/publicationdetail/page1/dcsf-01143-2009

Department for Education (1994) *Code of practice on the identification and assessment of special educational needs*. London: HMSO.

Department for Education (2011) Support and aspiration: A new approach to special educational needs and disability, a consultation (Green Paper) Cm8027. London: HMSO. Retrieved from www.education.gov.uk/publications/standard/publicationDetail/Page1/CM%208027 (Accessed October 27, 2019).

Department for Education (2015) SEND Code of Practice: 0–25 Years, London: DfE.

Department for Education (2019a) *Special education needs in England*. January. Retrieved from www.gov.uk/government/statistics/special-educational-needs-in-england-january-2019 (Accessed October 27, 2019).

Department for Education (2019b) *School workforce in England*. November 2018. https://assets.publishing.service.gov.uk/government/uploads/system/uploads/attachment_data/file/811622/SWFC_MainText.pdf

Department for Education (DfE) and Department of Health (DfH) (2015) *Special educational needs and disability code of practice: 0 to 25 years*. London: DfE.

DfES (Department for Education and Skills) (2015) *Special educational needs code of practice*. Nottinghamshire: DfES. Retrieved from http://webarchive.nationalarchives.gov.uk/20130401151715/www.education.gov.uk/publications/eOrderingDownload/0581-2001-SEN-CodeofPractice.pdf

Done, E. J. and Knowler, H. (forthcoming) Painful invisibilities: Roll management or 'off-rolling' and professional identity submitted to *British Education Research Journal*.

Done, E. J. and Murphy, M. (2018) The responsibilisation of teachers: A neoliberal solution to the problem of inclusion. *Discourse: Studies in the Cultural Politics of Education*, 39(1), pp. 142–155, DOI: 10.1080/01596306.2016.1243517

Done, E. J., Murphy, M. and Knowler, H. (2015) Mandatory accreditation for Special Educational Needs Co-ordinators: Biopolitics, neoliberal managerialism and the Deleuzo – Guattarian 'war machine'. *Journal of Education Policy*, 30(1), pp. 86–100.

Elliott, J. and Grigorenko, E.L. (2014) *The dyslexia debate*. Cambridge: Cambridge University Press.

European Agency for Special Needs and Inclusive Education (2015) *Empowering teachers to promote inclusive education: A case study of approaches to training and support for inclusive teacher practice*. Odense, Denmark: European Agency for Special Needs and Inclusive Education. www.european-agency.org/sites/default/files/Empowering%20Teachers%20

to%20Promote%20Inclusive%20Education.%20A%20case%20study.pdf (Accessed October 22, 2019).

Gazeley, L. (2010) The role of school exclusion processes in the re-production of social and educational disadvantage. *British Journal of Educational Studies*, 58 (3) pp. 293–309. ISSN 0007-1005

Graham, L. (2008) From ABCs to ADHD: The role of schooling in the construction of behaviour disorder and production of disorderly objects. *International Journal of Inclusive Education*, 12 (1), pp. 7–33, DOI: 10.1080/13603110701683311

Hattie, J. (2009) *Visible learning: A synthesis of over 800 meta-analyses relating to achievement.* 1st edition. London: Routledge.

Hellawell, B. (2019) An ethical audit of the SEND CoP 2015: Professional partnership working and the division of ethical labour. *Journal of Research in Special Educational Needs*, 19 (1), pp. 15–26.

House of Commons Education and Skills Select Committee. (2006) *Special educational needs: Third report of session 2005, 2006* (Volume 1) Report, together with formal minutes. London: Stationery Office.

Hutchings, J. and Crenna-Jenkins, W. (2019) *Unexplained exits from school: Further analysis by multi academy trust and local authority Education Policy Institute.* https://epi.org.uk/wp-content/uploads/2019/10/Unexplained-pupil-moves_LAs-MATs_EPI-2019.pdf

Knowler, H. (2009) Where should pupils who experience social, emotional and behavioural difficulties be educated? In Gibson, S. and Haynes, J. (eds.), *Perspectives on participation and inclusion engaging education.* London: A&C Black.

Knowler, H. and Done, E. (2019) Exploring senior leaders' experiences of off-rolling in mainstream secondary schools in England. *BERA Blog Post.* www.bera.ac.uk/blog/exploring-senior-leaders-experiences-of-off-rolling-in-mainstream-secondary-schools-in-england (Accessed October 28, 2019).

Lehane, T. (2017) "SEN's completely different now": Critical discourse analysis of three "Codes of Practice for Special Educational Needs" (1994, 2001, 2015). *Educational Review*, 69 (1), pp. 51–67, DOI: 10.1080/00131911.2016.1237478

Local Government & Social Care Ombudsman (LGSCO) (2019) *Not going to plan? – Education, health and care plans two years on.* Coventry: Local Government and Social Care Ombudsman. www.lgo.org.uk/information-centre/news/2019/oct/a-system-in-crisis-ombudsman-complaints-about-special-educational-needs-at-alarming-level (Accessed October 22, 2019).

Lough, C. (2019, October 21) Should we keep sending NQTs 'over the top'? *Times Education Supplement.* www.tes.com/news/should-we-keep-sending-nqts-over-top (Accessed October 28, 2019).

Mills, M. and Thomson, P. (2018) Investigative report into alternative provision reference. DFE-RR859 https://assets.publishing.service.gov.uk/government/uploads/system/uploads/attachment_data/file/748910/Investigative_research_into_alternative_provision.pdf

National Autistic Society (2016) *School report 2016: Two years on, how is the new special educational needs and disability (SEND) system meeting the needs of children and young people on the autism spectrum in England?* London: NAS.

Norwich, B. (1996) Special needs education or education for all: Connective specialisation and ideological impurity. *British Journal of Special Education,* 23, pp. 100–104, DOI: 10.1111/j.1467-8578.1996.tb00957.x

Norwich, B. (2013) *Addressing tensions and dilemmas in inclusive education.* Abingdon: Routledge.

Norwich, B. and Eaton, A. (2015) The new special educational needs (SEN) legislation in England and implications for services for children and young people with social, emotional and behavioural difficulties. *Emotional and Behavioural Difficulties*, 20 (2), pp. 117–132.

Norwich, B. (2019) From the Warnock report (1978) to an education framework commission: A novel contemporary approach to educational policy making for pupils with special educational needs/disabilities. *Frontiers Education*, 4 (72), DOI: 10.3389/feduc.2019.00072

OECD. (2005) *Teachers matter: Attracting, developing and retaining effective teachers*. Paris: OECD Publishing.

Oftsed (2019) *The education inspection framework*. Manchester: The Office for Standards in Education, Children's Services and Skills. https://assets.publishing.service.gov.uk/government/uploads/system/uploads/attachment_data/file/801429/Education_inspection_framework.pdf (Accessed October 22, 2019).

Pantić, N. and Florian, L. (2015) Developing teachers as agents of inclusion and social justice. *Education Inquiry*, 6 (3), pp. 333–351, DOI: 10.3402/edui.v6.27311

Pulsford, M. and Rizvi, S. (2019) Becoming an inclusive educator: Developing your practice as a mainstream teacher of pupils with SEND. In Capel, S., Lawrence, J., Leask, M. and Younie, S. (eds.), *Surviving and thriving in the secondary school: The NQT's essential companion*, 1st edition. London: Routledge.

Social Metrics Commission (SMC). (2018) *A new measure of poverty for the UK*. London: Social Metrics Commission.

Thomas, D. (2019, May 9) A data history of permanent exclusions and school moves [blog]. Retrieved from https://ffteducationdatalab.org.uk/2019/05/a-data-history-of-permanent-exclusions-and-school-moves/

Tomlinson, S. (2017) *A Sociology of special and inclusive education: Exploring the manufacture of inability*. Abingdon: Routledge.

UNESCO (1994) *The Salamanca statement and framework for action on special needs education*. Paris: UNESCO, Ministry of Education, Spain.

United Nations (2006) *Convention on the rights of persons with disabilities*. New York: United Nations. www.un.org/development/desa/disabilities/convention-on-the-rights-of-persons-with-disabilities.html (Accessed October 29, 2019).

Warnock Report (1978) *Special educational needs. Report of the committee of enquiry into the education of handicapped children and young people*. London: Her Majesty's Stationery Office.

Winch, C., Oancea, A. and Orchard, J. (2015) The contribution of educational research to teachers' professional learning: Philosophical understandings. *Oxford Review of Education*, 41 (2), pp. 202–216, DOI: 10.1080/03054985.2015.1017406

11

ADULT AND FURTHER EDUCATION

The impact of austerity on life chances and wellbeing

Sharon Clancy

Introduction

> Research from academic and institutional sources, over several decades, has shown that participation in all forms of post-compulsory education has a range of potential benefits relevant to health outcomes, such as stimulating further personal development which may provide the opportunity to progress in the labour market, as well as other individual benefits such as increased confidence and self-efficacy.

This chapter examines adult education and the impact of austerity on the provision and the need to prioritise lifelong learning in a new national education system.

Lifelong learning has a profound impact on individual lives and communities – politically, socially, economically and educationally – yet it remains the 'Cinderella' of the education system. We learn at times of transition and change; we learn to adapt to new work or to develop new skills; we learn for pleasure, for mental and physical wellbeing and for social contact, to assimilate new ideas and to understand our place in the world and how governance, power and resources are organised. Adult education has been historically, and remains, vital to democratic life, social cohesion, economic prosperity, and individual wellbeing.

In *Fair Society, Healthy Lives* (2010), Michael Marmot identified the critical importance of education as a means of empowerment – conferring a sense of control over one's life – and suggested that positive health outcomes are significantly more influenced by social than by clinical determinants. In his subsequent work, Marmot's evidence showed that an individual's health and wellbeing is 70% driven by social determinants and only 30% by clinical factors.[1] These, in turn, are positively associated with health behaviours and increased social capital, which is also associated with better health. Learning as a form of empowerment creates a virtuous circle. Research from academic and institutional sources, over several decades,[2] has shown that participation in all forms of post-compulsory education has a range of potential benefits relevant to health outcomes, such as stimulating further personal development which may provide the opportunity to progress in the labour market, as well as other individual benefits, such as increased confidence and self-efficacy.

Yet, despite a critical focus on lifelong learning within the European Union since the 1990s and growing research evidence on the wider benefits of adult learning, successive governments and policy makers over the last three decades have failed to grasp conceptions of learning beyond skills and the workplace, taking an increasingly market-driven perspective on education (see Holford, 2016).[3] The UK is now the most profoundly unequal society in Europe (see Dorling, 2017[4]), and as Marmot identified in his Review, the social gradient of health inequalities and the deleterious impact of a lower social and economic status on an individual's overall health and wellbeing demonstrates the impact of place and poverty. Inequalities arise from a complex interaction of factors – housing, income, education, social isolation, disability – all of which are strongly affected by an individual's economic and social status. Professor Philip Alston, the Special Rapporteur on extreme poverty and human rights, stated in 2018 that the Austerity agenda, with its emphasis on work at all costs in the face of swingeing cuts, has left swathes of the least visible people in the UK in extreme precarity and is in danger of destroying the post-war British welfare state. Austerity measures do not tackle the underlying causes of inequality and create a dangerous foment:

> by emphasizing work as a panacea for poverty against all evidence and dismantling the community support, benefits, and public services on which so many rely, the government has created a highly combustible situation that will have dire consequences.[5]

Yet in England, much of the civil society and community infrastructure that we built together in the second half of the 20th century, in the post-war settlement period, is disappearing before our eyes, overtly or by stealth. Civic spaces, outside the market, where informal, community-based learning has flourished, are in jeopardy. The reading groups, community groups, faith groups, activist projects which are based on shared interests, concerns and ideas and spring from grass roots needs and initiatives struggle for funding whilst the large state-sanctioned charities grow and prosper. Residential adult education colleges, such as Ruskin and Northern College, offering short- and long-term courses for non-traditional students, have dwindled in number from 35 in the post-war period to four. Such colleges, historically, developed strong links with both the trade union and labour movements in terms of their educational offer, what Pollins described as "the promotion in a residential setting of liberal education for working class students, recruited mainly from the trade unions" (Pollins, 1984, p. 63[6]). Universities no longer work with local communities delivering extra-mural courses or evening classes and schemes connected with the trade unions and the Workers Educational Association (WEA).

Instead, the number of part-time and mature students aged 17–60 in England who previously attended Higher Education institutions, many through extra mural and continuing education routes, has halved in a decade: from 96,575 in 2006/07 to 44,110 in 2016/17 (Department for Education, 2017[7]). Participation rates in adult learning and education have fallen across all levels of education and across the entire UK: with ongoing decline in government-funded part-time educational provision, fewer opportunities are available in particular for the most disadvantaged adults. In 2017, Les Ebdon, Director of Fair Access to Higher Education, urged colleges and universities to 'reach out to prospective adult learners', who are more likely to be part-time learners and from specifically under-represented groups – such as students from white working-class backgrounds, from certain BME groups and students with disabilities:

> We do know that they are disproportionately more likely to be from disadvantaged backgrounds than those who enter higher education straight from school. We also know that adult learners are far more likely to study part-time. And with the dramatic decline in part-time numbers since 2010 showing no sign of levelling off, numbers of adult learners look set to continue dropping unless drastic action is taken.
>
> *(OFFA – Office for Fair Access, 2017, Foreword[8])*

Further education

For a time the UK was at the top of the European league in terms of lifelong learning, with around 20% of working-age adults participating in learning by the early 2000s. However, these short-term gains have been comprehensively lost in the last 10 years. This is particularly notable in colleges of Further Education (FE), in which the number of adults (aged 19 and over) on FE courses in England fell from 3.16 million in 2010/11 to 2.18 million in 2017/18 (Higher Education Statistics Agency, 2018[9]).

Part of this results from the introduction of fees in 2010, which has had a dramatic impact, in Further as well as Higher Education. For many part-time and mature learners in FE, often juggling competing financial demands, there may be a genuine fear of taking on loans and of incurring debt. Drawn predominantly from the locality – in contrast to many students in Higher Education[10] – FE students may face multiple disadvantages economically and socially. Levels of participation in lifelong learning are profoundly unequal among different groups in society, with the most disadvantaged people the most severely affected. While 46 per cent of those who had left full-time education at the age of 21 or later were still participating in learning, only 21% of those who left school at 16 or earlier said they were engaged in learning. At the same time, in relation to basic skills in literacy and numeracy, the UK compares poorly internationally, with 9 million adults of working age with low basic skills.

We are also facing a crisis in mental health, much of which impacts directly on adult education providers and is often a result of the ruthless speed and pace of life today which many people feel leaves them behind. An Association of Colleges (AoC) survey (2015) found that in 66% of respondent colleges "the number of students with mental health difficulties had 'significantly increased' in the previous three years". In addition, "75% felt that their college had 'significant numbers' of students who had undisclosed mental health difficulties", while all reported having students with depression, anxiety or who were self-harming (Association of Colleges, 2015[11]).

A brief history . . .

The Further Education sector in the UK has a proud history of serving local people and of responding to industry and technical needs, coming into its own after the Second World War. In Britain, before the 1944 Education Act, many young people left school at 14, often to seek work, in order to contribute to the economic needs of the family; the Education Act decreed that attendance in full-time education for 15- to-18-year-olds would no longer be entirely voluntary. From the 1950s to the 1970s the FE sector enjoyed a boom period. A major white paper, *Technical Education*, in 1956, offered targeted spending of over £70 million over eight years to help counter the lack of skilled workers in technologies across the board, in key urban centres and regional and local satellite colleges. FE colleges built strong links with local businesses and employers. By the 1970s, after much of the restructuring and rebuilding work which had taken place in the two decades following the war, there was a shift in emphasis towards teaching a wider range of courses, both academic and vocational, including A-levels and BTEC (Business and Technology Education Council) qualifications. This period also marked a move away from skills training in traditional trades where lifelong jobs were no longer the norm, at a time when heavy industry and manufacturing were in decline.

The period of financial difficulty began for many FE colleges in the 1980s and 1990s during a time of increasing unemployment for young people, a fall in student numbers and the collapse of apprenticeship schemes. These developments helped fuel a government belief that colleges ran better governed independently as incorporated bodies, as evidenced in the 1992 Further and Higher Education Act, which removed colleges from Local Education Authority (LEA) control (and funding) and led to a spate of college mergers. Funding instead came directly from the government-appointed Further Education Funding Council (now the Education and Skills Funding Agency – ESFA, a merger of the Education Funding Agency and the Skills Funding Agency[12]). Finance was based explicitly on output and performance (the numbers of students enrolling, the amount of teaching/learning time and the number of courses completed, qualifications gained and jobs secured).

Since incorporation, the language of business has become much more prevalent in the FE sector, with competition and "market forces and managerial logics" (Scott, 2016, p. 57[13]) at the forefront. Before the Act, demands for services came from employers and the local educational marketplace through the LEA, though there was considerable local variation and inconsistency in terms of LEA interest, support and expenditure across the country. In the main, colleges had been historically left "to take their own routes and devise their own futures" (Ainley and Bailey, 1997, p. 11[14]), despite ties to education/training and employment policy objectives.

Incorporation placed a compulsion upon individual college senior management teams to secure and develop new sources of finance, in order to remain solvent and to compete on a commercial basis with other colleges and providers. Incorporation demonstrated an ideological faith by the then Conservative government in market forces as the best means of driving up both the quality and efficiency of educational provision, and a political determination to reduce the power and influence of LEAs, many of which were then controlled by either Labour or the Liberal Democrats. In the 2014 *College Governance: A Guide*, the Foreword makes it clear that the then Coalition government was still concerned that colleges placed too much emphasis on 'government' and state engagement and too little on being competitive within the educational market. They couched the renewed emphasis on the market in terms of 'freedom and flexibility':

> These freedoms and flexibilities allow colleges to act as autonomous institutions, providing the education and training that individuals, employers and the nation need to succeed in the global race. With this increased freedom comes increased responsibility within a clear accountability framework.[15]

FE now . . .

In the early 1990s there were almost 500 colleges in England. The figure is now 257 colleges in England and 303 across the whole of the UK (February 2019[16]). Currently FE Colleges offer education and training in industry-standard facilities, usually delivered by teaching staff who have professional experience in a given field – such as engineering, hospitality, IT, construction and the creative arts. FE Colleges teach across a range of abilities and skills, offering academic and vocational teaching, from basic skills, particularly English and maths, through to postgraduate qualifications. According to the UK government website, FE is now defined as including "any study after secondary education that is not part of higher education (that is, not taken as part of an undergraduate or graduate degree)".[17] FE also includes three types of technical and applied qualifications for 16-to-19-year-olds, including level 3 technical level qualifications which enable students to specialise in a specific technical job, level 2 technical certificates to help students to gain

employment or to progress to another technical level and applied general qualifications, which support continued general education at advanced level through
applied learning.

A refocussing of budgets towards apprenticeships means that adult education
relating to basic skills, school level qualifications, vocational courses delivered by
colleges and personal and social learning (community education and learning for
interest) is becoming less prevalent in England. Government cutbacks following the
economic downturn have led to a drop in training four times greater than in any
other European country, according to the Institute for Public Policy Research.[18]
According to Association of Colleges data analysis (May 2017), one million adult
education and training places have been lost in the 10 years from 2005–2006 to
2015–2016 with total numbers outside apprenticeships falling from 2.7 million
to 1.6 million. Furthermore, the growing internet-based economy in the United
Kingdom and the strong recovery of construction markets have created a serious
shortage of related skills within the UK workforce. This skills shortage, possibly
fueled by the huge loss in adult education and training places over the last decade,
has resulted in a renewed focus on vocational training from the government and has
fuelled demand for courses specialising in new skill sets.[19]

Whilst much of the current emphasis in Further Education is on young adults,
the learner picture is complex, with a very diverse group of adult learners seeking
to learn at different points in their lives. According to the Association of Colleges (AoC),[20] in 2018/19 FE colleges prepared 2.2 million students with valuable
employability skills, helping to develop their career opportunities. A total of 685,000
16-to-18-year-olds study in colleges and an additional 76,000 16-to-18-year-olds
undertake an Apprenticeship course. The FE sector has a strong diversity remit and
the student population reflects this. Some 92,000 college students are aged 60 and
above, while 25% of students are from an ethnic minority background and 23%
have a learning difficulty/disability. The average age of a college student is 29 and
the vast majority of students are over 25 – with 761,000 16–18-year-olds studying
in an FE college, 378,000 19–24-year-olds and 1,022,000 over 25.

There have been major shifts in how adult education is funded over the past two
decades. In the early 2000s, "the government spent around £3 billion a year . . .
on education and training for those over 19" (Association of Colleges, 2018, p. 1).
The Coalition government's *Further Education – New Horizon: Investing in Skills
for Sustainable Growth*, published in November 2010, announced that full funding
would be available to only those students with very low skills, with the expectation that learners and employers would contribute to the costs of intermediate and
higher level courses. The document also ushered in the abolition of grant funding
and introduced loans. The 2010 Comprehensive Spending Review set out the
parameters for public spending over the period 2011–2012 to 2014–2015. Under
the settlement, the adult FE resource budget was to fall by 25% from a baseline of
£4.3 billion in 2010–2011 to £3.2 billion in 2014–2015.[21] This process was then
extended and intensified in the 2013 Spending Round in which it was announced

that the spending review settlement would continue to 2015–2016 and that further savings to the FE budget of "at least £260 million" in 2015–2016 were to be made, "by prioritising higher value qualifications, and reducing non-participation spending".[22]

In 2016/2017, although the government allocated £3 billion to the Skills Funding Agency, comparable to the allocation in the early 2000s, this was to be split in "very different ways": £260 million was allocated via FE loans (and "not all of it is being used"), and £1 billion to apprenticeships for those aged over 19. Effectively, therefore, non-apprenticeship funding now comprises a much smaller proportion of an already reduced adult education budget. Due to the mismatch between student demand and resource allocation, £200 million – 13% of the £1.5 billion adult education budget – went unspent within the FE sector in 2016/2017 (Association of Colleges, 2018, p. 2).

Devolution is another factor in the current crisis. Until the period 2019–2020 the government, through the ESFA, offered funding to Local Authorities, Further Education Colleges and other adult education providers in England for the provision of what has been designated as 'Community Learning'. Now, however, with the devolution of Adult Education to six combined authority areas and the Greater London authority this provision is under serious threat and in some cases there are concerns that this type of learning will no longer be funded nor provided. This will have a major impact both on the number of students who have benefited from these types of courses, often the hardest to engage in learning, and also on local communities, especially those in the most disadvantaged areas. The Community Learning budget has helped adults through cultural engagement locally and on a wider societal level, and has dealt explicitly with issues related to health and well-being. The reduction in this type of learning is likely to reduce civic engagement, including volunteering, to impact on social integration, and to increase health and welfare costs.

Greed and inequality – the wages scandal

According to *The Guardian*, "Further Education has experienced an 8% real terms cut since 2010/11 causing course closures, job losses and reductions in student support services" (*The Guardian*, 18 September 2018). Continuing financial and resourcing issues and a shift in focus towards apprenticeships have also impacted significantly on staffing levels and the number of staff overall, and teaching staff in particular, has declined. According to the Further Education Workforce Data for England (2017),[23] looking at trends over time, we can see that the FE workforce has been declining at an average rate of around 3% per year. Between 2011–2012 and 2014–2015, the number of full-time equivalent employees in FE Colleges fell by 12,300 FTEs.

Cuts to spending in the FE sector have come at a time of increasing divisions relating to terms and conditions for staff on the ground, particularly teaching staff, and those in the top tier of management. Seventy percent of colleges reported having offered voluntary redundancies and 61% reported having undertaken compulsory redundancies in 2015/16. The past few years have increasingly seen jobs offered on fixed-term contracts, usually for one or two years, and part-time work for lecturers has become the norm, with many now finding themselves working across schools, FE colleges and community learning centres on a range of contracts. Around half of all FE contracts are part-time, a proportion considerably higher than in the general UK workforce which stands at 27%.[24] In the AoC/TES's 2018 survey of staff perceptions of the most problematic issues in FE, the top three concerns related to funding restrictions, a lack of capital funding and staff pay.[25] Although there are guidelines on pay and conditions of service recommended by the union (UCU), colleges are able to set their own salary scales and many do. The College Workforce survey shows that 95% of colleges use flexible contracts and the average college has 21% of its staff on such contracts. Added to this sense of precarity, entitlement to sick pay and holiday pay and access to pension schemes depends on whether staff are employed directly or through an agency and varies between employers.

At the same time, inflated pay for principals has become an ongoing issue. An article from the TES in 2017 indicates that, according to data from the ESFA, 12 colleges paid their leaders £200,000 or more – up by 50% from the previous year. Andrew Harden, head of Further Education at the University and College Union, stated in the article that: "College leaders who tell staff that the money is not there for a fair pay rise – all while pocketing massive pay rises themselves – are an embarrassment to the sector".[26] This is at the same time as demands relating to terms and conditions for general staff fell on stony ground and a series of strikes took place (see Nottingham College – www.tes.com/news/15-days-strikes-threatened-over-college-contracts).

Reflections

The issues raised in this chapter have aimed to demonstrate the vital role FE plays for local people and local economies. This leads to a number of policy options. Your choice will depend on the kind of society that you want to create: one which supports lifelong learning opportunities for people from all backgrounds and or one that limits opportunities for most of the population.

Policy options

The issues raised in this chapter lead to a number of policy options:

   Policy Option 1: status quo
   Policy Option 2: reform: address the issues raised in the chapter

Make lifelong education widely available with scholarships/fee waivers for those who meet particular criteria: refocus FE/vocational colleges to ensure they are responsive to local needs and recognise the need for democratic accountability in their governance structures, requiring representation from relevant local authorities, and recommending membership from local community organisations and trades unions. Monitor access and provision to ensure countrywide equity including for rural and remote areas perhaps by developing online provision. Introduce national standards for working conditions and senior pay levels.

The penultimate chapter provides further reflections and an executive summary of options, consequences and cautionary tales.

Notes

1 *Fair Society, Healthy Lives* (2010), The Marmot Review, Strategic Review of health inequalities in England post-2010
2 Mental Health Foundation (2011), *Learning for Life: Adult learning, Mental Health and Wellbeing*. London: Mental Health Foundation; Association of Colleges (2015), "Survey on Students with Mental Health Conditions in Further Education", Association of Colleges, London; Mezirow, J. (1997), *Transformative Learning: Theory to Practice*. New Directions for Adult and Continuing Education, No. 74, Summer. San Francisco, CA: Jossey-Bass Publishers.
3 Holford, J. (2016), The Misuses of Sustainability: Adult Education, Citizenship and the Dead Hand of Neoliberalism. *International Review of Education, 62*(5), 541–561. doi:10.1007/s11159-016-9591-4
4 Dorling, D. (2017), Turning the Tide on Inequality. In H. Meyer (Ed.), *Inequality in Europe* (pp. 35–43). Berlin: Social Europe.
5 Statement on Visit to the United Kingdom, by Professor Philip Alston, United Nations Special Rapporteur on extreme poverty and human rights, 16 November 2018, United Nations Human Rights, Office of the High Commissioner, p. 16.
6 Pollins, H. (1984), *The History of Ruskin College*. Oxford: Ruskin College Library Occasional Publication No. 3.
7 Department for Education (2017), "Further Education and Skills in England", No. SFR07/2017, Table 1.1, available at: www.gov.uk/government/uploads/system/uploads/attachment_data/file/5990 57/SFR07–2017-vocational-qualifications-update.pdf (accessed 6 March 2018)
8 Office for Fair Access (OFFA) (2017), "Understanding the Impact of Outreach on Access to Higher Education for Adult Learners from Disadvantaged Backgrounds: An Institutional Response", OFFA, London, available at: www.OFFA.org.uk/wp-content/uploads/2017/07/Final-Report-Understanding-the-impact-of-outreach-on-access-to-higher-education-for-disadvantaged-adultlearners-docx.pdf (accessed 31 July 2017).
9 Higher Education Statistics Agency (2018), "Higher Education Student Data", available at: www.hesa.ac.uk/data-and-analysis/students (accessed 6 March 2018).
10 AoC College Key Facts – 2018/19, available at: www.aoc.co.uk/sites/default/files/College%20Key%20Facts%202018-19.pdf
11 Association of Colleges (2015), "Survey on Students with Mental Health Conditions in Further Education", Association of Colleges, London.
12 The Education and Skills Funding Agency is an executive agency of the Department for Education and exercises functions on behalf of the Secretary of State for Education. It is also a European Social Fund co-financing organisation and helps deliver the learning and skills elements of local European Structural and Investment Fund strategies. The ESFA works through a set of training organisations. These organisations are mainly colleges, training organisations and employers that have a funding agreement to provide education and training.

13 Scott, W.R. and Biag, M. (2016), "The Changing Ecology of U.S. Higher Education: An Organization Field Perspective", Research in the Sociology of Organizations, v. 46, 2016

14 Ainley, P. and Bailey, B. (1997), *The Business of Learning*. London: Cassell.

15 Department for Business, Innovation and Skills, College Governance: A Guide, August 2014.

16 AoC, available at: www.aoc.co.uk/about-colleges/research-and-stats/key-further-edu cation-statistics

17 Gov.uk, available at: www.gov.uk/further-education-courses

18 IPPR, 18/2/17 Skills gap threat to post-Brexit economy – UK employers spend £6bn less on skills than Euro average, available at: www.ippr.org/news-and-media/press-releases/skills-gap-threat-to-post-brexit-economy-uk-employers-spend-6bn-less-on-skills-than-euro-average

19 Technical & Vocational Education in the UK: Market Research Report, SIC P85.410, Jan 2017.

20 AoC College Key Facts – 2018/19, available at: www.aoc.co.uk/sites/default/files/Col-lege%20Key%20Facts%202018-19.pdf

21 Department for Business, Innovation and Skills Spending Review Settlement, BIS, 20 October 2010.

22 HM Treasury, Spending Round 2013, Cm 8639, June 2013, p. 40.

23 Further Education Workforce Data for England, Analysis of the 2015–2016 Staff Indi-vidualised Record (SIR) data, Frontier Economics – June 2017.

24 ONS UK Labour Market Statistics: March 2017, available at: www.ons.gov.uk/employ mentandlabourmarket/peopleinwork/employmentandemployeetypes/bulletins/ukla bourmarket/mar2017 (Tes – formerly known as the Times Educational Supplement)

25 "Issues facing colleges" An Association of Colleges (AoC) survey in partnership with Tes May 2018

26 TES, 28th April 2017 Julia Belgutay, Will Martin & Stephen Exley, Colleges spend more on principal pay while staff face pay freeze – College chief pay rises an 'embarrassment for the sector'

SECTION 4

Curriculum, assessment, leadership and accountability

Section 4 focuses on issues and policy options in relation to curriculum, assessment, leadership and accountability.

Chapter 12 reviews curriculum options and is set against the background of the current policy context in in England. The Three Futures model developed by Young (2014) in his discussion of 'powerful knowledge' is taken as a starting point. It examines these futures as potential policy options with a preferred future based on the development of both 'powerful knowledge and creative know-how'.

Chapter 13 considers complex issues surrounding national assessment drawing on both research and practice from various international assessment systems. It considers three policy options based on firstly high-stakes testing only, secondly on external examinations combined with formative assessment and thirdly on cumulative assessment which is both cumulative and synoptic.

Chapter 14 addresses school leadership and the role of school leaders as innovators within a national education service. It explores the interface between policy, place, professionals and performance with reference to national education services. In turn it argues that where governments pursue the ideology of the small state and marketisation in education that privatisation, regional inequality, managerialism and inequitable outcomes follow.

Chapter 15 considers an alternative approach to accountability and inspection in Initial Teacher Education. It does so by considering the case of Finnish Teacher Education which is an exemplary case study of an enhancement-led quality assurance approach. It offers the option of an approach to accountability based on trust that is seen as an aspect that requires continuous work.

Chapter 16 discusses different models for accountability and inspection of schools. The chapter highlights two contrasting value sets underpinning decisions about how to manage people in order to achieve high quality outcomes. By drawing on management theory these are categorised as 'authoritarian' and 'common good'. Policy options include the replacement of the tarnished Ofsted brand with a system based on peer review, peer challange, external data gathering for benchmarking and trend identification, accompanied by support.

Section 5 which follows examines issues and policy options related to initial teacher education and professional development.

12

THE CURRICULUM

Developing powerful knowledge and creative know-how

Brian Hudson, with Chris Shelton

Introduction

The nature of the term 'curriculum' is complex, multi-layered and contested, being "conceived differently at different times by different scholars working in different countries and regions, working in different institutional settings with differing demands: universities, governments, schools, and corporations" (Jung and Pinar, 2016). As Stenhouse (1980) observed:

> What is curriculum as we now understand the word? . . . It is not a syllabus – a mere list of content to be covered – nor even is it what German speakers would call a Lehrplan. . . . Nor is it in our understanding of a list of objectives. Let me claim that it is a symbolic or meaningful object, like Shakespeare's first folio, not like a lawnmower; like the pieces and board of chess, not like an apple tree. It has a physical existence but also a meaning incarnate in words or pictures or sound or games or whatever . . . by virtue of their meaningfulness curricula are not simply means to improve teaching but are expressions of ideas to improve teachers. Of course, they have day-to-day instructional utility: cathedrals must keep the rain out.
>
> *(Stenhouse, 1980, p. 40)*

The word itself derives from the Latin word *currere* meaning 'to run the course'. It can be thought about in terms of the *planned curriculum* which sets out what is intended to be taught and learned overall; the *enacted curriculum* in terms of what is actually taught and also the *experienced curriculum* in terms of what is learned. However, it is also a multi-layered concept that can be seen to be operating at a number of levels i.e. the *policy level*, the *programmatic level* and the *classroom level* (Westbury, 2000, p. 33). With regard to the first, the *policy level* operates at the intersection between schooling, culture and society and defines the purposes and expectations of schools. Secondly the *programmatic level* relates to the analysis of content for and in school subjects and in the construction of appropriate content for classroom use. Thirdly there is the *classroom level* as the programmatic curriculum is further elaborated, enacted and connected to events and the worlds of real students. It is at the classroom level that "curriculum and pedagogy effectively merge" (Westbury, 2000, p. 34). It is also this level that was the focus of the influential pioneering work of Stenhouse (ibid.) on classroom-based action research – hence the reference at the start of this chapter to the claim that curricula are not simply means to improve teaching but are expressions of ideas to improve teachers. In this chapter we focus primarily on the policy level but aim to keep the complex and multi-layered nature of the curriculum at the foreground of our thinking.

The chapter is set against the background of the current policy context in England, which has become something of an 'outlier' in recent years. This context has been critically analysed by Michael Young (2014) in his well-known work on 'powerful knowledge', the curriculum and social justice in the future school. This was published in the book *Knowledge and the Future School: Curriculum and Social Justice* co-edited with David Lambert together with Carolyn Roberts and Martin Roberts. An important contribution of this work is the 'Three Futures Model' based on a recognition of the shifts in international policy over recent years from content knowledge to generic skills and also an analysis of the national policy context in the UK since the election of the Coalition Government in 2010 in particular. This chapter takes as its starting point the Three Futures model and examines these futures as potential policy options.

> **Policy Option 1:** The Future 1 scenario as described by Young (ibid.), refers to the curriculum inherited by secondary schools from the nineteenth century. This is symbolised by the typical curriculum of the grammar schools and public schools against which many teachers in England reacted from the 1970s onwards, in particular "those teaching slow or disadvantaged learners" (ibid., p. 58) because of its elitist nature. Under a Future 1 scenario knowledge is treated as largely given and established on the basis of tradition and also by the route it offers high achieving students to the leading universities in the country. Accordingly, a Future 1 curriculum is seen as an extended version of the English curriculum of the past and based on serving the interests of an elite. Recent curriculum policy since 2010 is seen as a deliberate policy of returning to Future 1.

> **Policy Option 2:** The Future 2 scenario curriculum gradually emerged in England over a period of time in response to the rigidity of Future 1 and, initially, to better cater to the needs of lower achievers. Curriculum boundaries between school subjects were loosened in order to open up new forms of interdisciplinary studies. Also, the insulation of subjects from everyday knowledge was loosened through a new emphasis on subject knowledge

application in everyday life e.g. science could be taught through its application to the development and function of medical, cosmetics or everyday products as the curriculum was opened up to practical applications of knowledge. These changes were made as part of policies of social inclusion and widening participation. In parallel there was a weakening of the boundaries between the worlds of school and work as an increasingly vocational curriculum was introduced for lower achieving students, many of whom were from disadvantaged backgrounds. This change was seen as part of "an increasingly instrumental view that education was a means to an end – usually expressed as the expectation of future employment" (Young, 2014, p. 60). This represented a shift away from an emphasis on content knowledge towards generic skills.

Policy Option 3: The Future 3 scenario arises out of the critique and analysis made of both Futures 1 and 2 (Young and Muller, 2010). The argument for such an alternative Future 3 scenario is presented on the basis that "both Future 1 and 2 views of knowledge are partly right but fundamentally mistaken" (ibid., p. 65). It points towards an alternative curriculum of the future based on an idea of knowledge that differs from Future 1 and Future 2 in a number of ways. Firstly, it explicitly locates knowledge in the specialist communities of researchers in different fields and consequently does not treat knowledge as given but as fallible and open to challenge through dialogue and debate within the specialist communities. It follows that Future 3 treats *subjects* as the most reliable tools that have been developed for enabling students to acquire knowledge and make sense of the world. The idea of "powerful knowledge" was introduced by Young (2009) as a curriculum principle underpinning the Future 3 model. In discussing the question of what knowledge school students are entitled to have access to he argues that "in all fields of enquiry, there is better knowledge, more reliable knowledge, knowledge nearer the truth about the world we live in and to what it is to be human" (Young, 2013, p. 107). Access to such knowledge is seen as an issue of social justice. In contrasting the ideas of "knowledge of the powerful" and "powerful knowledge" it is argued that knowledge is powerful "if it predicts, if it explains, if it enables you to envisage alternatives" (Young, 2014, p. 74). The idea is based on two key characteristics expressed in the form of boundaries. Firstly, this knowledge is specialised both in how it is produced and transmitted and this specialisation is expressed in terms of the boundaries between disciplines and subjects which define their focus and objects of study. Secondly, it is differentiated from the experiences that pupils bring to school or older learners bring to college or university and this differentiation is expressed in the conceptual boundaries between school and everyday knowledge (Young, 2013). In this chapter we look ahead to Future 3 and develop the idea of powerful knowledge further by extending it to one of *powerful knowledge and creative know-how.*

Definitions[1]

Curriculum: what is intended to be taught and learned overall (the planned curriculum); what is taught (the curriculum as enacted); what is learned (the curriculum as experienced).

Subject: an organisational or conceptual segment of the planned curriculum in school; may be disciplinary-, cross-disciplinary- or thematically based.

Discipline: a branch of academic knowledge as systematised into distinct ways of enquiring, knowing, exploring, creating, explaining and making sense, each with their own key foci, preoccupations, concepts, procedures and products.

Knowledge: the process and outcomes of coming to know, or the combination of what is known and how such knowledge is acquired. It encompasses knowledge both propositional and procedural, and both public and personal, and it allows for reservation and scepticism as well as certainty. It is neither synonymous with subjects nor all that a curriculum contains, though it is nevertheless a central goal of all education.

Powerful knowledge: knowledge that predicts, explains and enables one to envisage alternatives.

Propositional knowledge: 'knowing that' in terms of facts and concepts.

Procedural knowledge: 'knowing how' in terms of both *inferential know-how* and *procedural know-how.*

Inferential know-how: knowing how the conceptual knowledge (the 'know that') hangs together, and how to negotiate the epistemic joints that link the various pieces of knowledge together.

Procedural know-how: a more risky and uncertain kind of knowledge where the newcomer learns how to find out new things, finds out which warrants and tests work under what circumstances, what the tolerances and limits are in real situations, forming new judgements that lead to solutions that work in the world.

Skill: the ability to make or do something, especially of a practical kind; requires knowledge but is distinct from it.

The context of England

Recent curriculum policy in England since 2010 has involved a strong political steer towards a so-called knowledge-rich or knowledge-based curriculum.[2] However, in this context, knowledge is taken as given at the policy level and is based on a false dichotomy between knowledge and skills. This policy has been strongly influenced by the thinking arising from the Core Knowledge Foundation, the resources of which have been imported from the United States and published in partnership with the think tank CIVITAS based at 55 Tufton Street in Westminster. The associated approach has been strongly promoted in English schools over recent years directly from the Department for Education in Westminster, in particular through the Academies Programme. As a result, there is a very strong emphasis on factual knowledge or simply 'knowing that' i.e. propositional knowledge (Winch,

2013). This policy shift is seen as retrograde in neglecting creativity and 'knowing how' i.e. procedural (ibid.) and inferential knowledge and as a policy of back to Future 1.

In a key speech, the Minister for School Standards[3] stressed the importance of "knowledge-based education", which reflects the strong influence of the theory of Cultural Literacy (including 5,000 essential names, phrases, dates and concepts that every American needs to know) by Hirsch (1988). In particular it draws heavily on a monograph published by the Centre for Policy Studies[4] based at 57 Tufton Street in Westminster in terms of policy implications. In this publication it is argued that the "strongest policy lesson" is the danger of "throwing out authority in schools, and especially getting rid of knowledge-based, teacher-dominated instruction" (ibid., p. 64). It asserts incorrectly that "the story from Finland backs up the increasing amount of evidence, which suggests that pupil-led methods, and less structured schooling environments in general, are harmful for cognitive achievement". In turn England is used as an example of a context in which "pupil-led methods and a less authoritative school culture have been on the rise for decades, reflecting everything from teacher education to Ofsted orthodoxy". However, this "policy lesson" is based on an exaggeration of the fall in Finland's PISA performance trajectory in recent years and also on a misreading of recent curriculum policy changes in Finland. Rather than moving away from emphasising knowledge, the recent changes to the curriculum in Finland emphasise both the role of subjects and also transversal competences.

> The national core curriculum provides a uniform foundation for local curricula, thus enhancing equality in education throughout the country. The curricula of each municipality and school steer instruction and schoolwork in more detail, taking local needs and perspectives into consideration. If necessary, the local curriculum may also revised later. The aim is that the curriculum serves as an active and flexible support for teaching and school activities.
>
> *(Finnish National Agency for Education,[5] 2014)*

Furthermore, it is stated explicitly that "the national core curriculum is still based on the subjects specified in the Basic Education Act for all grades".

Against this background, recent professional debates about curriculum in England have been dominated by the ill-defined concept of the 'knowledge-rich' curriculum. Proponents of knowledge-rich curricula argue that the schools must ensure that pupils develop deep and detailed knowledge. This is presented as both a progressive argument by some and as a traditionalist argument by others. For too long, it is argued by both sides, children from more privileged backgrounds have accessed forms of knowledge that have been denied less advantaged children. For some, the 'knowledge-rich' curriculum is understood as a contrast to a 'skills-based' or 'competency' curriculum that focuses on the skills and attributes that children should master during their education. This is sometimes envisioned as developing a set of '21st century' skills where the ability to find and critically evaluate knowledge sources (particularly via the internet) is seen as more vital than retaining a store of factual knowledge.

As recent curriculum research from Ofsted has shown,[6] in actual practice, the differences between a 'knowledge-rich' and 'skills-focused' curriculum are much less than might be imagined. Proponents of a 'knowledge-rich' curriculum argue that you can't think critically about a topic without sufficient knowledge and understanding of the topic and the implementation of a 'knowledge-rich' curriculum can involve plentiful opportunities to think critically about the knowledge being learnt. Equally, schools implementing 'skills-based' curricula are frequently very clear about the knowledge that students need to have in order to develop the skills they promote – no schools aim for pupils not to know more at the end of their schooling. In popular discussion, both of these approaches have been caricatured and simplified in ways that their proponents frequently object to:

> A muddled discourse about subjects, knowledge and skills which infects the entire debate about curriculum, needlessly polarises discussion of how it might be organised, parodies knowledge and undervalues its place in education and inflates the undeniably important notion of skill to a point where it, too, becomes meaningless.
>
> *(Alexander 2010, p. 252)*

However, notwithstanding these problems, these simplifications are both prevalent and powerful. As a result, we argue that it is necessary to pay closer attention to what we mean by 'knowledge' and the various types of knowledge and also to consider the ways in which teachers transform subject knowledge into curriculum content in practice.

Accordingly, a future policy agenda needs to strike a balance between *knowledge that* and *knowledge how* (Winch, 2013). In relation to the latter, there are two different kinds of '*know-how*' knowledge that are important for the curriculum. Firstly, this is about "knowing how the conceptual knowledge (the '*know-that*') hangs together, and how to negotiate the epistemic joints that link the various knowledge bits together" – i.e. *inferential know-how* (Muller, 2016, p. 103). Secondly, is a more risky and uncertain kind of knowledge where the newcomer "learns how to find out new things, finds out which warrants and tests work under what circumstances, what the tolerances and limits are in real situations, forming new judgements that lead to solutions that work in the world" (i.e. *procedural know-how* [Muller, 2016, p. 103]). From this perspective, we can see that domains of knowledge are not lists of facts as they are sometimes dismissed but rather represent distinct ways of knowing and understanding. This knowledge is not simply to be memorised but rather to be evaluated, engaged with and questioned. The following example explains what this means in practice.

If the central purpose of education is the development of students' intellectual and moral capacities, then disciplinary knowledge should not be seen as an end in itself or something merely for delivery or transmission but a powerful resource for such development.

(Deng, 2015, p. 782)

This aspect of the quality of knowledge in the curriculum is considered as one of *epistemic quality* by Hudson (2019). This is related to a continuum that reflects a trajectory of the 'epistemic ascent' (Winch, 2013) in the development of expertise from the novice towards higher order 'knowledge that' and 'knowledge how' of an expert in the subject. It is illustrated by comparing high and low epistemic quality in school mathematics with the former involving problem solving, critical thinking, creative reasoning and learning from errors and mistakes in contrast with the latter that emphasises rule following and memorisation of strict procedures, algorithmic and memorised reasoning and right or wrong answers. Not only does this resonate with the distinctions between simply *knowing that* and *knowing how* but also highlights the complexity and creative potential of placing an emphasis on the latter. Accordingly, with regard to ensuring equitable access to quality education, there is a need to consider the *epistemic quality* of what students come to know, make sense of and are able to do in school with the aim of maximising the chances that all pupils will have *epistemic access* (Morrow, 2008) to a school curriculum of *high epistemic quality*.

It is further argued (Hudson, 2019) that high epistemic quality is promoted through an approach based on assessment *for* learning involving low stakes formative and self-assessment – for further consideration, see Chapter 13 "Assessment". Research (Hudson et al., 2015) indicates this approach is engaging and motivating for individual learners and can create the conditions leading to a sense of enjoyment and fulfilment of mathematics as a creative human activity. In contrast, the excessive pressure from high stakes external testing and inspection and the associated heavy emphasis on memorisation, drill and practice establish circumstances that can degrade epistemic quality into an experience for learners of mathematics that is fearful and anxiety-inducing, boring, demotivating and alienating from the subject itself.

The significance of "epistemic knowledge" is reflected in the recent position paper (OECD, 2018) on the future of education and skills to 2030. This is described as knowledge about the disciplines, such as knowing how to think like a mathematician, historian or scientist. The importance of procedural knowledge is also recognised which is described as being acquired through understanding how something is done or made – the series of steps or actions taken to accomplish a goal. It is seen to develop most often through practical problem-solving, design thinking and systems thinking. Furthermore, it identifies the importance of young people being able to mobilise their knowledge, skills, attitudes and values to meet complex societal demands – for further consideration see Chapter 2 of this book "Aims and values: direction with purpose". Thus, we argue that the development of 'powerful knowledge' is best achieved alongside the development of 'creative know-how' that also addresses attitudes and values through a curriculum for the 21st century of high epistemic quality.

Principles

This section aims to set out principles to give direction for developing the curriculum that emphasises *powerful knowledge and creative know-how*. In doing so it draws on principles from a long tradition of curriculum thinking. In relation to this, we consider these as 'principles of procedure' (Stenhouse, 1975) which can be seen as standards of individual or collective conduct. Such principles help to focus attention "on the ethical basis on which schools, teachers and pupils (and, for that matter, governments) act *now*" (Alexander, 2010, p. 195). As such these principles are underpinned by associated values, central to which is an aim to ensure social justice. In doing so we draw on those outlined by Alexander (2010, p. 175) and highlight those we consider as being primarily concerned with social inclusion and in ensuring social justice for all.

1   **Democratic engagement**

The way in which a government acts in the realm of education is a good indicator of the seriousness of its commitment to democratic principles (Alexander, 2010). A curriculum is too important to be left to the whim of whoever happens to be the current Secretary of State. Recent curriculum changes in England have been marked by controversy and conflict which reflected opposing views about the purposes of education (Ross, 2000). Furthermore, as Alexander (2010) points out, the English National Curriculum proposals of 1987 were imposed by government, the 1997–1998 review included no significant debate and the 2008–2009 'Rose Review' allowed for only brief and restricted consultation. Opportunities for consultation were also severely restricted when the curriculum was most recently reviewed in 2014. This stands in stark contrast to the approaches taken in some other countries, for example, the Netherlands.[7] We argue that a National Curriculum should be the responsibility of Education England (see Chapter 6) under the NES Board of Education in order to ensure transparency, debate and critique through extensive and meaningful consultation.

2   **Purpose**

A curriculum can be thought of as a "selection from culture" (Lawton, 1975) guided by clear curriculum purposes and aims. The content selected should be that which will enable pupils to attain the aims set out for them. It should be based on 'powerful knowledge' which will enable pupils to develop the 'powers' necessary to contribute to society. A clear focus on long-term aims and purposes will ensure that the curriculum is sufficiently rigorous and challenging. As Reiss and White suggest: "schools should be left free, within a relatively substantive overall national aims framework, to decide how and where to teach whatever best promotes these aims" (Reiss and White, 2014).

3   **Entitlement**

We propose that Education England specifies in broad terms the character of the education to which all children in England are entitled. In doing so there is a need to avoid "the neo-Victorian opposition between the 'basics' and the rest, which the. . . [current] . . . national curriculum perpetuates in its sharper-than-ever distinction between 'core' and foundation subjects" (Alexander, 2014, p. 160).

4   **Flexibility – guidance not prescription**

The curriculum should not over specify content and it should not prescribe pedagogy through micro-management. The entitlement for all pupils should be balanced with sufficient freedom for schools or groups of schools to design a curriculum that takes account of the student, teaching context and content. This requires a high level of teacher expertise – the subject knowledge to recognise the essential elements of the curriculum.

5   **Continuity and consistency**

A curriculum should ensure continuity and progression. In previous years, revisions of Early Years, Primary and Secondary curricula have been conducted separately leading to unclear priorities and imprecise or unhelpful notions of school-ready or secondary-ready.

6   **Recognise the reciprocal relationship between knowledge and skills**

In reforming the curriculum, it is necessary to avoid the unhelpful polarisation of knowledge and skills. As Alexander (2010) points out, "All but the most elemental skills . . . require knowledge" (p. 249) and skills "must complement knowledge and understanding rather than supplant them" (p. 250).

Quality and standards

In England, the latest education inspection framework by Ofsted has made curriculum a key focus for school inspections. Following a programme of research by inspectors, Ofsted has chosen to assess the quality of a school curriculum from September 2019 with reference to three elements: intent, implementation and impact. These three criteria can equally be used to consider the quality of a national curriculum:

- Firstly, the curriculum can be assessed as to the extent that its aims and intentions are clear, communicated and a product of consensus.
- Secondly, the implementation of the curriculum can be judged, in terms of how consistently it is adopted and how successfully this adoption addresses the principles set out previously.
- Thirdly, the impact of the curriculum can be judged in terms of outcomes for pupils and outcomes for schools and teachers.

It is proposed that quality and standards be overseen by Education England as a national education service Board of Education in partnership with the Regional Education Boards and school boards in conjunction with a reformed Inspectorate.

Reflections

In England, the 2014 National Curriculum reforms and the Free School programme have been the main vehicles for pushing the government's agenda towards Core Knowledge, an emphasis on cultural literacy and a narrow view of knowledge. There is a need to reform the current National Curriculum as a whole into "a looser, less prescriptive framework" (see Wolfe, 2013, p. 113) that balances the attention given to propositional, procedural and inferential knowledge across a broad curriculum and also to legislate so that this applies to all state-funded schools including all academies. This chapter does not set out to provide a blueprint for a revised curriculum. Rather it provides an exemplar of one policy context that has undergone considerable change in recent years as a backdrop to provide an analysis of these changes and a direction for the choice of alternative future scenarios. In developing the Future 3 scenario we argue for the need to consider knowledge as a complex phenomenon and for the need to strike a balance between 'knowing what' and 'knowing how'. In other words, we argue for a balance between propositional knowledge and procedural and inferential knowledge. We argue further for the need to address some fundamental principles in the process of curriculum design planning at the national level in addition to the relationship between knowledge and skills which involves meaningful consultation, is based on the consideration of entitlement, is flexible, addresses the purposes of education and which ensures continuity and progression. What is proposed is a process and direction of travel towards a curriculum that aims to develop *powerful knowledge and creative know-how* for all.

Options, consequences and cautionary tales

The issues raised in this chapter lead to a number of policy options:

Policy options

In summary we have identified three policy options, each of which is linked to a future scenario:

> **Policy option 1:** The Future 1 scenario as described by Young (2014) refers to the curriculum inherited by secondary schools from the nineteenth century. This is symbolised by the typical curriculum of the grammar schools and public schools. Under a Future 1 scenario knowledge is treated as largely given and established on the basis of tradition and also by the route it offers

high achieving students to the leading universities in the country. Accordingly, a Future 1 curriculum is seen as an extended version of the English curriculum of the past and based on serving the interests of an elite.

Policy option 2: The Future 2 scenario curriculum gradually emerged in England over a period of time in response to the rigidity of Future 1 and in response initially to the needs of lower achievers. Curriculum boundaries between school subjects were loosened in order to open up new forms of interdisciplinary studies. Also, the insulation of subjects from everyday knowledge was loosened through a new emphasis on subject knowledge application in everyday life. This change was seen by Young (2014) as part of "an increasingly instrumental view that education was a means to an end" (p. 60). This represented a shift away from an emphasis on content knowledge towards generic skills.

Policy option 3: The Future 3 scenario arises out of the critique and analysis made of both Futures 1 and 2. It points towards an alternative curriculum of the future based on an idea of knowledge that differs from Future 1 and Future 2 in a number of ways. Firstly, it explicitly locates knowledge in the specialist communities of researchers in different fields and consequently does not treat knowledge as given but as fallible and open to challenge through dialogue and debate within the specialist communities. It treats *subjects* as the most reliable tools that have been developed for enabling students to acquire knowledge and make sense of the world. The idea of "powerful knowledge" was introduced by Young (2009) as a curriculum principle underpinning the Future 3 model. Access to such knowledge is seen as an issue of social justice. In this chapter we look ahead to Future 3 and develop the idea of powerful knowledge further by extending it to one of *powerful knowledge and creative know-how*.

Consequences

Each policy option is seen to have a set of consequences, as outlined:

Policy option 1: Future 1 places too much emphasis on simply knowing that [propositional knowledge] e.g. an over-emphasis on factual knowledge, rule following of strict procedures, right or wrong answers and memorisation.

Policy option 2: In contrast Future 2 places too much emphasis on simply knowing how [procedural knowledge] e.g. an over-emphasis on generic skills and instrumental view of education as a means to an end.

Policy option 3: Future 3 is bounded by the epistemic rules of particular specialist communities and treats subjects as the most reliable tools that have been developed for enabling students to acquire knowledge and make sense of the world. The idea of powerful knowledge was introduced as a curriculum principle underpinning the Future 3 model.

Cautionary tales

> **Policy option 1:** A Future 1 curriculum is seen as an extended version of the past based on serving the interests of an elite and not a curriculum for all.
>
> **Policy option 2:** Future 2 risks losing the potential for disciplinary knowledge to be used as a resource for learning. It also risks a caricatured view of knowledge that renders the contours of knowledge and learning invisible to the very learners that the pedagogy was designed to favour and limiting access to 'knowledge of the powerful'.
>
> **Policy option 3:** Future 3 carries the risk of over-emphasising knowledge at the expense of skills and so we argue that the idea of 'powerful knowledge' should be developed further by extending it to one of *powerful knowledge and creative know-how*.

The penultimate chapter provides further reflections and an executive summary of options, consequences and cautionary tales.

Notes

1 Drawing on Alexander (2010), Muller (2016), Winch (2013) and Young (2014)
2 www.independent.co.uk/news/education/education-news/nick-gibb-teach-children-important-facts-not-joyless-processes-minister-urges-a6859401.html
3 www.gov.uk/government/speeches/nick-gibb-the-importance-of-knowledge-based-education
4 www.cps.org.uk/files/reports/original/150410115444-RealFinnishLessonsFULLDRAFT COVER.pdf
5 www.oph.fi/english/curricula_and_qualifications/basic_education/curricula_2014
6 www.gov.uk/government/speeches/hmci-commentary-curriculum-and-the-new-education-inspection-framework
7 www.curriculum.nu/het-proces/

References

Alexander, R. (2010) *Children, their World, their Education: Final Report and Recommendations of the Cambridge Primary Review*. Abingdon: Routledge.
Alexander, R. (2014) The Best That Has Been Thought and Said? *FORUM*, 56 (1).
Deng, Z. (2015) Content, Joseph Schwab and German Didaktik. *Journal of Curriculum Studies*, 47, 773–786. doi:10.1080/00220272.2015.1090628
Finnish National Agency for Education (2014) *New National Core Curriculum for Basic Education*, Retrieved from https://www.oph.fi/english/curricula_and_qualifications/basic_education/curricula_2014
Hirsch, E.D. (1988) *Cultural Literacy: What Every American Needs to Know*. New York, NY: Random House USA Inc.
Hudson, B. (2019) Epistemic Quality for Equitable Access to Quality Education in School Mathematics. *Journal of Curriculum Studies*. https://doi.org/10.1080/00220272.2019.1618917
Hudson, B., Henderson, S. and Hudson, A. (2015) Developing Mathematical Thinking in the Primary Classroom: Liberating Teachers and Students as Learners of Mathematics.

Journal of Curriculum Studies, 47 (3), 374–398. http://dx.doi.org/10.1080/00220272.20 14.979233

Jung, J-H. and Pinar, W. (2016) Conceptions of Curriculum. In D. Wyse, L. Hayward and J. Pandya (Eds.) *SAGE Handbook of Curriculum, Pedagogy and Assessment*. Thousand Oaks, CA: Sage Publications, 107–124.

Lawton, D. (1975) *Class, Culture and The Curriculum*. London: Routledge.

Morrow, W. (2008) *Bounds of Democracy; Epistemological Access in Higher Education*. Pretoria: HSRC Press.

Muller, J. (2016) Knowledge and the Curriculum in the Sociology of Knowledge. In D. Wyse, L. Hayward and J. Pandya (Eds.) *SAGE Handbook of Curriculum, Pedagogy and Assessment*. Thousand Oaks, CA: Sage Publications, 92–106.

OECD (2018) *The Future of Education and Skills: Education 2030*. OECD Publishing.

Reiss, M. J. and White, J. (2014) An Aims-based Curriculum Illustrated by the Teaching of Science in Schools. *Curriculum Journal*, 25 (1), 76–89.

Ross, A. (2000) *Curriculum: Construction and Critique*. London: Falmer Press.

Stenhouse, L. (1975) *An Introduction to Curriculum Research and Development*. London: Heinemann.

Stenhouse, L. (1980) Curriculum Research and the Art of the Teacher. *Curriculum*, 1 (1), 40.

Young, M. (2009) Education, Globalization and the 'Voice of Knowledge'. *Journal of Education and Work*, 22, 193–204.

Young, M. (2013) Overcoming the Crisis in Curriculum Theory: A Knowledge-Based Approach. *Journal of Curriculum Studies*, 45 (2), 101–118.

Young, M. (2014) Why Start with the Curriculum? In M. Young and D. Lambert with C. Roberts and M. Roberts (Eds.) *Knowledge and the Future School: Curriculum and Social Justice*. London: Bloomsbury Academic.

Young, M. and Muller, J. (2010) Three Educational Scenarios for the Future: Lessons from the Sociology of Knowledge. *European Journal of Education*, 45, 11–27.

Westbury, I. (2000) Teaching as a Reflective Practice: What might Didaktik Teach Curriculum?' In I. Westbury, S. Hopmann and K. Riquarts (Eds.) *Teaching as a Reflective Practice: The German Didaktik Tradition*. Mahwah, NJ: Erlbaum, 15–40.

Winch, C. (2013) Curriculum Design and Epistemic Ascent. *Journal of Philosophy of Education*, 47 (1), 128–146.

Wolfe, D. (2013) Schools: The Legal Structures, the Accidents of History and the Legacies of Timing and Circumstance. *Education Law Journal*, 100–113.

13

NATIONAL ASSESSMENT CHOICES

Nikki Booth

Introduction

Is the purpose of national assessment to support learning? Or is it an end of learning check for learners, teachers, and schools? To help address these questions certain key points need to be considered:

> Assessment is not an exact science, and we must stop presenting it as such.
> *(Gipps, 1994, p. 167)*

> Schools which deliberately "game the system" cannot be truly labelled as "high-performing" on, for example, nationally published league tables.

> There is approximately fifty-years' worth of research evidence to suggest that formative assessment, when used effectively, can have a significant impact on learner outcomes.
>
> An assessment system which relies on making inferences about an individual's attainment from just end-of-course examinations can be hugely problematic.

Assessment is a multifaceted, hotly debated, yet integral topic in education. This chapter considers complex issues surrounding national assessment drawing on both research and practice, and three policy options are identified and discussed:

- **Policy Option 1** – High-stakes testing: sets out some of the consequences of current national examination methodologies in England and draws attention to the issues surrounding the ability to make accurate valid and reliable inferences from such data.

- **Policy Option 2** – External examinations with formative assessment: although not completely separate from Option 1, this approach explores how the effective use of formative assessment, at all levels of an education service, can drive up learner standards, increase teacher quality, and meaningfully improve educational policy.
- **Policy Option 3** – Cumulative assessment: suggests the development of an assessment system which is both distributed and synoptic (Wiliam, 2007). In attempting to address *construct under-representation* as a key threat to the validity of assessment outcomes, a more balanced assessment system allows for evidence of learning to be done throughout a course of study (rather than just at the end of it) and allows for learning to accumulate over time.

In England, high-stakes, nationally reported summative 'products', in the form of national examinations, include, for example; Key Stage 2 SATs at ages 10–11, GCSE examinations at ages 15–16, and A-Level examinations, for many, at ages 17–18. What makes these assessments particularly high-stakes, and perhaps why they have higher value in society, is that the final results are used for admission into further and higher education, by Ofsted, albeit now partially, to judge the quality of education in schools, as well as, in some cases, by senior leadership teams (SLTs) to judge the effectiveness of their teaching staff. Whilst it is often the case that schools formatively use summative information from national examinations to develop ongoing school improvement plans, the same needs to be done at policymaker level also to continuously support the improvement of an education service as well as national educational outcomes for learners. At present, however, there is too much emphasis on final results from national examinations; there are serious questions as to whether such data can be used effectively to make valid and reliable inferences about learning, learners, teachers and schools.

Policy option 1: reducing the emphasis of national examination results

Since government is accountable for how it spends public money, schools, similarly, are made answerable for their results. However, in an environment, such as England, where what is measured has greater value, there are several issues which need exploring, as Table 13.1 summarises.

Based on Campbell's law,

> [W]hen test scores become the goal of the teaching process, they both lose their value as indicators of educational status and distort the educational process in undesirable ways.
>
> *(Campbell, 1976, p. 52)*

When data from summative assessments have higher value not only do they dominate political debates over education, they also impact on the day-to-day business of schooling, as the consequences that are discussed in the following sections demonstrate.

TABLE 13.1 Consequences of high-stakes testing

	Cost	Evidenced example of consequences, for many learners in schools, if emphasis on results is not reduced.	Reasons why making valid and reliable inferences from examination results is problematic.
KS1 & 2	Approximate annual cost to education budget: £44 million (Times Educational Supplement [TES], 2017).	• Off-rolling (see Chapter 16). • Attempting to meet national averages. • Learners developing mental health issues. • Teachers "teaching to the test".	• Reliability of the process of examinations. • Margin of error. • The adolescent brain.
GCSE	Approximate cost to school budget: £38 per learner, per subject studied, per year.		
A-Level	Cost to school budget: £135 per learner, per subject studied, per year.		

Attempting to meet national averages

Since 2016, both England's Department for Education and Ofsted shifted their focus from attainment to progress. What this meant for schools (in the context of GCSEs, for example) was that instead of focussing on the percentage of learners achieving 5+ A*-C grades (including English and mathematics) as a headline measure, learners' progress across their eight best qualifications (thus the name Progress 8) since their last national examination would be averaged to calculate a school's overall average Progress 8. The notion of Progress 8 is a step in the right direction on the previous 5+ A*-C headline; it "is designed to reward schools for the progress made by all pupils across the ability range, compared to pupils nationally with similar starting points" (Department for Education, 2018, p. 9).

Other previous policy-maker thinking in relation to calculating average progress needs further consideration, however. For example, when questioned by the Education Select Committee, it was revealed that former Conservative Secretary of State for Education, Michael Gove, did not understand the concept of averages when he said he expected *all schools* to make above-average progress, as the dialogue shows:

Chair: If "good" requires pupil performance to exceed the national average, and if all schools must be good, how is this mathematically possible?
Michael Gove: By getting better all the time.
Chair: So it is possible, is it?
Michael Gove: It is possible to get better all the time.

Chair: Were you better at literacy than numeracy, Secretary of State?
Michael Gove: I cannot remember

(UK Parliament, 2012)

Learners developing mental health issues

Research (National Association of Headteachers, 2015) shows that, in England, there are increasing numbers of learners who are suffering from school-related mental health issues due to the increasing pressure to perform well on examinations. The rise in the number of diagnoses of ADHD, in particular, has been shown to be linked with high-stakes testing. Further examples show that thoughts of suicide relate to educational problems; "[t]he pressure and stress of exams and not being able to deal with failure was another reason young people wanted to escape, seeing suicide as their only option" (For example, Childline, 2014, p. 37). In the context of England's GCSEs, for example, research (Denscombe, 2000) suggests that there are four reasons why learners at this age find examinations stressful, as Table 13.2 shows:

TABLE 13.2 Reasons and examples as to why GCSE examinations can be stressful

Reason why examinations are stressful	*Example why this might be*
Consequences	If a learner does not have enough "passes" at GCSE then a consequence might be rejection to enter college or Sixth-Form for further education in particular courses.
Markers of self-esteem	Learners judge themselves on the basis of the scores or grades they receive. A "good" grade, for example, is likely to result in one having high self-esteem.
Judgements by others	Following receipt of grades learners may well be judged by others, for example family members or peers.
Fear appeals	Teachers, for example, may well frequently reiterate the importance of the examinations and the *need* to get certain grades in certain subjects. Such 'fear appeals' like these are usually intended to be motivational, but do not always have the desired effect on learners.

What is interesting about the previous information is that the effects of mental health seem to come from how examination results are *used*, not the examinations themselves per se. This is an important distinction because, as the Director of Education for the OECD, Andreas Schleicher, has commented:

> [Some people say] tests drive students' anxiety these days. We don't have much evidence to support that actually – there's no correlation across countries between the prevalence of tests in a system and students' anxiety.
>
> *(Times Educational Supplement [TES], 2019, p. 13)*

Teachers "teaching to the test"

Research (Brill et al., 2018) by the UK's National Foundation for Educational Research (NFER) has shown that some schools reduce their curriculum and focus on getting learners to perform well on subjects and content which will be examined at the expense of mastering new knowledge in a broad range of subjects. As the National Association of Head Teachers (NAHT) observe: "The nature and wealth of the accountability system has encouraged schools to focus on those areas that are critical as school performance indicators, such as Key Stage 2 SATs, EBacc [English Baccalaureate] or Progress 8" (National Association of Headteachers, 2018, p. 9).

Such narrowing of the curriculum to focus on key performance measures has been noted by, for example, Ofsted:

> We saw curriculum narrowing, especially in upper key stage 2, with lessons disproportionately focused on English and mathematics. Sometimes, this manifested as intensive, even obsessive, test preparation for key stage 2 SATs that in some cases started at Christmas in Year 6. Some secondary schools were significantly shortening key stage 3 in order to start GCSEs. This approach results in the range of subjects that young people study narrowing at an early stage and means that they might drop art, history or music, for instance, at age 12 or 13. At the same time, the assessment objectives from GCSE specifications were being tracked back to as early as Year 7, meaning many young people spend their secondary education learning narrowed and shallow test content rather than broader and more in-depth content across a subject area.
>
> *(Ofsted, 2018)*

Despite this important finding there are, of course, examples of schools who do not reduce their curriculum and who do value the educational growth of the whole learner in a variety of subjects. As such, schools which deliberately "game the system" cannot be truly labelled as "high-performing" on, for example, nationally published league tables.

Reliability of the process of examinations

Reliability often refers to the consistency of a learner's outcome that would be observed from an assessment process were it to be repeated. This presents an issue because no single test or examination can ever be 100% reliable, and classifying learners (by grading them, for example) will always consist of a certain amount of error. The discussion and openness about these errors within national examination data is important because they can have implications for schools as well as individual learners.

There are several factors which can affect a learner's performance on the day of an examination, as Table 13.3 illustrates:

TABLE 13.3 Factors which can affect a learner's performance in an examination

Factor	What this means in context
The learners themselves	Due to lack of sleep or stress, for example, a learner may happen to feel particularly tired on the day which could affect their performance. Furthermore, due to slow retrieval strength a learner may not recall some content during the test but it might come back to them two hours after it has finished.
The choice of content examined	Given that only a small sample of the domain is actually examined, if a learner had different questions on different parts of the curriculum they may well have performed better (or worse) than on the questions actually given at that time.
The assessor	There can be variability between different assessors' scoring decisions, particularly for more subjective subjects like English, as opposed to mathematics, for example.
The national standard	Due to the yearly variability of grade boundaries (in the case of England's GCSE and A-Level examinations, for example), a learner who was awarded a particular grade in one year may have actually performed one grade better or worse in the previous year – even if they achieved the same mark.

These factors are important when considering making inferences from national examination data; it could make a difference as to whether some learners "pass" or "fail", or whether some schools are in line with national standards or not. In England, this is even more relevant now in GCSEs, for example, since, under examination reforms, the UK Conservative government completely removed coursework, for almost all courses, in favour of 100% end-of-course examinations.

Margin of error

A *margin of error* (also referred to as a Standard Error of Measurement [SEM]), considers the degree of uncertainty that a single examination might represent between learners' "observed scores" (the scores gained from taking an examination) and their "true scores" (the average of the individual's scores if the same examination was administered several times). This becomes somewhat problematic when, in the case of England, grades are awarded to classify how well learners performed, particularly for those who are, for example, close to the grade boundaries. This has already been acknowledged by Ofqual, who state: "clearly, candidates with scores near the grade boundaries are going to be more at risk of misclassification than those with scores in the middle of the band" (Ofqual, 2013). Furthermore, Ofqual also reports that "the more grades that are available for an exam, the greater the unreliability associated with the grade because the grade is covered by a smaller mark range and so is more susceptible to misclassification" (Ofqual, 2013).

In the US, as well as other countries, the notion of the margin of error is not shied away from because results from national examinations are reported as raw scores *with* a margin of error. This is not the case in some other countries like England, for example, where grades are reported instead of raw scores and without any indication of the likely error that might be involved. This is hugely problematic when using national examination data for important decisions about learners and schools. What needs to happen, therefore, as Ofqual recognises, is that the 'inconsisten[cies] in test and examination results [are] investigated, interpreted and understood properly' (Opposs & He, 2011, p. 5). As such, every effort should be made to clearly communicate this to all those involved in education (decision makers, learners, and parents alike) as well as the general public.

The adolescent brain

Research (Gärtner et al., 2014) has revealed that elevated levels of cortisol can have a negative effect on an individual's cognitive function and memory. Small amounts of cortisol are always in the bloodstream, and this is good because it helps the brain to stay alert and perform tasks. Cortisol can also be problematic, however, especially when a learner's anxiety levels rise because they are taking an important examination. What research has shown is that, because of elevated anxiety levels, the adrenal glands pump more cortisol around the body because it is undergoing stress (Slavin, 1980). This, then, impacts on the learner's short-term memory which, instead of focusing on the examination, calls on the long-term memory to help deal with the stress the body is undergoing. What happens is that frustration sets in and the learner can experience difficulty in retrieving information from an already pre-occupied long-term memory.

Research (for example, Stickgold et al., 2000, pp. 1237–1238) has also shown that sleep deprivation can have a negative effect on task performance. According to Sarah-Jayne Blakemore, a professor of cognitive neuroscience, when adolescents go through puberty, their circadian rhythms alter by a couple of hours compared to adults because melatonin (the hormone which makes us feel sleepy) is produced later in the evening. As a result of their altered biological clocks, many teenagers often feel less tired in the evening and, therefore, struggle to get up early in the morning for school (Blakemore, 2018). This is an important point when thinking about learners taking, for example, GCSE or A-Level examinations at 9 o'clock in the morning because, from a neuroscientific perspective, teenagers should, in fact, be still asleep.

Thus, if valid and reliable inferences cannot be accurately made about individual students and, by extension, teachers and schools, then the issues cited previously provide a good basis as to why their high-stakes emphasis should be reduced for schools.

Policy option 2: enhancing the use of formative assessment

There is considerable quantitative and qualitative research evidence to suggest that formative assessment, when used effectively, is a highly cost-effective process which has substantial impact on learner outcomes (OECD, 2005), as Table 13.4 summarises:

TABLE 13.4 Summary of formative assessment and how it can be used effectively

Approximate cost to schools	Evidence of impact from research	How formative assessment can be used effectively to help improve educational outcomes
According to the Education Endowment Fund (EEF), the *Embedding Formative Assessment* professional development programme for a school would cost £3,895 (approximately £1.20 per learner, per year when averaged over three years).	According to research conducted by Paul Black and Dylan Wiliam, the effects of the effective use of formative assessment is "among the largest ever reported for educational interventions. As an illustration of just how big these gains are, an effect size of 0.7, if it could be achieved on a nationwide scale, would be equivalent to raising the mathematics attainment score of an 'average' country like England . . . into the 'top five' after the Pacific Rim countries of Singapore, Korea, Japan and Hong Kong" (Black and Wiliam, 1998, p. 61).	• According to the OECD, information collected from national examinations can be used to shape strategies for improvement at all levels of an education service. • Policy makers can use information to set broad priorities for education policies as well as provide support for what investments, training, and support are required for school leaders and teachers.

The value of formative assessment is that it aims to promote a positive and constructive culture of evaluation and improvement (see Finnish and Scottish accountability services in Chapters 15 and16 and Wales in Chapter 1), and although it perhaps has the biggest impact on learning at the school and classroom-level, it can also be highly effective at the policy-level also. That said, despite the wealth of research into and exemplification of good practice, is seems that formative assessment, at present in the UK, "has [had] no (or at best limited) effect on learning outcomes nationally" (Coe, 2013. p. 10). This is because, as research has found (for example, Fautley & Savage, 2008), some SLTs value their teachers producing regular "products" as evidence which demonstrates high learner attainment and, as a result, teachers consciously neglect their own valued beliefs in formative assessment for data tracking purposes. This is not to say that inferences from summative assessments are not important – of course they are – but results from classroom-based tests and national examinations are only part of the story and will not improve an education system by themselves; something needs to be done with the information – i.e. it needs to be used *formatively* – for the service to improve.

The OECD (2005) suggest that information collected from national examinations can be used to shape strategies for improvement at all levels of an education service. For example, they recommend that, at the classroom-level, information

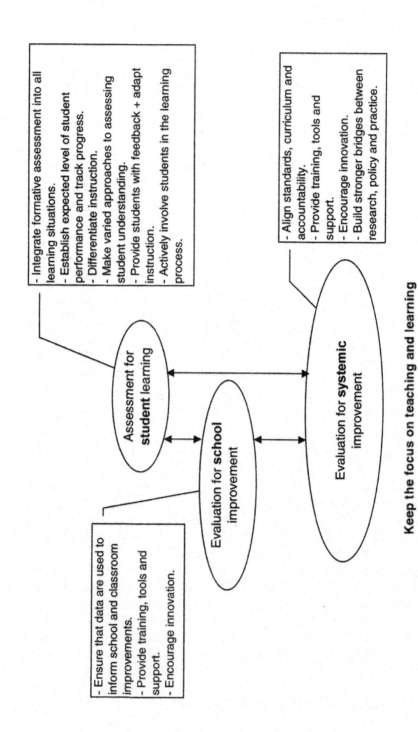

FIGURE 13.1 Co-ordinating the elements of formative assessment (OECD, 2005, p. 84).

can be elicited and used to change the direction of teaching to better meet learning needs. At the school-level, leaders can identify areas of strength as well as develop meaningful strategies, specifically relevant to the school, from identified areas for improvement. In a similar fashion, with a strong focus on teaching and learning, policy makers can use information gathered from national examinations to set broad priorities for education policies as well as provide support for what investments, training and support are required for school leaders and teachers. As the OECD make clear, "[s]ystems that address tensions that prevent wider practice of formative assessment and that foster cultures of evaluation are likely to make much greater progress" (OECD, 2005, p. 27). The ideas suggested by the OECD are shown in Figure 13.1.

The notion of providing quality formative assessment training for school leaders and teachers is important because, as has been revealed (see, for example, Carter, 2015; DfE, 2015; LKMco/Pearson, 2017), assessment (including formative assessment) is the greatest weakness. This is significant; since the removal of National Curriculum levels, for example, "many schools have adopted ineffective assessment systems" (House of Commons Education Committee, 2017, p. 8). What needs to happen, therefore, is that all leaders and teachers, at all levels of expertise, should have the opportunity to become skilled and confident assessors of learning. This requires strong support and leadership, not just from peers and school leaders, but from policy leaders also. In other words, valuable resources should be used in developing better teaching and learning, and not on the sorting and ranking of schools.

Policy option 3: developing a broader and more balanced system where assessment of learning is distributed and synoptic

An assessment system which relies on making inferences from just end-of-course examinations can be seen as hugely problematic; to an assessment expert, one of the main issues is that, by doing so, a serious threat to validity has occurred: *construct under-representation*. What this means is that because only a small part of the entire Key Stage or specification is assessed, other equally important learning outcomes go untested. Furthermore, even with the content being tested, it is done in a very superficial way. To address the notion of *construct under-representation*, a broader and more balanced system needs to be considered where assessment of learning is more *distributed* (where evidence of learning is done during and throughout a course of study and not just at the end of the phase of study) and *synoptic* (where learning is accumulated over time). In short, the present assessment system in England, for example, can be described as providing a "snapshot" of learning, when what we need, as Brookhart and colleagues make clear is a "photo album" (Brookhart et al., 2019, p. 21).

In 1988, in England, the original Standard Assessments Tasks, which were written by the Task Group for Assessment and Testing, were more broadly based and practical allowing the inclusion of formative, summative, and evaluative purposes of assessment. Here, this also meant an increase in the validity of the inferences made from the assessment judgements. The desire for more valid tests, however, "got caught up in the quagmire of manageability" (Weeden et al., 2002, p. 20) where despite the fact that learners were able to demonstrate their knowledge and understanding, the tests took too long to administer as well as there being questions regarding the reliability of their administration by different teachers. As such, these tests were abandoned and cheaper and more "reliable" pencil-and-paper externally set tests replaced them. It is important to note that while these pencil-and-paper tests may have increased the reliability of the assessments, their validity, however has decreased; within all time-constrained tests, "no test can cover all the learning that is set out in the curriculum" (Harlen, 2007, p. 23). As a result of this important limitation, in addition to externally set national assessments, teacher assessment should be included as an important part of the national assessment system. What this means is that, as Wiliam states, "it has the effect of lengthening the test" (Wiliam, 2007, p. 1). For example, during the normal course of teaching and learning, teachers gather evidence from a range of regular activities by the coverage of a more varied, and more complete, set of learning goals which can then be integrated into the normal teaching and learning cycle. This is a particular strength for an effective assessment system as it includes important information which externally set tests cannot capture. In principle, this means that a much wider variety of learning outcomes can be assessed (for example, deeper assessment which includes creativity and problem solving in more "authentic" contexts) and not just those that can be easily tested. It should be emphasised, however, that threats to the reliability of the information gathered need to be reduced. For example, research has shown (for example, as cited in Wiliam, 2007) that not only do some teachers give their learners higher scores or grades, but that they give higher marks to the students they like. As such, in order for the reliability of teacher judgements to be increased, there is the need for internal, as well as external, quality assured moderation to take place to confirm teachers' judgements which, compared to external testing, can enhance teaching and learning *during* the teaching and learning cycle. An important point to mention is that teacher assessment should not add to teacher workload. What should happen is that distributed and synoptic evidence of learning should be part of the normal teaching and learning cycle, not an addition to it. Furthermore, as has already been discussed in option 2, for any teacher assessment to be meaningful and effective, training in assessment literacy should be a point for national development for both beginning and more expert teachers and leaders.

Reflections

* The effective use of examination results is crucial for moving learning, teaching, and an education service forward.

This provides answers to key questions such as: Where are we? Where do we need to be? leading to, How are we going to get there? In England, for example, while assessment information from the Key Stage 1 phonics check (Year 1) and SATs (Year 2) are used by teachers to identify learning needs and provide necessary support to improve learning (which are not reported nationally), end of phase Key Stage 2 SATs, GCSE and A-Level examination results, however, are used for the sole aim of "summing up" learning and not for the purpose of how an individual's learning can be made even better for their next phase of education or, in some learners' cases, work.

• An education service, like England's, which is high-stakes and based on the notion of performativity will always have negative consequences on learners, teachers and the day-to-day business of schooling.

Such consequences can include: teachers being told to chase learner targets in order to meet the national average; learners developing mental health issues; and schools narrowing their curriculum in important examination years where teachers "teach to the test". It is important to note that the taking of the examinations is not the cause of these consequences per se, but how the information is *used*. In England, results from national examinations (Key Stage 2, GCSE, and A-Level) are used to not only "sum-up" a learner's end of phase examination performance as to whether they have "passed" or "failed", but also to label schools for the same purpose (for example, whether a school is in line with national average or not). To use examination results in this way can be hugely problematic because there are fundamental reasons, beyond a school's control, which can affect the outcome of these results.

• There is approximately 50 years' worth of research evidence to suggest that formative assessment, when used effectively, can have a significant impact on learner outcomes.

As cited and discussed in this chapter, research has found that the constant drive for improving examination results or "products" has resulted in teachers neglecting their formative assessment practices. As a result, what has happened, in some schools, is that there might be frequent testing, but little action on how the results can be made even better; tests are just to prove that progress is being made. In promoting an educational culture where formative assessment is at the heart, results from national examinations can be effectively used to identify national gaps in learning and provide strategies as to how these might be overcome.

• An assessment system which relies on making inferences from just end-of-course examinations can be seen as hugely problematic.

Given the limitations of time for end-of-course examinations, only a small part of an entire Key Stage or specification can ever be examined. As such, since other equally important learning outcomes go untested, the validity of the inferences made has to be questioned due to the amount of *construct under-representation*.

Teacher assessment is an important consideration where, during the course of teaching and learning, teachers would gather evidence from a range of regular activities by the coverage of a more varied, and more complete, set of learning goals which can then be integrated into the normal teaching and learning cycle. This is a particular strength for an assessment system; it means that a much wider variety of learning outcomes can be assessed (for example deeper assessment which includes creativity and problem solving in more "authentic" contexts) and not just those that can be easily tested.

Policy options

Policy Options have been outlined in detail throughout the chapter:

- **Policy Option 1:** High stakes testing: the removal of national examinations is not recommended, but the emphasis on the results they produce should be reduced as fundamental issues, beyond a school's control, affect outcomes: reliability, "margin of error" and, adolescents' biological and neurological changes.
- **Policy Option 2:** External examinations with formative assessment.
- **Policy Option 3:** Cumulative assessment.

These are discussed further with other policy options in the penultimate chapter.

Further Reading

Koretz, D. (2008) *Measuring up: What educational testing really tells us.* Cambridge, MA: Harvard University Press.

Koretz, D. (2017) *The testing charade. Pretending to make schools better.* Chicago, IL: University of Chicago Press.

Wiliam, D. (2018) *Creating the schools our children need. Why what we're doing now won't help much (and what we can do instead).* West Palm Beach, FL: Learning Sciences International.

References

Black, P., & Wiliam, D. (1998) *Inside the black box: Raising standards through classroom assessment.* London: King's College School of Education.

Blakemore, S. J. (2018) *Inventing ourselves: The secret life of the teenage brain.* London: Doubleday.

Brill, F., Grayson, H., Kuhn, L., & O'Donnell, S. (2018) *What impact does accountability have on curriculum, standards and engagement in education? A literature review.* Slough, UK: NFER.

Brookhart, S., Stiggins, R., McTighe, & Wiliam, D. (2019) *The future of assessment practices: Comprehensive and balanced assessment systems.* Online, available at: www.dylanwiliam center.com/whitepapers/assessment/ [last accessed 1 August 2019].

Campbell, D. (1976) Assessing the impact of planned social change. In G. Lyons (Ed.) *Social research and public policies: The Dartmouth/OECD Conference.* Hanover, NH: Public Affairs Centre, Dartmouth College.

Carter, A. (2015) *Carter review of initial teacher training.* Online, available at: https://assets. publishing.service.gov.uk/government/uploads/system/uploads/attachment_data/ file/399957/Carter_Review.pdf [last accessed 5 August 2019].

Childline (2014) *Can I tell you something?* ChildLine Review 2012–13. Online, available at: www.nspcc.org.uk/globalassets/documents/research-reports/childline-review-2012-2013.pdf [last accessed 1 August 2019].

Coe, R. (2013) *Improving education: A triumph of hope over experience.* Durham, UK: Centre for Education and Monitoring, Durham University.

Denscombe, M. (2000) Social conditions for stress. *British Educational Research Journal*, 26(3), 259–374.

Department for Education (DfE)(2015) *Final report of the commission on assessment without levels.* London: The Stationary Office.

Department for Education (DfE) (2018) *The government's response to the Education Select Committee's fifth report of session 2017 to 2019 on alternative provision.* Online, available at: www. gov.uk/government/publications/alternative-provision-response-to-the-select-commit tee-report [last accessed 1 August 2019].

Education Endowment Fund (EEF) (2019) *Embedding formative assessment.* Online, available at: https://educationendowmentfoundation.org.uk/projects-and-evaluation/projects/ embedding-formative-assessment/ [last accessed 1 August 2019].

Fautley, M., & Savage, J. (2008) *Assessment for learning and teaching in secondary schools.* Exeter, UK: Learning Matters Ltd.

Gärtner, M., Rohde-Liebenau, L., Grimm, S., & Bajbouj, M. (2014) Working memory-related frontal theta activity is decreased under acute stress. *Psychoneuroendocrinology*, 43(May), pp. 105–113.

Gipps, C. (1994) *Beyond testing: Towards a theory of educational assessment.* London: Palmer Press.

Harlen, W. (2007) *Assessment of learning.* London: Sage Publications.

House of Commons Select Committee (2017) *'High-stakes' testing harming teaching and learning in primary schools.* Online, available at: www.parliament.uk/business/committees/ committees-a-z/commons-select/education-committee/news-parliament-2015/pri mary-assessment-report-published-16-17/ [last accessed 5 August 2019].

LKMCO/Pearson (2017) *Final reports: Testing the water: How assessment can underpin, not undermine, great teaching.* Online, available at: www.lkmco.org/wp-content/uploads/2017/11/ Testing-the-Water-Final-Report-WEB.pdf [last accessed 5 August 2019).

National Association of Headteachers (NAHT) (2015) *Exam factories: The impact of accountability measures on children and young people.* Online, available at: www.teachers.org.uk/ files/exam-factories.pdf [last accessed 1 August 2019].

National Association of Headteachers (NAHT) (2018) *Improving school accountability.* Haywards Heath, UK: NAHT.

OECD (2005) *Formative assessment. Improving learning in secondary schools.* Paris, France: OECD Publishing.

Ofqual (2013) *Introduction to the concept of reliability.* Online, available at: www.gov.uk/gov ernment/publications/reliability-of-assessment-compendium/introduction-to-the-con cept-of-reliability [last accessed 5 August 2019].

Ofsted (2018) *Ofsted's Chief Inspector, Amanda Spielman, discusses findings from recent curriculum research, curriculum design and the new education inspection framework.* Online, available at: www.gov.uk/government/speeches/hmci-commentary-curriculum-and-the-new-edu cation-inspection-framework [last accessed 1 August 2019].

Opposs, D., & He, Q. (2011) *The reliability programme: Final report.* Coventry, UK: Ofqual, Online, available at: https://dera.ioe.ac.uk/2568/1/11-03-16-Ofqual-The-Final-Report.pdf [last accessed 5 August 2019].

Slavin, R. (1980) Effects of individual learning expectations on student achievement. *Journal of Educational Psychology*, 72, 520–524.

Stickgold, R., James, L., & Hobson, J. A. (2000) Visual discrimination learning requires sleep after training. *Nature Neuroscience*, 3, 1237.

Times Educational Supplement (TES) (2017) *Sats costs revealed: £44m in first year of new system*. Online, available at: www.tes.com/news/sats-costs-revealed-ps44m-first-year-new-system [last accessed 1 August 2019].

Times Educational Supplement (TES) (2019) *The week in quotes* (p. 13). 25 January 2019.

UK, Parliament (2012) *Uncorrected transcript of oral evidence*. Online, available at: https://publications.parliament.uk/pa/cm201012/cmselect/cmeduc/uc1786-i/uc178601.htm [last accessed 1 August 2019].

Weeden, P., Winter, J., & Broadfoot, P. (2002) *Assessment: What's in it for schools?* London: Routledge.

Wiliam, D. (2007) *Comparative analysis of assessment practice and progress in the UK and USA*. Presentation at Westminster Education Forum Seminar on Assessment, 10 October.

14

LEADERSHIP, INNOVATION AND CHANGE

Rosie Raffety

Introduction

> Learning how to define a problem, creatively break it into manageable parts, and systematically work towards a solution has become the core skill for the twenty-first century workforce.
>
> *Conn & McLean (2019, p. xiii)*

The purpose of this chapter is threefold:

Firstly, to contextualise discussion of generic problems within the UK education system as a feature and consequence of 'small state' education policies and economic assumptions;

Secondly, to present a 4P Conceptual Model that identifies specific problems and maps where shifts need to occur in the design of systemic solutions;

Finally, to share a prototyped programme for leadership development within the 4P model that builds capacity for problem-solving, innovation and change at scale.

School leadership in the context of austerity

School leaders everywhere occupy a mediational role between governments and the communities they serve. That role is frustrated and diminished when it becomes state policy to under-fund the public sector, axe coordinating public-bodies and accelerate privatisation. The economic model of free markets and the small state has accelerated policy defined by new public management theory (Lubienski, 2009) and high accountability school systems (Barber, Chijioke & Mourshed, 2010). This policy preference for education within a quasi-market, accelerating since the seventies, signifies a shift away from the value of education as a 'public good' in favour of education as a privatisable commodity (Offe & Ronge, 1975).

In the chapter that follows, I present a 4P conceptual model to enable thinking about where critical shifts in need to occur to enable a self-renewing education system. I argue, with reference to England as a case in point, that where governments pursue the ideology of the small state & marketisation in education that privatisation, regional inequality, managerialism and inequitable outcomes, follow. In construing education system re-design as a public sector transformation project, it follows that school leaders need to be skilled as design & change catalysts who can problem solve at scale. Reality, however, paints a bleaker picture. In March 2018 the Headteachers' Roundtable, a UK think-tank, hosted a summit to explore solutions to common challenges. The problems they list (SchoolsWeek, 2018) arise from directly from the policy values of the small state and free markets in education, namely:

1   insufficient funding;
2   excessive accountability;
3   poor retention;
4   limited school autonomy & agency

These concerns highlight the relentless challenge of balancing budgets, problems in retaining staff and a sense of professional disempowerment. In combination, they signal a UK system under stress and leaders on the verge of despair. The think-tank challenged the *"damaging culture created by high stakes, cliff edge accountability; insufficient funding of schools and short-sighted, poorly evidenced policies"*. It is a damning verdict on policy that construes both the state and education leaders as 'fixers' and firefighters instead of value-creators. Post Covid, these issues are only set to increase exponentially.

Austerity presents very particular challenges for leaders globally. It reflects assumptions about economic models, short-termism and tolerance for inequity (UNCTAD Report, 2019) that impact leadership morale, the education project and social stability. In England, austerity has resulted in rising inequalities from early years to post-16, with funding per primary and secondary pupil 4% below its peak in 2015 (Britton et al. 2019). Leadership is, by definition, about adding-value and getting results (Feser, Mayol & Srinivasan, 2015). Given the mediational role of school leaders, the architecture of education policy making merits review, alongside discussions of how best to equip leaders to serve learners in an age of robotics. The twin issues of public sector value-creation and policy values are the very crux of the matter.

The architecture of school leadership in the UK

The UK is the most geographically unequal economy in Europe (Jacobs, 2018). McCann (2019) in comparing the UK to 30 other OECD countries against 28 indicators, concludes that the UK is one of the most regionally unbalanced countries in the industrial world. Similarly, in his introduction to the UK2070 Commission Report (2019), Lord Kerslake asserts that deep-rooted regional inequalities across the UK demand 'long term thinking and a special economic plan to tackle them'. The report concludes that inequalities are exacerbated by "underpowered 'pea-shooter' and 'sticking-plaster' policies". A case is made for future policy to be "structural, generational, interlocking and at scale". Within advanced economies poverty and inequality are now political flash points (G-7 summit, Biarritz, 2019). Joseph Stiglitz, Nobel Prize-winning economist, observes that in structuring markets 'to serve those at the top' (2019, p.43) successive governments in the US and UK have made cardinal mistakes that perpetuate economic inequity and social instability, namely:

1   Failure to understand the importance of *long-term* thinking;
2   Lack of sensitivity to the eviscerating effects of economic *inequity*;
3   An ambiguous role for Government in achieving *equitable growth*;
4   Failure to understand the importance of *knowledge, learning and education* in supporting economic sustainability and innovation.

Such policy miscalculations add to the burden of school leaders seeking to mitigate child poverty effects in classrooms. What transpires is a set of inter-dependent variables in the architecture of public sector leadership at macro, meso and micro levels that frustrate and disempower the leadership role whilst diluting the transformative power of education as a public good. What is argued for here is a re-thinking of economic values and models regarding the size of the state, (Jacobs and Mazzucato, 2016; Mazzucato, 2018), the role of markets (Mazzucato, 2019; Stiglitz, 2019) and of communities (Rajan, 2019) that in turn define education purposes and the remit of its leaders.

A national education system as a public sector innovation project

Labour's proposal to establish a National Education Service (Labour 2019 Manifesto) aims to reverse austerity and stimulate equitable education outcomes. The core promise of the National Education Service Charter he is to deliver '*education that is free at the point of use, available universally and throughout life . . . (that will) 'create a strong and inclusive economy, enhance social cohesion and achieve greater equality'*. This new service is to be structured to 'enhance cooperation amongst all parts of the education system and across different boundaries and sectors'. Clearly, what is proposed is a public sector innovation programme with major implications for leadership development and system re-design.

Conceptualising public sector innovation

So what might public sector innovation involve with reference to education system re-design? A proposed definition is '*the design of new education services at different geographic and socio-structural levels that enhance learning, changing power relations and processes through which services are co-designed and delivered*'. The diagram below helps to conceptualise the three levels of innovation that require alignment within any public sector innovation project.

TABLE 14. 1 Levels of public sector innovation

Type	Aim	Outcome
Macro – *Disruptive*	To change conceptual frames of reference & challenge established narratives around size & role of the state, public sector and its leaders to shape new economic & educational structures	New economic, education & public value models incorporate system redesign. Leaders are skilled in problem-solving and deliberate design of learning ecosystems
Meso – *Institutional*	To challenge dominant economic models that restrict the role of the state and public sector to 'fixing' rather than innovating	State investment to create and shape markets & innovation networks where leaders sponsor bottom-up change
Micro – *Incremental*	To address unmet educational, leadership and community needs at the front line	Service re-design construed around human-centred processes & relationships

Critical shifts towards system innovation – the 4P conceptual framework

To help unpack what these levels of alignment above might mean in practice, it is helpful to focus on four very specific areas of systemic challenge, that I call the 4Ps:

1   Policy: To identify the economic assumptions driving government education policy;
2   Place: to consider how such policy translates at the level of place and regions;
3   People: to review evolving talent & professional development needs of leaders;
4   Performance: to consider how public value might be measured

I present below a conceptual framework that maps the problems arising across these four areas of challenge (4Ps) and charts what solutions might entail, given critical shifts in threshold concepts (Cousin, 2006) and the leveraging of enabling factors in practice. The aim is to generate fresh debate on education system re-design, drawing on a holistic conceptual model that links the design of solutions with enabling systemic resourcing.

A whole book could be written on the model above, but in the interest of brevity, I draw attention to the key concept of the *'entrepreneurial state'* as an investor in public sector innovation, enabling regional enterprise, working in partnership with education leaders, skilled in the design of education services that deliver real impact. The ongoing challenges of Covid-19 highlight the criticality of change-capable leaders and of system adaptability, currently massively under-resourced. The whole discussion that follows is located within a *systems of innovation* theoretical stance (Freeman 1995; Lundvall, 2007) which posits a role for the entrepreneurial state as both investor in innovation and enabler of innovative ecosystems across regions. The remainder of the chapter amplifies the 'people dimension' in system innovation with respect to deliberate 'design for impact' and leadership efficacy.

TABLE 14. 2 The 4P model – critical shifts from problems to solutions

4P AREAS	PROBLEM	SOLUTION	CONCEPT	ENABLER
POLICY	**Ideology drives Policy** Role of state confined to 'fixer' of failed markets. Little investment in public sector growth/ innovation.	**Policy prioritises investment** in education service innovation and innovation networks.	**Investment** *Entrepreneurial state* (Mazzucato, 2018) as investor in education & public sector innovation	**Dynamic innovation networks** enable flow & scaling of knowledge across national and local ecosystems.
PLACE	**Austerity fuels Inequality** School leaders 'fix' & firefight around welfare cuts & growing economic inequity.	**Long-term planning to stimulate *entrepreneurial regions*,** devolution, address inequity & digital dis-connectivity.	**Inclusive Ecosystem** Entrepreneurial regions drive innovation, enterprise, social justice & inclusion.	**Digital Connectivity** Services designed to enable anywhere, anytime access to lifelong learning.
PEOPLE	**Professional development fragmented** Isolation, firefighting and 'fixing' the norm for leaders. CoPs not facilitated or funded.	**Investment in development of *entrepreneurial leaders* who can problem solve,** innovate & add-value.	**Innovation** Entrepreneurial leaders sponsor R&D, bottom-up innovation & scale solutions.	**Deliberate Design** informs leadership development. Leaders shape local learning ecosystems.
PERFORMANCE	**Performance measures** No Public Value Framework (PVF) to measure efficacy of government and schools.	**PVF evaluates impact of education** & its capacity for innovation. Better understanding of how & where impact is generated	**Impact** Leaders skilled and up-skilled in deliberate design for impact & innovation.	**Data** Leadership impact enriched by access to live data & research.

Deliberate design for system innovation

System innovation demands a shift away from old models of *top-down reform* to one of *bottom-up service re-design*. The latter demands that leaders are sensitive to context, can energise schools, problem-solve and design solutions. Design is, primarily, a human-centred and multidisciplinary process with relationships (Cottam, 2019) and experiences at its core. It is increasingly recognised as a rigorous process for problem solving and surfacing unmet needs (Edson et al., 2017). This simplicity of definition belies a highly structured process and end-to-end cycle of observation, inquiry and problem-solving to prototype scalable solutions. It hinges on iterative inquiry to inform organisational change that is a world away from one-off transformation projects that leave culture utterly untouched.

Principles and values of system re-design

In drawing on design thinking precepts (NESTA/IDEO, 2009; Brown, 2009; Raffety, 2017) we are introduced a set of constructs that topple the tired discourse of 'fixing' and patching-up things up in favour of a humanistic methodology for deliberate design and personalisation of services. System re-design needs to satisfy five quality design values to ensure it is:

- **stakeholder-facing** placing professionals & communities at the heart of service redesign;
- **inclusive** and a force for social inclusion & regional regeneration;
- **adaptive** in providing for unmet learning needs of leaders & all stakeholders;
- **generative** of new professional knowledge, evidence and scalable solutions;
- **critical and creative** as a force for the creation of public value, human capital and impact.

Complex problem solving as a key leadership skill

The lexicon of deliberate design is all about the formation of leaders who can inquire, listen and problem solve – critical skills in public sector transformation. Research by Checinski (2019) reports that the failure rate for public-sector transformation projects is 80% and 74% for private-sector transformation efforts. Neither statistic is impressive. However, what the research does highlight is that the *'people'* factor - the skill of leaders in problem-solving and leading change - is the critical element in determining the success of transformation projects in any sector.

The World Economic Forum in its Future of Jobs Report (2016) placed complex problem solving as the number one skill for the 2020s. Critical thinking and creativity skills come next. Research undertaken by Feser et al. (2017) cite problem-solving, focus on results, seeking different perspectives and providing support to colleagues as prime attributes of high-performing leaders, irrespective of sector. Leaders who do well on problem-solving typically base decisions on sound analysis and are mindful of unconscious bias in decision-making (Kahneman et al, 1982).

Challenges in system innovation

However, there are challenges in introducing and scaling skills for change and problem solving across any national education system. They include the persistence of change resistant mindsets and silos; lack of national institutions to broker leadership training and facilitate innovation networks; and patchy investment in programmes for research, problem-solving, change management and leadership of innovation.

Siloed Mindsets

Currently, UK education is a highly siloed sector with diverse funding and transition arrangements at every level. Globally, leadership development over decades has prioritised management skills over creative problem-solving skills (see Table 14.3 below).

Unlike private sector organisations, education leaders must serve everyone within their universal remit, which demands service personalisation. However, it is recognised that within schools and many public sector organisations skills in deep analytics or human-centred design are in short supply (D'Emidio et al., 2019). Within any education system re-design project addressing leadership deficits in design and analytics skills-set is key.

Uncoordinated leadership development opportunities

Since 2010 centrally-funded institutions in the UK such as the National College for School Leadership (NCSL) and the Training Development Agency (TDA) have been progressively axed. The coordinating role and funding of Local Authorities has been reduced. Simultaneously, access to centrally-funded leadership development programmes and professional networking opportunities have been restricted. Wenger (2000) evidences that organisational success depends on leadership access to wider learning systems. Similarly, Freeman (1995) stresses the importance of government sponsored innovation networks. Within education system re-design, provision for centrally-funded organisations to co-ordinate leadership development and innovation networks is a must.

R&D and problem-solving deficit

There is some agreement that teachers should be *engaged* in research (CEBE, 2017; (BERA/RSA, 2014) which is not quite the same thing as generating it. Poor

TABLE 14.3 Managerial skills evolution (Adapted from Conn and McLean, 2019)

Phases	Strategy	Execution	Problem Solving
Time–Frames	1970s–1980s	1990s–2015	2015 onwards
Foci	Where & how to compete	Getting things done	Complex problem solving

investment in R&D was recognised by the OECD almost two decades ago as a major barrier to innovation in education (Maass, 2004) and continues to be a systemic deficit (Mehta, 2015). An evaluation of teaching as an evidence-based profession (Coldwell, Greaney et al., 2017) reported that whilst the need to solve problems provided the stimulus for teachers to draw on research, few had the confidence to interrogate research findings, instead looking to leaders to interpret research for them. Until R&D is integral to school practice, leaders will persist in missing the links between research, problem-solving, change and innovation.

Shift to prototyped programme for leadership development

The creation of a national education system demands that leaders not only learn about problem solving (Martin, 2009; NESTA/IDEO, 2009) but that they experience it (Raffety, 2015). John Fallon, former Chief Executive of Pearson, describes leadership in terms of 'defining a problem that's worth solving, bringing together the most talented people you can and then giving them the resources to go on and solve it' (The Times, August 9th 2014). Leaders need training in problem-solving processes and in sponsoring cultures (Brown, 2009) where R&D teams address strategic problems (Moldoveanu & Martin, 2008) and co-design scalable solutions.

What follows is such a blueprint for leadership development, grounded in empirical research (Raffety, 2015; 2017) and theoretical rigour (Breschi et al., 2017; Martin & Modeaveanu, 2007). In 2012, the Academy for Innovation, of which I am a Founding Director, developed the methodology of *'deliberate design for impact and innovation'* (2D2i), as part of an MA in Leadership and Innovation, validated by the University of West London. Following a year-long consultation with leaders, the part-time MA programme was designed, to:

- Provide access to modular, postgraduate accreditation;
- Enable part-time delivery in Innovation Hubs in twilight hours in term-time;
- Support local leaders to work together in Hub-based R&D teams;
- Address and align strategic school improvement priorities and role-specific problems;
- Develop skills in project design, problem-solving and strategic research to drive change;
- Generate and apply new knowledge to secure impact;
- Build capacity for scalability of solutions and innovation across schools and networks;
- Contribute to a community of practice (CoP);
- Produce termly stakeholder reports on research in progress;
- Present work in progress at an Annual Innovation in Practice Conference.

Methodology of 'deliberate design for impact and innovation' (2D2i)

In developing the process for problem solving (2D2i) within the MA programme, a number of methodological strands were synthesised such as *integrative thinking*

(Martin & Modeaveanu, 2007) spear-headed by the University of Toronto and *design thinking constructs* pioneered by Buchanan (1992) and Brown (2009). The programme drew on findings from my doctoral research (Penny, 1999) on micro-political issues in using research to drive change in schools. It incorporated practical insights from my experience as a change consultant to the National Remodelling Team (2005–2008) and Innovation Unit (2008–2010). Key principles in the design of leadership programmes (Feser et al., 2015) also informed the evolution of the 2D2i model, namely that:

1   learning is grounded in adult-learning principles and tailored to participants' needs;
2   the programme addresses real-world problems and organisational challenges;
3   participants develop skills as change catalysts which are applied;
4   learning is implemented at both individual and organisational levels;
5   learning is directly linked to value creation and scalable impact;
6   attention is paid to tools, processes and organisational culture to drive change.

A prototyped process for problem solving

The programme was delivered from 2013–18 in five Innovation Hubs in London and one near Birmingham. Critical thinking scaffolds were used to help make explicit disciplined processes in the design, review and reporting of projects. Performance coaching was a key feature of pedagogy. Year 1 focused on the *problem* and Year 2 on the *solution*, drawing on Sinek's (2011) sequenced leadership foci of *why, how and what*. Table 14.4 below summarises the 'Deliberate Design for Impact and Innovation' (2D2i) process and programme to equip leaders to solve real-world problems:

The programme included intensive training in research methodologies, pilot design, iterative prototyping and project evaluation, alongside skills development in premortem design (Klein, 2007), the micropolitics of change and cultural issues in leading and scaling innovation. Table 14.5 is a summary of how leadership skill development was targeted to secure intentional organisational effects:

It is important not to overclaim the efficacy of an approach to problem-solving derived from a 5-year MA programme across 6 Innovation Hubs in England. Leadership programmes can fail (Gurdjian et al., 2014) due to weak contextual relevance, decoupling reflection from the day-job, ignoring mindsets and failing to address impact. The MA programme intentionally addressed these four critical variables. We also devised a model to discuss and review leadership development with specific reference to context, community, collaboration and coaching. I'm writing a book to elaborate on all these approaches and models. For brevity's sake, Figure 14.1 below signals this personal, professional and community terrain in simple, diagrammatic form.

Programme insights

Problem solving requires the ability to inquire, analyse and synthesize ideas, whilst challenging assumptions and testing prototype solutions. It means that leaders must be able to conceptualise and critique their journey in learning, whilst reflecting on

TABLE 14.4 2D2i problem-solving programme

Year 1 Problem	Module Focus	Question	Year 2 Solution	Module Focus	Question
Term 1	**Design Project** – analyse context, organisation, role challenges. Clarify vision. Identify key problem. Align with strategic objectives. Specify intended impact. Review literature. State project assumptions, research question and initial intervention. Consider sample, stakeholders & potential for scaling.	Why?	Term 1	**Re-design Project** – test and prototype solution. Re-design project in light of new insights and data. Develop case for change, consider micro-political and cultural challenges. Conduct a Pre-mortem. Engage stakeholders. Present paper.	Why?
Term 2	**Design Methodology** – reflect critically on research design process as end-to-end project. Understand methodological pluralism. Design, define, defend methodology. Present paper.	How?	Term 2	**Refine Solution** – iterate and refine prototype solution. Elicit stakeholder feedback. Analyse data and consider strategy for scaling. Evaluate interim impact. Present paper	How?
Term 3	**Design Pilot** – test intervention, clarify project assumptions and project question. Analyse and reflect on data and feedback. Redefine/reframe problem in light of new insights. Present paper.	What?	Term 3	**Scale Solution** – test project solution and approach to scaling. Review project learning and insights. Define problem and solution, assess impact and claims in terms of new practice, theory or innovation. Final academic paper & conference presentation.	What?

TABLE 14.5 2D2i leadership skills development for organisational effects

Leadership Skills	Organisational & Cultural Effects	Mode
Analyse & think creatively	Analyse context, reflect & diagnose **problem**	BE
Design & trial solutions	R&D team inquire, co-design & test **solutions**	ASK
Design change strategy	R&D team develop strategy for change & scaling	DO
Evaluate impact	Evaluate levels of impact & apply insights	KNOW
Scale and adapt	Scale innovation & adapt as cultural norm	ENACT

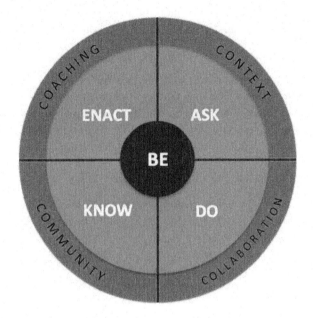

FIGURE 14.1 Contextual variables and leadership modes

processes. The key learning was that leaders required very focused training in four executive behaviours, to enable them to:

- Co-create vision and sponsor horizontal teams to drive strategic R&D across hierachies;
- Ask questions to expand mindsets, knowledge & skills;
- Coach teams to learn, problem solve & collaborate on strategic priorities;
- Enable organizational models, structures and culture to make innovation the day job.

Ancillary Learning Points

1   Enhanced recruitment and retention were unanticipated programme benefits.
2   It took time and skill to distinguish between symptoms and substantive problems.
3   Problem definition and re-framing became key to prototyping successful solutions.

4 Research design and project management required scaffolding and external support.
5 Leaders needed help to align R&D, professional learning and strategic change initiatives.
6 R&D teams required external facilitation to form, storm, norm and perform.
7 Successful leaders empowered R&D teams to connect with, and span, hierarchies.
8 Leaders benefitted from peer-feedback in prototyping solutions and confron ting biases.
9 Projects scaled well where change proposals aligned with schools' CPD ecosystems.
10 Over time, leaders became more skilled in evaluating insights, impact and innovation.

Kotter (2011) argues that organisations need *both* networks and hierarchy to evolve. We also found that school hierarchies optimise efficiency when aligned with horizontal R&D remitted to drive change. However, Innovation Hubs did need coaching to appreciate the mutuality of agile R&D teams within hierarchical systems, coupled with specific skills development in negotiating the politics of change.

Performance and the public value of education

Enabling change, impact and innovation are reasonable performance expectations of any leadership role in the 21st century. A benefit of equipping education leaders to design learning around intended impact is that it positions them to potentially engage with policy-makers regarding the public value of education and its funding. However, the study of public value is very complex as identified by Jørgensen & Bozeman (2007). Public value is not easily defined (Alford & Hughes, 2008) nor is there an agreed methodology for measuring public sector performance. Most countries assume that public sector outputs equate with inputs, implying the only way to improve education is to throw more money at it. We know that is too simplistic.

One way through this impasse might be to think in terms of a Public Value Framework (PVF) that is inclusive of Government, the public sector and schools. Such an exemplar framework trialled and reported by Barber (2017) charts the terrain of public value and offers a credible starting point on which to build. He proposes (Barber, 2017, p.27) the four pillars of "pursuing goals, managing inputs, engaging users and citizens and developing system capacity". As we scrutinise the detail under the four pillars of goals, it is clear that the exemplar Public Value Framework is premised on building system 'capacity to innovate', 'learn from innovation', 'work across organisational boundaries' and 'evaluate impact'. Such a Public Value Framework may map well onto the domain of a national education system and a more entrepreneurial leadership function at the level of both state and schools, trained in innovation by design.

Cautionary tale

The dominance of free market discourse and new public management theory has eclipsed values associated with equity, social justice and professionalism (Gewirtz et al., 1995). A new national education system must attend not only to structural changes but critically to values and discursive regimes.

Reflections

An aim of this chapter has been to stimulate thinking and critique around the symbiotic roles of state, leaders and communities in education service and system re-design. Education is a humanistic project. It contributes to public value (Mazzucato, 2018) & human capital (Samek et al., 2019). It raises fundamental questions about economic models & the interests they serve, alongside our values for society, the planet we inhabit & our shared future. Within any national education system, viewed here as ongoing transformation project, the resourcing of leaders as problem-solvers and innovators is critical. The chapter concludes by recommending four policy shifts as a package for systemic innovation premised on the *core value of long term investment in education as a public and social good.*

Radical Change Recommendations

The issues raised in this chapter lead to a number of policy options:

Policy Option 1: Long term investment by an entrepreneurial state in education system innovation and innovation networks.

Policy Option 2: Long-term investment and planning to stimulate entrepreneurial regions, addressing economic inequity and enabling digital connectivity.

Policy Option 3: Log term investment in education and public sector leadership development, prioritising training in problem solving and service re-design to meet the needs of lifelong learners.

Policy Option 4: Commissioning of a Public Value Framework to help evaluate impact across a national education system and enable access to live, high-quality data on sector performance.

The penultimate chapter provides further reflections and an executive summary of options, consequences and cautionary tales.

References

Alford, J., & Hughes, O. (2008) Public Value Pragmatism as the Next Phase of Public Management. *The American Review of Public Administration, 38*(2), 130–148.

Barber, M., (2017) Delivering Better Outcomes for Citizens: practical steps for unlocking public value London: *Crown Copyright 2017.*

Barber, M., Chijioke, C., & Mourshed, M. (2010) *How the World's most Improved School Systems keep Getting Better.* London: McKinsey & Company.

BERA/RSA (2014) *Research and the Teaching Profession: Building the capacity for a self-improving education system - Final report of the BERA-RSA inquiry into the role of research in teacher education,* London: BERA.

Breschi, R., Freundt, T., Orebäck, M. & Vollhardt, K. (2017) The Expanding Role of Design in Creating an End-to-end Customer Experience *McKinsey and Company.*

Britton, J., Farquarson, C. & Sibieta, L. (2019) *The 2019 Annual Report on Education Spending in England,* London: Institute for Fiscal Studies.

Brown, T. (2009) *Change by Design: How Design Thinking Creates New Alternatives for Business Education Services and Society,* New York: Harper Collins.

Buchanan, R. (1992), Wicked Problems in Design Thinking, *Design Issues, Vol. 8, No. 2 (Spring, 1992), pp. 5–21 Published by: The MIT Press.*

CEBE (2017) Leading Research Engagement in Education: Guidance for organisational change, *CEBE/SSAT.*

Checinski, M., Dillon R., Hieronimus S., & Klier, J. Putting People at the Heart of Public-Sector Transformations, New York: *McKinsey and Company.*

Coldwell, M., Greaney, T., Higgins, S., Brown, C., Maxwell, B., Stiell, B., Stoll, L., Willis, B., & Burns, H. (2017) *Evidence-informed teaching: an evaluation of progress in England. Research Report July 2017.*London: Department for Education, 2017. DFE-RR-696.

Conn, C. & McLean, R. (2019) *Bulletproof Problem Solving: The One Skill That Changes Everything,* Hoboken New Jersey: John Wiley & Sons.

Cottam, H (2019) *Radical Help: How we can remake relationships between us and revolutionise the welfare state,* London: Virago Press.

Cousin, G. (2006) An introduction to Threshold Concepts, *Higher Education Academy.*

D'Emidio, T., Klier, J., Wagner, J. & Weber T. (2019) The Public Sector gets Serious about Customer Experience, *New York: McKinsey Quarterly.*

Edson, J., Kouyoumjian, G. & Sheppard, B. (2017) More Than a Feeling: Ten design practices to deliver business Education Services Value, *New York: McKinsey and Company.*

Feser C., Mayol, F. & Srinivasan, R. (2015) Decoding Leadership: What Really Matters, New York: *McKinsey Quarterly.*

Feser, C., Nielsen, N. & Rennie, M (2017) What's Missing In Leadership Development? New York: *McKinsey & Company.*

Freeman, C. The 'National System of Innovation' in Historical Perspective, *Cambridge Journal of Economics,* Volume 19, Issue 1, February 1995, Pages 5–24, https://doi.org/10.1093/oxfordjournals.cje.a035309.

Gewirtz, S., Ball, S. & Bowe, R., (1995) *Markets, Choice and Equity in Education* Buckingham: Open University Press.

Gurdjian, P., Halbeisen, T. & Lane, K. (2014) Why Leadership Development Programmes Fail *New York: McKinsey Quarterly Jan 2014.*

G7 Leaders' Summit 2019: https://sdg.iisd.org/events/g7-leaders-summit-2019/.

Jacobs, M. (2018) *Prosperity and Justice - A Plan for the New Economy: The Final Report of the IPPR Commission on Economic Justice* London: IPPR/Polity Book.

Jacobs, Michael & Mazzucato, Mariana. (2016). 1. Rethinking Capitalism: An Introduction. *The Political Quarterly. 86. 10.1111/1467–923X.12230.*

Jørgensen, T. B., & Bozeman, B. (2007). Public Values: An Inventory. *Administration & Society, 39*(3), 354–381. https://doi.org/10.1177/0095399707300703.

Kahneman, D., Slovic, P. & Tversky, A. (1982) *Judgment Under Uncertainty: Heuristics and Biases.* New York: Cambridge University Press.

Klein, G. (2007) Performing a Project Premortem *Harvard Business Review, Sept 2007 Issue.*

Kotter, J. (2011) Hierarchy and Network: Two Structures, One Organisation *Harvard Business Review https://hbr.org/2011/05/two-structures-one-organizatio.*

Labour Party Manifesto (2019) https://labour.org.uk/manifesto/.

Lubienski, C. (2006) *Do Quasi-markets Foster Innovation in Education? A Comparative Perspective, OECD Education Working Papers,* No. 25, OECD Publishing, Paris.

Lundvall, Bengt-Åke (2007) National Innovation Systems—Analytical Concept and Development Tool. *Industry & Innovation. 14. 95–119. 10.1080/13662710601130863.*

Maass, G. (2004) Funding of Public Research and Development: Trends and Changes, *OECD Journal on Budgeting,* vol. 3/4, https://doi.org/10.1787/budget-v3-art22-en.

Martin, R. & Modeaveanu, M. (2007) Designing the Thinker of the Future *pp.5–8, Rotman Business School, Winter 2007.*

Martin, R. (2009) *Design of Business: Why Design Thinking is the Next Competitive Advantage,* Harvard: Harvard Business Review Press.

Mazzucato, M. (2018) *The Entrepreneurial State: Debunking Public vs. Private Sector Myths,* London: Penguin.

Mazzucato, M. (2019) *The Value of Everything: Making and Taking in the Global Economy,* London: Penguin.

McCann, P. (2019) Perceptions of Regional Inequality and the Geography of Discontent: Insights from the UK, *UK2070 Commission Think Piece.*

Mehta, J. (2015) From Quicksand to Solid Ground: Building a Foundation to Support Quality Teaching, *Harvard Graduate School of Education* http://www.totransformteaching.org/wp-content/uploads/2015/10/From-Quicksand-to-Solid-Ground-Building-a-Foundation-to-Support-Quality-Teaching.pdf.

Moldoveanu, M. C. & Martin, R. (2008) *The Future of the MBA: Designing the Thinker of the Future* Oxford: Oxford University Press.

National Education Service Charter https://www.labour.org.uk/wp-content/uploads/2018/09/Charter-of-the-National-Education-Service.pdf.

NESTA (2009) *Designing for Public Services: A Practical Guide* NESTA/IDEO https://www.nesta.org.uk/toolkit/designing-for-public-services-a-practical-guide/.

Offe, C. & Ronge, V. 1975 (1975). Theses on the Theory of the State. *New German Critique.* 6. 10.2307/487658.

Penny, R. (1999) *A Case Study of the Micropolitics of Change: Perspectives on Policymaking and Teacher Professionalism in a Comprehensive School in the 1990s,* Unpublished PhD Thesis. University of Exeter.

Rajan, R. (2019) *The Third Pillar: How Markets and the State leave the Community Behind,* London: Penguin Random House.

Raffety, R., (2015) Work-based Research in Primary Leadership Education, *New Vistas Journal, Volume 1 Issue 1, University of West London.*

Raffety, R. (2017) School-based Research, using the Methodology of Deliberate Design for Impact and Innovation (2D2i): Think Piece *London: Academy for Innovation.*

Samek, L., Darko, C., King, W., Sidhu, S.V., Parmar, M., Foliano, F., Moore, F., O'Mahony, M., Payne, C., Rincon-Aznar, A. & Vassilev, G. (2018) Provision of Human Capital Evidence Review - A Report for the Office for National Statistics, *London: ONS.*

SchoolsWeek April 27th 2018: Headteachers Roundtable Summit 2018 https://schoolsweek.co.uk/headteachers-roundtable-summit-2018-be-bold-stay-ethical-and-keep-learning-at-the-heart-of-solutions/.

Sinek, S. (2011) *Start With Why: How Great Leaders Inspire Everyone To Take Action* London: Penguin.

Stiglitz, J. (2019) *People, Power and Profits: Progressive Capitalism for an Age of Discontent,* London: Allen Lane.

UK2070 Commission (2019) Fairer and Stronger: Rebalancing the UK Economy – The First Report of the 2070 Commission, *UK2070 Commission.*

UNCTAD (2019) *Trade and Development Report: Financing a Global Green New Deal,* UNCTAD.

Wenger, E. (2000) Communities of Practice and Social Learning Systems. *Organization, 7(2), 225–246.*

World Economic Forum (2016) Global Challenge Insight Report: The Future of Jobs - Employment, Skills and Workforce Strategy for the Fourth Industrial Revolution, *World Economic Forum.*

15

AN ALTERNATIVE APPROACH TO ACCOUNTABILITY AND INSPECTION

Evaluation for improvements in Finnish Teacher Education

Brian Hudson, Marilyn Leask with Hannele Niemi and Jari Lavonen

Introduction

This is an abridged version of a chapter by Hannele Niemi and Jari Lavonen (University of Helsinki) that was first published in 2012 (Niemi & Lavonen, 2012). It is entitled "Evaluation for improvements in Finnish Teacher Education" and is reproduced with the kind agreement of Peter Lang publishers and the authors. We use it as an exemplary case study of an enhancement-led quality assurance approach to demonstrate there are alternative approaches to accountability and inspection to those used in England. Moreover, such an alternative approach can be seen to be demonstrably highly effective, as it works well in Finland: one of the most successful education systems in the world. The authors draw attention at the outset to Scotland also having a system of enhancement-led institutional (ELIR) reviews since 2003. The case study focuses on the main structures and processes by which quality in Teacher Education particularly has been assessed at the national, institutional and programme levels in Finland. It also draws on the results of recent evaluations and the outcomes of a national-level QA-related research project. We draw on this chapter in the final section on reflections to highlight policy options that relate to particular sets of values in relation to conceptions of professionalism in education and teacher education in particular.

> Concepts like quality control and quality management are often perceived as technocratic top-down approaches which frequently fail in . . . education. It is suggested that in recent times the field of quality management in . . . education has changed. The new era – uses . . . more holistic quality approaches in order to develop an organisational culture of quality . . . focussing on change instead of control, development rather than assurance and innovation

more than standards compliance. In this process quality management systems and instruments, competencies, and individual and collective values, are not seen as separate entities of quality development but are combined into a holistic concept – the concept of quality culture.'

(Ehlers, 2009, p. 359)

Trust is not a status quo, it requires continuous work.

(Niemi & Lavonen, 2012, p. 182)

Three levels of quality assurance in Finnish teacher education

In Finland, the national evaluation policy, and quality assurance part of it, is enhancement-led, meaning that evaluation is a tool for improvements. This is also the leading principle in Higher Education (HE). In Finnish HE there are three main levels of Quality Assurance (QA) as shown in Figure 15.1:

1 National level. There are audits and other external reviews. QA in teacher education (TE) follows the national common frameworks for HE. It is mainly based on audits in six-year cycles organized by the Finnish Higher Education Evaluation Council (FINHEEC) and strategic negotiations of accountability with the Ministry of Culture and Education (MCE). The first round of audits in all Finnish HE institutions were completed by 2011. In addition, TE has also been a special interest area of the MCE and it has initiated or supported several national evaluations or reviews during the last few years. (2)

2 Institutional level: The main responsibility for TE quality lies with individual universities. TE is part of HE. All primary and secondary school teacher education is carried out in universities. This means that teacher education is also part of universities' own QA policy. Each university has its own strategic plans for the development of teaching and research. Universities set up their own QA methods and TE must follow these common guidelines. TE is assessed as all other university disciplines or programmes in the reference frame of their own discipline criteria.

3 Department and programme level: there are processes at the grassroots level for improving the quality of student learning. These QA methods are the closest to TE students and teachers. TE staff use several QA tools and practices, like collaborative programme planning with staff and stakeholders. The systematic collection of student feedback and its collaborative analysis is another example of department QA.

This chapter presents the main structures and processes by which quality in TE is assessed at the national, institutional and even programme levels in Finland.

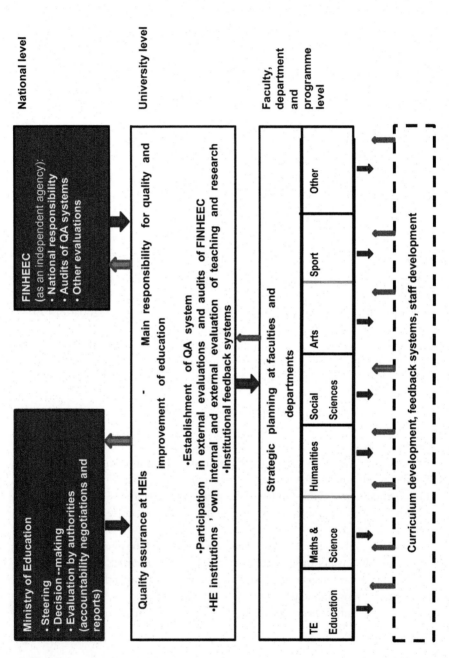

FIGURE 15. 1 The quality assurance system in teacher education in Finnish HE

The Finnish evaluation policy in HE – an enhancement-led approach at the national level

The Finnish evaluation policy and QA are based on improvement-led principles. This is frequently called an enhancement-led policy. The main aim is to use evaluations to raise quality in operational processes and to seek efficient and effective ways to achieve high outcomes in teaching and learning. These have been FINHEEC's principles since its establishment in 1996:

> FINHEEC evaluations use an enhancement-led approach. The aim is to help HE institutions to identify the strengths and good practices in their operations as well as development targets. Enhancement-led evaluation supports the institutions in realising their own strategic aims and targeting their future development and also engenders constant development. The key procedures in enhancement-led evaluation are varied, inclusive evaluation methods and the incorporation of external evaluation into the everyday work and normal development of the higher education institutions. The enhancement-led approach is used in all the phases of the FINHEEC evaluation process: as part of planning, implementation, reporting and follow-up.

Scotland also has enhancement-led institutional reviews (ELIR) as one component of its Quality Enhancement Framework (QEF). Introduced in 2003, they are seen there as a radical approach to QA and enhancement in HE. The main focus of the ELIR method is to review an institution's approach to improving the student learning experience. It also examines an institution's ability to secure the academic standards of its awards and to manage the quality of the learning opportunities it provides to its students. In the Finnish system auditing covers all university operations including teaching, research, interaction with society, infrastructure and administration.

FINHEEC conducts an auditing process for each HE institution every sixth year. FINHEEC is an independent expert body assisting HE institutions and the Ministry of Education and Culture in evaluation matters. The Council members represent universities, universities of applied sciences, students and working life. Decisions made by the Council are prepared and implemented by a Secretariat, led by a Secretary General (Government Decree on FINHEEC 794/2009).

In the Finnish HE audits focus on a university's QA methods and procedures, not outcomes: the QA methods should ensure high quality outcomes. Every audit has an external review team and an external evaluation process starts with an internal self-evaluation or a kind of SWOT analysis made by the institution's staff. The staff present their objectives, recognise strengths and weaknesses in their self-evaluation and present evidence which supports the findings. The external evaluators or an evaluation panel become familiar with the self-evaluation documents and prepare questions for the next step, interviews and discussions. Finally, the panel prepares an external evaluation report based on the self-evaluation report and interviews. Even though the main focus is on the institutions' own aims and activities, the Finnish auditing model is based on the Standards and Guidelines for QA in the European HE Area (ENQA, 2011).

Teacher education faculties have given feedback that they had already documented their processes before because they are accountable to society as a whole for their outcomes. The same feedback has emerged from those involved in medicine as it also has a very close relationship with employers and the health care sector (Haapakorpi, 2011).

Audits in teacher education

Universities with a legal right to award degrees are responsible for the quality of those degrees. Teacher education follows the same QA processes as all HE in Finland. The main QA method at the national level is auditing, which means assessing the methods by which higher education institutions assure their own quality.

All primary and secondary school teachers have received their education in eight universities since the 1970s. Vocational teachers have received their education in one of five teacher education HE units since 1995 which are closely related with universities of applied sciences (polytechnics). According to teacher education decrees issued in 1995 and 2005, all teachers must attain a master's degree to receive a teacher qualification.[1]

In Finland there is neither a Teacher Council nor any other external agency that awards certificates or licences to teach in schools after graduation. The Decree on Teacher Qualifications defines what is required for teaching posts at different levels and sectors of the education system, while the Teacher Education Decree regulates how the BA and MA degrees must be composed if someone wants to become a teacher. When hiring a new teacher, employers check that the applicant has these studies in their academic degree.

The audits ensure that the general structures are relevant and well-functioning in teacher education in Finland; but they cannot assure what happens in teaching and learning in a local context. This means that we also need other methods for ensuring quality in teacher education. Auditing allows universities a high degree of freedom to create their own methods for QA and particularly for providing a quality culture. Teacher education includes very complex study programmes which need collaboration with many disciplines as well as many university departments. Programmes also consist of teaching practice in university teacher training schools or local schools. Promoting a quality culture means that the relevance of studies, structure of degrees and quality of leaning outcomes must be assessed with methods other than just audits. National evaluations of TE and research projects on TE are important sources to be used in the further development of TE.

National evaluations, research and networks for promoting QA in teacher education

During the last 20 years, Finnish teacher education has been evaluated systematically in many national and international external evaluations. Further, many research projects and doctoral dissertations have provided important knowledge for further development. The following major evaluation processes have been carried out during this time:

- 1989 National Committee for Developing Teacher Education
- 1993–1994 National and international evaluation of educational sciences and teacher education (The Committee Report, 1994; Buchberger et al., 1994; Niemi & Kohonen, 1995)
- 1995–1998 Research project 'Effectiveness of Teacher Education' as part of a large national research programme 'Effectiveness of Education' (Niemi, 1996, 2002; Niemi & Kemmis, 1999)
- 1998 National evaluation of ICT in teacher education (Niemi, 1999)
- 1998–1999 National evaluation of teacher education (Jussila & Saari, 1999)
- Evaluation of the quality of research in the teacher education departments in the University of Helsinki 2000 and 2005
- Teacher education 2020 (Ministry of Education, 2007)
- Auditing of all Finnish universities 2005–2011 (FINHEEC, 2011).

Some of the national level evaluations have focussed on structural and HE policy issues and some have concentrated on themes of teachers' professional development in TE. The evaluations have revealed many positive outcomes of TE in Finland. Elementary teacher education has remained one of the most popular study options. TE has succeeded in recruiting high quality students. Graduated teachers have good classroom skills and content knowledge. There has not been a real problem of dropouts from the teacher-education programmes and teachers do not usually change from their teaching job to another profession. Teachers are committed to their work in schools after graduation. Only 10–15% of teachers have thought of changing to another career even though their academic MA level qualification would make them competent for a large range of different career options. Young teachers see their profession as lifelong learning and they have a very positive attitude to developing their job skills.

Although teacher education has succeeded in many respects, there are still many problems which need to be taken seriously. Many evaluations have pointed out that the lack of co-operation between different partners decreases the quality of teacher education. Co-operation should have been much better organised, more oriented towards common purposes and more intensive. These needs are apparent between academic disciplines and educational departments, teacher training schools and teacher education departments, local schools and university schools, teacher education institutions and local communities. Multicultural issues set new demands for Finnish schools as do the increasing numbers of children with special needs.

Informal benchmarking between universities provides one form of QA and also provides platforms to share urgent challenges as well as best practices. Regular national meetings among deans and heads of departments that are responsible for TE are important QA tools. Since 1987 it has also been a tradition that researchers of different subject matters hold national annual seminars, mostly organised in Helsinki. These forums provide researchers interested in subject didactics an opportunity to discuss and interact with other researchers and create research-based knowledge for the development of teacher education (e.g. Meisalo, 2007, p. 174). National co-operation has also been typical in reform processes that have brought about changes in the major structures or contents of TE.

Teacher education as part of universities' own QA

Finnish teacher education has received much attention because of the high learning outcomes of Finnish 15-year-old students in the international Programme for International Student Assessment (PISA). The students achieved the highest or second highest scores in reading, mathematics and scientific literacy assessment among students in OECD countries in the years 2000, 2003, 2006 and 2009.[2] Many researchers as well as Finnish policy makers regard high quality teachers and teacher education as one of the major factors in good learning outcomes (e.g., Lavonen, 2008).

Universities have a high degree of autonomy in designing their curricula. Therefore, no detailed 'curriculum of teacher education' covering all universities in Finland can be presented (Niemi & Jakku-Sihvonen, 2011). However, based on the Decree of Teacher Education (2005), the main elements of all teacher education curricula consist of studies in the following:

- *Academic disciplines:* as taught in schools. Class teachers have a major in educational sciences and minors in other disciplines. Class teachers also have a module 'Multidisciplinary Studies' (60 ECTS credits) which is a combination of different school subjects and their pedagogics.
- *Research studies:* methodological studies, a BA thesis and a MA thesis.
- *Pedagogical studies* (min. 60 ECTS credits): obligatory, includes teaching practice.
- *Communication, language and ICT*: obligatory.
- The preparation of *a personal study plan.*
- *Optional studies.*

These elements can be integrated in several different ways depending on students' career choices. Although a distinction between class teachers and subject teachers is retained, the structures of the respective degree programmes allow them to take very flexible routes to include both in the same programme or permit later qualification in either direction.

Class teachers

Students in class teacher education programmes take a five-year degree programme leading to Masters level.

Besides the major studies in education described previously, *multidisciplinary studies* as the first minor subject give a prominent knowledge-base to a class teacher.

Multidisciplinary studies consist of pedagogy of all primary school subjects as well as the cross-curricular themes to be implemented in varied school subjects.

Subject teachers

Subject teachers teach different subjects in secondary school. Their education requires co-operation between academic subject faculties or departments and teacher education departments. For instance, at the University of Helsinki the subject teacher education is organised in co-operation with six faculties and the Department of Teacher Education. Studies are divided into two parts: the subject is studied at the department of the particular subject (e.g. Physics), while the pedagogical studies are undertaken at the Department of Teacher Education and in two Teacher Training Schools. These pedagogical studies give the students the qualification necessary for teaching positions in all types of schools in their major and minor subject.

Students in the subject teacher education programme take a major and a minor in the subjects they intend to teach in school.

Pedagogical studies

The pedagogical studies are obligatory for qualification as a teacher and are approximately the same for primary, secondary teachers, vocational and adult education teachers.

Discussion

It is important to recognise the different levels in QA and the role of QA at each level and, moreover, the interaction between levels. At the national level, the audits and other external reviews offer feedback on national-level planning and allocation of resources as well as an external input to the continuous development of Teacher Education (TE) at the institutional, department and programme levels.

QA at the institutional level offers information for the development of co-operation and structures of TE. At the department and programme level, QA is important for the continuous development of the programmes. Vice versa, also grass-roots level feedback is needed for institutional and national level reforms.

The Finnish evaluation and QA policy emphasises improvement-led approaches. The purpose of all the evaluations is to enhance quality in teaching, learning and research in HE. In TE this requires systematic feedback loops and intensive co-operation with many actors and partners in TE. Teacher education has very ambitious aims. For decades the Finnish orientation toward TE has committed itself to the development of a research-based professional culture (Niemi & Jakku-Sihvonen, 2006). The aim of TE studies is to train students to find and analyse problems they may expect to face in their future work. In Finnish TE the aim is that teachers can work as independent professionals in schools and make their active contribution on educational issues including development of the school curriculum as well as formative and summative assessments of students' learning.

To achieve these objectives holistic QA and interactive processes between all levels of QA are needed. High quality TE requires that national, institutional, departmental and programme level actors continuously co-operate with regard to diagnosing, discussing and making decisions about the development of structures, contents and methods. It is also important that staff members at the institutional and department level and relevant stakeholders are aware of the role of the different levels and the role of QA at each level.

Ehlers writes (2009) referring to Wolff (2004) that we are entering a new era in quality management of HE. Much attention has been paid to mastering instruments of quality control or accreditation in the past decade. The focus is turning more and more to mastering change, allowing ownership for individual development, promoting champions in organizations and enabling professionals in HE.

In teacher education we need methods and practices that get deeper into organizations and closer to the teachers and learners.

In Europe many countries agree that the general idea of transforming national teacher education aims into the form of standards or learning outcomes is to enhance learning and to make learning explicit and accountable and, moreover, to increase the quality of learning (Spady, 2003). Defining learning outcomes has been emphasised as an important basis for the quality of education in educational policy papers in Europe. However, this approach is not without its problems, especially in terms of QA at the local level. The roots of defining the learning outcomes could be argued to come close to the behaviouristic tradition of teaching and learning where the main idea is to define the 'end behaviour' in precise terms in order to create a basis for optimal instructional treatment. This kind of straightforward idea of teaching could be harmful to understanding learning and the development of TE programmes as a process.

Finland has not followed the standardisation tradition as it has been pursued in many other countries by harmonising TE programmes, organising centralised assessment in TE and a heavy national-level QA policy. In Finland, the role of different levels and autonomy at each level in QA has been emphasised. For example, the role of QA at the department level is mainly for the continuous and collaborative development of TE programmes. Finland approaches QA by understanding quality in a broad way: quality in education leads to the intended learning outcomes either indicated in national-level documents or, like in the Finnish system, is decided on in a department and at the programme level in particular situations.

The Finnish model is based on a level of trust where all partners involved in TE make sure their processes are kept at a high level. It has so far worked since all levels of QA take their responsibility seriously. It also means that continuous interaction is needed between different partners. Trust is not a status quo; it requires continuous work.

Reflections

It is significant that the ambitious aims of teacher education in Finland are based on a commitment to the development of a research-based professional culture. In

Finnish teacher education the aim of teachers working as independent professionals in schools is stressed as is their active contribution to the development of the
school curriculum and to the formative and summative assessments of students'
learning. This perspective is based on a values judgement which rejects the narrow
instrumentalism of simply mastering instruments of quality control or accreditation
within a culture of managerialist control and imposed workforce technical compliance. A key issue is one of coming to terms with change, allowing ownership
for individual development, promoting champions in organizations and enabling
professionals in education contexts. As exemplified by Ehlers (2009, p. 344):

> A main problem which is addressed is that even though sometimes effec-
> tive organizational processes have been implemented, the educational quality
> (e.g. answering the question 'what is good learning?') is still lagging behind,
> and teaching strategies of educators or learning strategies of students have
> not been improved.

In teacher education and education more broadly methods and practices that get
deeper into organizations and closer to the teachers and learners are necessary.

It is also significant to note that Finland has not followed the standardization
tradition as it has been pursued in many other countries by harmonising TE programmes, organising centralized assessment in TE and a heavy national-level QA
policy. Rather in Finland, the role of different levels and the autonomy at each level
in QA has been emphasized. For example, the role of QA at the department level
is mainly for the continuous and collaborative development of TE programmes.
Finland approaches QA by understanding quality in a broad way: quality in education leads to the intended learning outcomes either indicated in national-level
documents or, as in the Finnish system, is decided on in a department and at the
programme level in particular situations.

Of special significance is the fact that the Finnish model is based on a level of
trust where all partners involved in education make sure their processes are kept at
a high level. This implies that continuous interaction is needed between different
partners and that trust is not a status quo but an aspect that requires continuous
work.

Looking at the context in England, differences in approach are immediately
apparent. As highlighted by Niemi and Lavonen (2012), mentioned previously,
Scotland has had a system of enhancement-led institutional (ELIR) reviews since
2003. The website for QAA Scotland describes Enhancement-led Institutional
Review (ELIR) as an evidence-based method of peer review, meaning that staff
and students from other institutions join a team of reviewers to assess what each
HE institution does. ELIR results in a judgement and a set of commendations and
recommendations relating to the way the institution is securing academic standards
and improving the student experience. As discussed in Hudson and Moran (2012),
with regard to programmes of Initial Teacher Education in Scotland, these are subject to validation and review processes under the auspices of a university or degree
awarding institution and must be accredited by the General Teaching Council for

Scotland (GTCS) as leading to registration as a teacher. Given the central place of HE in this process of registration, there is a dual system of QA in the case of Initial Teacher Education with the Quality Assurance Agency (QAA) Scotland having the responsibility for QA of HE. Thus procedures at the institutional level need to take account of this dual system in relation to their internal QA processes and procedures.

The central role of the GTCS as the professional body for teaching in Scotland with significant powers stands in sharp contrast to the situation in England where the General Teaching Council for England was abolished in 2012. Although the Chartered College of Teaching was formed in England in 2017 the remit of this body does not extend to that of the GTCS and it is still in the process of working to establish its standing and support in the profession as a whole. Some observers with experience of the system in Scotland have drawn attention to the significant level of trust that has been built into the system over a long period of time in Scotland between teachers and the GTCS. It also been observed that the system in Scotland has an advantage in this regard over England in being much smaller. At just under 5.5 million in 2017, the population of Scotland is one-tenth the size of England. However, this highlights the potential of establishing a similar system in England overseen by Education England but operationalized at a regional level. This would involve a system with input to QA systems in HE from representative bodies of profession at the regional level.

Policy options

The issues raised in this chapter lead to a number of policy options. The decisions made reflect the values of those making them. To make decisions about change, you are advised to consult stakeholders to find out what is working well and what needs changing. For example, in England, it is wasteful of time and resources to subject university teacher training to two different systems with regard to accountability: one being the Quality Assurance Agency processes applied to all universities and the other being the Ofsted system of external inspection that is principally applied to schools.

> **Policy Option 1:** Status quo
> **Policy Option 2:** Accountability based on trust as outlined previously with the recognition that 'trust is not a status quo but an aspect that requires continuous work.'
> **Policy Option 3:** Consultation to establish a system which focuses on national interest with due consideration of cost-benefits and input from representative bodies of profession at the regional level.

The penultimate chapter provides further reflections and an executive summary of options, consequences and cautionary tales.

Notes

1 As part of the Bologna Process, on 1 August 2005 teacher education in Finland moved to a two-tier degree system. In terms of the Bologna Process, the degree of qualified teachers is equivalent to a second-cycle degree in the European HE area. Teacher qualification requires BA 180 + MA 120 = 300 ECTS credits (1 ECTS credit is about 27 hours work).
2 Finnish MCE: www.minedu.fi/pisa/index.html?lang=n

References

Buchberger, F., De Corte, E., Groombridge, B., & Kennedy, M. *Educational Studies and Teacher Education in Finnish Universities*: A Commentary by an International Review Team p. 14. Helsinki, 1994: Ministry of Education, Division of Educational and Research Policy.

Ehlers, U. 'Understanding Quality Culture', *Quality Assurance in Education*, 17/4, 2009, 343–363. https://doi.org/10.1108/09684880910992322

ENQA. The European Association for Quality Assurance in Higher Education (www.enqa. eu/files/BergenReport 210205.pdf.) – Accessed 14 March 2011.

Haapakorpi, A. 'Quality Assurance Processes in Finnish Universities: Direct and Indirect Outcomes and Organisational Conditions', *Quality in Higher Education*, 17/1, 2011, 69–81.

Hudson, B., & Moran, T. 'Quality Assurance Systems in Teacher Education Reform for the 21st Century in Scotland', in J. Harford, B. Hudson & H. Niemi (Eds.) *Quality Assurance and Teacher Education: International Challenges and Expectations* (Oxford, Peter Lang, 2012). ISBN 9783034302500.

Jussila, J., & Saari, S. *Opettajankoulutus tulevaisuuden tekijänä* (Teacher Education as an Agency for the Future). Publications of the Finnish Higher Education Council, 11. Helsinki, 1999: Edita. Korkeakoulujen arviointineuvoston julkaisuja 11. Edita: Helsinki.

Lavonen, J. 'Finland in PISA 2006 Scientific Literacy Assessment', in J. Hautamäki, E. Harjunen, A. Hautamäki, T. Karjalainen, S. Kupiainen, J. Lavonen, E. Pehkonen, P. Rantanen & P. Scheinin (Eds.) *PISA 2006: Analysis, Reflections, Explanations* (Helsinki: Ministry of Education Publications, 2008), 44, 65–113.

Meisalo, V. 'Subject Teacher Education in Finland: A Research-Based Approach: The Role of Subject Didactics and Networking in Teacher Education', in R. Jakku-Sihvonen & H. Niemi (Eds.) *Education as a Societal Contributor* (Frankfurt am Main: Peter Lang, 2007), 161–180.

Ministry of Education. *Teacher Education 2020* (in Finnish Opettajankoulutus 2020, an abstract in English), Reports and reviews of the Ministry of Education 44: 2007, Helsinki (2007).

Niemi, H. 'Active Learning – A Cultural Change Needed in Teacher Education and in Schools', *Teaching and Teacher Education*, 18, 2002, 763–780.

Niemi, H. 'Effectiveness of Teacher Education: A Theoretical Framework of Communicative Evaluation and the Design of a Finnish Research Project', in H. Niemi & K. Tirri (Eds.) *Effectiveness of Teacher Education: New Challenges and Approaches to Evaluation*. Reports from the Department of Teacher Education in Tampere University, 1996, A6, 11–32.

Niemi, H. 'ICT in Teacher Education', in M. Sinko & E. Lehtinen (Eds.) *The Challenges of ICT*. (Juva: Atena, 1999), 145–173.

Niemi, H., & Jakku-Sihvonen, R. 'Research-Based Teacher Education', in R. Jakku-Sihvonen & H. Niemi (Eds.) *Research-Based Teacher Education in Finland: Reflections By Finnish Teacher Educators* (Turku: Finnish Educational Research Association, 2006), 31–50.

Niemi. H., & Jakku-Sihvonen, R. 'Teacher Education in Finland', in M. V. Zuljan & J. Vogrinc (Eds.) *European Dimensions of Teacher Education, Similarities and Differences* (Slovenia: University of Ljubljana & The National School of Leadership in Education, 2011), 33–51.

Niemi, H., & Kemmis, S. 'Communicative Evaluation: Evaluation at the Crossroads', *Lifelong Learning in Europe (LLinE)*, IV/1, 1999, 55–64.

Niemi, H., & Kohonen, V. *Towards New Professionalism and Active Learning in Teacher Development: Empirical Findings on Teacher Education and Induction* (University of Tampere, Department of Teacher Education, 1995, Research series A 2).

Niemi, H., & Lavonen, J. 'Evaluation for Improvements in Finnish Teacher Education', in J. Harford, B. Hudson & H. Niemi (Eds.) *Quality Assurance and Teacher Education: International Challenges and Expectations*. Rethinking Education, Vol. 6 (Oxford: Peter Lang, 2012), 159–186. ISBN 9783034302500.

Spady, W. G. 'Outcome Based Education', in J. W. Guthrie (Ed.) *Encyclopedia of Education* (2nd ed., New York: Macmillan Reference, 2003), 1827–1831.

The Committee Report. *Educational Sciences Towards the Future*: Final report of the Committee for the Evaluation and Development of Educational Sciences (p. 16). Helsinki: Ministry of Education, Division of Educational and Research Policy, 16. Helsinki, 1994) (in Finnish, abstract in English). Ehlers, U. D. 'Understanding quality culture', Quality Assurance in Education, 17/4, 2009, 343–363.

Wolff, K.-D. 'Wege zur Qualitätskultur. Die Elemente der Qualitätsentwicklung und ihre Zusammenhänge', in W. Benz, J. Kohler & K. Landfried (Eds.) *Handbuch Qualität in Studium und Lehre*, C 2.1 (Berlin, Josef Raabe Verlags, 2004), 1–20.

16

ACCOUNTABILITY SYSTEMS FOR SCHOOLS

Coercion or cooperation?

Marilyn Leask

Introduction: values and decisions about accountability systems

In England a high stakes accountability system – Ofsted – operates. Ofsted has been named as leading to a number of teacher suicides (Newmark, 2018), and even the right-wing press finds it of questionable value:

> Ofsted inspections [of English schools]: You'd be better off flipping a coin.
> *(Flanagan, reporting for the right wing Daily Telegraph, 2014)*

A survey of eight European countries for this book showed a number of similarities between accountability systems but considerable differences with the English system. Common features include school self-review, checks on the curriculum, national monitoring of data to look for trends as this contribution to the survey by Erika Löfström, University of Helsinki indicates. She describes the Finnish system as follows:

> In Finland, schools are left with substantial space to make decisions within the parameters of the national curriculum. This premise already makes "accountability" somehow problematic, or difficult, at least. Consequently, this terminology is not even used. The Finnish conception of responsibility could rather be described as an orientation towards school development. Rectors have a significant responsibility in enabling school development, and this is seen as the way to sound performance (or accountability, if you will). Also the work with school's own curricula (based on the national curriculum) is an important dimension as it involves practically most teachers as stakeholders in the processes of school development. It is also important to know that rectors and teachers enjoy significant public trust in Finland.

The Finnish Education Evaluation Centre (https://karvi.fi/en/) is an independent national body collecting and analysing data on schools, but this is always sample-based to give an indication of trends in school, no single teacher's performance is assessed, and no school is singled out as a poor school. Focus is not on individuals or single schools, but on phenomena and trends in schools at large.

The previous chapter provided a detailed example of the accountability system for teacher training and higher education in Finland which is based on agreed frameworks, mutual high expectations, benchmarking and trust.

The focus of accountability in an education system depends on the values and principles underpinning the education service. In some education services access for all to a broad curriculum is paramount, in others segregated schooling with different curricula for different learners is acceptable (See Chapters 8 and 9 on selection and segregation).

Management theory (MacGregor, 1966) describes two contrasting value sets underpinning decisions about how to manage people to get a high quality outcome, described by MacGregor as Theory X (authoritarian) and Theory Y (common good).

Theory X (authoritarian) is based on the belief that staff are not self-motivated to do the best job possible, and consequently leads to an authoritarian style of accountability. The English Ofsted inspection system of schools, colleges, early years settings and university teacher training, in existence since 1992, tends to fit Theory X's view of people – that they have to be coerced to do a good job.

Theory Y (common good) is based on the belief that staff are self-motivated to do the best job they can. This leads to an accountability system constructed on an ethic of trust, benchmarking, peer challenge, appreciative inquiry (see Coffield, 2019) and benchmarking as evidenced in the previous chapter. In Northern Ireland the long-term policy "Every school a good school"[1] seems to be based on Theory Y views of people while giving parents reassurance that high quality for all is the priority of the education service.

The UK NHS accountability system for doctors which monitors their ability to make life and death decisions seems based on Theory Y management tools with features being mutual responsibility, peer review and challenge from others with similar roles, coupled with data benchmarking to identify outliers in the operation of a practice, coupled with an annual CPD requirement, coupled with open access to summaries of the latest research through the National Institute for Health and Clinical Excellence[2] and systematic reviews through the independently run Cochrane Collaboration.[3]

Similarly, Theory Y principles seem to apply to accountability systems for Air Traffic controllers whose ability to get their decisions right first time, every time is tested publicly every day. They work within a system focussed on open, no-blame reporting of mistakes followed by analysis of problems supported by training and retraining.[4,5]

Some definitions

Accountability: There are different forms of accountability: individuals may be held to account, or hold themselves to account. Forms of accountability include *professional* (using reflective self-analysis, benchmarking and peer review/appreciative inquiry), *moral* (using reflective self-analysis to check adherence with ethics), *contractual* (duties as specified in a contract) (Goddard and Leask, 1992, p. 22).

Inspection by external bodies: there appear to be two contrasting models of inspection, and two different forms of follow-up following inspection.

Model A Inspection focusses on *process* checks, the inspection checks that an organisation has suitable evaluation processes in place to monitor and maintain quality (Boothroyd, 1998).

Model B Inspection focusses on *spot practice checks*, perhaps on a one- or two-day visit to check if everything is satisfactory on the days of the visit.

In terms of follow up to inspection, the inspectors take one of two roles:

Inspector Role 1, *inspection and support*: the inspector continues to work with the organisation to improve quality assurance processes process and assist the school to improve.

Inspector Role 2, *inspection only*: the inspector has no responsibility to demonstrate how improvements could be made and just makes a judgement and simply walks away. This can only work if schools can access suitable support for improvement (Goddard and Leask, 1992, p. 164).

Subject specialist knowledge: By this term we mean knowledge based initially on extensive practice in schools and then developed through engagement with research and benchmarking nationally and internationally. Roles which develop and require this knowledge from international and national benchmarking and from engagement with undertaking and commissioning of research are those of specialist inspectors, local authority or regional subject advisers and teacher educators in universities and teachers engaged in research and development typically with the previously mentioned stakeholders.

England – a case study

Prior to 1989, there were structures in place to support knowledge sharing and the development of subject pedagogy. There were subject specialist HMIs, subject specialist local authority advisors and advisory teachers (responsible for induction of new teachers in an area) and scholarships for teachers to undertake Master's level study.

Several major policy changes since the 1980s have eliminated these roles and opportunities for emerging subject leaders to develop such specialist subject expertise, which was previously used to support school development. Examples include:

• 1989 onwards: The Local Management of Schools initiative devolved budgets and staffing from LAs to schools shifting heads' attention and skills to finance,

HR and buildings rather than just teaching and learning. A consequence was that training funds were switched into leadership and away from subject specialist support provided by local authority advisers and inspectors at the local level. (These advisers were networked with subject specialist HMI who had a national view of practice and innovation in a subject area.)

• 1989: shifting some teacher training to schools led to immediate job cuts for specialist subject experts in teacher training institutions. 1992 onwards: the financing and focus of Ofsted.

• 1990: The Inner London Education Authority, a powerhouse of subject specialist curriculum development and innovation and for publishing resources used across England, was abolished.

• 2010 onwards: Knowledge about how to improve, once publicly shared as a public good has become privatised within academy chains. Limiting university teacher training was initiated by the Gove administration post 2010, leaving the education service in England with very limited research capacity in subject curriculum and pedagogy.

• 2010: Secretary of State Michael Gove and Schools Minister Nick Gibb dismantled the national bodies which had been charged with providing online support to schools through resources and networks, namely the National College for Teaching and Leadership,[6] Becta, QCDA and TDA.

• 2019: In a return to the pre-1989 practices, Ofsted has changed the inspection framework to focus on subject teaching. However, the process of privatising education services has continued and intensified up to the present, leaving local/regional authorities with extremely limited capacity and forcing schools to rely on commercial trainers and consultants in an unregulated quasi-market.

England's Ofsted system: what is the purpose of inspection if not school improvement?

Ofsted has been under repeated criticism since its foundation: from educators and from Parliament's cross-party committees set up to scrutinise policies and public services (Select Committee 1999; OFSTIN, 1996; National Association of Head Teachers' [NAHT] Accountability Commission [2018] and an enquiry led by Professor Frank Coffield [2019]).

Ofsted[7] makes a claim to be "A force for improvement through intelligent, responsible and focused inspection and regulation"[8] saying "we target our time and resources where they can lead directly to improvement". But the UK Government's National Audit Office found, after nearly 30 years of Ofsted, there is no evidence of positive impact:

> Ofsted's impact measurement
> 3.2 Ofsted does not know whether its school inspections are having the intended impact: to raise the standards of education and improve the quality of children's and young people's lives. It has not had clear performance

indicators or targets to track progress towards these high-level aims. Its performance measures have instead focused mainly on activity and processes.[9]

(National Audit Office May 24, 2018, p. 42)

The National Audit Office found that Ofsted did not have evidence that its
inspections were raising the standards of education provided to children and
young people. Until Ofsted is able better to assess its impact, it is difficult
for the National Audit Office to be satisfied that Ofsted provides value for
money to the taxpayer.[10]

(Public Accounts Committee 7 Sept 2018 citing the NAO).

It is time for a complete overhaul. Ofsted must be abolished and replaced with
a system of school self-review and peer evaluation, with quality assurance by
local inspectors (HMIs) and an HMCI that is unafraid to speak truth to power.[11]

(NEU 10 Sept 2018)

- It [Ofsted] limits ambition, incentivises self-interest and deters talented staff from working in more deprived communities.
- It narrows the curriculum and encourages teaching to the test and
diverts attention from teaching and learning.
- It drives good people from the profession and provides less assurance
of standards.

NAHT's Accountability Commission[12] (2018)

It is ironic that Ofsted now focusses on subject teaching when well established subject-
specialist advisory services in local authorities have been virtually eliminated.

As early as 1999, a headteacher, presenting evidence to the House of Commons
Select Committee, reported the lack of improvement focus, despite failing to challenge the assumptions of distrust which underpin Ofsted inspections:

We . . . believe in a model of school self-improvement, externally moderated
and inspected. That separateness [of external inspection] we would totally
agree with. It has to be there. Schools need that separate look. However, at
the same time, the actual improving must be done by the school, moderated
perhaps by a combination of a national inspectorate system with LEA support
to come in.

(McNicholas, in evidence to the House of Commons Select Committee, 1999)

Many years later, the National Association of Head Teachers seems to accept Ofsted's self-justification, namely that a strong eternal body was needed to ensure that
no child attends a poor school. However, it had come to the conclusion that Ofsted
was ineffective and indeed counterproductive.

Ofsted continues to perform a critical function by identifying failure in the
system so that no child attends a poor school. Yet the accountability system

provides little benefit to the pupils, parents and staff at the vast majority of schools in this country that are not failing. At best it is a distraction on the journey from good to great. At worst it works against improvement by incentivising the wrong actions and behaviours. At a system level, the approaches used by the government to hold schools to account are acting as a brake to overall improvement and are, on balance, doing more harm than good.

(NAHT Review, p. 4)

Ofsted delivers unreliable judgements according to the UK Parliament's watchdogs and right and left organisations

The introduction of Ofsted in 1992 was supported by cross-party concern for quality in education.

In England, in 1991 the major parties in the UK ([Straw, 1991], Labour; and Conservative Central Office, undated, p. 3) issued statements about how they intended to improve quality in education . . . based on the assumption that quality in education services are improved by making methods of accountability more rigorous – particularly through inspection. . . . [T]hose pronouncements assumed there is a direct relationship between external methods of accountability and quality. The assumption is that if the curriculum is also prescribed (through a national curriculum) high quality will automatically follow.

(Goddard and Leask, 1992, p. 18)

Ofsted was set up to replace Her Majesty's Inspectorate. It was established to operate on a cheap and barely professional basis: a privatised model whereby Ofsted contracted to over a hundred companies who in turn sub-contracted inspectors for so many days. Very few HMI remained to ensure continuity and knowledge transfer. From the start, Ofsted was unable to guarantee the quality of its teams, and consequently has had to depend on inspectors largely ratifying the school's test and exam data (Matthews and Sammons, 2004). It is hardly surprising that schools in poorer neighbourhoods, which tend to get lower test and exam results, are far more likely to receive failure notices from Ofsted. Even when Ofsted finally removed the intermediary agencies and contracted all its staff directly, the quality of individual inspectors and the reliability of their judgements has been uncertain. The number of suicides related to Ofsted inspections is noted.[13] These presumably have a long-term effect on the mental health and worldview of the children they taught and their communities.

This has led to repeated complaints by public bodies, as the following recent example illustrates:

The Committee's . . . report,[14] published in September 2018, concluded that Ofsted was not providing the level of independent assurance about the quality of education that schools and parents need.

(Parliament's Public Accounts Committee
7 September 2018 citing the NAO)

The *Daily Telegraph*, a right-wing newspaper published an article with the headline: "Ofsted inspections [of English schools]: You'd be better off flipping a coin" (*Daily Telegraph*, 2014).

Finally, on the Left of the Labour Party, Angela Rayner MP, Shadow Secretary of State for Education, announced in September 2019 that a Labour Government would abolish Ofsted as it is not fit for purpose.[15]

Ofsted's misuse of data

Philip Moriarty (2014), a parent and school governor, draws on his expertise as a physicist to highlight the misuse of data by Ofsted in reaching their judgements:

> A very large part of the reason [people support Ofsted] is that they naively, quaintly, yet dangerously assume that education is equivalent to a competitive sport where schools, teachers, and children can be accurately assessed on the basis of positions in league tables. What's worse – and this is particularly painful for a physicist or, indeed, anyone with a passing level of numeracy, to realise – is that this misplaced and unscientific faith in the value of statistically dubious inter-school comparisons is at the very core of the assessment culture of Ofsted.
>
> *(ibid., 2014, p. 1)*

> Ofsted's implicit assumption is that the value of a school . . . and, by extension, the value of the teachers and students in that school, can be reduced to a set of objective and robust 'metrics' which can in turn be used to produce a quantitative ranking (i.e. a league table). Even physicists, who spend their career wading through reams of numerical data, know full well that not everything that counts can be counted.

> During the governor training sessions I attended, I repeatedly asked to what extent the results of Ofsted inspections (and other Ofsted-driven assessment schemes) were reproducible. In other words, if we repeated the inspection with a different set of inspectors, would we get the same result? If not, in what sense could Ofsted claim that the results of an inspection were objective and robust? As you might perhaps expect, I singularly failed to get a particularly compelling response to this question. This was for a very good reason: the results of Ofsted inspections are entirely irreproducible.
>
> *(Moriarty, 2014, p. 1)*

Moriarty (ibid.) identifies the following flaws in Ofsted's use of data, describing them as " 'rookie' flaws in data analysis":

1 Inadequate appreciation of the effects of small sample size;
2 A lack of consideration of statistical significance/uncertainties in the data. (Or, at best, major deficiencies in communicating and highlighting those uncertainties);

3 Comparison of variations between schools when the variation within a given school (from year to year) can be at least as large;
4 An entirely misleading placement of schools in "quintiles" when the difference between the upper and lower quintiles can be marginal. Ofsted has already had to admit to a major flaw in its initial assignment of quintiles.

> What is perhaps most galling is that many A-level students in English schools will be taught to recognise and avoid these types of pitfall in data analysis. It is an irony too far that those teaching the correct approach to statistics in English classrooms are assessed and compared to their peers on the basis of Ofsted's pseudostatistical nonsense.
>
> *(ibid., p. 1)*

Moriarty accuses OFSTED as practising a form of "Cargo cult science".

Similarly, the NAHT has recently called for action by the Department for Education (DfE) to reduce the negative impact of the unintelligent use of performance data:

> As currently constructed, NAHT believes that the quality of education judgement is too complex and dense to be applied with consistency across the inspection workforce. This is a particular concern given the irregular deployment of most Ofsted Inspectors, and the continuing high turnover of HMI.
>
> *(NAHT response to the Education Inspection framework*
> *3 April 2019 P. 2)*[16]

The other major headteacher body, the Association of School and College Leaders (ASCL) makes basically the same accusation:

> Mistakes with [the data] checking exercise have happened before. However, where a system-wide error has been established it would be wrong of the DfE to insist that all errors are corrected at school level. In some cases, the resulting workload for schools would be considerable and unreasonable.[17]
>
> *(2019)*

The quality of inspectors

In Ofsted's early days, Professor Carol Fitzgibbon of Durham University argued: "people's lives and schools' futures [are] being determined by inspections. But if one inspector can make a different judgment to another, then it is meaningless. I have yet to see evidence of reliable consistency" (TES, 3 May 1996).

After multiple reforms and reorganisations, the situation remained the same 20 years later. Here is the voice of the official watchdog, the National Audit Office:

> In 2015, Ofsted brought all inspection work in-house with the aim of improving quality. . . . Previously it had outsourced much of its inspection work to private companies, but it was not satisfied with the level of control this arrangement gave it over quality. . . . Contracted inspectors [existing or retired practitioners] provide Ofsted with flexibility in staffing [i.e. a gig economy].
>
> *(National Audit Office May 24, 2018, p. 8)*

This suggests enormous flaws in the previous contracting and sub-contracting system, yet no account has been taken of the damage done to schools, the careers destroyed, the long-term psychological impact on communities, teachers, parents and children of being told that they are "Unsatisfactory" when in fact their inspectors weren't qualified to comment.

What are the alternatives?

Many suggestions have been made. Even the right-wing think tank Policy Exchange has proposed abandoning the Ofsted system and instituting a two-stage procedure:

1   a "short inspection" for all schools every two years, which would award an overall graded judgement (Outstanding to Inadequate)
2   a follow-up "tailored inspection" for all schools judged less than Good, with double the current inspector time in order to investigate in more depth (again, graded Outstanding to Inadequate).

In our view, this would not help but would make matters worse. Short Inspections are extremely superficial, based on one inspector (two in a larger secondary school) for a single day. That is no basis for badging a school Inadequate, and would result in even greater bias against schools serving disadvantaged neighbourhoods.

The NAHT's propose that schools collaborate in helping each other to improve. This is similar to the NHS GP practice accountability model mentioned earlier:

> We need to develop confidence in lateral accountability systems to peers that will, in time, enable the further reduction in vertical accountability systems to the government.
>
> The profession needs to be freed to work together, challenge one another, encourage innovation, share excellence, and focus on doing what is right for all pupils to succeed. The secret is not to be found in achieving an Ofsted label.
>
> *(NAHT, 2018)*

The following practical recommendations are drawn from those consulted in the writing of this chapter: teachers, head teachers, parents and governors.

1   Schools normally already engage in a formal ongoing process of self-evaluation or review: effective models exist. What is not needed is a prescriptive model that requires people to undo/change to prescribed models in which the form becomes much more important than the process. The process can be focused on particular issues, as they arise. This process of school review must involve gaining the perspectives of all staff, students, parents and the local community.

2   In order to ensure an objective, external contribution, a visiting headteacher and specialists from another schools should be involved as 'critical friends' (see the NHS GP accountability process).

3   A small but expert HMI should be re-established, as before Ofsted was created. It must be free from the pressure of government manipulation and interferences. A major role should be to check whether government policies are working, through thematic reviews and visits to a sample of schools. It should also learn from the best practice internationally, and provide advice and training to local authorities, schools and subject experts, particularly those in challenging situations. The audit function e.g. compliance with statutory requirements etc. could easily be part of a Local Authority conducted audit rather than wasting time in an Ofsted inspection trawling through safeguarding records etc.

4   The process should be monitored by the local authority and national HMI to ensure that it is rigorous and that the school gets expert advice and support to improve. Parents and governors should have a point of contact for raising issues and seeking help. The respective roles of HMI and LA would need to be clarified in order to avoid duplication

5   School review should result in recommendations for improvement, not a marketing label. All schools can be improved, and it is unhelpful and damaging to divide schools into different grades. Integral to this is the establishment of a culture which promotes and encourages open and frank discussion of areas for development, relative weaknesses as a positive as opposed to the blame culture that currently prevails. The evidence for base used in Ofsted inspections does meet the criteria for credible research.

6   Ofsted has tried to reform time and again, without success. Its recent attempt is doomed to fail, due to the variable quality of inspectors and too short a time to understand the school in depth. It should be abolished and the money spent on boosting the capacity of local authorities to assist school review.

To achieve this, there needs to be local support for school improvement. This would require professional staff working with local expertise of experienced teachers and heads.

Reflections

That external quality assurance systems are part of a national education service is accepted by stakeholders from across the spectrum of political views – what is contested is the form it should take, what if any support mechanisms should be in place and who provides and pays for these.

These decisions are informed by the values of those making the decisions: do they believe that teachers are motivated to do the best job possible (Management theory Y, i.e. teachers see themselves working to a common good) or do they believed teachers have to be coerced (Management theory X)?

In England, the current situation is toxic for children and teachers and unsustainable. As the NAHT review expressed it, the accountability system is failing on three counts:

- It is driving good people out of the profession: directly, as the consequence of perceived drops in performance and indirectly, through the unmanageable workload associated with it and a pervasive culture of fear
- It dissuades good teachers and leaders from working in challenging schools for fear of being treated unfairly by the inspectorate
- Perhaps most concerning of all, it has celebrated and encouraged defensive and insular leadership behaviours that, if unchecked, will limit our capacity to improve (p. 4)

Others point out that Ofsted's use of data is flawed.

The NAHT solution (p. 5) is a system with:

> robust peer-to-peer support and challenge, focused on encouraging collaboration and supporting all schools to greatness. Through the development of quality assurance processes for national peer review programmes, we will build confidence that reviews are consistent, robust and reliable.

And they challenge educators to change practices:

> Key to achieving this vision will be the profession itself. It requires a significant cultural and behavioural shift and for leaders and teachers to step up and take responsibility for one another and ownership over educational standards. This is not something that we, the profession, should wait for the government to mandate us to do. We do not need permission from the DfE to step into this space and do the right thing. And if we do not step forward, who will?
>
> *(p. 22)*

We believe the recommendations outlined previously would bring about a sea change in English schools, improving teacher retention and make teaching a profession which attracts the best, as in Finland and other high-achieving countries.

Policy options

The previous ideas lead to several policy options

Given the criticisms from all parties about the unreliability of judgements and the flawed methods used, we suggest the English Ofsted model does not lead to the education service delivering high quality education to all which is surely the rationale for an inspection system. On the contrary, the Ofsted system encourages the denial of schooling to children – through 'off-rolling' so schools appear high in national examination results tables – and encourages teachers to avoid teaching in challenging schools (see Chapter 6).

> **Option 1: Status quo**
> **Option 2: Reform and Refocus:** For England, we suggest the Ofsted brand
> is too tarnished for reform.
> **Option 3: Replace:** A number of successful accountability systems are based
> on peer review, peer challenge, external data gathering for benchmarking
> and trend identification, accompanied by support. See Chapter 19 for online
> knowledge services which could provide a core element of cost effective
> improvement support.

Policy options and their consequences are discussed in the penultimate chapter.

Acknowledgements

We acknowledge: the contributions of Brian Lightman, the NAHT Accountability Commission https://www.naht.org.uk/our-priorities/improving-school-account ability/ 14 September 2018, and the teachers and teacher educators attending the workshops linked with developing and testing ideas for this book during 2018 and 2019 which led to this text, as well as; the contributions of colleagues from the Teacher Education Policy in Europe (TEPE) network.

Notes

1 www.education-ni.gov.uk/articles/every-school-good-school-esags
2 www.nice.org.uk
3 https://uk.cochrane.org
4 www.faa.gov/documentLibrary/media/Order/JO_7210_633.pdf
5 www.caa.co.uk/Commercial-industry/Airspace/Air-traffic-control/Air-navigation-services/The-Air-Traffic-Management-Common-Requirements-Implementing-Reg ulation/
6 www.gov.uk/government/organisations/national-college-for-teaching-and-leadership
7 Up to 1992, to support school improvement in England, there was an integrated sys-tem with teacher subject specialists employed by local authorities inspecting/advising and providing training and benchmarking across a region via other local authorities with HMI providing independent inspection/advice providing training and benchmark-ing across regions via other local authorities. There were tensions then about whether

inspection or advice provided the best basis for improvement with different LEAs taking different approaches. The select committee in 1996 described the system as "cosy".

8 https://assets.publishing.service.gov.uk/government/uploads/system/uploads/attach ment_data/file/648211/Ofsted_strategy_summary.pdf

9 National Audit Office May 24, 2018 www.nao.org.uk/report/ofsteds-inspection-of-schools/

10 www.parliament.uk/business/committees/committees-a-z/commons-select/public-accounts-committee/inquiries/parliament-2017/ofsted-inspector-17-19/

11 https://neu.org.uk/press-releases/public-accounts-committee-report-ofsted-raises-sig nificant-concerns

12 NAHT (14 September 2018) Accountability Review (www.naht.org.uk/our-priorities/improving-school-accountability/)

13 Further details are on the website: www.independent.co.uk/news/uk/home-news/pri mary-school-teachers-suicide-rate-double-national-average-uk-figures-a7635846.html www.theguardian.com/uk-news/2015/nov/20/headteacher-killed-herself-after-ofsted-downgrade-inquest

In 2009 more than one teacher a week committed suicide. www.channel4.com/news/teachers-suicide-rates-double-in-a-year.

14 www.parliament.uk/business/committees/committees-a-z/commons-select/public-accounts-committee/inquiries/parliament-2017/inquiry118/

15 www.theguardian.com/politics/2019/sep/21/labour-we-will-scrap-ofsted-radical-election-pledge

16 www.naht.org.uk/_resources/assets/attachment/full/0/89501.pdf

17 www.ascl.org.uk/Help-and-Advice/Accountability-and-inspection/Performance-measures/September-pupil-level-data-checking-exercise-and-p

References

Boothroyd, C. (1998) Focus Management on Learning. In Horne, H., *The School Management Handbook*, fifth edition. London: Kogan Page.

Coffield, F. (31 January 2019) 7 Problems with Inspections Ofsted Must Fix. *Times Educational Supplement*, https://www.tes.com/news/coffield-7-problems-inspections-

Conservative Central Office (undated) *Local Government Brief: Number 38: Citizen's Charter.* London.

Flanagan, P. reporting for the *Daily Telegraph* (2014) *Ofsted Inspections [of English schools]: You'd be Better Off Flipping a Coin.* https://www.telegraph.co.uk/education/10701613/Ofsted-inspections-youd-be-better-off-flipping-a-coin.html

Goddard, D. and Leask, M. (1992) *The Search for Quality: Planning for Improvement and Managing Change.* London: Paul Chapman

MacGregor, D.(1966) The Human Side of Enterprise. *The Management Review*, 46, no. 11, 22–28. https://www.kean.edu/~lelovitz/docs/EDD6005/humansideofenterprise.pdf

Matthews, P. and Sammons, P. (2004) *Improvement Through Inspection: An Evaluation of Ofsted's Work.* London: Institute of Education and OFSTED HMI2244. https://dera.ioe. ac.uk/4969/3/3696.pdf

Moriarty, P. (2014) *Lies, Damned Lies, and Ofsted's Pseudostatistics.* Institute of Physics https://blog. iop.org/?s=LIES%2C+DAMNED+LIES%2C+AND+OFSTED'S+PSEUDOSTATIS TICs; www.teachers.org.uk/files/ofsted-pseudostatistics-by-philip-moriarty_0_0.doc; https://muircheartblog.wordpress.com/2014/07/23/lies-damned-lies-ofsteds-pseu dostatistics/. Note: Moriarty is Professor of Physics at the University of Nottingham, where his research focuses on nanoscale science.

NAHT Accountability Commission (14 September 2018) *Improving School Accountability.* https://www.naht.org.uk/our-priorities/improving-school-accountability/

National Audit Office. (24May 2018) *Ofsted's Inspection of Schools.* https://www.nao.org.uk/report/ofsteds-inspection-of-schools/

Newmark, B. (3 June 2018) *Why Are Teachers so Scared of Ofsted?* https://bennewmark.wordpress.com/2018/06/09/why-are-teachers-so-scared-of-ofsted/

OFSTIN (June 1996) *Conference Proceedings: How Sound OFSTED's Methodology is, how Helpful it is as a Model for School Improvement and whether it Offers Value for Money.* Oxford: New College.

Select Committee on Education and Employment (20 January 1999) *Minutes of Evidence.* https://publications.parliament.uk/pa/cm199899/cmselect/cmeduemp/62/9012001.htm

Straw, J. (1991) *Raising the Standard: Labour's plan for an Education Standards Commission* (Labour Party press release). London. 25 June.

SECTION 5

Teacher education

Section 5 focuses on the issue of professionalism for teachers as no education system can outperform the quality of its teachers.

Chapter 17 considers issues of recruitment and retention in relation to the professionalism of teachers, from the beginning of their professional training, during their induction into professional practice and continuing throughout their careers. Starting with an acknowledgement of the UNESCO Incheon Declaration (2015): "We will ensure that teachers and educators are empowered, adequately recruited, well trained, professionally qualified, motivated and supported within well resourced, efficient and effectively governed systems", this chapter outlines how this may be achieved. There is also an exploration into the shift in the values of professionalism and an examination of the debates about the status of teachers, including issues of recruitment and retention.

Chapter 18 considers issues related to what matters most and has worked well in strategies to promote teacher development. The chapter starts by examining how teacher education has been framed as a policy problem, and how different conceptualisations of teaching lead to radically divergent policy alternatives.

Chapter 19 begins by highlighting how OECD TALIS research (2009) has found that no country has yet solved the problem of keeping all its teachers up-to-date through continuing professional development, due to the challenge of scope and cost. As yet, the problem of CPD for teachers has not been solved by the current policy of leaving this issue to the market, so instead a coordinated, coherent national strategy is proposed to create an independent Education Knowledge Service (EKS) to co-ordinate development of a regularly updated, open access, research-informed online education resources bank supporting CPD for teachers, trainee teachers and teacher educators.

In this way, subject content and pedagogic approaches could be kept up-to-date and relevant. Providing teachers with the agency to direct their own professional learning, with recognition and accreditation through CPD points, which could enhance retention and support teacher well-being.

17

REFRAMING THE PROFESSIONALISM OF TEACHERS

Linda la Velle and Kate Reynolds

UNESCO Incheon Declaration (2015): We will ensure that teachers and educators are empowered, adequately recruited, well trained, professionally qualified, motivated and supported within well resourced, efficient and effectively governed systems.

Introduction

Internationally influential bodies (UNICEF, 2001; UNESCO, 1966, 2015a, 2015b, 2016, 2018) have agreed that every child has a right to a good teacher and that good teachers have the interests of their learners at the centre of their practice. However, if the current trajectory is followed, 74 countries worldwide face an acute shortage of teachers, 33 of which will not have sufficient teachers of any quality to provide their children with primary education (International Taskforce on Teachers for Education 2030, 2015). Long working hours during term-time and rising pupil numbers, both of which lead to teacher stress, are cited as the underlying reasons for poor recruitment and retention. The key recommendation of a report of the National Foundation for Educational Research (NFER, 2019) is that recruitment of teachers to UK schools is a matter for urgent action.

Why do people choose to teach? Many enter the teaching profession for altruistic reasons, hoping to make a difference to people's lives, both individually and at a broader, societal level. Becoming a teacher is a complex process, involving the acquisition of much knowledge, many skills and both personal and professional attributes. But is learning to teach a training or an education? The first would imply a technical manual methodology in which competences are box-ticked and mechanical skills honed. We argue here that the second approach to the inculcation of teachers' professionalism is one that will raise the cerebral level at which they tackle each element of their work, producing greater job satisfaction and pupil outcomes and thus enhance the attraction to the profession and retention within it. However, an underlying tension about the nature of education is revealed in relation to teacher education and this chapter aims to illustrate the historic and deeply embedded values that have a bearing on teachers' professionalism.

Successive UK governments have made education a centrepiece of their 'reforming' policies. Over the past 20 years, as is mentioned in several other chapters of this book, this has resulted in an unprecedented level of policy churn that, at the classroom level, has in general had a less than productive effect. Although the situation in other jurisdictions of the UK is less extreme, the effect of educational policy changes on teacher education in England has been profound. A move away from Higher Education Institution (HEI) courses towards a school-based model of initial teacher education has seen a reduced emphasis on a notion of teaching as an autonomous, intellectual activity (Sorensen, 2019) and greater importance given to accountability through such measures as league tables and inspection outcomes. Thus, there has been a shift in the values of professionalism. The international debates about the status of teachers (Hargreaves, 2009; la Velle and Kendall, 2020) and teaching as a master's-level profession (la Velle and Kendall, 2019; la Velle, 2013) have shown a wide disparity of views from across the world about what it is to be a teacher. This chapter will further elucidate the professional realities of being a teacher in the 21st century and argue for a balanced educational ecology in which teachers and learners can flourish within a diverse, equal and decolonialised ecosystem.

The UNESCO declaration quoted previously reiterates the importance of teachers for education across the world. The United Nations has gone further and under sustainable development goal number four countries are committed to:

> ensur[ing] inclusive and equitable quality education and promot[ing] life-long learning opportunities for all by 2030. In order to achieve this sustainable development goal, countries will need to consider internationalising the teacher workforce and ensuring that teachers are fit for the 21st century.
> *(UNESCO, 2019)*.

The central role of teachers in making a difference to children's education is now no longer doubted. Building on work following the McKinsey Report (Mourshed et al., 2010) governments across the world have recognised the importance of investing in the teaching workforce and ensuring they have up-to-date skills and knowledge to support teaching in the 21st-century. However, the global framework of accountability and testing reinforced by the PISA league tables, which has been pushed by so many governments internationally, has restricted teachers' professional autonomy, assuming a 'one size fits all' model for teaching in countries across the world. The pressure of accountability and testing frameworks has led to increased levels of stress within the teaching workforce (NFER, 2019). This is exacerbated by the increase in the numbers of teachers leaving the profession early, and the reduction in the supply of teachers, highlighted previously. A UK report from the National Audit Office (NAO, 2017), reporting to Parliament, showed that the Department for Education, which is responsible for the supply and demand of teachers in schools, had singularly failed to reach its targets for the past five years (BBC, 2017).

Therefore, there is a need both to reinvigorate the teaching profession and to ensure it is an international profession that can meet the demands of UNESCO's SDG 4. This chapter discusses these issues in relation to teachers' professionalism with a focus upon recruitment and initial teacher education, with some discussion of the experiences of being a teacher and building a career as a teacher.

Becoming a teacher

In the context of the United States, a report asked: "what would it take systematically to attract – and retain – top students to a teaching career?" (Auguste et al., 2010). In his briefing paper to the UK parliament, Don Foster (2018) has highlighted a continuation of the long-term trend of falling numbers of student teachers in training and of those awarded qualified teacher status (QTS) in the UK. Even in this climate of high employability of newly qualified teachers (NQTs), recruitment, especially in shortage subject specialisms (maths, physics, computing, design technology, modern foreign languages), teaching as a profession is not attracting well-qualified graduates in sufficient numbers. In the UK, a number of initiatives, for example the Troops to Teachers, Teach First, Return to Teaching programmes, various bursaries and scholarships, early career payments, etc. have failed significantly to address this recruitment crisis. It is suggested (Paine and Zeichner, 2012) that part of the answer to the question opening this paragraph lies in the international quality of teacher education.

This begs the question of how to make teaching a more attractive career. In countries such as Portugal, Australia, Ireland and Canada teaching is a high status profession and, unsurprisingly, there is no issue of recruitment such as that seen in the UK. Notably, these counties offer initial teacher education (ITE) courses at master's level (McLean Davis et al., 2013; la Velle and Flores, 2018). The need for this in England has been argued over the past two decades (Totterdell et al., 2011; la Velle, 2013; la Velle et al., 2018), but these calls have been ignored by successive UK governments since 2010.

A good initial teacher education lays the foundation for a successful professional career. Principally among its hallmarks are the development and enhancement of teachers' knowledge bases, including not only subject knowledge and how to impart it, but also those of the curriculum, classroom management, pupils as learners, the national educational landscape and how practice is informed by research (Shulman, 1987; la Velle and Kendall, 2019).

There is certainly a major policy debate to be had nationally, and indeed internationally, about the efficacy of different approaches to teacher education in the light of the challenges of preparing teachers for 21st-century schools. In its crudest terms, this has often been reduced to a dualistic opposition of HEI-led versus school-led approaches to the preparation of teachers. Yet within this apparent binary are important ethical, conceptual and empirical questions about the nature of professional formation, the governance of the sector, the balance between theoretical and practical knowledge and arguments about the best ways to ensure teacher supply, teacher quality and the achievement of the desired outcome (Whitty, 2019).

In the UK, education, including teacher education, is devolved to the national governments of Wales, Scotland and Northern Ireland. Therefore, the reforms of 2010 (as enshrined in *The Importance of Teaching* [DFE, 2010]) onwards had impact only in England. These reforms led to an increasing diversification of routes to becoming a teacher with a wide range of teacher training providers appearing in a more explicitly "market led" approach. The Diversity in Teacher Education (DiTE) project undertook a mapping exercise to produce a topography of initial teacher training (ITT) in England (Whiting, 2016), where the significant finding was the complexity in provision.

In England, the curriculum of the postgraduate certificate of education (PGCE) and access to places on initial teacher training courses is subject to policy initiatives by the Department for Education and the Office for Standards in Education (Ofsted). Teacher training providers are inspected on a roughly five-year cycle by Ofsted to ensure that they are working within the parameters set by government. These factors include the amount of time spent in school (practising teaching) and the subject matter to be studied (curriculum knowledge). In neither case is the subject of global or international contexts included (as the OECD recommends – see Chapters 1 and 2).

In England, the teaching profession is predominantly made up of white, degree educated women. Under the previous Labour government specific schemes had been put in place to increase the number and proportion of black and male teachers. The coalition government of 2010 and onwards closed such schemes but universities have widening participation initiatives to ensure greater representation of underrepresented groups. At present, there are no specific schemes to encourage black students or male students to enter the teaching profession (Bhopal, 2015). Not only does this lack of diversity limit innovation and creativity, it also robs children and young people of role models and a wider representation of contemporary society and what it means to be a teacher in the 21st century.

In the UK, as in a significant number of other nations in the developed world, several key policy changes are urgently needed:

1   invest in teacher education in universities, ensuring that it becomes a Master's level profession in line with good practice across the world;
2   revise the curriculum, with advice from the international community, to ensure it is broad, balanced and takes into account both the need for an international outlook for children and young people and the need for teachers to have the skills to teach globally
3   decrease the different routes to achieving qualified teacher status to ensure that the process is simple, consistent and easily understood
4   develop sustainable initiatives to help to redress the lack of diversity in the teaching profession.

Being a teacher

The reality for the newly qualified teacher (NQT) in England, as in many other countries, is often one of culture shock characterised by a very heavy workload. Research supported by the Nuffield Foundation has provided evidence that 25% of teachers in England work more than 60 hours per week (Allen et al., 2019).

In England, the retention rate for teachers continues to spiral downwards. According to the National Education Union (NEU), over 81% of 8,000 teachers surveyed were considering leaving the profession (NEU, 2018; Worth and van den Brand, 2019) and the *Times Educational Supplement* reported that one in three teachers leaves in the first five years (TES, 2019). Combined with an extension to the age of retirement, teachers are now expected to work not only longer days, but also for more years. A report from the OECD shows that out of 48 countries secondary school teachers in England had one of the highest workloads and increasing low levels of job satisfaction (TALIS, 2018; National Education Union, 2019). Fewer and fewer teachers want to reach levels of senior leadership or to become head teachers. According to a survey from the National Association of Head Teachers more than a quarter of schools could not fill their head teacher vacancies, double the rate in 2017 (NAHT, 2019).

All this paints a consistently gloomy picture in relation to the current working conditions and state of the teaching profession in England. This is replicated in other developed countries, for example, America (García and Weiss, 2019). British politicians are made clearly aware of the fact that recruitment and retention in teaching is approaching the "perfect storm" (ibid.) of crisis.

Making schools resilient and life enhancing organisations has to be key to ensuring that people wish to become teachers and want to stay in the teaching profession for their career once they join. In the UK, as in a significant number of other nations in the developed world, a number of fundamental policy changes are urgently needed:

1   bring all teachers' terms and conditions under a nationally negotiated framework
2   include teacher well-being *and teacher education* as part of the inspection/accountability measures of schools (Ofsted in the UK)
3   tackle excessive workload and the framework of testing and accountability
4   provide career-long professional support

Building a career as a teacher

The provision of consistent, high quality professional development is the hallmark of a good profession. In teaching, this is patchy at an international level (Makopoulou and Armour, 2014). Apart from the economic argument (in some low GDP countries, there simply aren't the resources) one reason for this may be that, in the UK at least, education is a political football. Successive governments use education to make their mark with resulting policy churn. The effect of this is that curriculum and its assessment measures are prescribed and accountability increased. This decreases teachers' autonomy and has the effect of diluting the potential effectiveness of CPD. In countries such as Finland, Japan and Singapore, CPD is robust and effective, enabling the positive development of both practice and policy (Williams, 2013). Whether the CPD is formal, as is the case for example in Japan, where lesson study has been a feature for many decades, or less formal, as in Finland, where there is an emphasis on professional responsibility and where the national educational system is less top-down and accountable, success relies on the development of a professional ecology of mutual support: a community of practice (Lave and Wenger, 1991) (see chapter 19).

The NQT starting on her teaching career in England is entitled to a funded two-year package of entitlements under the ECF (Early Career Framework, Gov. uk, 2019). This provides structured training and support and is linked to research-based evidence. The ECF was introduced in 2019 and it seems to respond to many of the calls for the underpinning and on-going provision of the intellectual and professional components of a teacher's work, as argued in the opening section of this chapter. However, its effectiveness in terms of recruitment, retention and job satisfaction of teachers will only be apparent in the subsequent years following an evaluation of its implementation.

Provision of good CPD, as in any educational endeavour, relies on the quality of teaching. However, within the UK at least, this is inconsistent. Coe (2013) has argued that although the right kinds of CPD have the potential to result in advantage for learners, most of that undertaken by UK teachers is not of this sort. Efforts are under way through such organisations as the International Council on Education for Teaching (ICET); the Universities Council for the Education of Teachers (UCET), the American Association of Colleges for Teacher Education (AATCE) among others to bring together a set of internationally recognised professional standards for teacher educators, but this is in its infancy. The Deans for Impact (2016) have suggested five general principles of effective practice relevant to teacher education: pushing beyond current performance; working towards well-defined, specific goals; focussed practice; response to high quality feedback and developing a mental model of expertise.

Although it is beyond the scope of this chapter, but discussed elsewhere in this book (Chapter 19), the affordances of digital technology cannot be ignored in a consideration of CPD for teachers (Leask, 2018). Many initiatives, e.g. the EU's Erasmus+ programme, have provided rich opportunities for the building of international communities of practice for teachers. One example of this is the work of the PhenoloGIT (2018) and Robo21C projects (2018), funded under this scheme, which connected schools across Europe to investigate seasonal changes of plants and animals using geographical information systems and robotics in primary schools, respectively. The outcomes of both these projects centred on valuable professional development for the teachers involved. Unfortunately, for the UK teachers, unlike many of their European counterparts, this is not recognised, except within their own schools. Chapter 19 outlines a model for CPD credentialing as a way of building a CPD portfolio, linked with a CPD points system.

Teachers wishing to avail themselves of a wide range of on-line provision have the opportunity to do so. Examples of ways that have been developed to enable this include the innovative MESH Guides (www.meshguides.org.uk; MESH-Guides, 2020), designed to support teaching as a research-informed profession. For example, if a teacher wants to find out how to intervene and address the common spellings errors made by children, this can be done within minutes, with the opportunity of delving further and deeper into the pedagogic research if they wish (see MESHGuides on Spelling).

In the UK, as in a significant number of other nations, a number of key policy changes are urgently needed in order to support the development of teachers' professionalism and autonomy:

- provide quality CPD by accrediting a wider range of opportunities, tailored to the teacher's needs and context
- ensure sustainability of provision that is both focussed and embedded in a school's culture and context
- ensure that CPD is always research-informed and evidence based

Reflections

This chapter has considered issues of recruitment and retention in relation to the professionalism of teachers at the start of their professional training, during their induction into professional work and continuing throughout the duration of their careers. The picture has been drawn up of a bleak landscape in relation to these matters in England, which appears to be becoming an increasing outlier in comparison with other nations in the developed world. This must be seen in relation to the developing world; however, in many low- and middle-income countries the challenge of providing quality teaching brings the thrust of this chapter back to UNESCO's SDG4. It is the responsibility of those nations with the resource to do so to lead the way in successfully recruiting, developing and retaining excellent teachers for the benefit of all learners, and as Chapter 19 points out, using digital tools to curate and share the latest research-based knowledge for teaching. This can then be accessed by other low- and middle-income countries.

Policy options

The issues raised in this chapter lead to a number of policy options.

Your choice from the following policy options will be influenced by the values and principles you have chosen (see Chapters 1, 2, 3) and your view of the role of national government in leading development for the national good.

Recruitment of teachers

Policy Option 1: Lead to ensure quality and diversity: Act to ensure the teacher workforce diversity reflects the diversity in the population. This will mean ensuring training routes are accessible in all regions so as not to exclude applicants in areas where universities/teacher training organisations are not accessible. Consider part-time routes to attract career changers – experienced parents and people with other skills and experience. This is likely to require provision of distance education perhaps through an Open University. Ensure a global curriculum and Master's level accreditation.

Policy Option 2: Leave to market forces: Deregulate teacher training and leave provision to the market. This has been a policy thrust in England since 2010 and the figures cited previously show this has not solved recruitment, retention and quality issues.

Retention of teachers and professionalising teaching

Policy Option 1: Work with teacher leaders to ensure realistic workloads and accountability processes, co-ordinate comprehensive research-based CPD provision

Policy Option 2: Leave to market forces

The penultimate chapter provides further reflections and an executive summary of options, consequences and cautionary tales.

References

Allen, R., Benhenda, A., Jerrim, J. and Sims, S. (2019) New Evidence on Teachers' Working Hours in England. An Empirical Analysis of Four Data Sets. https://johnjerrim.files.wordpress.com/2019/09/working_paper_teacher_hours.pdf. Accessed 20th September, 2019.

Auguste, B., Kihn, P. and Miller, M. (2010) Closing the Talent Gap: Attracting and Retaining Top-third Graduates to a Career in Teaching (McKinsey Report). www.mckinsey.com/~/media/mckinsey/industries/social%20sector/our%20insights/closing%20the%20teaching%20talent%20gap/closing-the-teaching-talent-gap.ashx. Accessed 19th September, 2019.

BBC (2017) Reality Check: Is the Government Missing its Teacher Targets? www.bbc.co.uk/news/education-42340798. Accessed 19th September, 2019.

Bhopal, K. (2015) Race, Identity and Support in Initial Teacher Training, *British Journal of Educational Studies*, 63:2, 197–211, DOI: 10.1080/00071005.2015.1005045

Coe, R. (2013) *Improving Education: A Triumph of Hope over Experience*. Durham: Centre for Evaluation and Monitoring.

Deans for Impact (2016) *Practice with Purpose: The Emerging Science of Teacher Expertise*. Austin, TX. http://deansforimpact.org/wp-content/uploads/2016/12/Practice-with-Purpose_FOR-PRINT_113016.pdf. Accessed 20th September, 2019.

DFE (2010) *Policy Paper: The Importance of Teaching: The Schools White Paper 2010*. https://www.gov.uk/government/publications/the-importance-of-teaching-the-schools-white-paper-2010. Accessed 4th August, 2020.

Foster, D. (10 December 2018) *Teacher Recruitment and Retention in England. House of Commons Briefing Paper No 7222*. House of Commons Library. https://commonslibrary.parliament.uk/research-briefings/cbp-7222/. Accessed 4th August, 2020.

García, E. and Weiss, E. (2019) The Teacher Shortage Is Real, Large and Growing, and Worse than We Thought: The First Report. In *The Perfect Storm in the Teacher Labour Market, Series*. Economic Policy Institute, 26 March. https://www.epi.org/publication/the-teacher-shortage-is-real-large-and-growing-and-worse-than-we-thought-the-first-report-in-the-perfect-storm-in-the-teacher-labor-market-series/. Accessed 4th August, 2020.

Gov.uk (2019) Supporting Early Career Teachers. www.gov.uk/government/publications/supporting-early-career-teachers. Accessed 20th September, 2019.

Hargreaves, L. (2009) The Status and Prestige of Teachers and Teaching. In Saha, L.J. and Dworkin, A.G. (Eds) *International Handbook of Research on Teachers and Teaching*, Vol. 21. Springer International Handbooks of Education. Boston, MA: Springer.

Incheon Declaration, Education 2030. World Education Forum (2015). *Towards Inclusive and Equitable Quality Education and Lifelong Learning for All*. Republic of Korea: UNESCO together with UNICEF, the Word Bank, UNFPA, UNDP, UN Women and UNHCR.

International Taskforce on Teachers for Education 2030 (2015) www.teachersforefa.unesco.org/v2/index.php/fr/newss-2/item/490-global-teacher-shortage-threatens-education-2030. Accessed 29th October, 2019.

la Velle, L. (2013) Masterliness in the Teaching Profession: Global Issues and Local Developments, *Journal of Education for Teaching*, 39:1, 2–8, DOI: 10.1080/02607476.2012.733186

la Velle, L and Flores, M.A. (2018) Perspectives on Evidence-based Knowledge for Teachers: Acquisition, Mobilisation and Utilisation, *Journal of Education for Teaching*, 44:5, 524–538, DOI: 10.1080/02607476.2018.1516345

la Velle, L. and Kendall, A. (2019) Building Research-informed Teacher Education Communities: A UCET Framework. *Impact*, 5, 66–69.

la Velle, L. and Kendall, A. (2020) Research-Informed Teacher Education Communities: The foundation for successful recruitment and retention? In Ovenden-Hope, T. and Passy, R. (Eds) *Exploring Teacher Recruitment and Retention: Regional Disparities and Key Challenges*. London: Routledge. In Press.

la Velle, L. Stenhouse, E. and Sutton. C. (2018) Masterliness: The Challenge for Professional Development. *Journal of Interdisciplinary Studies in Education*, 7:1, 54–66, DOI: 10.5281/zenodo.1869007

Lave, J. and Wenger, E. (1991) *Situated Learning: Legitimate Peripheral Participation*. Cambridge, UK: Cambridge University Press.

Leask, M. (2018) Teaching – A Self-improving Profession? Together We Can Do It. www.ewc.wales/site/index.php/en/about/events-and-blogs/son-archive/43-english/about/staff-room/blog-archive/766-professor-marilyn-leask-teaching-a-self-improving-profession-together-we-can-do-it-here-s-how.html. Accessed 20th September, 2019.

Makopoulou., K. and Armour, K. (2014) Possibilities and Challenges in Teachers' Collegial Learning, *Educational Review*, 66:1, 75–95, DOI: 10.1080/00131911.2013.768955

McLean Davies, L., Anderson, M., Deans, J., Dinham, S., Griffin, P., Kameniar, B., Page, J., Reid., C, Rickards, F., Tayler, C. and Tyler, D. (2013) Masterly Preparation: Embedding Clinical Practice in a Graduate Pre-service Teacher Education Programme, *Journal of Education for Teaching*, 39:1, 93–106, DOI: 10.1080/02607476.2012.733193

MESH Guides (Mapping Educational knowHow) (2020) www.meshguides.org/. Accessed 20th September, 2019.

Mourshed, M., Chijioke, C. and Barber, M. (2010) How the World's Most Improved School Systems Keep Getting Better. *The McKinsey Report*. www.mckinsey.com/~/media/McKinsey/Industries/Social%20Sector/Our%20Insights/How%20the%20 worlds%20most%20improved%20school%20systems%20keep%20getting%20better/ How_the_worlds_most_improved_school_systems_keep_getting_better.ashx. Accessed 19th September, 2019.

National Association of Head Teachers (2019) www.naht.org.uk/news-and-opinion/news/ pay-and-conditions-news/new-naht-research-shows-government-needs-to-move-faster-on-the-issues-that-damage-recruitment-and-retention/. Accessed 20th September, 2019.

National Audit Office (2017) Retaining and Developing the Teaching Workforce. Report by the Comptroller and Auditor General, 7th September, 2017. www.nao.org.uk/wp-content/uploads/2017/09/Retaining-and-developing-the-teaching-workforce.pdf. Accessed 19th September, 2019.

National Education Union (2018) Teachers and Workload: A Survey Report by the NEU on Teacher Workload in Schools and Academies. https://neu.org.uk/media/3136/view. Accessed 20th September, 2019.

National Education Union (2019) www.teachers.org.uk/pay-pensions-conditions/work load. Accessed 20th September, 2019.

National Foundation for Educational Research (NFER) (2019) https://nfer.ac.uk/news-events/press-releases/more-teachers-feel-tense-or-worried-about-their-job-than-those-in-comparable-professions/. Accessed 19th September, 2019.

Paine, L. and Zeichner, K. (2012) The Local and the Global in Reforming Teaching and Teacher Education, *Comparative Education Review*, 56:4, 569–583. *JSTOR*, www.jstor. org/stable/10.1086/667769.

PhenoloGIT (2018) PhenoloGIT: Spacial Data Analysis and Mobile Learning for Schools. www.phenologit.org/. Accessed 20th September, 2019.

Robo21C (2018) Robo21C: Robotics for Primary Schools in the 21st Century. http:// robo21c.com/. Accessed 20th September, 2019.

Shulman, L. (1987) Knowledge and Teaching: Foundations of the New Reform, *Harvard Educational Review*, 57:1, 1–22.

Sorensen, N. (Ed) (2019) *Diversity in Teacher Education: Perspectives on a School-led System.* Published: UCL IOE. ISBN: 9781782772521.

TALIS The OECD Teaching and Learning International Survey (2018) www.oecd.org/ education/talis/ Accessed 20th September, 2019.

Times Educational Supplement (2019) *One in Three Teachers Leaves within 5 Years.* www. tes.com/news/one-three-teachers-leaves-within-five-years. Accessed 20th September, 2019.

Totterdell, M., Hathaway, T. and la Velle, L. (2011) Mastering Teaching and Learning Through Pedagogic Partnership: A Vision and Framework for Developing 'collaborative resonance' in England, *Professional Development in Education*, 37:3, 411–437, DOI: 10.10 80/19415257.2010.510003

United Nations Economic, Social and Cultural Organisation [UNESCO] (1966) Recommendations Concerning the Status of Teachers: International Labour Organisation/UNESCO Special Intergovernmental Conference on the status of Teachers (Paris). https://unesdoc. unesco.org/ark:/48223/pf0000160495. Accessed 19th September, 2019.

UNECSO (2015a) Incheon Declaration and Framework for Action for the Implementation of Sustainable Development Goal 4. http://uis.unesco.org/sites/default/files/ documents/education-2030-incheon-framework-for-action-implementation-of-sdg4-2016-en_2.pdf. Accessed 19th September, 2019.

UNESCO (2015b) Sustainable Development Goal 4 and its Targets. https://en.unesco.org/ education2030-sdg4/targets. Accessed 19th September, 2019.

UNESCO (2016) Close to 69 Million Teachers Needed to Reach 2030 Education Goals. www.unesco.org/new/en/media-services/single-view/news/close_to_69_million_ new_teachers_needed_to_reach_2030_educat/. Accessed 19th September, 2019.

UNESCO (2018) International Taskforce of Teachers for Education 2030, Strategic Plan 2018–2021. www.teachersforefa.unesco.org/v2/index.php/en/. Accessed 19th September, 2019.

UNESCO (2019) Sustainable Development Goal 4. https://en.unesco.org/themes/educa tion2030-sdg4. Accessed 29th October, 2019.

UNICEF (2001) The State of the World's Children: Early Childhood. Author Carol Bellamy. UNICEF. ISBN: 92-806-3633-2.

Whiting, C. (2016) Towards a New Topography of ITT: A Profile of Initial Teacher Training in England 2015–16. http://researchspace.bathspa.ac.uk/8254/. Accessed 20th September, 2019.

Whitty, G. (2019) Foreword. In Sorensen, N. (Ed) *Diversity in Teacher Education: Perspectives on a School-led System*. London: UCL IOE Press. ISBN: 9781782772521. pp. xvii–xxv.

Williams, C. (2013) Professional Development: What Can Brits Learn from Schools Abroad? www.theguardian.com/teacher-network/teacher-blog/2013/oct/08/professional-develop ment-learn-schools-abroad

Worth, J. and van den Brand, J. (2019) Teacher Labour Market in England, Annual Report 2019. www.nfer.ac.uk/teacher-labour-market-in-england-annual-report-2019/. Accessed 19th September, 2019.

18

INITIAL TEACHER EDUCATION

What matters most and has worked well

Moira Hulme, Emilee Rauschenberger,
and Karen Meanwell

Introduction

Teacher education is receiving unprecedented attention in national policy making due, in large part, to the now widely accepted notion that high-quality teaching is the most important within-school factor influencing pupil achievement, especially for less advantaged pupils (OECD, 2012).

> High-quality teaching is the most important within-school factor influencing pupil achievement, especially for less advantaged pupils.
>
> *(OECD, 2012)*

> Yet, in England, as illustrated in the discussion below policy experiments in the diversification of providers has generated regressive inter-local competition, sector instability and contributed to recruitment and retention challenges. Equity in education for children is ill-served by inequitable access to teachers of quality.

As a result, there has been a shift in policy focus from the structural reform of education systems to teacher quality. Strengthening teacher education is regarded as a prerequisite for high-quality teaching, learning, and the development of the profession. The success of strategies to improve educational outcomes ultimately depends on the teachers who carry it out and thus on the dispositions and attributes of those attracted to the field, and the quality of their professional learning and development. Despite heightened policy attention there has not been a systematic programme of research to support innovation in teacher education policy and practice (OECD, 2019). The body of evaluative research to inform policy and programme development is growing, but limited. The aim of this chapter is to make a case for context-sensitive and evidence-informed deliberation on what matters most and has worked well in strategies to promote teacher development. To achieve this aim, it is first necessary to examine how teacher education has been framed as a policy problem, and how different conceptualisations of teaching lead to radically divergent policy alternatives. Some consequences of the latest policy choices are illustrated in a review of the impact of reform on the sector in England. The chapter concludes with consideration of seven options for future policy direction.

The politics of teacher education

When assessing alternative strategies to enhance teacher quality it is important to remember that the idea of 'quality' – and how to measure it – is a context-driven concept shaped by competing interests and the governance structure in a particular locality. Teacher education is the product of contestation. Policy interventions are not simply responses to self-evident problems but set the terms of reference for thinking about an issue. Policy pronouncements build collective understandings of how things are and what really matters with the public and those employed in an education service. An examination of international trends in policy talk and academic discourse reveals a series of recurring dichotomies that illustrate the various ways in which the teacher quality problem has been framed in different countries. These frames are underpinned by different notions of teacher expertise and give rise to different accountability mechanisms. Attention to framing is particularly pertinent in the context of the politicisation of teacher education in the preceding decades as competition between countries to achieve highly in the OECD PISA tests casts a spotlight on teaching.

For the purposes of illustration, competing positions in the struggle to influence teacher education can be summarised as follows:

- The professional project (professional capital) and the new modernisers (business capital) (Cochran-Smith, 2005; Hargreaves and Fullan, 2012; Hargreaves, 2013)
- The research literate professional and the 'classroom ready' new teacher (BERA-RSA, 2014)
- Models that proceed from a 'strong' or 'thin equity perspective' (Cochran-Smith et al., 2016)

The professional project starts from the premise that teaching is a complex and intellectually demanding professional undertaking, and consequently seeks to make strong teacher preparation and induction universally available. The professional project is evident in support for clinical practice models of teacher education; the promotion of professional learning across the career course; the cultivation of an enquiry disposition; an understanding of the need for critical and culturally responsive pedagogy, and capacity building for curricular and pedagogical innovation. From this perspective, beginning teachers need to develop an understanding of pedagogical content knowledge *and* policy and research literacy in order to operate as informed agentic and activist professionals (Sachs, 2016). In contrast, the new moderniser approach reflects the encroachment of market discipline and the promotion of alternative 'fast track' routes to qualified teacher status, or indeed the removal of the requirement for state-maintained schools to employ qualified teachers. The emphasis is less on career-long professional learning than classroom readiness at entry, training while teaching, and the use of compensatory funding mechanisms to attract teachers to high needs schools and shortage subjects. Both approaches tackle the issue of equity in education. However, while the new modernisers focus on the recruitment of high calibre entrants and financial incentives, those seeking to advance the professionalisation agenda draw attention to the need to create conditions where new teachers can teach well and thrive in learning communities committed to their continuing professional growth. From a strong equity perspective, deliberation on the quality of provision extends beyond narrow notions of teacher effectiveness to include consideration of wider social justice goals (see Table 18.1).

TABLE 18.1 Underpinning policy logic of teacher education reform strategies

Professional project	*New modernisers*
Central regulation of provision	De-regulation
University-led	Multiple sites, early entry/fast track routes
Emphasis on pedagogy, professional knowledge base	Emphasis on subject matter preparation (Cochran-Smith, 2005)
Strong equity perspective	*Thin equity perspective*
Teacher education for social justice	Teacher-as-problem
Aligned with wider social policy	Focus on workforce development
Democratic evaluation, professional accountability	Results-based accountability
'Inequality [is] rooted in and sustained by long-standing systemic societal inequities'	'School factors, especially teachers, are the major sources of educational inequality'
Intersecting systems of inequality reproduce inequity in education	Inequity created by unequal access to good teachers (Cochran-Smith et al., 2016: 17)
Professional capital	*Business capital*
'Getting good teaching for all learners requires teachers to be highly committed, thoroughly prepared, continuously developed, properly paid, well networked with each other to maximise their own improvement, and able to make effective judgements using all their capabilities and experience'	'A teaching force that is young, flexible, temporary, inexpensive to train at the beginning, un-pensioned at the end (except by teachers' self-investment), and replaceable where ever possible by technology. Finding and keeping good teachers then becomes seeking out and deploying (but not really developing or investing in) existing human capital – hunting for talented individuals, working them hard, and moving them on when they get restless or become spent'. (Hargreaves, 2013: 293–294)

Highly qualified	*Differently qualified*
Teaching as complex activity,	Classroom ready,
Focus on career-long professional learning,	Focus on performance, teacher effectiveness
Development of research literacy among teachers	Knowledge of 'what works'
Impact of ITE programmes on diversity & social justice goals.	Evidence of impact on measures of student attainment.

(BERA-RSA, 2014)

A strong equity perspective assumes that teachers and schools alone cannot achieve equity; rather, it requires educators working with policymakers and others in larger social movements to challenge the intersecting systems of inequality in schools and society that produce and reproduce inequity. Working from a strong equity perspective also includes focusing directly on creating the conditions for high-quality teaching, such as supports for teachers and students, stable and supportive leadership, intensive interventions to close opportunity gaps for students in the early grades, and well-supported teacher induction programs.

(Cochran-Smith et al., 2016: 4)

Policy options – the English political experiment in 'disruptive innovation' post-2010

Teacher education in England currently operates a pluralistic model that retains features of an enduring 'professional project' alongside diversification of providers and routes. Over two decades the sector has undergone radical change. In 1999, 75 higher education institutions provided the professional preparation required for England's prospective schoolteachers. By 2019, over 240 providers offer multiple pathways to qualification in a state regulated market. Despite the pace of change, and the proliferation of providers and pathways to qualification, state-led marketisation processes in teacher education in England have attracted little attention among policy researchers. The theory of quasi-market competition in the public sector rests on three suppositions: that competition will produce efficiency gains as providers focus on performance measures; that unpopular under-achieving providers will withdraw from the market; and, that providers will become more responsive to service users/clients (Ball, 2017). The following section addresses these assertions in relation to the introduction of market-like competition in teacher education in England.

First, if it is a market, it appears skewed and ineffective at addressing either of the key performance areas of teacher supply and teacher quality. The confusing array of routes impairs the operation of a market driven by informed consumer choice on price, quality, or location. It is not a self-regulating market. Centrally controlled financial incentives and sanctions discipline provision. Schools have been protected from the risks of entering the market. Within School Direct[1] partnerships schools recruit candidates but the higher education institution (HEI) is accountable to Ofsted for student performance. If schools withdraw a School Direct place, the HEI, as provider of the postgraduate academic component (PGCE), must accommodate the wash-back. School Direct is intended to be responsive to local needs, but 57% of state-funded schools (over 11,000 schools) are not involved in the programme. Rural primaries and secondary schools in areas of high deprivation are least likely to be involved (Public Accounts Committee, 2016). Teaching Schools were established on a funding model of diminishing returns – £150,000 over three years. Although intended to be self-supporting after five years, funding to support roles in teacher development and school-to-school improvement was extended. The required Ofsted Outstanding rating for the hub school in Teaching School alliances was dropped to at least Good to provide greater stability. Even so, smaller providers have found that incentives do not match the investment required and have sought additional income by moving into the market for the supply of continuing professional development (CPD) services. Where competition between providers is high, clusters of schools have fixed the price of services, skewing the local CPD market.

The insertion of market relations has produced 'gaming' i.e. opportunistic behaviour unrelated to quality enhancement. Schools are free to select ITE providers each year. Some HEIs pay more for student placements per head than others. Enterprising headteachers can wait until the start of the school year before accepting a student teacher to extract a higher price from a pressured HEI. (This can be the difference between £1,000 per student placement to £3,000). Local economies of differential trainee value have emerged. School-centred initial teacher training (SCITT) programmes offering a range of curriculum areas may temporarily reduce their SCITT provision to subjects within the English Baccalaureate (EBACC) (English, maths, a language, science and history or geography) to protect employability data, which is returnable to Ofsted. Opportunities for new teacher employment are typically higher in EBACC curriculum areas. Such tactics help to protect SCITT records for 'outstanding practice' in high stakes Ofsted appraisals. Providers receiving positive Ofsted inspection grades (in a six-yearly cycle) were rewarded by protected or increased allocations of student teachers. Their income varies with the number of students.

There is little evidence that these reforms have secured public value. The cost of training new teachers exceeds £700 million per annum. The Public Accounts Committee (2016: 3) observed that, 'The Department has been introducing new methods for recruiting teachers for some years but many of its plans are experimental, unevaluated and still evolving. Its approach is reactive and lacks coherence'. Moreover,

> the Department was unable to provide good evidence that the hundreds of millions of pounds spent on training routes and bursaries, some of which have been in place for a number of years, are resulting in more, better quality teachers in classrooms.

> *(ibid.)*

In 2016/17, the National College for Teaching and Leadership (NCTL) provided over £244 million funding in the form of grants and bursaries to incentivise recruitment (tax-free payments paid in instalments ranging from £3,000 to £30,000 depending on subject and degree class). There is no way of discerning whether applicants who received financial incentives had always intended to be teachers or chose teaching with an equivocal, or unassured commitment. The National Audit Office (NAO) report (2016: 11) confirms,

> The Department has not assessed the impact of bursaries on applicants' success or the number who go on to qualify and teach. . . . The longer-term impact should also be explored through qualitative research, along with the risks, for example that successful applicants may have applied anyway, regardless of the bursary.
>
> *(NAO, 2016)*

Future Teacher scholarships (to attract teachers in science, technology, engineering and maths) were introduced in 2017 without an explanation of how this would increase recruitment beyond what would otherwise be achieved. Basic salaries for Newly Qualified Teachers (NQTs) are now below the training bursaries received by some candidates. The cost to schools of under-recruitment is considerable. Spending on supply staff rose from £918 million in 2011–2012 to £1.2 billion in 2014–2015 (Dickens, 2017).

There is growing concern about teacher shortages in England, stimulated by rising pupil numbers, shortfalls in recruitment, and increases in the proportion of teachers considering leaving the profession (Worth et al., 2018). Target numbers for new trainees have not been met each year from 2013 and fall below the level needed to maintain future teacher supply in the state sector. The allocation process of training places has not supported efficient workforce planning. The allocation methodology in 2012 gave HEIs a maximum annual allocation that was not guaranteed; in contrast, schools were given a minimum guaranteed number. In November 2015, the allocations methodology for 2016/17 was changed with little warning to allow school-led providers to recruit freely until recruitment targets *overall* were achieved, while HEI numbers remained capped. All HEI recruitment closed when the *national* quota for subjects was close to being achieved, irrespective of whether candidates had been called for, or indeed were in the process of attending, interviews. As the pace of the admissions process accelerated, candidates were accepted who might have been rejected in previous rounds, and providers were unable to re-open admissions when candidates who were offered places later withdrew. In the absence of strategies to safeguard against attrition, the number of applicants starting in September 2016 fell by 7 per cent; primary undergraduate admissions fell by 16 per cent. In the face of an impending teacher shortage, in April 2017 NCTL took the unprecedented step of allowing providers that had recruited 90 per cent of their annual allocation to request an increase of up to 25 per cent above their original allocation, except in Physical Education and undergraduate courses. Then in September 2017, recruitment controls for most postgraduate courses for 2018/19 were lifted (NCTL, 2018).

In short, diversification of providers has generated regressive inter-local competition and sector instability. Moreover, the consequences of teacher shortages are being felt most acutely in schools judged by Ofsted to require improvement and often serving the most disadvantaged communities. Schools and universities are entangled in ever more complex and precarious relations of 'co-opetition' (Brandenburger and Nalebuff, 1996). In response to projected teacher shortages, attention is now turning from an overriding concern with diversification of routes and pathways towards early career support and retention (DFE, 2019). Although such recalibration will be welcomed by school leaders and teacher educators, prospects for genuine reflection and policy learning are likely to be restricted by the circular logic that has informed recent education reform: when markets fail to enhance service provision, market mechanisms need to be strengthened (Burch, 2009). Thirty years of such 'ratcheting of policy' has circumscribed public debate within narrow parameters (Ball et al., 2012). Edupreneurs within market-oriented think tanks (such as Civitas, Reform, Policy Exchange) act as lobbyists, pushing the case for reform, undermining opposition and excluding alternative voices (e.g. senior civil servants, local government representatives, and university faculty). They occupy a key role in the brokerage of radical policy ideas, preparing the ground, helping to render ideas thinkable. Boundaries become blurred with personnel moving between lobby groups and official positions in a tight-knit community of reformers. Such 'bounded density' between policy actors and opinion shapers presents challenges to deliberative democracy (Desai, 1994). In a highly polarised and politicised environment, systematic research-based evaluations of outcomes are needed to appraise the relative effectiveness, costs and benefits of education policy alternatives, including different routes to professional qualification.

Reflections

This chapter has explicated policy choices for teacher education. It has suggested that the marketisation of teacher preparation in England has not achieved its intended outcomes. Attrition rates indicate that many early career teachers are under-prepared for the demands of the role or the contexts in which they teach. The structural and conceptual fragmentation of teachers' professional education is a barrier to progress. The well-rehearsed division of theory and practice has been deployed by new modernisers advocating alternative pathways to qualification. Such rhetoric denies the relations of partnership that are at the centre of professional preparation. Strengthening teacher preparation requires intensive mentoring through close and proactive relationships with partner schools – moving beyond 'placement' schools and unguided practice to exploration of theory through practice. A strong equity perspective further demands that prospective teachers consider barriers to educational equity and reject deficit thinking. Educational equity for children demands equitable access to effective teachers. This, in turn, requires universal access to coherent and integrated professional preparation programmes followed by properly resourced mentored induction throughout the early career phase. The long-term public and personal cost of poorly prepared teachers should feature prominently in deliberation on the economics of early career support.

Policy options for the future

The issues raised in this chapter lead to a number of policy options:

This final section draws on the competing reform agendas outlined in the first part of the chapter, and the consequences of the English policy experiment outlined in the second part, to identify seven policy options for teacher education in England.

Policy Option 1: Maintain the status quo

Continue to accelerate moves towards a schools-led system with multiple routes. Further fragmentation of the sector will not address growing concern in regard to the recruitment and retention of high calibre candidates and the provision of equitable access to high quality training experiences across the sector.

Policy Option 2: Create a stable policy context

Accelerated moves towards a schools-led system of teacher education in England in recent years has not provided a stable context for service enhancement or evaluation. Providers must navigate a complex landscape in which change is a constant feature. Different official bodies (Ofsted, the Quality Assurance Agency for Higher Education) make multiple accountability demands. Incentives for robust evaluation and review of provision contract when change is instigated with such regularity and such speed at policy level. Promotion of an increasingly diverse market, particularly in times of challenging recruitment, leaves providers vulnerable to financial non-viability. This is most acute among (modern/post-1992) university departments of education where teacher development is their core business. As universities continue to provide the majority of training places, further de-stabilisation would be a particularly high-risk strategy.

Policy Option 3: Orient teacher recruitment for teacher quality

Workforce planning and recruitment strategies have not proven effective in matching supply and demand. Financial incentives for applicants have produced 'bursary tourism', with insufficient evidence of longer-term effects on retention and effectiveness. Allocation mechanisms have incentivised providers to recruit quickly (before national numbers were capped) rather than focus on a selection process to assure quality. Teacher supply should not be reduced to *getting* teachers (recruitment) but *developing* teachers of quality, including opportunities for lead practitioners to become mentors, curriculum specialists, or school leaders (Darling-Hammond, 2017).

Policy Option 4: Support professional learning across the career course
(see Chapter 19)

Teacher learning is properly understood as a process of development that continues across the career course: through initial teacher education, induction, peer mentoring, in-service professional development, and professional collaboration. Effective induction experiences are those that support new teachers to thrive and achieve in professional learning communities that lay the foundations for career-long professional growth. Extended periods of professional preparation are evident in moves towards two-year qualifying programmes e.g. MTeach. Collective responsibility for system improvement is evidenced in the development of immersive residency models e.g. cohort-placement hub schools. The redesign of teacher education and reconceptualisation of schools as learning organisations is a more ambitious enterprise than the crude instrument of deregulation (Ingvarson et al., 2014),

Policy Option 5: Look beyond new teachers for improvement

Change processes need to engage educators. Change strategies informed by a theory of collective improvement focus on schools and regions rather than individual teachers or initial teacher education. That is not to say that recent entrants to the profession have no influence on professional culture, but this is limited if new teachers do not stay. Developing expertise takes time and experience across a range of employment settings. In England, much school improvement is seen through the lens of improving individual teachers driven by National Teaching Schools. School-to-school support is overly reliant on geographical reach and relationships with those organisations.

Policy Option 6: Build research capacity in teacher education

Research engagement is likely to be strongest where the university connection is strong. Research policy can do more to support impactful close-to-practice educational research and to build capacity in the sub-field of teacher education research. Teaching Schools have struggled to fulfil a research role. Research Schools, and schools in designated 'opportunity areas', need to draw on a broader base of research to support professional growth and grow capacity or risk adopting a thin version of evidence-based practice. The guidance report, *Putting Evidence to Work: A School's Guide to Implementation*, goes some way to redress the pedagogical re-positioning (and marginalisation) of the profession in debates on evidence-based education in recent years (Sharples et al., 2018). The Chartered College of Teaching has an important role here.

Policy Option 7: Advance collaborative professionalism

Rather than repeat the teacher-as-problem narratives of the past, policy deliberation might adopt a nuanced approach to evidence of impact. Outcomes-based approaches to educational evaluation must attend closely to the question of impact, specifically impact on what? For whose benefit? Evaluation and competency frameworks can benefit from the input of multiple stakeholders with diverse experiences in establishing what matters most. Collective dialogue can promote shared understanding among stakeholders and serves to emphasise that preparing competent new teachers goes beyond building their subject and pedagogical knowledge. Effective ITE also requires providers to foster collaborative professionalism that values academic, practitioner, and community-based knowledge.

The penultimate chapter provides further reflections and an executive summary of options, consequences, and cautionary tales.

Further reading and resources

Allen, R., & Sims, S. (2018) *The Teacher Gap*. London: Routledge.
British Educational Research Association-RSA (2014) Research and the Teaching Profession. www.bera.ac.uk/wp-content/uploads/2013/12/BERA-RSA-Research-Teaching-Profession-FULL-REPORT-for-web.pdf
Chartered College of Teaching. https://chartered.college/
Cochran-Smith, M. et al. (2018) *Reclaiming Accountability in Teacher Education*. New York: Teachers College Press.
Hargreaves, A., & O'Connor, M.T. (2018) *Collaborative Professionalism*. London: Sage Publications.
La Velle, L., & Kendall, A. (2019) Building Research Informed Teacher Education Communities, *Impact*. https://impact.chartered.college/article/building-research-informed-teacher-education-communities-ucet-framework/

Note

1 School Direct, introduced in 2012, is a programme where schools recruit trainees directly and universities may provide accreditation of training via a postgraduate certificate or diploma.

References

Ball, S.J. (2017) *The Education Debate* (Third Edition) Bristol: Policy Press.
Ball, S.J., Maguire, M., & Braun, A. (2012) *How Schools do Policy: Policy Enactments in Secondary Schools*. Abingdon: Routledge.
Brandenburger, A.M., & Nalebuff, B.J. (1996) *Co-opetition*. New York: Currency Doubleday.
British Educational Research Association-RSA (2014) Research and the Teaching Profession. www.bera.ac.uk/wp-content/uploads/2013/12/BERA-RSA-Research-Teaching-Profession-FULL-REPORT-for-web.pdf
Burch, P. (2009) *Hidden Markets: The New Education Privatization*. New York: Routledge.
Cochran-Smith, M. (2005) The New Teacher Education: For Better or for Worse? *Educational Researcher,* 34(7): 3–17.
Cochran-Smith, M., Stern, R., Sánchez, J.G., Miller, A., Keefe, E.S., Fernández, M.B., Chang, W., Carney, M.C., Burton, S., & Baker, M. (2016) *Holding Teacher Preparation Accountable: A Review of Claims and Evidence*. Boulder, CO: National Education Policy Center.
Darling-Hammond, L. (2017) Teacher Education around the World: What Can We Learn from International Practice? *European Journal of Teacher Education*, 40(3): 291–309.
Desai, R. (1994) Second-hand Dealers in Ideas: Think-tanks and Thatcherite Hegemony. *New Left Review*, 203: 27–64.
DfE (2019) Teacher Recruitment & Retention Strategy. www.gov.uk/government/publications/teacher-recruitment-and-retention-strategy

Dickens, J. (2017) Government to Step in over Supply Teacher Costs, *Schools Week*, 19th May. https://schoolsweek.co.uk/government-to-step-in-over-supply-teacher-costs/

Hargreaves, A. (2013) Professional Capital and the Future of Teaching. In T. Seddon and J.S. Levin (eds) *Educators, Professionalism and Politics. Global Transitions, National Spaces and Professional Projects.* London: Routledge, pp. 290–310.

Hargreaves, A., & Fullan, M. (2012) *Professional Capital: Transforming Teaching in Every School.* New York, NY: Teachers College Press and Toronto, ON: Ontario Principals' Council.

Ingvarson, L., Reid, K., Buckley, S., Kleinhenz, E., Masters, G., & Rowley, G. (2014) *Best Practice Teacher Education Programs and Australia's Own Programs.* Canberra: Department of Education.

National Audit Office (NAO) (2016) Training New Teachers. www.nao.org.uk/wp-con tent/uploads/2016/02/Training-new-teachers.pdf

National College for Teaching and Leadership (NCTL) (2018) Annual Report and Accounts For the Year Ended 31 March 2017. https://assets.publishing.service.gov.uk/govern ment/uploads/system/uploads/attachment_data/file/673371/NCTL_16-17_ARA_-_ Web_version.pdf

OECD (2012) *Equity and Quality in Education: Supporting Disadvantaged Schools and Students.* Paris: OECD Publishing.

OECD (2019) *A Flying Start: Improving Initial Teacher Preparation Systems.* Paris: OECD Publishing. https://doi.org/10.1787/cf74e549-en

Public Accounts Committee (2016) Training New Teachers, 10 June 2016, HC 73. https:// publications.parliament.uk/pa/cm201617/cmselect/cmpubacc/73/73.pdf

Sachs, J. (2016) Teacher Professionalism: Why are We Still Talking About It? *Teachers and Teaching,* 22:4, 413–425.

Sharples, J., Albers, B., & Fraser, S. (2018) *Putting Evidence to Work: A School's Guide to Implementation.* London: EEF. https://educationendowmentfoundation.org.uk/public/files/ Publications/Campaigns/Implementation/EEF-Implementation-Guidance-Report.pdf

Stoll, L., & Kools, M. (2016) *What Makes a School a Learning Organisation: A Guide for Policy Makers, School Leaders and Teachers.* Paris: OECD with UNICEF.

Worth, J., Lynch, S., Hillary, J., Rennie, C., & Andrade, J. (2018) *Teacher Workforce Dynamics in England.* Slough: NFER.

19

CPD, KNOWLEDGE SERVICES AND RESEARCH

21st century solutions

Sarah Younie and Marilyn Leask with Jon Audain,
Christina Preston and Richard Procter

Introduction: CPD – an international problem

> The absence of a strong publicly stated knowledge base allows the misconception to continue that any smart person can teach.
>
> (Fullan, 1993 p. 111)

> The risk is that if good evidence is not available, bad evidence will be used instead . . . fundamental for education, perhaps, is the question how evidence can be improved in terms of reliability, thoroughness and accessibility.
>
> (Saussois, 2003 p. 1)

> Self-directed CPD through reading research papers, watching videos, attending online and face-to-face seminars is recognised by other professions as providing CPD.
>
> (Royal College of Surgeons, 2018)

There is the need to strengthen the connection between teachers' practice and educational research, whereby the latter informs professional practice. This requires the development of a coherent strategy for teachers to engage with educational research, which can be achieved through teachers' continuing professional development. This argument has been reinforced by recommendations in an OECD (Organisation for Economic Cooperation and Development) examination of educational R&D in England (OECD, 2002) and internationally (OECD, 2009).

According to OECD TALIS research (2009), no country has a good solution for the provision of up-to-date continuing professional development (CPD) for teachers.

For the purposes of this chapter we identify four main purposes of CPD:

1 CPD initiated by government for whole sector change
2 CPD provided by subject associations
3 CPD initiated by schools for within school change and
4 CPD self-directed: initiated by the individual teacher for personal professional development

We use the term 'online' CPD to refer to formal courses as well as self-directed CPD where teachers are acquiring new knowledge themselves through reading, listening to or viewing online content or actively through professional networks e.g. via subject association networks and social media.

Our policy option proposal in this chapter is for the establishment, at national level, of an Education Knowledge Service (EKS) that would:

- bring together research evidence dispersed across disparate organisations
- make research available in easily useable formats for teachers
- co-ordinate R&D across the sector through working with professional subject associations and school networks
- establish systems and processes supporting a self-improving system which values and co-ordinates the contributions of research-active teachers as well as other education researchers
- use digital technologies effectively to achieve these goals through providing CPD opportunities

Our policy proposal is to build a sustainable Education Knowledge Service, providing a national evidence centre for teachers and educators open to use anywhere. It would be designed to use resources within the education service already where possible to ensure sustainability. This would then tackle the issue of the long-standing problem of translating findings from educational research into practical applications.

Research-based lessons

Is there any reason that someone might disagree with the expectation that lessons should be based on the latest research-based knowledge? Can it ever be acceptable in the 21st century that learners are taught out-of-date knowledge?

Not so long ago, teachers and learners relied on textbooks which took years to produce. In the 21st century, new research-based knowledge in a topic could appear in a teacher's email immediately it is published and regardless of the country of origin. Language translation tools make knowledge transfer between languages relatively simple.

This apparently simple solution is however not quite the solution. Driscoll et al. (2004) in their systematic review of primary MFL pedagogy, which is important in teaching, found over 5,000 possibly relevant articles just from recent years. Other reviewers report similar problems. Educators acting individually can't actually manage to extract the knowledge they need from the volume of individual papers produced. There is also potentially a waste of resources where researchers are publishing articles which don't add significantly to the body of knowledge, when there are also significant gaps in the pedagogical knowledge base for teaching.

So encouragement of research synthesis as well as identifying and sharing gaps in research knowledge seems an obvious intervention to support self-directed CPD for teachers.

Perhaps new standards are needed for publication in some fields, with clear summaries and syntheses? That realisation has given rise to the systematic literature review processes and practices more recently.

Teacher CPD and accessing the research base for education: an international concern

Twenty years ago, the OECD began surveys of education services to examine knowledge management processes. Saussois (2003) in reviewing OECD findings identifies these challenges for education: 'The risk is that if good evidence is not available, bad evidence will be used instead. . . . Fundamental for education, perhaps, is the question how evidence can be improved in terms of reliability, thoroughness and accessibility' (Saussois, 2003: 1). Hargreaves (1996: 12) argues that the shortcomings in the knowledge base mean that teachers may justify practices by falling back on:

• tradition (continuing with the same approach even if it is based on outdated practice)
• prejudice ('my school district likes it done in this way. . . ')
• dogma (this is the way it should be done) and
• ideology (if enough teachers are made to do it by policy changes or through methods of destruction or construction, then this must be right?)

These constitute four pillars underpinning educational practice as outlined by Caroline Cox. Furthermore, Saussois (2003) cites a 1999 US government study which analysed education research papers and found: 'just 400 out of 20,000 academic papers that even potentially have practical applications, i.e. just 2% of the total'. Michael Fullan, who has a long history of researching quality in education, suggested in 1993 that the lack of an evidence base was holding back the development of teaching as a profession: 'The absence of a strong publicly stated knowledge base allows the misconception to continue that any smart person can teach' (Fullan, 1993: 111). Fullan challenged the teacher education community to identify the evidence underpinning their practice: 'a key obstacle in the evolution of teaching as a profession is an inadequately defined knowledge base about teaching and teacher education' (1993: 113). Lawrence Stenhouse, the founder of the teacher-researcher movement in the UK, in 1975 proposed teachers take control of pedagogic research, scaling up small-scale studies and synthesising across these (Stenhouse, 1975).

At the highest level of international organisations, there is concern that the education sector knowledge base is disorganised. The OECD (2009: 3) suggested 'education could be transformed by knowledge about the efficacy of (teaching) practices'. Irina Bukova, Director General of UNESCO, had a vision that to improve education worldwide, teachers and teacher-educators would have to act 'as change agents'.

> We need a new focus on the quality of education and the relevance of learn-
> ing, on what children, youth and adults are actually learning. . . . We need
> an ever-stronger focus on teachers and teacher educators as change agents
> across the board.
>
> *(Bukova, 2015: 4)*

Our analysis is that technologies offer the teaching 'profession' the opportunity to revolutionise the way knowledge is held and constructed 'by the profession, for the profession' but that a central co-ordinating body would need to lead on this, to guarantee quality, relevance and coverage.

So while in this chapter we can make the case for digital technologies offering the chance for teachers virtually anywhere[1] to be able to access online CPD materials either online or offline,[2] we are aware that the lack of quality assurance and an evidence base is apparent in online materials in a way that is hidden with face-to-face CPD where the spoken word is ephemeral. We are not suggesting there are universal truths but that online materials are easily subject to scrutiny. But who is to do it?

Whose knowledge informs CPD?

Leask and White's (2004) UK government funded research found little peda-gogic research exists which is relevant to the teaching of key concepts in specific subjects for the range of learner needs. Similarly, processes for teachers keep-ing up-to-date with new subject content from research units were found to be inadequate. The authors estimate that a comprehensive pedagogic knowledge repository for the teaching profession may contain 40,000 or more entries. This calculation is based on the core concepts for teaching covered in the indexes of educational texts like Capel et al. (2019) multiplied by the approximate num-ber of key concepts covered in each subject, from early years up to the end of secondary level, multiplied by the different types of assessment possible and the different types of learners.[3] A UK initiative established to improve relevance of research, the Education Endowment Fund, is not focusing on pedagogical research.

TABLE 19.1 Forms of knowledge for teaching (developed from Schulman, 1987, cited in Capel, Leask and Younie, 2019)

General Pedagogic Knowledge	i.e. the broad principles and strategies of classroom management and organisation that apply irrespective of the subject.
Subject Content Knowledge	i.e. research-based knowledge generated by specialist research units, e.g. in genetics, literature etc.
Subject Pedagogic Knowledge	i.e. the knowledge of what makes for effective teaching and deep learning of concepts in specific subjects at specific ages for particular learners.
Technology Pedagogic Knowledge	i.e. general and subject specific pedagogic knowledge about how to deploy technologies to support learning of concepts in specific subjects at specific ages for particular learners.
Curriculum Knowledge	i.e. the materials and the programmes that serve as 'tools of the trade' for teachers and which ensure progression in learning over the years.
Knowledge of Learners and their Characteristics	i.e. knowledge of child development from psychology, sociology and neuroscience.
Knowledge of Educational Contexts	i.e. cultural knowledge which impacts on schooling.
Knowledge of Educational Ends	i.e. purposes, values and philosophical and historical influences: both short- and long-term goals of education and of a subject.

Shulman's (1987) forms of knowledge for teaching (Table 19.1) provide an organising structure for the forms of knowledge required for teaching.

If you accept these forms of knowledge are necessary for teaching (and if not which would you leave out?), then consider the origins of the knowledge for practice in these fields: who is responsible for updating the knowledge and how can a teacher keep up-to-date in these fields without digital tools?

In the online world as with face-to-face CPD, the research and evidence base underpinning CPD may not be explicit and indeed in some cases may not exist.

How does an education sector create new knowledge?

Much is written exhorting teachers to improve learning outcomes, but you will find little analysis of how new knowledge is created and shared and indeed who creates it. Leask and White (2004) found that although the UK has the fifth largest economy in the world, there was not sufficient research capacity in the university sector to generate the wide-ranging pedagogic research to support comprehensive CPD for teachers. However, in the teacher community interest and capacity exists, but is not coordinated.

Digital networking and the creation and validation of new knowledge

There are existing models of how new pedagogic knowledge is created. For example, when computers were introduced into schools in the UK (early 1980s), new pedagogies had to be developed and the government funded a programme which brought together innovative educators to create and share new knowledge.[4] Reliance on print made this a slow and costly process. Within ten years the process was transformed by digital technologies. From the early 1990s there were successful experiments in education, networking researchers and teachers worldwide to share and build knowledge. In 1992, MirandaNet, an international knowledge sharing network of ICT innovators in education, was established to share practices internationally. In 1996 the UK government agency, Becta, established a SENCO forum which is now managed by volunteers by the professional association NASEN. These initiatives showed the power of online networking for knowledge sharing across national boundaries.

Teachers will be aware of social-constructivism learning theory and Vygotsky's 'zone of proximal development' – that learning requires a more knowledgeable leader. In the previous cases, there were no more knowledgeable others and the term 'communal constructivism' was coined to describe the process of collaboratively creating and testing new knowledge (Leask and Younie 2001). Fifteen years ago, the UK local government sector, with approximately 600 specific areas of responsibility, developed online communities of practice to network local authority specialists across the four home countries. Users now come from 80 countries. Members of the communities benchmark practice, share and develop new practices and induct new colleagues into the shared knowledge of the network (KHub.net). The health sector also has had longstanding collaborative online knowledge services such as the Cochrane Collaboration (www.cochranecollaboration.org) and the National Institute for Clinical Excellence pathways (https://pathways.nice.org.uk).

The majority of countries have national research and education networks[5] (NRENS) providing the broadband connections and some knowledge services for educational organisations. These are coordinated by the EU funded GEANT initiative (www.geant.org). The NRENs may be linked with closed educational intranets connecting classrooms such as the European SchoolNet (1995, www.eun. org), London Grid for Learning, and Scotland's Glow platform. The NRENs provide connectivity across all schools, universities and FE colleges but some knowledge services are not open for professional networking because of the need to protect users' identities.

Lessons from failures with online CPD to date

In the early days of the development of internet hosted resources for teachers, a number of governments invested heavily in online CPD resources (EdNA in

Australia; the QCDA, TDA, BECTA, DFE resources in England). Teachers then found changes of government meant resources were taken offline. Colleagues in Sweden and Scotland have reported similar actions.

Not only is this a significant waste of government funds, but curricula were built around the resources, and not just in the originating countries. South African colleagues reported that UK government funded National Curriculum resources which they had been using vanished overnight with no warning, with the shutting down of government agencies and the 'bonfire of the quangos' in 2010 by the coalition government (Blamires, 2015).

A lesson for the education sector is that where governments fund resources the resulting resources need to be protected from destruction.

CPD opportunities with digital networking

Knowledge and practice exist showing how to use internet connectivity to support rapid exchange and testing of new ideas between teachers and researchers, regardless of their location, followed by rapid publication and dissemination. Access to knowledge for self-directed professional development such as that needed when individual teachers face students with new challenges can be supported cost-effectively by personalised online CPD processes. For example, at the beginning of the school year, if teachers find they have students with specific individual needs the online SENCO forum[6] provides a first port of call for discussion with peers. Some teachers use Twitter for similar purposes, but we would not consider any service which allows content posted by anonymous users to be reliable.

Many of the smaller countries in the world do not have the resources to have specialist subject associations which typically run specialist networks. A third of the world's countries have a population lower than 3 million with many not being able to provide extensive higher education. Clearly with such small populations they need to depend on the knowledge generated across the disciplines in the more economically powerful countries to keep their professionals up-to-date.

In the UK, many professional networks seem to exist but there is no central register or co-ordination which would help new teachers to find online professional communities. In the education sector, it appears the lack of a dedicated body providing central organisation has left the education sector 10 years behind in using what are now basic digital tools for professional groups such as doctors and nurses (NICE, Campbell Collaboration), social workers (SCIE), lawyers (LEXUS-NEXUS) to use to improve the quality of professional practice by providing access to a research-informed knowledge base.

Imagining 'online' CPD in the future

Tried, tested and low-cost digital technologies support current online resources/ apps and 'courses' which typically use web publishing linked with two-way online communication tools. We look beyond this basic provision[7] and can imagine a world where:

- Class teachers periodically receive a text with links to brief summaries about new and substantial research relevant to their classroom practice and challenges. Such a knowledge service would provide summaries which were quality assured, authoritative with authors known, where alternative viewpoints were acknowledged, and where advice would be weighted for strength of evidence and transferability. These CPD resources might be presented as podcasts, video, texts, interactive resources, simulations – whatever is appropriate to the topic and would be accessible through different devices. Through our experiments with how to summarise research creating the knowledge needed for teaching, we have found that new knowledge created from years of research can often be simply expressed. In addition this can be easily incorporated into a teacher's existing professional practice: take, for example, the research that mind-mapping is a pedagogical tool which helps reluctant writers break through the barriers preventing them writing[8] or that neuroscientists find brain 'plasticity' allows lifelong learning[9] or, for biologists, that phages (viruses that eat only bacteria) are providing a means to defeat superbugs (bacteria).[10]
- In such a world, teachers, learners and parents would all have access to research summaries about the barriers to learning key concepts that individual children face and so could use these for planning interventions.
- In such a world, subject content knowledge experts, such as neuroscientists, would work with leading teachers to translate research findings into practical classroom applications, publishing a summary which could be translated into many other languages at the touch of a button.
- Leading teachers would be part of specialist national and international teacher researcher/researcher networks, creating new research-based pedagogic knowledge, benchmarking practices and sharing the results with colleagues; such networks would publish and update summaries developed cost-effectively using online communication and collaboration tools.
- In this world, high quality resources covering all lesson subject content, such as those developed by Open Universities around the world, would be freely available to subject specialist teachers to support their self-directed CPD and professional updating.
- Personal video analysis of practice could be undertaken routinely as part of professional development and practice refinement coupled with personal, perhaps online, mentoring available (see the existing IRISConnect model).
- Smart glasses allow specialists remote to a school, to join in discreetly and directly, a teacher's conversations with learners who have particular barriers to learning.

This world is within the grasp of those entering teaching now through existing current digital tools but individual teachers cannot realise the vision alone.

Accrediting online CPD: 'CPD points' systems

Self-directed CPD through reading research papers, watching videos, attending online and face-to-face seminars is recognised by other professions as providing CPD (Royal College of Surgeons, 2018).

We suggest it is only a matter of time before governments start to require teachers to demonstrate that they are undertaking CPD in order to retain their teacher registration. Other, professions already operate self-managed 'CPD points' systems independent of government.

However, repositories of articles, podcasts or videos are not the full answer to keeping teachers up-to-date. Such repositories abound e.g. the US's ERIC (https://eric.ed.gov/pdf/ERIC_Retrospective.pdf), which provides open online access to articles. Professional associations and teachers' councils usually provide members with online access to articles (www.subjectassociations.org).

UK government funded research (Leask 2004; Leask and White, 2004) found open access to academic articles was not particularly helpful to teachers:

- Academic articles are not written for a 'user' teacher audience
- There is a massive oversupply of articles in some areas. See for example, the UK government's commissioned systematic review of research on primary modern foreign language pedagogy (Driscoll et al., 2004). Reviewers found 5,184 potentially relevant articles. How does a teacher decide which to read? And, few articles were found to be relevant.

During 2001–2004 educators, charity officials, public and civil servants from UK government agencies (TDA, GTCE, DFE and QCDA) met to review the state of educational research and found that in the UK there was no systematic funding of research into pedagogy and no coordination of such research (Leask, 2004). This study found that most research was funded to meet the needs and priorities of funders, which were not the same as those of classroom teachers. Hence for much CPD there was just anecdotal evidence of impact.

So who is to act?

Leask and White's (2004) research found no UK body which took responsibility for ensuring that research was available to support teaching subject-specific knowledge. Post-2010, UK investment has focused on randomised control trials which do not appear to address subject specific pedagogy.[11] Leask and Younie's research (2013) found no international body with the remit to ensure teachers everywhere can access the latest knowledge to keep up-to-date.

The current free market system for funding educational research where funders or individual researchers choose research topics themselves may be valuable for innovation and personal interest, but it works against a need to have a comprehensive research base for teaching.

The MESH (Mapping Educational Specialist knowHow) experiment – learning from success and failures

The authors of this chapter have been involved in experiments with digital technologies to support lifelong teacher learning since the 1980s and have, with colleagues around the world, developed a prototype knowledge mobilisation system to address the criticisms of knowledge management in the education sector. The system is called MESH – **M**apping **E**ducational **S**pecialist know**H**ow.

While the UK had extensive open online educational resources for CPD prior to 2010, the websites where they resided were closed down following a change in government. In the years that followed, a network of colleagues consulted with teacher and teacher education colleagues about online CPD provision from countries as diverse as Australia, Afghanistan, Bhutan, Cameroon, Croatia, the Czech Republic, New Zealand, Malaysia, Pakistan, Poland, South Africa, Thailand and the United States. They found colleagues faced similar problems about the lack of research and lack of access to useable knowledge for teachers' professional practice. There was a willingness to work together to address these problems.

MESH also consulted with OECD and UNESCO colleagues and found no organisation with a remit or the capacity to focus on building and making public the knowledge base underpinning educational practice. (Note: this is not the same as giving teachers open access to research articles.)

Here are the points of consensus that developed from the consultation:

- No initial training can provide teachers with the knowledge needed for teaching over a whole career. In both developed and developing countries, there appears to be a consensus around initial teacher training models – three or four years of training with concurrent teaching of pedagogy and subject content training or a $3 + 1$ model with some countries e.g. Finland, also requiring Master's level training (this was proposed in England in 2008[12]). However, in times of shortages of teachers, standards for entry are usually dropped. This means that CPD provision cannot be based on assumptions about what teachers know already and supports the case for self-directed CPD to be organised. We propose integrating ITT and CPD online provision linked with CPD points type accreditation,[13] in order to provide a continuum for professional learning. Teachers who are members of the Royal Society of Biology already undertake self-directed accredited online CPD.[14] Given the pace of change in different subject disciplines (as well as in pedagogy, neuroscience, psychology and so on) keeping teachers up to date is a significant challenge.
- Knowledge resources need regular updating.
- A–Z lists of research summaries are needed – specifically for teachers – accessible at the touch of a button and regularly updated.
- Small changes in publishing practices could lead to production and updating of such research summaries.

- Other professions with similar knowledge services provide funding models educators could follow.

The MESH initiative (Hurley 2019; Younie et al., 2019) combines online collaborative knowledge-building models with 'translational research'[15] publishing models to create prototypes of new ways of working to provide up-to-the-minute CPD materials. Examples have been developed with

1 regional/local networks with university, school and local authority staff working together
2 specialist research institutes
3 professional subject associations
4 non-governmental organisations (NGOs)
5 PhD supervisors and their students (via a national validating group)

A MESH international advisory council[16] was formed with colleagues from the countries above in 2018 to share knowledge across different countries. What is now called the MESH knowledge mobilisation system focuses on networking teachers and researchers to bring together and keep updated syntheses, summaries and online knowledge maps of existing research-based knowledge.

A sixth model – coordinating the work of leading teachers as change agents – is the next development. Practice exists but is dispersed. It needs systemic co-ordination to have system-wide impact. We argue such a network would lead to a dynamic and agile sector, able to respond rapidly to change with change supported by research. We argue that change should be introduced on the basis of research evidence for sound educational reasons rather than on the whim of politicians with particular vagaries.

Online networking supporting peer research collaboration scaling up promising small-scale research is what we propose is necessary for building the pedagogic research base for CPD – for every subject area, every concept, every type of learner. But we also suggest these ways of working are incorporated into normal professional practices for nominated staff. Such embedding is necessary, given that funding from external bodies seems to rarely support sustainability as practices stop when funding stops. If enough leading educators adopt a self-improving profession stance then these ways of working might achieve the prize of a global research informed knowledge base for the teaching profession which can be updated regularly and be free at the point of access: the vision of the MESH international network.

Quality provision of CPD

Online CPD means that no longer is a teacher or school tied to a local provider. As long as the school has internet access or access to downloading tools[17] to provide offline provision, no longer does the remoteness of the school mean CPD is not available to staff. With over 80 languages able to be automatically translated via Google Translate, no longer is language of publication the major barrier it once was to accessing research knowledge to inform professional practice.

Digital technologies support teachers' open access to online research summaries and can support self-directed personal professional development. In the scenario of ubiquitous international connectivity the quality of the knowledge accessed through online CPD could be genuinely world leading. We are not suggesting there are universal truths but that through the technology access to world leading knowledge is possible and that alternative viewpoints and emerging knowledge can be easily included so that a teacher can weigh up the research evidence before making an informed decision about his or her practice.

However, our research indicates that no one country working alone (except perhaps Russia or China) is likely to be able to coordinate the resources necessary to realise the opportunities for online CPD. The knowledge base for teaching is just too extensive and dispersed currently, with pockets of new knowledge being developed in research units, NGOs, dataset repositories and universities across the world.

Reflections

Without action at the national and international level, the problem of CPD for teachers will not be solved – the market has not delivered, so if the country wants an education service preparing young people for the future, not the past, the state needs to develop a strategy for making this happen.

We propose that government establish an independent Education Knowledge Service (EKS) to co-ordinate development of a regularly updated, open access, research-informed online education resources bank supporting CPD for teachers, trainee teachers and teacher educators.

The EKS would not duplicate existing provision but would work with specialist subject/professional associations, research units (across all disciplines), government, businesses, commercial knowledge services and most importantly examination boards to ensure full coverage of topics relevant to teaching, providing open access for teachers to summaries of the latest research. We propose that the EKS be independent so as to be able to take decisions based on professional rather than political grounds. It could come under the jurisdiction of the national education board outlined in Chapters 3 and 6.

In this way, lesson content and teaching approaches could be kept up-to-date and relevant. Providing teachers with the agency to direct their own professional learning, with recognition and accreditation through CPD points, this could enhance retention and support teacher well-being.

Policy options

Three options for providing resources which support quality assured research-informed CPD. These are as follows:

Policy Option 1: Status quo. Some political parties have the philosophy that the market will sort all problems. This does not seem to have worked in England for the issue of making syntheses of educational research accessible to teachers. Michael Gove, the Secretary of State for Education in 2010, closed down all Department for Education funded work in this area as part of his philosophy of 'putting a bush fire through the education sector so that green shoots may emerge'. As it turns out, it is not within the remit or resources of individual teachers, schools, researchers, professional associations or universities to provide a national service – but each can play its role.[18]

Policy Option 2: Status quo with some statutory direction and startup funding. Politicians can set the criteria for the award of government research funds: through prioritising synthesis and gap analysis, together with co-ordination with other research funders, the filling of gaps may be a relatively easy policy decision to take and to implement. In the UK, the Research Excellence Framework criteria for judging university research provides a lever for change.

Policy Option 3: Radical solution which happens to support the UN's Sustainable Development Goal 4c – ensure high quality teaching: Recognise that the task of creating and publishing research syntheses/groundbreaking research relevant to teaching is a task beyond the knowledge resources of any one country and create, perhaps with the OECD or UNESCO, an international collaboration to enable teachers around the world to access the latest research in the topics they are teaching, in their own language. An example of such collaboration between ministries is the European SchoolNet, connecting classrooms across Europe with core funding from 30 ministries of education.

The consequences of these policy options are discussed in the next chapter.

Acknowledgements

This chapter is adapted with permission from The Council for Subject Associations, Technology Pedagogy in Education Association and Education Futures Collaboration Policy briefing 19/02.

Notes

1 In developed and developing countries, smartphone ownership levels are high.
2 Digital tools exist to download whole repositories and transfer these to devices used offline. See e-granary www.widernet.org/egranary/. Transfer of files from digital device e.g. phone to other devices can be achieved without Wi-Fi using for example, USTAD mobile software.
3 NASEN, the UK professional association for educators interested in special needs and disabilities, identifies 50 forms of special educational needs that teacher may come across in their career.
4 TVEI: the Technical and Vocational Education Initiative (1983–1997)
5 NRENs https://en.wikipedia.org/wiki/National_research_and_education_network
6 www.sendgateway.org.uk/whole-school-send/sencos-area/
7 The Mapping Educational Specialist knowHow initiative, MESH, can be found on www.meshguides.org.
8 Reluctant writers www.meshguides.org/guides/node/38

9 Neuroscience and Neuromyths for teachers: www.meshguides.org/guides/node/287
10 http://sitn.hms.harvard.edu/flash/2018/bacteriophage-solution-antibiotics-problem/
11 https://educationendowmentfoundation.org.uk
12 See www.independent.co.uk/student/postgraduate/postgraduate-study/do-teachers-need-to-take-masters-863540.html
13 See Royal College of Anaesthetists www.rcoa.ac.uk/content/continuing-professional-development
14 See Royal Society of Biology www.rsb.org.uk/careers-and-cpd/cpd
15 Translational research is applied research – translating theory to practice.
16 www.meshguides.org/home/international-advisory-board/
17 Such as eGranary www.widernet.org/egranary/
18 Funding models for open-access high-quality resources for teachers are problematic. The UK Local Government Association (LGA) approach to managing innovation sustainably is worth considering: where an initiative is a national priority, startup funding is negotiated with Government; then if the initiative is a success, the local authorities fund the initiative from their own resources, if they wish it to continue, often through subscription.

    In the education sector, the ministry for education would need to lead on this and negotiate with relevant bodies such as subject or professional associations, but ongoing funding in education on a subscription model is problematic. Schools where the resource might make the most difference might be those least able to subscribe to a national resource. Teachers who might most benefit may not be able to afford fees. For the medical sector in the UK, the Government funds the National Institute for Health and Clinical Excellence.

References

Blamires, M. (2015) Building portals for evidence-informed education: Lessons from the dead. A case study of the development of a national portal intended to enhance evidence informed professionalism in education, *Journal of Education for Teaching*, 41:5, 597–607, DOI: 10.1080/02607476.2015.1105532

Bukova, I. (2015) *The Right to Education for all Children*. Paris: UNESCO.

Capel, S., Leask, M. and Younie, S. (2019) (8th edition) *Learning to Teach in the Secondary School*. Abingdon: RoutledgeTaylorFrancis.

Driscoll, P., Jones, J., Martin, C., Graham-Matheson, L., Dismore, H. and Sykes, R. (2004) A systematic review of the characteristics of effective foreign language teaching to pupils between the ages 7 and 11. In *Research Evidence in Education Library*. London: EPPI-Centre, Social Science Research Unit, Institute of Education. Available at: https://eppi.ioe.ac.uk/cms/Portals/0/PDF%20reviews%20and%20summaries/MFL_2004review.pdf?ver=2006-03-02-125233-317 (accessed on 17 June 2019).

Fullan, M. (1993) *Change Forces: Probing the Depths of Educational Reform*. Abingdon: RoutledgeFalmer.

Hargreaves, D. H. (1996) *Teaching as a Research Based Profession: Possibilities and Prospects*. London: Teacher Training Agency. Available at: https://eppi.ioe.ac.uk/cms/Portals/0/PDF%20reviews%20and%20summaries/TTA%20Hargreaves%20lecture.pdf (accessed on 14 June 2019).

Hurley, S. (2019) *In Conversation with the MESH Executive Board. voicEd Radio Podcast*. Available at: www.spreaker.com/episode/18295429 (accessed on 17 June 2019).

Leask, M. (2004) *Using Research and Evidence to Improve Teaching and Learning in the Training of Professionals: An Example from Teacher Training in England*. London: Teacher Training Agency. Available at: www.leeds.ac.uk/educol/documents/00003666.htm (accessed on 17 June 2019).

Leask, M. and White, C. (2004) Initial Teacher Training (ITT) Professional Resource Networks (IPRNs) – rationale and development. Leeds: Education-line. Available at: www.leeds.ac.uk/bei/Education-line/browse/all_items/136757.html (accessed on 17 June 2019).

Leask, M. and Younie, S. (2013) National models for continuing professional development: The challenges of twenty-first-century knowledge management, *Professional Development in Education*, 39:2, 273–287, DOI: 10.1080/19415257.2012.749801

Leask, M. and Younie, S. (2001) Communal constructivist theory: Pedagogy of information and communications technology & internationalisation of the curriculum, *Journal of Information Technology for Teacher Education*, 10:1 & 2, 117–134.

OECD (2002) *Educational Research and Development in England*. Examiners' Report. CERI/CD (2002)10. Paris: OECD Publishing.

OECD (2009) *Creating Effective Teaching and Learning Environments: The First Results from the TALIS Survey*. Paris: OECD Publishing. Available at: www.oecd.org/edu/school/43023606.pdf

Royal College of Surgeons (2018) *Reading for CPD: How Our Reflective CPD Form Can Help*. London. Available at: www.rcseng.ac.uk/library-and-publications/library/blog/reading-for-cpd/ (accessed on 17 June 2019).

Saussois, J. (2003) *Reflections on OECD Studies on Knowledge Management and Related Issues: Implications for Schooling for Tomorrow*. Paris: OECD Publishing.

Shulman, L. S. (1987) Knowledge and teaching: Foundations of the new reform. *Harvard Educational Review*, (February), 1–22.

Stenhouse, L. (1975) *An Introduction to Curriculum Research and Development*. London: Heineman.

Younie, S., Audain, J., Eloff, I., Leask, M., Procter, R. and Shelton, C. (2019) Mobilising knowledge through global partnerships to support research-informed teaching: Five models for translational Research, *Journal of Education for Teaching: International Research and Pedagogy*, Special Issue on 'Perspectives on Evidence-based Knowledge for Teachers: Acquisition, mobilisation and utilization'. Available at: https://doi.org/10.1080/02607476.2018.1516348 (accessed on 17 June 2019).

SECTION 6

Policy options and consequences

Chapter 20 reviews the Policy Options proposed in the chapters covering the foundations of a new national education system and discusses the consequences of these policies, including their consequences for young people, their communities and the well-being of society.

Chapter 21: As this book was going to press in 2020, a global pandemic erupted, and around the world, schools, colleges and universities (along with all businesses except for essential services) were closed for weeks initially and then months, as countries went into 'lockdown', to limit transmission of the coronavirus through the population.

This chapter provides an analysis of early lessons for the education sector from this global pandemic.

20

POLICY OPTIONS AND CONSEQUENCES

What has to be done, when and with whom

Sarah Younie, Marilyn Leask and Brian Hudson

Introduction

> Education systems provide the foundations for the future wellbeing of every society. In addition, teaching is the one profession that makes all other professions possible.

> The rhetoric that there is a simple solution to ensuring a national education service and system that delivers a world-class education for all is entrancing.
>
> *Younie and Leask (2019a)*

The international context for this book is the ongoing preoccupation of governments to improve their education systems and the lack of publications on education system design, as mentioned in the preface.

Internationally, UNESCO's new Sustainable Development Goals challenge developed and developing countries to provide high-quality education for all children by 2030. Additionally, international measurements of the effectiveness of school education systems such as the OECD, PISA and TIMSS benchmarks have created a highly competitive environment between the countries involved. There is a danger that such measures, which are naturally limited in scope, lead to unintended consequences as politicians opt to adopt quick fixes so that they are seen by the electorate to be improving the country's place in the international league tables. It is important to guard against this. This book suggests an education system be viewed as an ecosystem with interdependencies between many different components needing to be considered when change is contemplated. This will lead to a more in-depth and nuanced understanding of the complexity when developing education policy.

England, a cautionary tale: England is used as a case study in a number of chapters as it presents a system which has become an extreme outlier among developed nations. The context for England is that many of the initiatives and changes introduced by the current government are considered not to be working by Parliament's own regulatory bodies. In England, the education system was opened up to a free market early in the 21st century, and chaos of provision has ensued together with a crisis of teacher recruitment and retention (DfE, 2019b). This has led to a parental and political backlash and the main opposition party, the Labour Party, promoting the concept of a National Education Service as the model for the system of the future. This is an extreme example of a society going around in circles. In 1833, the MP for Wigan brought the first documented proposals before Parliament to establish a National Education Service. Many subsequent Education Acts made significant changes to the service only to have the changes swept away by the next government (see Chapter 5). This adversarial approach has wasted resources and challenges the notion of a democracy being a system where Parliament and Government work for all the people.

The nature, pace and complexity of change in societies and economies are posing fundamental questions about the purposes of school education.

In our analysis we argue that democracies are best served by open and detailed debate managed by a national body at arm's length to government tasked to work with parties and stakeholders to achieve a genuine majority view about the purposes of school education and the services and systems necessary to support these purposes. The school curriculum should promote deep learning and the development of capacities that will help equip young people for their future lives. Systems of governance of the education service are needed that are suited to the maintenance of stability yet which allow for innovation in the emerging environment going forward.

Currently, conventional research, development and dissemination strategies are insufficiently agile and penetrative for periods of disruptive change such as societies are now experiencing. The consequences of the changes in England have been damaging to the profession and the experiences of those in the system, with a rise in mental health issues, not only for children and young people, but for teachers too, leading to a retention crisis (Perryman and Calvert, 2019), perhaps a consequence of the destruction deliberately caused by the incoming Secretary of State for Education in 2010, who announced to ministry staff that he wanted to 'put a bushfire through education, to let the green shoots rise' (Gove, cited in Younie and Leask, 2019b), in the form of the market forces shaping education. This has sadly left many young people 'off-rolled' without schooling (DfE Timpson Review of School Exclusion, 2019a) and without experienced teachers (Harrison, 2012) and those in school following a system described by those in it as 'unknowable', 'unmanageable' and 'unfixable' (Whalley and Greenway, in Chapter 5). The consequent crisis in the recruitment and retention of teachers, which has persisted for a number of years, is reaching a 'perfect storm' (García and Weiss, 2019; Younie and Preston, 2020).

Instead, England could have an open culture founded on mutual and collaborative learning as in other European countries, which offers a better opportunity to create necessary relevance and agility and ownership of high-quality education.

Our analysis is that future approaches to governance and change must secure the active engagement of those who will make change a reality. Future change strategies will require investment in building a workforce rooted in extended professionalism. Parents, carers and the wider community should be seen as stakeholders with the right to be involved in decisions about education in their community. Accountability should be integral to a culture committed to learning and improving rather than high-stakes compliance. (See Chapter 16 on accountability systems for schools.)

Values and principles

It is important to consider your values and whether they support a shared conception of citizenship in contemporary society. For us these include the importance of all citizens understanding and appreciating the role of 'deliberative democracy' (Fishkin, 2018) and the deliberate including of voices of different groups, which includes understanding participatory democracy and representative democracy.

Value of consensus

Decisions about education services are based on the values of those making the decisions. These are then transmitted overtly or covertly to children and young people thereby shaping society. To give an example, from Matthews in Chapter 2, if equality is valued, then children and young people should develop an understanding that we are living in an increasingly diverse world with gender, 'race', cultural and religious variations. Taking gender equality as an example, defining one's sexuality is increasingly seen as crucial to social and emotional development, and LGBT views are progressively being more understood. Often individualism is accepted as being important. However, for equality across sexualities and cultural differences, individualism should be tempered with accepting that the individual only exists within a community, and so forms their identity as an individual-in-group. At the root of this is the development of factors such as empathy, self-reflection with others, consideration and resilience. The consequences of taking a different stance are likely to be ghettoisation and intolerance.

Managing competing expectations: stakeholder engagement and consensus

Nations aspiring to be democratic face the challenge of how to balance competing values and demands of different groups in society. A consequence of not managing these is social conflict and alienation if one set of values clearly dominates policy, provision and expenditure to the exclusion of others. At the same time, accommodating diverse views without creating an education service and system which institutionalises segregation (see Chapter 8) is a challenge. The 'Deliberate Democracy' process (Fishkin and Lushkin, 2005) offers a way to manage competing expectations of stakeholders when national education policy is being set. In

Chapter 6, we highlight the importance of the governance of a national education service and system to include stakeholder engagement: the concept of 'Education England' is proposed as a way forward.

To provide transparency in decision making and the allocation of resources we suggest the general principles for the operation of such a body (a national education council or board) be based on the notion of deliberative democracy i.e. consultation with all major stakeholders.

Foundation 1: an innovating education service and system for the future – aims, values and principles

Fundamentally, the foundations of policy are decided by your values and will affect the type of education service and system that you develop.

Whether you believe in notions of superiority, underpinned by beliefs of fixed intelligence, leading to academic selection, with the consequence of a segregated schooling system, or whether you believe in equality and diversity with schools offering the same opportunities for all, will significantly affect the type of education service and system you create.

Integral to this are your beliefs about the role and responsibilities of private and public sector funding, with the former letting the market reign and the latter with a sense of collective public good.

Your policy options are:

Policy option 1: develop an elitist system
Policy option 2: develop a system based on meritocracy with equality of opportunity
Policy option 3: abdicate any responsibility for national leadership of the system; let the market have a free hand in determining what education is provided, and use minimal state funds to provide provision of no interest to the market

Consequences: Each of the aforementioned policy options leads to significantly different consequences.

The elitist system allows for a minority to benefit from a system that is designed to enable the 'most able' to flourish and functions to protect power and privilege. This leads to policy making that is developed through the underlying principles of a neoliberalist philosophy where the market is best placed to provide provision.

The more meritocratic system enables more standardised schooling, providing greater equity between schools and parity of opportunities.

In the interests of developing a more equal and stable education provision, we propose that a new, national education service and system is developed for England. Essentially, this would be managed by an independent education council, which sets policy priorities, builds cross party agreement and is committed to long-term planning (a minimum 10-year plan), in order to create stability, consistency and coherence.

Foundation 2: Education England – a vision and design for a new national education service

With the cautionary tale from England, which sees a highly fragmented and varied range of types of schools operating, we argue for a new provision, with consistent leadership offering coherence and stability.

The role of government in education could be from the choices that follow:

Policy Option 1: Power over educational matters is largely devolved to local government

Policy Option 2: Central government assumes some powers over particular priorities

Policy Option 3: Central government assumes total control in most areas, with the role of the markets and managerialism to the fore

Policy Option 4: Central government takes a strategic leadership role finding consensus in partnership with major political parties, education stakeholders, local and regional bodies, with a standing national advisory council (see Chapter 6).

Our proposal for Educational England, with a national advisory council, has similarities to Norwich's (2019) conception of an Education Framework Commission (EFC) with a 10-year 'buy in', established and operated independently from government with membership extending to all relevant stakeholders. The national advisory body or board (or commission) should be viewed as a way to facilitate consultation between different political parties on key issues. This approach could engender 'deliberative democracy' (Fishkin, 2018).

The policy options for the schools' system are:

Policy option 1: Status Quo remains, with a diversified schooling system.

For England, this will lead over time to further inequalities in resourcing and outcomes. The system will remain fragmented and meaningful improvements to the picture nationally are unlikely to occur.

Policy option 2: All schools are in a national, resilient system.

A new, national education service and system could proceed through consultation and consensus to bring coherence, stability and high quality to every element of the sector.

Foundation 3: social justice and inclusion

If your values are for a more inclusive society with fewer divisions, then the following policy options will address your priorities. These are drawn from 'Every Child Included in Education' (outlined by Blandford in chapter 7).

Policy Option 1: *Respect and pupil well-being*: Promote kindness and wellbeing in education, business and third sector settings, where every child and young person is included every day, addressing mental health, character and resilience through culture and mutuality, celebrating tolerance, patience, friendship, creativity and problem solving.

Policy Option 2: *Focus funding on early years and a relevant curriculum*: Increase investment across all phases of education, beginning with the early years that results in a socially and culturally relevant curriculum, increasing attainment in reading, writing and maths, enhancing life chances and culminating in a meaningful destination for every child.

Policy Option 3: *Teacher training*: Put greater focus on teachers as professional learners through recruitment, retention, and professional development that includes an enhanced understanding of the way disadvantaged and vulnerable children learn.

Policy Option 4: *Inclusion*: Reduce children and young people being excluded in education: increase responsibility for children at risk of exclusion through cross-agency collaboration and close the gap for SEND. (See chapter 10 for further specific policy options on SEND.)

Policy Option 5: *Community engagement*: Increase recognition of parents, carers and wider communities, valuing all parents and carers as crucial partners in the improvement of learning and life chances for every child.

Policy Option 6: *school provision*: Establish as free and open to all a new national education service and system to build a more meritocratic society. This would require phasing out all state support for private education including the removal of tax exemptions, grants, subsidies or other privileges which in the UK are currently extended to both private schools and the pupils' parents. Work from the general principle that public money should only be spent on education that is free and open to all regardless of wealth, current ability or aptitude and pass legislation (see Chapter 8).

Policy Option 7: *lifelong learning*: Make lifelong education widely available with scholarships/fee waivers for those who meet particular criteria: refocus FE/ vocational colleges to ensure they are responsive to local needs and recognise the need for democratic accountability in their governance structures, requiring representation from relevant local authorities, and recommending membership from local community organisations and trades unions. Monitor access and provision to ensure countrywide equity including for rural, remote and coastal areas, including by developing online provision. Introduce national standards for working conditions and senior pay levels.

Foundation 4: curriculum, assessment, leadership and accountability

With respect to the *curriculum*, policy options are structured around the 'Three Futures' model, developed by Michael Young (2014) in his consideration of knowledge and the future school. This provides opportunities to reform the curriculum into a looser, less prescriptive framework (see Wolfe, 2013, p. 113) that balances the attention given to propositional, procedural and inferential knowledge across a broad curriculum. Then, set this curriculum reform within a wider review of the aims and purposes of education e.g. in terms of 'qualification' (knowledge and skills), 'socialization' (orientation in tradition and practices) and 'subjectification' (the formation of the person) (see Biesta, 2010).

In his 'Three Futures' model Young (2014) discusses 'powerful knowledge', which is examined by Hudson in Chapter 12 as a potential policy option. Access to 'powerful knowledge' is seen as an issue of social justice, and Hudson develops the idea further by extending it to one of 'powerful knowledge and creative know-how'.

With respect to *assessment*, three policy options are identified and discussed, the first of which focuses on high stakes testing that sets out some of the consequences of current national examination methodologies in England and draws attention to the issues surrounding the ability to make accurate, valid and reliable inferences from such data. The second policy option explores how the effective use of formative assessment, at all levels of the education system, can drive up learner standards, increase teacher quality and meaningfully improve educational policy. Then, the third suggests the development of a cumulative assessment system which is both distributed and synoptic.

With respect to *accountability*, the policy options for England are: one, to have the status quo and maintain the Ofsted system. The second policy option is radical, to abolish the process, which we call policy option two: *reform, refocus and replace*. For England, we suggest the Ofsted brand is too tarnished for reform and must be replaced. A number of successful accountability systems (see Chapter 15 for alternatives) are based on peer review, peer challenge, external data gathering for benchmarking and trend identification, accompanied by support. See Chapter 19 for online knowledge services which could provide a core element of cost-effective support focusing on improvement.

All of the aforementioned requires *leadership*, which Raffety (in Chapter 14) argues needs to be innovative. We propose that the resourcing of leaders as change catalysts and innovators is critical in a new national education system. If we conceive of education as a humanist project contributing to public value (Mazzucato, 2018) and human capital (Samek et al., 2018), which in turn relates to a set of values about economic funding models and understanding whose interests they serve, we argue for collective good and society, rather than privatisation for profit for a minority. Following this, we recommend four policy options as a package for systemic innovation premised on the core value of long-term investment in education as a public and social good.

The radical change recommendations we make are all of the following: Policy option one: The state invests in education system innovation and learning ecosystems; policy option two: investment is made in regions to address economic inequity and enable digital connectivity; policy option three: leaders receive intensive training in problem solving and system re-design; policy option four: a new Public

Value Framework evaluates the impact of the national education service and enables access to live, high-quality data on sector performance.

Foundation 5: teacher education, research and online knowledge services

The importance of highlighting the need to enhance the professionalism of teachers is due to the fact that no education system can outperform the quality of its teachers. To this end, an education system fit for purpose needs to be ensuring inclusive and equitable quality education for all by training and keeping up-to-date its teaching profession.

Again, taking a cautionary tale from England, the impact of policy reform on teacher training routes has led to a significant diversification, which lacks coherence and has failed to address the crisis in teacher recruitment and retention (DfE, 2019b). Consequently, Hulme et al., in Chapter 18 identify seven policy options for teacher education and provide a coherent approach to developing teacher professionalism.

> **Policy Option 1:** *Maintain the status quo*: with multiple routes into initial teacher education. Bearing in mind, however, that fragmentation will not address growing concern in regard to the recruitment and retention of high calibre trainees and the provision of equitable access to high quality training experiences across the sector.
>
> A number of alternatives to the status quo are considered as follows.
>
> **Policy Option 2:** *Create a stable policy context*: Through working with an independent, national education council on a coordinated 10-year programme, coherence can be established.
>
> **Policy Option 3:** *Orient teacher recruitment for teacher quality*: with more effective workforce planning and recruitment strategies to match supply and demand.
>
> **Policy Option 4:** *Support professional learning across the career course*: Teacher learning is properly understood as a process of development that continues across a teacher's career: through initial teacher education, induction, peer mentoring, in-service professional development and professional collaboration. Effective induction experiences are those that support new teachers to thrive and achieve in professional learning communities that lay the foundations for career-long professional growth.
>
> **Policy Option 5:** *Look beyond new teachers for improvement*: Change processes need to engage educators. Change strategies informed by a theory of collective improvement focus on schools and regions rather than individual teachers or initial teacher education.
>
> **Policy Option 6:** *Build research capacity in teacher education*: Research policy can support impactful close-to-practice educational research and to build capacity in teacher education research. Teaching Schools have struggled to fulfil a research role. Research Schools, and schools in designated 'opportunity

areas', need to draw on a broader base of research to support professional growth and grow capacity or risk adopting a thin version of evidence-based practice.

Policy Option 7: *Advance collaborative professionalism*: Rather than repeat the teacher-as-problem narratives of the past, policy deliberation might adopt a nuanced approach to evidence of impact. Evaluation and competency frameworks can benefit from the input of multiple stakeholders with diverse experiences in education of what matters most. Collective dialogue can promote shared understanding among stakeholders, and foster collaborative professionalism that values academic, practitioner and community-based knowledge.

As the UNESCO Incheon Declaration (2015) states: 'We will ensure that teachers and educators are empowered, adequately recruited, well trained, professionally qualified, motivated and supported within well resourced, efficient and effectively governed systems'.

One radical policy option, which supports the UN's Sustainable Development Goal 4c, to ensure high quality teaching, is creating an accessible knowledge-base for the profession. This recognises that the task of creating and publishing research syntheses relevant to teaching is a task beyond the knowledge resources of any one country. This necessitates the creation of an international collaboration to enable teachers around the world to access the latest research on the topics they are teaching, alongside research into the pedagogical practice (see Chapter 19).

Following on from this, we envisage the following opportunities for educators:

Opportunities

- Be part of developing international teacher standards to support UNESCO SDG4.
- Collaborate to develop research-based knowledge to strengthen initial teacher education worldwide and strengthen serving teachers' professional practice.

The case study of England: lessons learnt

Cautionary tales from England provide evidence to support the removal of education policy reform from government ministers pursuing political agendas. Instead we propose establishing Education England as an independent body managed through political and professional consensus.

In the UK where the education system was opened up to a free market early in the 21st century, chaos of provision has ensued together with a crisis of teacher recruitment and retention. This has led to a parental and political backlash, and the Labour Party promoting the concept of a National Education Service as the model for the system of the future.

We note that such fragmentation is not accidental; it is fragmented by design (see Wolfe, 2013). Wolfe has analysed successive education acts since the early 2000s and shown that legislation has brought more and more fragmentation – so much so that the system is becoming so broken that the damage is fast approaching irreparable, or as Whalley and Greenway argue in Chapter 5, 'unmanageable', 'unknowable' and 'unfixable'. Arguably the loss of the post-war collective vision, which led to the introduction of a welfare state, with the national health service, free state secondary schooling, better housing and working conditions, has decayed in the rise of rampant individualism and neoliberalist values, with their origins in Reagan-Thatcherite economic policies. We are left with the survival of the richest and potential for growing civil unrest.

However, it is not too late to claim a space and opportunity for a fresh start. To reinvigorate deliberative democracy, we propose it is possible to create a national, coherent and self-improving education service through a collaboration between different agencies and stakeholders. But such an initiative needs determined leadership, deep commitment and a preparedness to compromise and support diversity.

It is important to reiterate that politicians and their advisors do not have the specialist depth of knowledge to understand how their policies will be operationalized and what the unintended consequences will be.

This book, we hope, will provide an understanding that education as a system, with structures and processes, and as a service, is a complex and nuanced phenomena that cannot be reduced to quick fixes or political whims of ministers. Instead, we propose a new, national education service with an independent council or body (called Education England), like Norwich's (2019) commission, with a 10-year plan for public good; to set policy priorities, including reconciling plural and contrary positions: in short, to design a cross-party consensual education policy framework, within which political parties and multiple education stakeholders will work in partnership.

Reflections[1]

From the analysis undertaken across all the chapters there is a common critique that the education system in England is currently broken, with differential provision preventing children and young people from having equity of experiences. To this end we argue for a new, national education service designed around shared values with cross-political party support that allows for the following opportunities:

Opportunities

- Create a much more dynamic education system with learning at all levels at its heart.
- Develop more rounded young people who are ready to embrace the complexities and challenges of change, with robust resilience.

- Join a number of countries that are leading thinking about future education, as reflected in the OECD's 2030 Project and its work on leadership in complex systems.
- Counteract trends towards teacher alienation arising from an education policy-making process that is seen as remote and even quixotic.

It is hoped that the ideas in this book firstly provide a framework for designing, developing and then implementing a new national education service and system for England and that secondly the ideas about education system design are helpful for those in other countries wishing to improve their education services.

Note

1 This book builds on the book Goddard, D. and Leask, M. (1992), *The Search for Quality, Planning for Improvement and Managing Change*, a review of the English Education system written following Leask's research for the DES School Development Plans Research Project (1989–1990) – a major national DES research project. Del Goddard was an innovative educator and Chief Adviser for education in the London Borough of Enfield.

References

Biesta, G.J.J. (2010) *Why "What works" still won't work: from evidence-based education to value-based education*, Vol. 29, pp. 491-502. Studies in Philosophy and Education, Springer.

Department for Education (2019a) *Timpson Review of School Exclusion: Technical Note*, May 2019. London: Department for Education.

Department for Education (2019b) 'School workforce in England'. November 2018. https://assets.publishing.service.gov.uk/government/uploads/system/uploads/attachment_data/file/811622/SWFC_MainText.pdf

Fishkin, J.S. (2018) 'Random assemblies for law making? Prospects and limits'. *Politics & Society,* 46: 359–379. doi:10.1177/0032329218789889.

Fishkin, J.S. and Luskin, R.C. (2005) 'Experimenting with a democratic ideal: Deliberative polling and public opinion'. *Acta Politica,* 40 (3): 284–298. doi:10.1057/palgrave.ap.5500121.

García, E. and Weiss, E. (2019) 'The teacher shortage is real, large and growing, and worse than we thought: The first report'. *The Perfect Storm in the Teacher Labour Market' Series,* Economic Policy Institute, 26 March.

Harrison, A. (2012) 'Academies told they can hire unqualified teachers'. London. BBC news www.bbc.co.uk/news/education-19017544. Accessed 5 October 2019.

Mazzucato, M. (2018) *The Entrepreneurial State: Debunking Public vs. Private Sector Myths.* London: Penguin Books.

Norwich, B. (2019) 'From the Warnock report (1978) to an education framework commission: A novel contemporary approach to educational policy making for pupils with special educational needs/disabilities'. *Frontiers Education,* 4 (72). doi:10.3389/feduc.2019.00072.

Perryman, J. and Calvert, G. (2019) 'What motivates people to teach, and why do they leave? Accountability, performativity and teacher retention'. *British Journal of Educational Studies.* doi:10.1080/00071005.2019.1589417.

Samek, L., Darko, C., King, W., Sidhu, S.V., Parmar, M., Foliano, F., Moore, F., O'Mahony, M., Payne, C., Rincon-Aznar, A. and Vassilev, G. (2018) *Provision of Human Capital Evidence Review – A Report for the Office for National Statistics.* London: ONS.

Wolfe, D. (2013) 'Schools: The legal structures, the accidents of history and the legacies of timing and circumstance'. *Education Law Journal*, 100–113.

Young, M. (2014) Why start with the curriculum? In Young, M. and Lambert, D.; with Roberts, C. and Roberts, M. (Eds.) *Knowledge and the Future School: Curriculum and Social Justice*. London: Bloomsbury Academic.

Younie, S. and Leask, M. (2019a) 'The bonfire of the quangos'. *Society for Education Studies Colloquialism*, Oriel College, Oxford, 26 September.

Younie, S. and Leask, M. (2019b) *Lessons from the bonfire of the quangos: The case for legislation to provide checks and balances to the powers of the Secretary of State for Education*. SES (Society for Education Studies) Colloquium on 'Education reform legislation in a changing society', Oxford University, Oriel College, 26–27 September 2019.

Younie, S. and Preston, C. (2020) Understanding the contribution of professional communities of practice in education technology in influencing teacher recruitment and retention. In T. Ovenden-Hope and R. Passy (Eds.) *Exploring Teacher Recruitment and Retention: Contextual Challenges from International Perspectives*. London: Routledge.

21

EDUCATION IN EMERGENCIES

Pandemic/disaster planning for education sector continuity

Sarah Younie, Marilyn Leask and Stephen Hall

Introduction and context

> There are decades when nothing happens and there are weeks when decades happen.
>
> *(Friedman, 2014 quoting Vladimir Ilyich Lenin in an article referencing medical breakthroughs)*

> Education systems provide the foundations for the future wellbeing of every society. In addition, teaching is the one profession that makes all other professions possible.
>
> *(Chapter 20)*

As this book was going to press in 2020, a global pandemic erupted, and around the world, schools, colleges and universities (along with all businesses except for essential services) were closed for weeks initially and then months, as countries went into 'lockdown', to limit transmission of the coronavirus through the population.

Closing of schools had different consequences for different stakeholders – parents, teachers, pupils – and brought into sharp relief inequalities in societies: children who had personal internet connected devices were able to continue their education at home where their teachers moved swiftly to teaching online. Other children from poorer families or with special needs simply missed out (UNESCO 2020), or were disadvantaged through inequalities in provision.

This chapter provides an analysis of early lessons emerging from this situation of a global pandemic – the most significant of which was, how well prepared was the schooling system for times of crisis and managing continuity of learning when school closures, the need for which was anticipated in national and international pandemic planning (WHO 2005), were called for? We argue that such planning is an essential prerequisite for robust education system design particularly, given that virologists predict that epidemics and pandemics will continue to occur periodically as new viruses emerge: recent examples being Ebola, SARS, MERS, Swine Flu, measles and HIV.

Pandemic planning is one of the responsibilities of governments, and guidance from WHO (2005) and the European Commission (ECDC 2006; EC 2009a, 2009b; NZ 2011, 2020), referenced in what follows, outlines good practice. Planning for the continuance of education is recommended as one element of national plans with consideration of interdependencies between sectors being essential in pandemic planning.

As an example of a failure to plan for a pandemic appropriately, in England, education pandemic plans had not been updated for over a decade (DES 2006; DCSF 2008). The outdated plans were not fit for new structures in the education sector, following a change of government in 2010, which led to the diminishing of local education authorities. In addition, in 2010 all the government funded (for England) online educational resources – lesson plans, resources and teaching advice – had been mothballed by the incoming government (Blamires 2015; Younie and Leask 2019).

With the 2020 coronavirus pandemic, in England, an announcement was made at 5 p.m. on 18 March that schools would be closed from the end of the day on 20 March 2020 until further notice, except for children identified as vulnerable and those of key workers. Consequently teachers themselves were designated as 'key workers' to work in those few schools that remained open; however, for the majority of children, face-to-face teaching ended overnight. This required individual teachers to radically change their practice to meet the needs of remote schooling. Careful planning as recommended by the WHO (2009) and the European Commission (2009a, 2009b), alongside updating the existing documents (DfES 2006; DCSF 2008), could have avoided a situation where teachers and pupils, particularly pupils preparing for final exams of their school careers, were placed under considerable stress.

There is, of course, no guarantee that another pandemic won't occur in months or within a few years, so up-to-date contingency planning is essential.

School closures: pandemic/disaster plans for education sector continuity

While the coronavirus pandemic and the subsequent national lockdowns including closures of schools may have come as a surprise in 2020 to many, a simple internet search shows that governments, regional authorities and some schools (Uscher-Pines et al., 2018; MESHGuides 2020a, 2020b; NZ 2011, 2020) have had pandemic management plans ready for decades. However, few provide advice on how teachers and schools can ensure continuity of learning and equity of access to education provision during pandemics.

The World Health Organisation (2005) and linked European Commission's advice for managing and assessing readiness for pandemics in 2007 and 2009 updated earlier advice and outlined steps which those who have experienced national lockdowns in 2020 will recognise. School closures feature as one of the containment measures: 'Influenza spread will be accelerated in schools and other closed communities leading to a potential need to close schools' (European Centre for Disease Prevention and Control, 2006, p. 45). The advice over a decade old for England, as mentioned previously, (DCSF, 2008) was that every school should have a pandemic plan linked with regional and national plans. The United States, Canadian and New Zealand government advice was similar and schools, regional and national bodies made their plans freely available on the internet (see MESHGuides, 2020a and b for a list of examples).

A generic framework for pandemic plans

European Commission (2009a, 2009b) advice provides a generic framework for developing national pandemic plans 'which strengthen current systems':

'Pandemic preparedness is most effective if it is built on general principles that guide preparedness planning for any acute threat to public health. This includes the following:

1   Pandemic preparedness, response and evaluation should be built on generic preparedness platforms, structures, mechanisms and plans for crisis and emergency management.
2   To the extent possible, pandemic preparedness should aim to strengthen existing systems rather than developing new ones, in particular components of national seasonal influenza prevention and control programmes.
3   New systems that will be implemented during a pandemic should be tested during the inter-pandemic period.
4   Adequate resources must be allocated for all aspects of pandemic preparedness and response.
5   The planning process, implementing what is planned, testing and revising the plan in order for key stakeholders to familiarise themselves with the issues at hand, may be even more important than the pandemic plan itself.
6   Pandemic response requires that *business continuity plans and surge capacity plans* [author's emphasis] be developed for the health sector and all other sectors that could be affected by a pandemic to ensure sustained capacity during a pandemic.
7   The response to a pandemic must be evidence-based where this is available and commensurate with the threat, in accordance with the IHR. Planning should be based on pandemics of differing severity while the response is based on the actual situation determined by national and global risk assessments.' (European Commission, 2009a, p. 1).

Interestingly, whilst calling for pandemic planning, when it comes to the education sector, there is actually very little detail provided (WHO 2009; European Commission, 2009a, 2009b).The MESHGuides (2020a, 2020b) Coronavirus Briefing lists the reports reviewed. In identifying this gap, we aim to address this omission in this chapter by providing a framework for policy makers to prepare for emergencies. Education continuity plans should kick in then immediately for whatever type of crisis may emerge, whether pandemics, natural disasters, terrorism or other conflicts that may arise.

In identifying the concept of 'business continuity planning' we argue that for the education sector this means plans must focus on the continuing education of learners. We focus on specific elements of practice which together provide a framework for emergency planning for the education sector.

Elements of an education sector framework for planning for pandemics (and natural disasters)

Table 21.1 lists educational elements to be included in any crisis plan based on the experience of educators in different countries during the 2020 Covid-19 pandemic. (Specifically this list is derived from our analysis of existing plans (MESH 2020a, 2020b) and the MESH International Council, weekly meetings during the

TABLE 21.1 Examples of core educational elements of education pandemic/disaster plans – national, regional, local

The Foundation for your policy and plans is determined by your underpinning philosophy and goals

Elements
1   Maximising learner experiences and ensuring marginalised learners are provided for
2   Teaching and learning pedagogy, including remote pedagogies
3   Curriculum resources: online/TV/radio content
4   Assessment
5   Equipment provision
6   Parental/carer involvement strategy
7   Home worker strategy
8   Community/NGO/Charity roles and resources
9   Mental health and wellbeing of staff, students, families
10 Special cases
11 Challenges: Losses and risks
12 Initial Teacher training
13 Mapping educators' specialist expertise and networks: linking local and national level plans
14 Ensuring continuity and synergy between national strategy and local plans
15 Infrastructure review
16 Exit from lockdown: Re-entry plan for reopening schools
17 Pandemic/disaster recovery readiness checklist

coronavirus crisis. Council members [see Acknowledgements] collaborated across UN regions to analyse practices occurring during the lockdown period and school closures).

The following sections pose questions to consider for each of these elements in Table 21.1 when drawing up an Education Pandemic/Disaster Plan.

In considering each element we suggest you note:

- Who needs to be engaged in this provision?
- How can you use existing infrastructures?
- How will you refresh your plans?
- How will you communicate your plans?
- What children are not catered for in your plans?
- What unintended consequences may there be?

Overview: policy foundation: underpinning philosophy, principles and goals

In developing an Education Emergency Plan, you will be making decisions which will be influenced by the values, culture/s and resources specific to your country and your decision makers. You will need to consider:

1   **Equity:** How will you manage equitable access to schooling for all learners including those in impoverished homes, rural areas and those with special needs? How will you ensure continuation of support services to those receiving, for example, free meals, support for special needs, psychological support and so on? How will you ensure equity of access to knowledge? Is knowledge valued as a public good and therefore freely available for all to access, or is knowledge viewed as a private commodity?
2   **Access:** consideration needs to cover access to any technologies required and any specialist services. How will you ensure access to the technologies you use to support continuity of schooling?
3   **Curriculum/assessment and teacher empowerment**: How can teachers be supported at a local level to adjust the curriculum, expectations and assessments to meet the needs of their pupils? Can they use a range of pedagogies, for example, including online, 'free-choice learning' (Falk and Dierking 2002; Dierking 2005) and intergenerational pedagogies?
4   **Infrastructure:** What infrastructure is needed to support your plans specifically to support equitable access to continuity of learning?
5   **Communications:** Do you have designated risk management/disaster recovery staff who provide the link between government communications and local communities and schools? If existing communication channels are blocked, what alternative means of communication do you have in place? Are all involved aware of these?

6   **Community/volunteer engagement:** What resources human (networks/
organisations/individuals) and materials are available in communities to help
in times of crisis?

7   **Evaluation strategy:** how will you evaluate your plan to check that no child
is left behind and that teachers are able to work as well as is possible?

8   **Leadership:** to ensure confidence of the population: Who/what organisation/s
will make the decisions about schooling? The balance of experience they have
will either ensure advice works in different communities or not: if, as is not
uncommon, decisions are made by an educated urban elite, such decisions
may just work, for example, in urban settings. The credibility of those making
decisions may impact on adherence by the population to the decisions. Do you
know the educational organisations that command respect in your context?

For additional guidance see the documents produced by the Inter-Agency Standing Committee-UNICEF, WHO and IFRC (2020), and the International Labour
Organisation (2020).

Operationalising the policy elements: education continuity planning for times of crisis

Taking each element of education emergency planning that follows, we raise key
questions that require addressing in your plan.

1 Maximising learner experiences

Continuity of learner experience: How will you ensure continuity of learner experiences as much as is possible with use of appropriate pedagogies? How will you link
learning to resources aligned to the curriculum normally experienced by learners
but which may require adaptation for learning outside school e.g. to be project
based, to have an intergenerational focus? How many children are *not* going to be
catered for through your strategy? Which students are most at risk of becoming
marginalised?

What has been evident from the current outbreak of Covid-19 and the need to
provide alternative learning via online/radio/TV/printed materials as a substitute
for face-to-face teaching in schools is that:

Teachers are highly innovative and creative at designing online/radio/TV/
printed learning materials in order to sustain opportunities for pupils' learning
experiences and, as a result, teachers have been appreciated by parents and society
for these skills and qualities. How does your plan capitalise on this expertise such
that it can easily be shared with other teachers and parents at a local level?

Not all pupils may have access to the internet or to a device that can be used
to receive, respond to, create or modify learning materials for individual and/or
collaborative use. How will you ensure sustained learner experiences for all learners where possible by providing ready access to internet-connected devices for

'attending' online lessons? The children most in need in any country are those least likely to have internet access and most likely to need high levels of support to achieve success in education (World Economic Forum, 2020).

2 Teaching and learning pedagogy, including remote pedagogies

This section considers the continuity of teaching and learning for when there are school closures, including the need to plan for remote pedagogies.

When drawing up future Education Emergency Plans, the following considerations need to be taken into account with regards to teaching remotely (this may be online or through radio, TV, printed materials or other media):

Pedagogies for online/remote learning: Is there a shared definition and understanding of the pedagogical model that is to be implemented in the event of any new pandemic, emergency or disaster? Has the model been updated in the light of research and evidence into the use of new and emerging technologies? Have all stakeholders such as teachers, learners and parents/carers been consulted and have contributed to any adopted pedagogies for online/remote learning? How has the issue of the 'digital divide' been assessed and addressed? (West, 2015). Have you considered 'free-choice learning', where children work on substantial projects on issues of their choice, which are particularly relevant to what they wish to learn about (Falk and Dierking, 2002; Dierking, 2005) and intergenerational pedagogies? See the MESHGuides website page 'Pedagogies for community supported learning in crises' (see meshguides.org.uk).

How has teachers' ability to ensure progression through teaching online and remotely been updated, particularly in terms of advances in technology and the need for up-skilling teachers digital literacies? What training is needed so that teachers can deliver in different learning environments, incorporating learner-centred and learner-initiated approaches, project-based learning and intergenerational learning etc.? What training is being given to teachers regarding differentiation of volume of work and levels of challenge according to the needs and abilities of individual learners?

Is there sufficient access to software materials to enable up-skilling if required, including access to a range of digital technologies and multiple platforms to trial and see what is workable in a local context? Are there sufficient checks and balances that commercially available materials, which use a 'sit and follow' pedagogical approach to learning, will work for all learners rather than only work for some learners with a certain level of skills, knowledge and support?

In some cases, during the coronavirus pandemic teachers and pupils have experienced 'overload', due to a lack of forward planning for remote schooling in times of crisis, which has led to the need for uncoordinated rapid responses from individual teachers, schools and homes during the current Covid-19 outbreak. This is leading to potential burn-out through the effort that has been put into transferring traditional materials into a remote schooling environment (Spec, 2020).

During the current period of school closures due to the pandemic, parents have found a home-schooling pedagogy (highly structured, formal learning) to be more of a challenge than the home-educating pedagogy (more flexible, spontaneous and informal learning) (see also Jeffs and Smith, 2011). Parents and their children have previously demonstrated (Morton, 2010) that they can be highly innovative, imaginative and creative at seeing opportunities for intergenerational, informal learning both online and 'at home'. This has not been consistently true for every household, and many children in developed and developing countries do not enjoy either the support and encouragement from parents or other members of their family, or access to continued learning provision.

Home-schooling or home-education?

Whilst the terms home-schooling and home-education are used quite interchangeably in the current coronavirus crisis, it is pertinent to state that there is no agreed or definitive distinction between the two terms. However Devitt (2018) writing on the website www.howdoihomeschool.com offers the following observation about this confusion.

> What is homeschooling? Is it simply school at home or is there more to it than that? If you're asking these questions, you're not alone as the definition is murky due to the variety of methods with which a child can be educated at home. While many parents employ the traditional method that mimics the public school setup, others employ a more flexible and natural way of learning.

This reflects the experience of many parents across countries during the coronavirus lockdown, with some children experiencing school replicated within the home, other children experiencing a rich diversity of both formal and informal learning experiences and some children having no education at all.

Parent/carer understanding of pedagogy – teaching and learning: What support is offered to parents/carers regarding home education to avoid children switching off? How are misconceptions and misunderstandings about how to teach addressed, such as structuring learning at home differently from the structure of school lessons and avoiding the counter-productive outcomes from too high a volume of work and not enough rest time for processing what has been learned? Is information freely and readily available to parents/carers on maximising environmental conditions for learning at home, wherever possible? Issues such as temperature, lighting levels, levels of CO_2 in unventilated rooms etc. can be critical to effective learning.

Online pedagogies: There is little or no consensus on what pedagogy is best suited to online learning for children. The Education Endowment Foundation (2020) published a Rapid Evidence Assessment: Distance Learning document that examines the existing research (from 60 systematic reviews and meta-analyses) for approaches that schools could use, or are already using, to support the learning of pupils while schools are closed due to Covid-19, but the findings would require further interpretation to be applicable for parents working in a home schooling environment. In preparation for future epidemics/pandemics/disasters there is a need to search out best practice for online pedagogies in relation to both school teaching and home learning across the ages.

How does your plan accommodate emerging pedagogies that build on effective practice that the current crisis has uncovered? How is research into what effective pedagogies look like within an online environment utilised within your plan?

How does your plan ensure that politicians and public servants develop an understanding of relevant pedagogies so they are not as likely to be persuaded by 'non-experts' to adopt a particular product or approach (with their associated consultancy fees) by commercial bodies looking to profit from the confusion of ignorance?

3 Curriculum/Online Content

Remote teaching is very demanding for teachers and learners, and co-ordinated national/regional/local provision of resources should help with equitable access to ongoing learning and minimise pressure on teachers who are having to take on new responsibilities and ways of working. Issues to consider include:

- Media: What media can be used for remote schooling in your context: Radio? TV? Internet-based online (which technologies)? Paper-based and posted? A combination of methods?
- Knowledge: in your context is the knowledge needed for teaching a public good or private commodity? Is teacher knowledge freely shared (perhaps online or on radio or TV) for the benefit of all and built collaboratively, or is it commercialised and privatised? How might you mobilise research-informed, quality-assured knowledge/resources? How might it be structured to be accessible and usable by parents/carers as home educators as well as teachers?
- Reviewing readiness to adopt remote learning: Professor Tracey Tokuhama-Espinosa (2020) has a well developed decision tree for checking readiness for online classroom teaching.

4 Assessment

A fundamental part of any continuity plan for education is how online and remote learning pedagogies might recognise and validate achievement in different forms through a new process of evaluation and assessment that has a closer fit with the principles of online learning.

- Adjustments: What adjustments to assessment requirements may need to be made?

- Equity and access: How will learners' access external assessments or public examinations?
- Accrediting informal learning: What different forms of assessment might be employed during the crisis to accredit informal learning/intergenerational learning e.g. pupil diaries (written, audio or video diaries), online show and tell, performances and so on.

5 Equipment provision

Supplementary to equipment that schools might offer their pupils, there may be a need to provide, at short notice, certain equipment to ensure continuity of educational provision both for pupils at home and those attending a setting that is different to their normal experience. In a world of rapidly developing technology which relies heavily on sustained connectivity to the Internet, 'equipment' may include mobile devices that have such operational connectivity. This gives rise to the following questions regarding equipment provision with any national plan:

- Commercialisation opportunities: commercial offers may often have hidden costs. For example, in the coronavirus crises, a search engine revealed over 1,000 'free materials' which were offered by a variety of companies which turned out to be – free trials for a week, free for the period of crisis and which were linked to paid for materials. Out of 1,047 'free' resources, only 28 were genuinely 'free for all time' to the end use (date of search 20 April 2020).
- What provision can be provided for off-grid connectivity to maintain communication and access to online learning materials and support?
- Printed packs: For those without internet, plans we have reviewed suggested printed packs, posted to pupils. Would your plan cater for this and are funds and resources to print packs available? Gentles (MESH, 2020a) reported that some teachers paid for such materials from their own pockets. What distribution plans are in place that do not require pupils or their parents/carers to travel personally to collect such learning materials and resources? (see DCSF advice 2008).
- Equipment provision: in the event of another pandemic what provision of personal protective equipment (PPE) is to be made available to teachers, other staff and pupils? Where will this be kept? Are instructions available to make PPE? During the coronavirus, schools have used design and technology equipment to make protective visors, community groups have made masks and indeed gowns for medical staff, goggles used for science lessons have been used for protection against virus transfer.

6 Parental/carer involvement strategy

Questions to consider:

- Equity: In what ways does the plan consult with parents and other agencies about continued provision for those children with no access to learning at home, or those parents/carers whose role within emergencies or pandemics prohibits them from home educating their children? In what ways does the plan support children who cannot access either the support and encouragement from parents or other members of their family, or access internet-connected devices that support online learning?

- What support and guidance is available for parents/carers who might find homeschooling (highly structured, formal learning) to be more of a challenge? What support is there for a more flexible, spontaneous and informal learning approach in the home setting?
- Parents and their children can be highly innovative, imaginative and creative at seeing opportunities for intergenerational, informal learning both online and 'at home'. Does the strategy incorporate and capitalise upon greater parental and intergenerational involvement in learning along with recognition for the value of both formal learning and informal learning?

7 Home worker strategy (see also mental health, which follows)

Questions to consider:

- How can you ensure that home workers are appropriately supported to maintain learning – if they need to home-school their own children and work from home at the same time as in a pandemic lockdown?
- If parents are expected to work from home while also homeschooling their children, have you identified pedagogies that support independent learning? Are the expectations for homeschooling respectful of parents' needs to perform adequately in their jobs?

8 Community readiness/NGO/charity role and resources

Education is both a national and a local responsibility – national to ensure equity and standards and community, because poorly educated community members put everyone at risk in a pandemic. MESHGuides (2020b) lists pedagogies for learning which can be supported by communities.

Questions to consider:

- Are there community organisations, NGOs or charities with human or material resources which can support homeschooling so that no learner is left behind? Such resources e.g. buildings/halls/cinemas/open spaces may help with social distancing when schooling returns.
- Might local mapping of community resources provide a way of identification of additional local resources to supplement school resources?
- As with the containment of the Ebola virus, might an effective containment strategy involve mobilising staff from areas not yet affected to support staff in areas when challenges are hardest?

9 Mental health

Questions to consider:

- Does your plan acknowledge mental health issues arising from the impact of a crisis on those involved in providing education provision/homeschooling as well as coping with family and community challenges?
- Have you strategies to ease stress?

Networking teachers to share solutions may ease pressures. Creating easy access to tools and resources supporting teaching as well as individual well-being is another. (There are specific charities providing expertise for mental health with resources available through their websites.) Provision for key workers to ease the burden of ensuring essentials are provided in the home, like basic shopping and accessing medicines, may relieve pressures. In the UK during the coronavirus crisis, schools remained open for children of key workers. In terms of Maslow's (McLeod, 2007) hierarchy of needs, those at the bottom of the triangle need to be met first.

10 Special cases

Each community will have unique opportunities for supporting schools in times of crises e.g. spaces for safe continuing of schooling as well as challenges e.g. key workers' children, the education of children in care, children with special needs, other vulnerable children. The identification of special cases should be addressed as part of the planning process. Ensuring that marginalised learners do not become further disadvantaged is key.

11 Losses, risks and challenges

The following list outlines some of the risks and challenges to be faced:

- Misinformation, misconceptions and myths, including conspiracy theories – these can be potentially dangerous – in a pandemic. How do your plans mitigate these? How do your plans ensure accurate knowledge that is evidence-informed is available?
- Children who miss out or get left behind; how do they 'catch up'?
- Avoiding chaos – do your plans make maximum use of networks and existing resources/organisations to coordinate efforts? Or does your plan mean every teacher inventing the means of remote teaching for him- or herself?
- Do you have backup plans to accommodate failure of leadership?
- Does your plan consider quality assurance of education experiences during the crisis?
- Does your plan envisage education as a public good – so resources paid for by taxpayers are not hoarded but are shared?

12 Initial Teacher training

Faced with the aforementioned issues, there is clearly a need for the training of teachers, now and in the future, to include relevant and appropriate skills, knowledge and understanding in order to be prepared for:

- teaching within a world that is subject to the sudden disruption to 'formal' education due to emergencies such as pandemics, epidemics and natural disasters which includes being able to mix online/remote learning with both face-to-face teaching and intergenerational learning at home
- a different approach to evaluation, assessment and validation of achievement in online/distance learning environments and informal settings as well as more traditional formal learning environments.

Therefore, do your teacher training programmes include study of pedagogical models and approaches that are suitable for online/distance learning, formal and informal learning and intergenerational learning to an equal level and standard as their specialist subject knowledge?

Teacher training will need to equip teachers with the ability to draw on learners' own interests and motivations, as well as the part that parents, siblings and other family members can play in teaching and learning and the specialist knowledge and support that schools and outside professional agencies can provide as and when necessary.

Countries might do well to look to Finland's approach to teacher training, with the study of pedagogies included to an equivalent level and standard as subject specialisms (Halinen, 2016). Teacher training needs to also include the value and importance of social and cultural capital as a fundamental dimension to the role of schools and education in general within the community.

13 Mapping educators' specialist expertise and networks: linking local and national level plans

Does your plan include how you will access experts and networks of educators who can support online/distance/home learning? Being able to provide access locally and nationally to expert and credible knowledge may foster calm and help teachers to draw on 'trusted' knowledge with confidence; this can help to challenge fake news and myths and misconceptions. See the MESHGuide on COVID-19 that contains a strand on science, including myth-busting.

14 Ensuring continuity and synergy between national strategy and local plans

Are your schools continuity plans realistic? Are there links between national and local plans? This ensures that there is coherence between a national strategy and links to operational plans at a local level.

15 Infrastructure review

Is the infrastructure there to carry the plans out? If not, what can be done to address this?

16 Exit from lockdown: re-entry plan for reopening schools

Does your plan for re-opening schools after school closures ensure due diligence and duty of care to all staff and pupils, including catch-up classes and phased re-entry if necessary? Points to consider in a national co-ordinated re-entry plan would include: a local level/individual school re-entry plan, which would need to consider at the local context managing the transition from lockdown/homeschooling back to full-time school.

For continuity of learning, teachers may need to organise compensatory sessions for supporting disadvantaged learners to fill the gap of learning losses. Curriculum and assessments may need adjusting to support transitioning back into school, including a 'recovery curriculum' for a period of time. See the UNESCO International Teacher Task Force Advice (2020) and UNESCO et al. (2020).

17 Pandemic/disaster recovery readiness checklist

Questions to consider:

- Do you have an assessment tool for evaluating plans and a strategy for reviewing and updating plans?

The European Centre for Disease Prevention and Control (ECDC, 2006) proposes that plans are checked regularly and updated. They provide an assessment tool which would need adaption for education specific plans. Table 21.2 shows the headings they suggest for such a plan.

Do you have a school closure exit strategy? The UNESCO et al (April 2020) Framework for reopening schools provides guidance (Leask and Younie, in press).

TABLE 21.2 Example – Assessment planning tool with a main focus on pandemic or natural disaster preparedness from ECDC, 2006

Goal	KEY INDICATOR	CURRENT STATUS	*Instructions in italics* *Comments and notes by those filling in*

Policy options

Policy option 1: top-down model

Develop a national education 'business continuity plan' for the school sector through national emergency/natural disasters/pandemic plans.

The national plans on crisis management during a pandemic that we have looked at are missing detail on how the education sector manages specific issues: how to ensure equity for children in disadvantaged situations, equal access to resources, expectations for forms of remote teaching and learning, managing public examinations/national assessments when children are out of schools.

Any education plans need to be detailed – to ensure continuity of learning as much as possible. The issues raised in this chapter provide a checklist. Plans need to be regularly updated and communicated to all stakeholders.

Policy option 2: bottom-up model

This for the central and regional government is the do-nothing model – leave the education of children in a crisis to individual teachers, schools, commercial bodies, NGOs.

The Covid-19 pandemic 2020 tested national disaster plans, and teachers' reports from many countries (MESH, 2020a) indicate individual teachers were expected to carry the load of maintaining education on their own, using their own resources: financial and technical.

This ad hoc model does not take advantage of a systematic approach to knowledge sharing that is possible with advanced digital technologies, but relies on a less coordinated approach from individuals sharing what they know or have found out, leaving the education of children to chance. Where individuals start to broadcast their views there may be no quality assurance and few checks and balances. By way of contrast, materials from subject and professional associations and teacher training departments which are quality assessed by peers can be rapidly harnessed and disseminated.

One consequence of this approach is that it is 'uneven': for some the plethora of options and learning materials is too great and teachers, pupils and parents become overwhelmed with choice. For others there are very limited, if any, options with very limited material available thus widening the divide between the 'haves' and 'have nots'.

Policy option 3: hybrid collaboration model

Work collaboratively with professional education organisations, such as teachers' subject associations, teacher unions, national and regional networks – of headteachers and local authorities and teacher training institutions.

All the government advice on pandemic planning we reviewed urges caution in the closing of schools, because of the disruption. Having national and local expert groups ready to lead on carefully worked through plans for each phase and subject could be expected to mitigate some of the damage. The European Commission advice (EC 2009a, 2009b) outlines options:

> During pandemics with lesser severe disease and of fewer falling sick, such as those seen in 1957 and 1968, some possible community measures (proactive school closures, home working, etc.), though probably reducing transmission, can be more costly and disruptive than the effects of the pandemic itself. Hence such measures may only have a net benefit if implemented during a severe pandemic, for example one that results in high hospitalisation rates or has a case fatality rate comparable to that of the 1918–19 'Spanish flu'.
>
> *(EC 2009a, p. 1)*

A benefit of such formal professional collaboration may be the development of understanding of pedagogy in politicians and public servants so they are not prey to 'snake oil' merchants and lone ranger charismatic 'experts' who may step to the fore in crises – for commercial gain.

Reflections: Future-proofing education for times of crisis – ensuring learning continues for all

The World Health Organisation (2009) advises governments and ministries of education to provide a national strategy for remote schooling during a time of emergency, whether a pandemic or natural disaster. That not all governments have implemented this advice has become apparent during the 2020 worldwide Covid-19 pandemic when within a couple of weeks of rising political concern of a global health crisis, schools were closed.

A robust education system design would identify the need for a nationally rigorous emergency contingency planning element, which accounted for risks (known and unknown/sudden) that may require immediate action and lead to a national closure of all schools and cancellation of all public exams, like in the pandemic of 2020. Such plans have to be updated regularly as all the advice in government documents in the references suggest.

Where a national strategy is seen as too centralist by the population, then a minimum would be a systemic coordinated approach to ensure parity and inclusivity across all local areas and to ensure equity of educational experience for all children, across all ages and phases.

Lessons learned – from the Covid-19 pandemic

The seriousness of the coronavirus contagion rates were identified in January 2020 in the *Lancet* (Wang et al., 2020) and in any case virologists (WHO, 2009) say that epidemics/pandemics are to be planned for as a factor of life. In some countries, leaders were slow to react.

Taking England as a case study provides an example of what happens when there is insufficient planning for times of crisis in education. The sudden lockdown of schools, with no prior warning to school leaders and teachers, sent many teachers, parents/carers and pupils into a whirlwind of uncertainty. Schools were told to close indefinitely. The cancelling of all public exams and shutting of all classrooms for up to 8 million pupils was nationally unprecedented in the history of public-funded schooling in England.

There should have been a national education strategy for times of crisis and an 'emergency schooling plan' already written and ready to be operationalised in every school. There was not. The 2006 and 2008 plans, prepared under a previous government, were no longer fit for purpose because of infrastructure changes to education; specifically the demise of local education authorities and the fragmented rise of 'Multi-Academy Trusts', which lack any centralised or systemic coordination (see Chapter 5).

If the government had the foresight and planned a strategy for schools and had a well-coordinated response for education in emergencies, there would have been a bank of online resources for teaching the national curriculum, readily available, to roll out across the country for all schools and homes. This would have appropriately supported CPD materials and online courses for teachers to 'get up to speed' with remote learning, if required, to become familiar with different digital technologies and platforms to support online pedagogies. In the event, the government provided some funding to a few schools, while the professional organisations worked with teacher volunteers at their own expense with the BBC to create a BBC Bitesize quality assured solution. This lack of co-ordinated planning is mystifying. As Younie and Leask point out (2019), all these resources existed but were taken offline after the 2010 election by Michael Gove, incoming Secretary of State, and his special adviser Dominic Cummings, who implemented a 'bonfire of the quangos' (Institute for Government 2012).

At the outset of school closures in England, schools and teachers were suddenly scrabbling around to transfer their lessons into online content without due guidance and support from the government. Schools were thrown into overdrive, as were universities and colleges, in trying to quickly adapt their face-to-face teaching to learning at a distance. The lack of preparation is forgivable from frontline educators used to working in classrooms directly with learners; however, for a government to have not prepared for such a national emergency, which virologists had long predicted and for which the EU prepared detailed guidance (European Centre for Disease Prevention and Control, 2006), remains arguably unforgivable. For England, we propose that the government establish an independent Education Knowledge Service (EKS) to coordinate development of a regularly updated, open-access, research-informed online education resources bank, supporting learners of all ages and phases. A national strategy to provide a fully functioning EKS, to support education during emergencies and crises must be called for, as a minimum requirement of government, to ensure the learning of a generation is not compromised by school lockdowns.

Every education system should be able to answer the questions: What steps are being taken to ensure there is continuity of learning for all? What steps are there to ensure there is *stability* and *equity* of access to pedagogically appropriate resources? These should be answered with confidence so that teachers can access materials needed to teach their curriculum. This will also require the concomitant need for online CPD too, for all teachers and support staff, to be briefed and upskilled in the latest digital technologies to support remote learning. This should also be available to trainee teachers and teacher educators to help plan for any such future events too.

To conclude, we acknowledge the need to future-proof education for times of crisis, as there will be other pandemics, inevitably, as viruses either mutate or new viruses jump species, alongside the possibility of natural disasters, such as wide-scale flooding, or fires, taking out schooling as a viable option and needing to move rapidly into remote online learning.

Ensuring the provision of continued learning for all children is a national concern; no country's education system should be unprepared for a national crisis, ever. Risk management requires us to plan for worst-case scenarios. So, if the country wants an education system preparing all children and young people for the future, each country's government needs to develop a strategy for making education happen during times of crisis.

In short, strategies for crisis management for schooling need to assess risk, whether for global pandemics, national epidemics or natural disaster/s, and provide online resources or viable alternatives (TV, radio or printed packs) that could be immediately called upon to support learners across all ages and phases.

Recognising that the situation is different in different countries, we stress the need for governments to understand that teaching is a profession with recognised experts, whose work is quality assured through recognition by professional subject associations, which have, as a core purpose, identifying and promoting excellent teaching of their subjects.

Continuity and contingency planning are vital for a robust education system design, for every region and country. As European Commission (2009a, 2009b) documentation recommends, there should be national strategies in place for education for times of crisis. Governments may have previous examples of guidance (e.g. in England DfES 2006; DCSF 2008), but these must be refreshed and not, as happened in England, ideologically rejected due to a change in political party following an election; education and children's lives are worth more than that.

We propose from now on, that educators look to their governments to provide a well-planned national strategy for education that is operationalizable at the local level for schools for times of crisis.

Opportunities and gains

UNECSO and Google have partnered during the Covid-19 crises to provide an education home schooling portal – is this going to be sustainable? Surely such an initiative has the potential to support learners across the world, whether in crises (and thereafter too) and emergency settings or not, and support the achievement of UNESCOs sustainable development goals – of high quality learning for all children. We are investigating this option. Results will be reported on the MESH-Guides website (www.meshguides.org).

Acknowledgements

Thanks are given to the MESH International Council members whose contributions to the coronavirus weekly meetings enabled us to draw up these guidelines for planning continuity for education in emergencies; specifically: Dr Bc Akin-Alabi (Nigeria); Dr Linda Devlin (Wolverhampton University, UK); Professor Irma Eloff (Pretoria University, South Africa); Dr Temechegin Engida (UNESCO-IICBA, Ethiopia); Carol Gentles (International Council on the Education of Teachers and University of the West Indies, Jamaica); Stephen Hurley, (VoicEd, Canada); Professor N.B. Jumani (International Islamic University, Pakistan); Khalid Khan (Ministry of Education, Pakistan); Mohamed Mukhtar (Development Line, Somalia); Professor Ruksana Osman (UNESCO Chair, Witwatersrand University, South Africa); Purna Shrestha (Voluntary Services Overseas International, NGO member UNESCO International Teacher Task Force); Dr Ling Siew Eng (Universiti Teknologi MARA, Malaysia); Professor Tracey Tokuhama-Espinosa (Ecuador and Harvard University, USA).

Thanks also to the MESH Executive Board members: Jon Audain (chair of Technology, Pedagogy and Education Association, University of Winchester, UK), Mike Blamires (RIPPLE, UK), Richard Procter (De Montfort University).

This chapter was first published as a paper on the MESHGuides website www.meshguides.org and licensed for reuse under a creative commons licence.

Following a series of international webinars undertaken by Leask and Younie, on behalf of MESH, from April to October 2020, further research data has been gathered on managing education during a pandemic, which has led to the forthcoming book (Leask and Younie, in press). All of the major concerns raised in this chapter are analysed and examined in further depth in the book.

References

The special edition of the Journal for Technology, Pedagogy and Education (to be published in 2021), (www.tandfonline.com/toc/rtpe20/current) provides detailed records and analysis of practices which emerged across the education sector in different countries at this time, with particular reference to the use of technologies to support learning during the pandemic.

Blamires, M. (2015) 'Building portals for evidence-informed education: Lessons from the dead. A case study of the development of a national portal intended to enhance evidence informed professionalism in education'. *Journal of Education for Teaching: International Research and Pedagogy*, 41(5) [Special Issue], 597–607.

DCSF (Department for Children, Schools and Families) (2008) *Supporting learning if schools close for extended periods during a flu pandemic* (December). www.wokingham.gov.uk/ EasysiteWeb/getresource.axd?AssetID=192722&type=full&servicetype=Attachment. Accessed 22 April 2020.

Devitt, R. (2018) *What is home schooling?* www.howdoihomeschool.com https://howdoihomeschool.com/2018/07/30/what-homeschooling-definition/. Accessed 29 April 2020.

DfES (Department for Education and Skills) (2006) *Planning for a human influenza pandemic guidance to schools every child matters.* https://schools.oxfordshire.gov.uk/cms/sites/schools/files/folders/folders/documents/healthandsafety/main_schools_guide.pdf. Accessed 22 April 2020.

Dierking, L. (2005) 'Lessons without limit: How free-choice learning is transforming science and technology education'. *História, ciências, saúde – Manguinhos,* 12, 145–160. 10.1590/S0104-59702005000400008. Accessed 22 April 2020.

EC (European Commission) (2009a) *Why is pandemic preparedness planning important?* www.ecdc.europa.eu/en/seasonal-influenza/preparedness/why-pandemic-preparedness. Accessed 22 April 2020.

EC (European Commission) (2009b) *Guide to public health measures to reduce the impact of influenza pandemics in Europe – 'The ECDC Menu'.* www.ecdc.europa.eu/en/publications-data/guide-public-health-measures-reduce-impact-influenza-pandemics-europe-ecdc-menu. Accessed 22 April 2020.

ECDC (European Centre for Disease Prevention and Control) in collaboration with the European Commission and the World Health Organisation Regional Office for Europe (September 2006 edn), *Assessment tool for influenza preparedness in European countries – with a main focus on pandemic preparedness.* www.ecdc.europa.eu/sites/default/files/media/en/healthtopics/seasonal_influenza/Documents/Tool/0609_Pandemic_Influenza_Assessment_Tool.pdf. Accessed 22 April 2020.

Education Endowment Foundation (2020) *Rapid evidence assessment: Distance learning.* https://educationendowmentfoundation.org.uk/public/files/Publications/Covid-19_Resources/Remote_learning_evidence_review/Rapid_Evidence_Assessment_summary.pdf. Accessed 22 April 2020.

Falk, J. and Dierking, L. (2002) *Lessons without limit: How free-choice learning is transforming education.* Lanham, CA: AltiMira Press.

Friedman, S. L. (2014) 'There are decades where nothing happens; and there are weeks where decades happen" – Vladimir Ilyich Lenin'. *Journal of Hepatology,* 60(3), 471–472. Accessed 22 April 2020.

Halinen, I. (2016) *Collaborating to create a relevant curriculum based on well-being for all.* Keynote address to Learning Teacher Network Conference, Tallinn, Estonia.

Institute for Government (2012) *Bonfire of the quangos.* London. www.instituteforgovernment.org.uk/news/latest/bonfire-quangos. Accessed 22 April 2020.

Inter-Agency Standing Committee-UNICEF, WHO and IFRC (2020) *Interim guidance for Covid-19 Prevention and control in schools,* March 2020. Accessed 22 April 2020.

International Labour Organisation, (2020) *ILO sectoral brief: COVID-19 and the education sector.* www.ilo.org/wcmsp5/groups/public/ – ed_dialogue/ – sector/documents/briefingnote/wcms_742025.pdf. Accessed 22 April 2020.

Jeffs, T. and Smith, M. K. (2011) 'What is informal education?', *The encyclopedia of pedagogy and informal education.* https://infed.org/mobi/what-is-informal-education/. Accessed 26 April 2020.

Leask, M. and Younie, S. (in press) *Ensuring Schooling for All in Times of Crisis: Lessons from Covid-19.* London: Routledge.

McLeod, S. A. (2007) *Maslow's hierarchy of needs.* www.simplypsychology.org/maslow.html. Accessed 26 April 2020

MESHGuides (April 2020a) *Covid-19 support: MESH international advisory council reports and meetings.* www.meshguides.org/covid-19-support-mesh-international-advisory-council-reports-and-meetings/. Accessed 22 April 2020.

MESHGuides extra (May 2020b) Pedagogies for Community supported learning in crises. Accessed 22 April 2020.

Morton, R. (2020) 'Home education: Constructions of choice'. *International Electronic Journal of Elementary Education,* 3(1), October 2010.

New Zealand Government (updated August 2011) *Influenza pandemic planning guide for early childhood education services, schools and tertiary organisations.* www.education.govt.nz/assets/Documents/Ministry/Initiatives/Health-and-safety/PandemicPlanningGuideForEdSectorAug2011.doc. Accessed 23 April 2020.

New Zealand Government (updated 30 March 2020) *Planning for an epidemic/pandemic event* (quick guide). www.education.govt.nz/school/health-safety-and-wellbeing/emergencies-and-traumatic-incidents/pandemic-planning-guide/. Accessed 23 April 2020.

Spec, D. (30 April 2020) 'A third of teachers have Covid-19 mental health fears'. London. Times Educational Supplement. www.tes.com/news/third-teachers-have-covid-19-mental-health-fears. Accessed 22 April 2020.

Tokuhama-Espinosa, T. (2020) *Decision tree for going on line: The virtual classroom.* https://thelearningsciences.com/site/portfolio-items/virtual-class-organization/?lang=en. Accessed 22 April 2020.

UNESCO (2020) *Half of world's student population not attending school: UNESCO launches global coalition to accelerate deployment of remote learning solutions.* https://en.unesco.org/news/half-worlds-student-population-not-attending-school-unesco-launches-global-coalition-accelerate. Accessed 23 April 2020.

UNESCO, UNICEF, World Bank (April 2020) *Framework for reopening schools.* https://en.unesco.org/news/back-school-preparing-and-managing-reopening-schools. Accessed 22 April 2020.

UNESCO International Teacher Task Force (April 2020) *Policy note – guidance for school leaders and teachers for schools re-opening.* Paris: UNESCO.

Uscher-Pines, L., Schwartz, H. L., Ahmed, F. et al. (2018) 'School practices to promote social distancing in K-12 schools: Review of influenza pandemic policies and practices'. *BMC Public Health,* 18, 406. https://doi.org/10.1186/s12889-018-5302-3. Accessed 23 April 2020. Accessed 22 April 2020.

Wang, C., Horby, P. W., Hayden, F. G. and Gao, G. F. (2020) 'A novel coronavirus outbreak of global health concern'. *The Lancet,* 395(10223), 470–473. https://doi.org/10.1016/S0140-6736(20)30185-9. Accessed 23 April 2020.

West, D. M. (2015) *Digital divide: Improving internet access in the developing world through affordable services and diverse content.* Brookings Center for Technology Innovation. www.brookings.edu/wp-content/uploads/2016/06/West_Internet-Access.pdf. Accessed 23 April 2020.

World Economic Forum (2020) *3 ways the coronavirus pandemic could reshape education.* www.weforum.org/agenda/2020/03/3-ways-coronavirus-is-reshaping-education-and-what-changes-might-be-here-to-stay. Accessed 23 April 2020.

World Health Organisation (2005) *Checklist for influenza pandemic preparedness planning.* www.who.int/csr/resources/publications/influenza/FluCheck6web.pdf. Accessed 23 April 2020.

World Health Organisation (2009) *Reducing transmission of pandemic (H1N1) 2009 in school settings.* www.who.int/csr/resources/publications/reducing_transmission_h1n1_2009.pdf. Accessed 22 April 2020.

Younie, S. and Leask, M. (2019) *Lessons from the bonfire of the quangos: The case for legislation to provide checks and balances to the powers of the Secretary of State for Education.* SES (Society for

Education Studies) Colloquium on 'Education reform legislation in a changing society', Oxford University, Oriel College, 26–27 September 2019.

Younie, S., Leask, M. and Hudson, B. (2020) 'Policy options and consequences: What has to be done, when and with whom'. Chapter 20 in B. Hudson, M. Leask, and S. Younie (Eds) *Education system design: Foundations, policy options and consequences*. Abingdon: Routledge.

INDEX

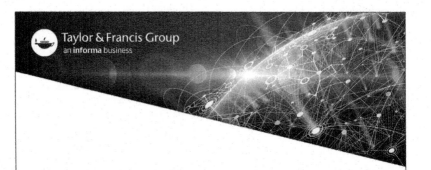